The Christian Doctrine of God,
One Being Three Persons

D1081881

The Christian Doctrine of God, One Being Three Persons

Thomas F. Torrance

t & t clark

T&T CLARK LTD
A Continuum imprint

The Tower Building,   80 Maiden Lane,
11 York Road,   Suite 704
London, SE1 7NX   New York, NY 10038

First published 1996
Paperback edition 2001
Reprinted 2004, 2006

ISBN 0 567 08829 4

British Library Cataloguing-in-Publication Data
A catalogue record for this book is available from the British Library

Typeset by Trinity Typesetting, Edinburgh
Printed an bound in Great Britain by Biddles Ltd., King's Lynn, Norfolk

To

Thomas Spear Torrance,

Economist and Philosopher of Science

Contents

Preface

THIS monograph is devoted to clarifying understanding of the most profound article of the Christian Faith, the doctrine of the Holy Trinity. The exposition takes place within the frame of the biblical and Nicene tradition of the One Holy Catholic and Apostolic Church. It is heavily influenced by Greek patristic and Reformed theology, with particular acknowledgement of debt to Athanasius the Great, Hugh Ross Mackintosh and Karl Barth. My argument and presentation have taken an open-structured form in the conviction that the truth of the Holy Trinity is more to be adored than expressed. The Holy Scriptures do not give us dogmatic propositions about the Trinity, but they do present us with definite witness to the oneness and differentiation between the Father, the Son and the Holy Spirit, under the constraint of which the early Church allowed the pattern and order of God's Triune Life to impose themselves upon its mind. There took shape within the ecumenical thinking of the Church a specifically apostolic frame of understanding the truth of the Gospel which soon came to be revered as the distinctive *mind* or φρόνημα of the Catholic Church. It was to this *mind* that the great fathers and theologians of the Church intuitively appealed in forming theological judgments and making conciliar decisions.

It was thus that something of immense significance for the whole life, worship and mission of the Church took place, the formation of a theological paradigm of understanding which became more and more articulate as the Church sought to expound, clarify and integrate the truths of the Gospel, and defend them from damaging misinterpretation. I believe it is important to recognise that in these early centuries, as the truth-content of apostolic Scriptures unfolded within the understanding of the Church, something of definitive and irreversible significance took place. This is very evident in the Nicene confession of belief in 'one Lord Jesus Christ ... of one substance with the Father (ὁμοούσιος τῷ Πατρί)'. In that conciliar formulation of the *homoousion* the fathers of the Nicene Council were articulating what they felt they *had to* think and say under the constraint of the truth and in fidelity to the biblical witness to Christ and the basic interpretation of it already given in the apostolic foundation of the Church. The explicit formulation of the *homoousion* at the Council of Nicaea was an absolutely fundamental event that took place in the mind of the early Church. It was a decisive step in deeper understanding of the Gospel, giving precise expression to the all-important relation between the incarnate Son and God the Father, which they made in obedience to God's saving revelation in Jesus Christ and in continuity with the apostolic tradition upon which the Church could not go back. With it a giant step was taken in grasping and giving expression to the internal relation of the incarnate Son to the Father, and thereby to the ontological substructure and coherence of the Gospel. It proved to be an inerasable and irreversible event in the history of Christian theology.

In its way the Nicene formulation of the *homoousion* may be said, *mutatis mutandis*, to be not unlike some of the great events in the history of science in which the rational structure of human knowledge of the created universe has been profoundly revised in a way upon which we cannot go back, even if our understanding of nature may have to be reformulated in the light of the deeper knowledge of the universe to which the revised structure of science gave rise. This is not to claim of the Nicene term *homoousios* that it is somehow sacrosanct and beyond reconsideration, for all theological terms and concepts fall short of the realities they intend and are open to further modification in the light of it. Like any other creative 'definition' of this kind, owing to its essentially semantic and interpretative function, this formulation must also be continually tested and revised in the light of what it was coined to express in the first place, as well as in the light of its fertility in the subsequent history of thought. But apart from the linguistic expression coined by the Nicene Fathers the formulation of the *homoousion* proved to be of astonishing generative and heuristic power, for it was so well rooted in the source of the Church's faith that it was pregnant with intimations of still profounder aspects of divine reality in Jesus Christ pressing for realisation within the mind of the Church.

Elsewhere I have likened the irreversible nature of such an event in the history of Christian theology to what we do with a jig-saw puzzle.

> We assemble the scattered pieces together, fitting them appropriately to each other until the pattern they conjointly make comes to view. If then we break it all up and throw the pieces back into disorder, we may have little difficulty in fitting them all together again, but it will be impossible for us to do that without recalling the picture we reached the first time. Something irreversible would have taken place in our mind and memory, which could not but influence all subsequent attempts to recover the coherent pattern made by the different parts.[1]

Although the formulation of the *homoousion* was a turning point of far-reaching significance in the development of Christian theology it cannot be isolated from what happened in the early centuries in the mind and memory of the Church as a whole. It belonged to the decisive movement of thought in which the conceptual content of the Gospel mediated to the Mediterranean world through the apostolic tradition was unfolded within the preaching and teaching of the Church in the course of its transforming impact upon the thought of the Hellenic world. There resulted throughout the Church a development of the distinctive doxological and theological outlook canonically upheld and regularly cultivated in its sacramental and liturgical life. This was an apostolically mediated participation by the Church in the very Mind of Christ, which grounded, shaped and integrated the mind of

---

[1] *The Trinitarian Faith* (T&T Clark, Edinburgh, 1988), p. 144.

the Church in its grasp and confession of the supreme truths of the Gospel. In this way there came to prominence what was known as the Catholic as well as Apostolic *mind* or φρόνημα to which the theologians and bishops like Athanasius regularly appealed in expounding and defending the Faith once delivered to the saints.

Thus, as I understand it, there arose in the early era of the Christian Church a fundamental orientation and theological structure of a conceptually irreversible nature. It belongs to the very *esse*, and not just to the *bene esse* of the Church, and as such constitutes the intellectual as well as spiritual basis upon which the whole historic Church throughout the centuries rests. It is not surprising that the Nicene Council was soon regarded with awe as divinely 'inspired', for it was recognised as uniquely constitutive for all subsequent theological and conciliar activity. It is certainly upon the Nicene-Constantinopolitan Creed that all Christendom in the West as well as the East has rested and continues to rest. I myself appreciate Nicene-Constantinopolitan theology as still having a decisive and formative role to play in all Christian theology, and find myself turning particularly to the great Greek Fathers in that tradition as providing me with the incisive insights I find most helpful today in rethinking and reformulating Christian theology, not least in the field of trinitarian theology. Hence I make no apology for my constant concern with Greek patristic theology in this book, and in making use of some of the main insights it offers for an exposition of Christian doctrine.

The account of the doctrine of the Trinity offered here is not analytical, deductive, or discursive, but holistic. It is an attempt to be faithful to the way in which the Holy Trinity is presented to us in the Gospel, if only implicitly, as a Whole but as a differentiated Whole. This means that exposition must proceed in a circular way, in which understanding of the whole is not built up from a prior grasp of its constituent parts, but in which the whole while understood out of itself is nevertheless understood with subsidiary attention to its parts, and the parts are properly understood in the light of the whole. Circular procedure of this kind cannot but involve repetition, for an account of any one Person of the Holy Trinity cannot be given without relation to the other two Persons. Not a little repetition is also involved in this book due to my urge to make theological statements as rounded or complete as possible in themselves. But I hope that repetition of this kind, in which the same truth is restated in cognate forms, instead of annoying readers may help them toward a better understanding of the main contentions of the monograph, and even mitigate for them my rather difficult style. I would claim, however, that the difficulty of my style is sometimes due to the difficulty of the subject-matter! In order to help the understanding of the reader I have included references throughout to several other books of mine where the same trinitarian concepts are given another or fuller exposition.

Readers should note that the theological terms employed here in the doctrine of the Holy Trinity (not least 'being' and 'person') are to be understood, not in accordance with some later use or current sense, but in the transformed meaning they are given within the doctrine of the Trinity itself and under the impact of the reorganised consciousness of God brought about in the Church through the Gospel. While Greek words are used in many references, I have added transliterations in Roman letters to help readers. It should be emphasised that the word 'man' is used throughout this book in the *inclusive biblical sense* and not in a sexist way, and thus with no confusion between linguistic gender found in this or that language and personal gender. Gender belongs only to the creaturely world and may not be read back into God.

I would like to express great indebtedness to my dear son Thomas, not only with his assistance in handling computer software in the production of this book, but for the great help he has been to my wife and myself in untold ways.

Edinburgh,
Advent, 1994.

Introduction

THE Christian doctrine of God is to be understood from within the unique, definitive and final self-revelation of God in Jesus Christ his only begotten Son, that is, from within the self-revelation of God as God become man for us and our salvation, in accordance with its proclamation in the Gospel and its actualisation through the Holy Spirit in the apostolic foundation of the Church. It is in the Lord Jesus, the very Word and Mind of God incarnate in our humanity, that the eternal God 'defines' and identifies himself for us as he really is. Only in Christ is God's self-revelation identical with himself, and only in Christ, God for us, does he communicate his self-revelation to us in such a way that authentic knowledge of God is embodied in our humanity, and thus in such a way that it may be communicated to us and understood by us. Jesus Christ is at once the complete revelation of God to man, and the perfect correspondence on man's part to that revelation required by it for the fulfilment of its own revealing movement. As the faithful answer to God's self-revelation Jesus Christ yields from out of our human existence and life the fulfilled reception and faithful embodiment which belongs to the content of God's revelation of himself to man. Moreover, it is only in Christ in whom God's self-revelation is identical with himself that we may rightly apprehend it and really know God as he is in himself, in the oneness and differentiation of God within his own eternal Being as Father, Son and Holy Spirit, for what God is toward us in his historical self-manifestation to us in the Gospel as Father, Son and Holy Spirit, he is revealed to be inherently and eternally in himself. It is thus in and through Jesus Christ and the Holy Spirit that the distinctively Christian doctrine of God in his transcendent triunity is mediated to us.

It is certainly the incarnation of the eternal Word of God made flesh in Jesus Christ which prescribes for us in Christian theology both its proper matter and form, so that whether in its activity as a whole or in the formulation of a doctrine in any part, it is the Christological pattern that will appear throughout the whole body of Christian dogmatics. This does not mean, however, that all theology can be reduced to Christology, but that because there is only one Mediator between God and man, the Man Christ Jesus, in the presentation of the doctrines of the Christian faith, every doctrine will be expressed in its inner coherence with Christology at the centre, and in its correspondence with the objective reality of God's self-revelation in Christ. On the other hand, because in Jesus Christ God reveals himself through himself and as he is in himself, the ultimate ground upon which our knowledge of Jesus Christ himself and of God's self-revelation through Christ rests becomes disclosed as trinitarian. It is thus that the doctrine of Christ and the doctrine of the Holy Trinity belong intrinsically and inseparably together, and are to be coordinated in any faithful account of them.

While the Lord Jesus Christ constitutes the pivotal centre of our knowledge of God, God's distinctive self-revelation as Holy Trinity, One Being, Three Persons, creates the overall framework within which all Christian theology is to be formulated. Understandably, therefore, the doctrine of the Holy Trinity has been called the innermost heart of Christian faith and worship, the central dogma of classical theology, the fundamental grammar of our knowledge of God. It belongs to the Gospel of God's saving and redeeming love in Jesus Christ who died for us and rose again and has given us the Holy Spirit who has shed the love of God abroad in our hearts. The doctrine of the Trinity enshrines the essentially Christian conception of God: it constitutes the ultimate evangelical expression of *the Grace of the Lord Jesus Christ* who though he was rich for our sakes became poor that we through his poverty might become rich, of *the Love of God* who did not spare his own Son but delivered him up for us all, for it is in that personal sacrifice of the Father to which everything in the Gospel goes back, and of *the Communion of the Holy Spirit* through whom and in whom we are made to participate in the eternal Communion of the Father and the Son and are united with one another in the redeemed life of the people of God. Through Christ and in the Spirit God has communicated himself to us in such a wonderful way that we may really know him and have communion with him in his inner life as Father, Son and Holy Spirit.

Consider the familiar teaching of the Epistle to the Ephesians.[1] In accordance with the eternal purpose which he has set forth in Jesus Christ, God has destined us in love before the foundation of the world to be holy and spotless, adopted as his children through union with Christ in whom we have redemption through his blood, the forgiveness of our sins according to the riches of his grace, and has sealed us with the promised gift of the Holy Spirit who is the pledge of our inheritance in God as those whom he has redeemed and appropriated for his very own. And so in fulfilment of his predetermined design to gather up all things in Christ, things in heaven and things on earth, God himself has drawn near to us and drawn us near to himself through the blood of Christ, in order to break down the barriers of enmity between us (Jews and Gentiles alike) and himself, so that 'through Christ we both have access by one Spirit unto the Father'.[2] This means that owing to the atoning reconciliation which God has worked out in Jesus Christ in the midst of our human historical existence, he has established an intimate two-way relation between himself and us and us and himself, making himself accessible to us and giving us entry into the inner fellowship of his divine Life by allowing us to share in God's own eternal Spirit. Expressed otherwise, knowledge of God the Father is mediated to us through Christ and is imparted to us in the Spirit within the new state of affairs brought about by the Cross of Christ. "'Through him we have access by one Spirit unto the Father'", as H. R. Mackintosh once wrote, 'is a great comprehensive Pauline word; and in such a verse the experience out of which

---

[1] Eph. 1 & 2. I have in mind the exposition of Athanasius in *Contra Arianos* 2.76.
[2] Eph. 2.18.

flowed the New Testament faith in a Triune God grows transparent. It is the experience of a differentiated yet single Divine causality in redemption.'[3] 'Only through God is fellowship with God accessible to man.'[4] It is through this doctrine of the Trinity distilled from the New Testament witness that we are enabled to relate Jesus Christ and the Holy Spirit intelligibly to the inmost Being and eternal Life of God, and thereby to deepen and strengthen our faith in Jesus Christ as Lord and Saviour from its ultimate ground in God's revelation of himself through himself.

This self-revelation of God in the Gospel amounts to the greatest *revolution in our knowledge of God*. It is precisely when we grasp its truth that we discern the enormous significance of the doctrine of the Holy Trinity. For Judaism or for Greek philosophy, or indeed for every religion apart from Christianity, God remains ultimately incomprehensible to men and women in the bare and unfigured simplicity of his Being – he is the Nameless One who cannot be apprehended in himself or be conceived in the personal relations of his inner life as a Communion of Love. Hence statements made about God, apart from his active personal self-revelation, as many ancient and modern philosophers would have it, are non-cognitive – they are at best of no more than tangential borderline significance. It is quite otherwise in the Gospel when we say that the Father, the Son, and the Holy Spirit are God, the One God whom we know and with whom we have to do as the God of our salvation. The three divine Persons are the Triune Being of God; the Triune Being is three Persons.[5]

In sharp contrast with every other religion, Christianity stands for the fact that in Jesus Christ God has communicated to us his *Word* and has imparted to us his *Spirit*, so that we may really know him as he is in himself although not apart from his saving activity in history, for what he is toward us and for us in history he is in himself, and what he is in himself he is toward us and for us in history. The Word of God and the Spirit of God are not just ephemeral modes of God's presence to us in history; nor are they transient media external to himself through which God has revealed to us something about himself; they belong to what God ever is in his communion with us. They are the objective ontological personal forms of his self-giving and self-imparting in the dynamic outgoing of the holy Love which God himself is. It thus belongs to the essential faith of the Church that through his Word and his Spirit who are of one and the same being with himself God has really communicated *himself* to us in his own eternal and indivisible Reality as God the Father Almighty, the Creator of heaven and earth and of all things visible and invisible. That is why we believe that what God is toward us in Jesus Christ, the Word made flesh, he is in himself, antecedently and eternally in himself; and that what he imparts to us through the Spirit who sheds the love of God into our hearts, he is in himself, antecedently and eternally in himself. It is thus that through Jesus Christ God has given himself to us and through the Holy Spirit takes us up

---

[3] H. R. Mackintosh, *The Doctrine of the Person of Jesus Christ* (Edinburgh, 1913), p. 509.
[4] Ibid. p. 194.
[5] Cf. Augustine: '*trina unitas et una trinitas Deus ... trinitas in unitate et unitas in trinitate*', *Confessiones*, 1.7.7.

3

into communion with himself as Father, Son and Holy Spirit, the one God of all grace whom we know as the God of our salvation.

Think of the immense revolution this means for our understanding of God.

It means that God is not some remote, unknowable Deity, a prisoner in his aloofness or shut up in his solitariness, but on the contrary the God who is free to go outside of himself, to share in the life of his creatures and enable them to share in his own eternal Life. It means that God is not limited by our feeble capacities or incapacities, but that in his grace and outgoing love he graciously condescends to enter into fellowship with us, to communicate himself to us, in such a way as to be received and be known by us. But of course the doctrine of the Holy Trinity means that the more we know God in himself in this way the more wonderful we know him to be, a God who in his inexhaustible Nature infinitely transcends all our thoughts and words about him, but who in spite of that reveals himself tenderly and intimately to us through his only Son and in his one Spirit who are of the same divine Nature as God the Father.

It also means that God is not some immutable, impassible deity locked up in his self-isolation who cannot be touched with our human feelings, pains and hurts, but on the contrary is the kind of God who freely acts and passionately interacts with us in this world, for in his own eternal Being he is the ever living, loving and acting God who will not be without us but who in his grace freely determines himself for us as our God and Saviour.[6] This is not to say that God is constituted in his Being or in the personal nature of his Being through the relations of his love toward us, any more than he is constituted in his Being through relation to the universe which in his ungrudging love he has created out of nothing.[7] In his love of us and for us God freely wills not to be without us and wills to be with us as those whom he has eternally chosen to coexist with himself and share his eternal love. It is the sheer gratuitous grace of God, the transcendent freedom of his self-determination in love for us, which is so wonderful, for he does not need relation to us to be what he is as the living acting God. In his superabounding and overflowing love he does not want to be alone without us or want us to be alone without him. According to the Christian Gospel, then, there is and can be no other God than this God whose very Being is the One who loves us and will not be without us, for the Being of God and the Activity of God in loving may not be separated. God's Being is not some abstract impersonal essence, but dynamic personal Being, for God is who he is in the Act of his revelation, and his Act is what it is in his Being, which Karl Barth used to speak of as 'Being in Person'.[8] Just as we

---

[6] Karl Barth has written of this as 'the Being of God as the One who loves in freedom', *Church Dogmatics* II.1 (Edinburgh, 1957), pp. 257ff, 272ff. See also Heinrich Vogel, *Gott im Christo* (Berlin, 1951), pp. 282ff, 346ff.

[7] The idea held by Origen that God's relation to the created universe is necessary to his own Being was comprehensively destroyed by Athanasius, see Georges Florovsky, 'The Concept of Creation in Saint Athanasius', *Studia Patristica*, vol. 4 (1962), pp. 16–57. Cf. also my discussion, *The Trinitarian Faith*, pp. 76ff.

[8] *Church Dogmatics* II.1, p. 208. See the sections 'The Being of God in Act', and 'The Being of God as the One who Loves', and 'The Being of God in Freedom', pp. 257–321. It was this volume of the *Kirchliche Dogmatik* which I heard as lectures in Basel in 1937–38, and which left an indelible print on my mind.

can never go behind God's saving and revealing acts in Jesus Christ and in the mission of his Spirit, so we can never think or speak of him truly apart from his revealing and saving acts or behind the back of Jesus Christ, for there is no other God.

It is of course because God actively loves us, and actually loves us so much that he has given us his only Son to be the Saviour of the world, that he reveals himself to us as the Loving One, and as he whose Love belongs to his innermost Being as God. If he were not Love in his innermost Being, his love toward us in Christ and the Holy Spirit would be ontologically groundless. God is who he is as he who loves us with his very Being, he whose loving is as inexhaustible as his infinite Being for his Love is his Being in ceaseless triune movement and activity. It is precisely as this living, loving, and acting God that he has come to us in Jesus Christ and unites us to himself by his one Spirit, interacting with us in creation and history, and in our human and physical existence in time and space, all in order to be *our* God and to have *us* for his people.

It is thus that we understand why Christians believe the God and Father of Jesus Christ to be the one and only God and Saviour of the world. He is not different in himself from what he is in the activity of his saving and redeeming love in the singularity of the incarnation and crucifixion of Jesus Christ, the God who in loving and saving us has once for all given his very Self to us in his Son and in his Spirit, and who in giving himself freely and unreservedly to us gives us with him all things. It is in the Cross of Christ that the utterly astonishing nature of the Love that God is has been fully disclosed, for in refusing to spare his own Son whom he delivered up for us all, God has revealed that he loves us more than he loves himself.[9] And so it is in the Cross of Jesus Christ above all that God has both exhibited the very Nature of his Being as Love and has irrevocably committed his Being to relationship with us in unconditional Love. In Jesus Christ and in the Holy Spirit we know no other God, and believe that there is no other God for us than this God, who freely seeks and creates fellowship with us, utterly undeserving sinners though we are.

The fact that, as St John tells us,[10] God *is* Love, who has manifested his love to us in sending his only Son into the world so that we might live through him, does not mean that God is Love in virtue of his love for us, but that God is in himself the fullness and perfection of Love in loving and being loved which out of sheer love overflows freely toward others. It means that the Love that God is, is not that of solitary inactive or static love, whatever that may be, but the active movement of reciprocal loving within the eternal Being of God which is the one ultimate Source of all love. That God is Love means that he is the eternally loving One in himself who loves through himself, whose Love moves unceasingly within his eternal Life as God, so that in loving us in the gift of his dear Son and the mission of his Spirit he loves us with the very Love which he is. In other words, that God is Love as this loving One in Christ and in the Spirit, means that in their interpersonal reciprocal

---

[9] This is the implication of Rom. 8.31f. Cf. also the words of St Paul addressed to the bishops of Ephesus regarding 'the Church of God which he has purchased with his own blood' (Acts 20.28).
[10] 1 John 4. 8ff.

relations the Father, the Son and the Holy Spirit are the Communion of Love which the One God eternally is in himself, and indeed is also toward us. It is as this ever living and acting Communion of loving and being loved that God is who he is, the perfection and fullness of Love that will not be confined within the Godhead but freely and lovingly moves outward toward others whom God creates for fellowship with himself so that they may share with him the very Communion of Love which is his own divine Life and Being.

It is the message of this Triune Love that constitutes the very heart of the Gospel: 'God so loved the world that he gave his only begotten Son, that whoever believes in him should not perish but have eternal life.'[11] The eternal Lord God lives and is he who he is in the free unstinting outflow of that limitless love toward us exhibited and enacted at infinite cost to himself in the sending of his beloved Son to be the propitiation for our sins. It also belongs to the very heart of the Gospel that by his Triune Nature as a Communion of Love in himself, as Father, Son and Holy Spirit, God is the kind of God who as a fullness of personal Being in himself not only creates personal reciprocity between us and himself but creates a community of personal reciprocity in love, which is what we speak of as the Church of the Lord Jesus Christ living in the Communion of the Spirit and incorporated into Christ as his Body. It is this triune God who lives and is actively present in the fellowship which he creates with others whom we believe to be the God of infinite personal care for each of us his dear children and for every created being. The Holy Trinity is the ever-living Trinity who personally listens to our petitions and answers our prayers and sustains us in all the vicissitudes of our daily life within the embrace of his presence and power.

It is certainly true that our theological conceptions of God as Father, Son and Holy Spirit derive from and are essentially coordinated with what God has manifested of himself in the historical events of which we read in the New Testament. Those evangelical events are empty if they are sundered from their roots in history. They have saving import for us only if the historical presentations of God as Father, Son and Holy Spirit flow from and direct us back to personal realities inside the divine Life. That is to say, the historical manifestations of God as Father, Son and Holy Spirit have evangelical and theological significance only as they have a transhistorical and transfinite reference beyond to an ultimate ground in God himself. They cannot be Gospel if their reference breaks off at the finite boundaries of this world of space and time, for as such they would be empty of divine validity and saving significance – that would be to leave us trapped in some kind of historical positivism. The historical manifestations of the Trinity are *Gospel*, however, if they are grounded beyond history in the eternal personal distinctions between the Father, the Son and the Holy Spirit inherent in the Godhead, that is, if the Fatherhood of the Father, the Sonship of the Son, and the Communion of the Spirit belong to the inner Life of God and constitute his very Being.

In view of this oneness of the Being and Activity of God made known to us through Christ and in the Spirit, it is understandable that Hugh Ross Mackintosh

---

[11] John 3.16.

(my old teacher of Christian Dogmatics in Edinburgh), used to insist that we hold inseparably together Christian conceptions of God *for us* and of God *in himself,* that is, conceptions of God that arise out of the evangelical pattern or economy of God's saving revelation in history and conceptions of God which are expressions in time of eternal personal distinctions in God. And so he steered a course in his lectures through any divergence between what are called notions of 'the economic Trinity' and notions of 'the immanent or ontological Trinity.'[12] In the Gospel God does not just *appear* to us to be Father, Son and Holy Spirit, for he really *is* Father, Son and Holy Spirit in himself, and reveals himself as such. 'Our believing apprehension of Father, Son and Spirit, is not in contact with appearances only, but with reality. If God shines through Christ to our believing apprehension, then by way of this historic medium we see into the Divine Nature.'[13] The economic Trinity and the ontological Trinity are not to be separated from one another for they are locked together in God's threefold *self*-revelation and *self*-communication to us as Father, Son and Holy Spirit.

The economic Trinity might well be spoken of as the *evangelical Trinity* and the ontological Trinity as the *theological Trinity.* 'Evangelical' in this sense refers to the truth content of the Gospel as it is revealed to us through the incarnate or human economy (ἡ ἀνθρωπίνη οἰκονομία) which Christ undertook toward us, in the midst of us, and for our sakes (εἰς ἡμᾶς, ἐν μέσῳ ἡμῶν, δι' ἡμᾶς);[14] and 'theological' in this sense refers to the truth of the eternal Being and Activity of God as he is in himself, the essential Deity (οὐσιώδης Θεότης), or 'Theology' (Θεολογία, which Athanasius equated with divine worship).[15] While for Athanasius *economy* and *theology* (οἰκονομία and θεολογία) must be clearly distinguished, they are not to be separated from each other.[16] If the economic or evangelical Trinity and the ontological or theological Trinity were disparate, this would bring into question whether *God himself* was the actual content of his revelation, and whether *God himself* was really in Jesus Christ reconciling the world to himself. That is the evangelical and epistemological significance of the *homoousion* ('consubstantial', of one substance, or of one and the same being with the Father) formulated by the Council of Nicaea in AD 325. If there is no real bond *in God* between the economic Trinity and the ontological Trinity, the saving events proclaimed in the economy of the Gospel are without any divine validity and the

---

[12] H. R. Mackintosh, *Doctrine of the Person,* p. 512f. Thus also Heinrich Vogel, *Gott im Christo,* pp. 254ff.

[13] H. R. Mackintosh, *Doctrine of the Person,* p. 515.

[14] This was Athanasius' way of expressing it, e.g. *Contra Arianos,* 2.12, 44–45, 51–52 or *In illud, omnia,*1.

[15] Athanasius, *In illud, omnia, 6; Contra Arianos,* 1.15; 2.12, 45, 51; 3.15; *De synodis,* 51. See T. F. Torrance, *The Trinitarian Faith,* 1988, p. 302f.

[16] Consult again Georges Florovsky, op. cit., p. 48. Due to the epistemological dualism (χωρισμός) pervading Hellenistic thought the Church had constantly to struggle against a threat to sever 'economy' from 'theology' (οἰκονομία from θεολογία), for it would have done away with the ontological reference of the Gospel and of faith to any real ground in the being and activity of God. See further my discussion in 'The Implications of Oikonomia for Knowledge and Speech of God in Early Christian Theology', in *Oikonomia, Heilsgeschichte als Thema der Theologie,* ed. F. Christ (Hamburg-Bergstedt, 1967), pp. 223–238.

doctrine of the Trinity is lacking in any ultimate divine truth. The trinitarian message of the Gospel tells us that the very contrary is the case, for in Jesus Christ and in the Holy Spirit we really have to do with the *Lord God himself* as our Saviour. Thus, as we shall see, the designation of Jesus as 'Lord', i.e. Κύριος = YHWH, is found more than a hundred times in the New Testament Scriptures.[17]

The economic Trinity and the ontological Trinity overlap with one another and belong to one another, and can no more be separated than the Act of God can be separated from his Being or his Being from his Act. It is in that interrelation between the two that the redemptive significance and evangelical relevance of the Holy Trinity become disclosed. What God is toward us and for us in his revealing and saving acts in the incarnate economy undertaken for our sakes he is in his personal divine Being as Father, Son and Holy Spirit, and what he is in his personal divine Being as Father, Son and Holy Spirit he is toward us and for us in the revealing and saving acts of his incarnate economy.[18] This is very evident, as we have noted above, in the New Testament witness to the fact that God is Love, and indeed a Communion of Love, out of which his love overflows freely and gratuitously toward us through the Son and in the Spirit as the Love of God for us, in a redeeming movement of Love in which God through his Son and in his Spirit gathers us into union and communion with himself. It is significant, however, that in his first Epistle in which St John writes of this movement of the Life and Love of God and of our communion with the Father and with his Son Jesus Christ, he deliberately speaks of their original apostolic experience and knowledge of Jesus Christ the incarnate Son of God in audible, visible and tangible terms that are clearly meant to reject any spiritualising a-historical conception of God's self-communication and the communion which it involved.[19] We have here to do with the lofty yet down-to-earth truth of the Gospel. Hence for St John, divine redemption and actual historical reality are held inseparably together throughout the Epistle, as in the Fourth Gospel.[20] Moreover, for St John the meaning of 'love' is defined not in general terms of what we may think or do but in concrete terms of the actual love of God for us exhibited in the atoning death of his dear Son.[21]

In modern times it is unfortunately the case that the enormous importance of the doctrine of the Trinity, and its revolutionary implications, have tended to be lost from sight, and sometimes to be treated as rather irrelevant, or only of peripheral significance for Christian faith and living. Much of the reason for this is that people have worked for so long in the Western world with a notion of God who is somehow inertially detached from this world, exalted inaccessibly above it, and remote from our creaturely cries and prayers. And so in Western theology particularly it has

---

[17] See C. B. Kaiser 'The Biblical and Patristic Doctrine of the Trinity. In what ways can the relationship be established?', in T. F. Torrance, *Theological Dialogue between Orthodox and Reformed Churches*, vol. 2 (Edinburgh, 1993), pp. 166 & 189–192.
[18] This was the main point of Athanasius' exposition of Luke 10.22 (Matt. 11.27), *In illud, omnia*, 1–6.
[19] 1 John 1.1ff.
[20] 1 John 1.1f.
[21] 1 John 4.10.

become too common for theologians to separate the doctrine of the One God from the doctrine of the Triune God.[22] That gives expression to a deistic disjunction between God and the world, far removed from what God has revealed of himself in the ancient Hebrew Scriptures or in the New Testament as the God whose covenant love undergirds the whole creation and embraces all humanity with his mercies, and as the God who, far from holding himself aloof from us, has himself once for all become one with us in the world and one of us in the Lord Jesus Christ. This understanding of the redemptive Love of God implies that our knowledge of God is irrevocably correlated with the world as his creation and as the medium designed for his self-revelation and self-communication to mankind. The very fact that God reveals and communicates himself *to us in the world* which he loves and seeks to save means that he does not give us a knowledge of himself merely as he is in himself but only a knowledge of himself and his inner divine Life through his actual and dynamic relation to the world. Everything God has revealed of himself through Israel and in the incarnation has to do with the purpose of his redeeming love for us and for the whole of his creation. We know nothing of God and can know nothing of him completely isolated in himself and apart from the fulfilment of his creative and redeeming purpose. Whatever that might be, it would be of a God who is not Love.

In our day, however, the relegation of the doctrine of the Trinity to the periphery of the Church's life and thought is being radically challenged and to a large extent changed, owing very largely to the epoch-making work of Karl Barth who, on the basis of God's incarnate self-revelation, reintegrated the doctrine of the Triunity of God with the evangelical message of his saving and redeeming activity in Jesus Christ and the Holy Spirit, thereby restoring express knowledge of the Holy Trinity to its place in the centre of the Church's faith and worship not unlike the place given to it in the great Nicene theology and liturgy of the Early Church. Karl Barth developed his doctrine of the Trinity within the evangelical frame of thought brought about by the concentration of the Reformation on the Gospel of saving grace and of God's redemptive activity embodied in Jesus Christ, which had the effect of clarifying the understanding of the historic Faith and of setting Christian theology back upon its proper soteriological basis in line with the Nicene-Constantinopolitan Creed. The teaching of Karl Barth in the *Church Dogmatics* was welcomed and supported by other leading theologians in the Reformed and Lutheran traditions, notably by H. R. Mackintosh in Edinburgh and Heinrich Vogel in Berlin. Then in due course he was followed by the Roman Catholic theologian Karl Rahner who developed a parallel account of the Trinity within the mystery of salvation in which he sought to bring about an integration of two disparate strands in the doctrine of God that had been given authoritative form in the development of Augustinian and Thomist theology in the Latin West. There are certainly differences between

---

[22] This was far removed from the doctrine of the Trinity in the *Confessio Theologica* of Jean De Fécamp in the eleventh century (ed. J. Leclercq and Jean-Paul Bonnes, Paris, 1946, pp. 114ff.) In it the divine Trinity and Unity are addressed together in a sustained theological prayer: *Confiteor ... Totum Patrem in Filio et Spiritu Sancto, Totum Filium in Patre et Spiritu Sancto, Totum Spiritum in Patre et Filio, Sanctam et individuam Trinitatem, unum Deum omnipotentem.* 1.14, p. 119.

the thought of Karl Barth and the thought of Karl Rahner, reflecting the dogmatic structures of Reformed and Roman Catholic theology. However, both of them rejected the old Western habit, formalised by Thomas Aquinas, and developed in post-Reformation Roman Catholicism and Protestantism, in which the doctrine of the One God was divided from the doctrine of the Triune God, as though the doctrine of the One God could be set out rationally by itself, while the doctrine of the Triune God could be accepted only on the ground of divine revelation. That would be tantamount, as Karl Barth argued, to splitting the fundamental concept of God. By rejecting both the philosophy of dualism deriving from the medieval world and the philosophy of dualism built into the Enlightenment that lay behind ways of thinking of God which represented him as a remote, inertial and impassible Deity, Barth and Rahner have done much in the Reformed and Roman Communions to set aside a doctrine of the Trinity that has little perceptible relation to the history of salvation through Jesus Christ, and to restore the classical Greek patristic understanding of the Holy Trinity within the framework of the Church's confession of the Gospel of the incarnation and the mystery of divine salvation. Thereby they have shown once again that the doctrine of the Trinity belongs to the very heart of saving faith where it constitutes the inner shape of Christian worship and the dynamic grammar of Christian theology: it expresses the essential and distinctively Christian understanding of God by which we live, and which is of crucial significance for the evangelical mission of the Church as well.

In order to set the tone of the chapters that follow it may be helpful at this point to refer to several prime features that governed John Calvin's approach to the sheer Godness of God, and the Holy Trinity,[23] and allow them to guide us here, for along with Luther he had much to do with opening up the way in the West for a evangelical restructuring of the Church's understanding of the Faith once delivered to the Saints. Particularly characteristic of his devout attitude of mind was 'piety' or 'godliness' (*pietas* or *religio*) which he defined as 'that reverence joined with the love of God which knowledge of his benefits brings about'.[24] This was more or less his equivalent for the New Testament and patristic *eusebeia* (εὐσέβεια) which he also spoke of as the 'fitting worship of God'.[25] Coupled with this approach was his profound sense of 'God's unfathomable and spiritual Being' which wholly exceeds all human conception and imagination and is more to be worshipped than investigated.[26] The fact that the Being of God is intrinsically incomprehensible makes all our attempts to grasp the 'essence' or 'quiddity' of God as no more than cold and empty speculations.[27] Hence Calvin rejected the theological method of the Latin schoolmen that began with the abstract question 'What is God (*quid sit Deus*)?' and put in its place the concrete question 'What kind of God is he (*qualis*

---

[23] See my presentation of Calvin's trinitarian teaching in chs. 2 and 3 of *Trinitarian Perspectives, Toward Doctrinal Agreement* (T & T Clark, Edinburgh, 1994), pp. 21ff & 41ff.

[24] John Calvin, *Institutio*, 1.2.2; cf. 1.2.2.

[25] *Institutio*, 1.12.1.

[26] *Institutio*, 1.5.9; 1.13.1, 21.

[27] *Institutio*, 1.3.1; 1.5.1, 9; 1.13.1, 21.

sit Deus)?', a question about what accords with the Nature of God, or the personal question 'Who is God (*quis sit Deus*)?' That is to say, we may know God only in accordance with the One he reveals himself personally to be in his saving activity toward us and what he has revealed to us of his divine Nature through Christ, who as God and Man in his one Person has come as the sole Mediator between God and man to reconcile us to God.[28]

It was a fundamental principle of Calvin which he adopted from the teaching of Irenaeus and Hilary that since God alone knows himself, he may not be known by us except through himself and his own self-witness or testimony.[29] 'How can the human mind define the unlimited Being of God according to its own small measure?'[30] 'In this sense Irenaeus writes that, unlimited though he is, God is finite in his Son (*in filio esse finitum*), for he has accommodated himself to our small measure lest our little minds should be overwhelmed by his immeasurable glory ... God is comprehended in Christ alone.'[31] This means that we may know God only through sharing in the knowledge of the Son by the Father and of the Father by the Son, and the testimony he gives us of himself through his Spirit.[32] As such we disavow any understanding of the Holy Trinity or any formulation of the doctrine of the Holy Trinity that has no intrinsic relation to the saving revelation of God in the life, work and Person of the Lord Jesus Christ. Only he can reveal God truly and perfectly who is himself the very Son of God, only he can speak of God truly and perfectly who is himself the Word of God made flesh. Practically, Calvin says, this means that 'we must not be minded to inquire of God elsewhere than in his sacred Word, or think anything of him except under the guidance of his Word, or to say anything of him except it is taken from the same Word'.[33]

It was in strict adherence to this fundamental principle that Calvin set out his doctrine of the Trinity in the *Institute of Christian Religion*. While God is infinitely exalted above what we can ever conceive of him by ourselves, he nevertheless makes himself known to us through a twofold movement of revelation in which he *lifts us up* above the world and *descends to us* far beneath his own exaltedness, lisping to us, as it were, in words that we can grasp but that are not limpid expressions of what God is like so much as accommodations of his knowledge to the slightness of our minds.[34] Calvin warns that real as knowledge of this kind is, it is not to be confused with 'comprehension', for it is a kind of knowledge that surpasses all understanding, since the divine Reality that our minds embrace by faith in this way is infinite.[35] However, Calvin adds, while God discourses 'sparingly' about his own Being,

he also designates himself in a special way by which he may be known and by which he can be peculiarly distinguished, for he proclaims himself as the

---

[28] *Institutio*, 1.2, 1–2; 1.6.4; 1.10.2; 3.2.6.
[29] Hilary, *De Trinitate*, 1.18; 4.36.
[30] John Calvin, *Institutio*, 1.13.1.
[31] *Institutio*, 2.6.4.
[32] Matt. 11.27; Luke 10.22; 1 Cor. 2.9ff.
[33] *Institutio*, 1.13.21.
[34] *Institutio*, 1.13.1.
[35] *Institutio*, 3.2.14.

One in such a way that he presents himself to be contemplated distinctly in three Persons. Unless we hold fast to these, it is merely a naked and empty name of God without the true God, that flutters about in our brain.[36]

In other words, the 'Trinity' is not just a way of thinking about God, for the one true God is actually and intrinsically Triune and cannot be truly conceived otherwise. There is in fact no real knowledge of God as God except through his revealing or naming of himself as Father, Son and Holy Spirit, for the three Persons are the one true God[37] – apart from them God cannot be known in the truth and reality of his Being.[38] That is precisely the revelation of God that is mediated to us in Scripture: 'Say there is a Trinity of Persons in the one Being of God, and you will have said in a word what the Scripture says, and suppressed empty talk.'[39] 'Because God has manifested himself by his coming in Christ, he has also become known more familiarly in three Persons.'[40] For John Calvin this biblical, Christological and soteriological approach to God through his saving self-revelation as Father, Son and Holy Spirit in Scripture, is one in which we seek to know him strictly in accordance with what he is in his divine Nature and with who he is in his living and saving activity toward us. But it also provides us with a way to know God reverently and obediently in a truly godly manner appropriate to him. 'Scripture and pious experience themselves show us in the absolutely simple Being of God, the Father, the Son and the Holy Spirit.'[41] In this connection Calvin was fond of referring to the teaching of Gregory the Theologian that the Father, the Son and the Holy Spirit are the Godhead, and that we cannot think of One divine Person without immediately being surrounded by the radiance of the Three, nor discern the Three without being carried back to the One, for in their Triunity the Father, the Son and the Holy Spirit shine forth as one undivided Light.[42]

---

[36] *Institutio*, 1.13.2.
[37] Gregory Nazianzen, *Orationes*, 39.11.
[38] *Institutio*, 13.19–20.
[39] *Institutio*, 1.13.5.
[40] *Institutio*, 1.16.1.
[41] John Calvin, *Catechism* (1537), *Opera Selecta*, vol. 1 (Munich, 1926), p. 396; cf. *Institutio*, 1.10.2.
[42] John Calvin, *Institutio*, 1.13.17; *Commentary on John* 1.1; *Epistulae*, 607, etc.; Gregory Nazianzen, *Orationes*, 31.4; 39.11; 40.41. See again my essays on Calvin's Doctrine of the Trinity in *Trinitarian Perspectives*. The trinitarian teaching of Calvin was recognised during the Reformation as so close to that of 'Gregory the Theologian' that he also was spoken of as 'Calvin the Theologian'.

2

The Christian Perspective

GOD being God, all our knowledge of him comes by divine revelation, for it is impossible for us to know God without his willing to be known. *God may be known only through God*, and is known only as he makes himself known to us through the revealing and saving agency of his Word and Spirit. This biblically grounded principle, *without God, God cannot be known*, was clearly formulated by Irenaeus in the second century in a remarkable clarification of the foundations of Christian theology in the early Church.[1] God actively reveals himself through himself, through the incarnation of his Son among us as our Saviour and by the power of his Spirit. 'In all things, and through all things, there is one God the Father, and one Word and one Son, and one Spirit, and one salvation to all who believe in him.'[2] This does not imply a preconceived notion of God or any independent idea of God reached apart from the history of his saving revelation to the people of Israel or behind the back of his self-revelation through his Son Jesus Christ and in his one Spirit actualised in the midst of Israel. There is no God other than the self-revealed God, and no self-revelation of God apart from the fulfilment of his eternal purpose in his saving and reconciling acts in the life, death and resurrection of Jesus proclaimed to us in the Gospel. As Irenaeus taught, it is only with the incarnation of the only begotten Son, who declares the Father and interprets his Word, that the very God who made himself known in a seminal way through the Old Testament prophets foretelling the advent of his Son, is now made known to us in the saving economy of the New Testament revelation in this trinitarian way.[3] In Jesus Christ the Word of God made flesh, God the Father has taken the initiative, actively revealing himself to us through himself as the one and only Lord

---

[1] See especially Irenaeus' discussion of this principle with reference to Matt. 11.27 & Luke 10.22 in the opening chapters of book four of *Adversus haereses*. Thus 4.11: 'The Lord has taught us that no one can know God unless God himself is the Teacher, that is to say, without God, God is not to be known.' (Ἐδίδαξεν ἡμᾶς ὁ Κύριος, ὅτι Θεὸν εἰδέναι οὐδεὶς δύναται, μὴ οὐχὶ Θεοῦ διδάξαντος, τουτέστιν, ἄνευ Θεοῦ μὴ γινώσκεσθαι τὸν Θεόν.) Thus, as Hilary formulated it, God is known only through his witness to himself, for he is his own best Interpreter, *De Trinitate*, 1.18; cf. 4.36.

[2] Irenaeus, *Adversus haereses*, 4.11.

[3] Irenaeus, *Adversus haereses*, 4.18–20; & 4.34.10.

13

God who speaks to us from the free ground of his own self-existent and self-sufficient being, and makes himself known as the otherwise inaccessible, unknowable and unnameable One. He proclaims himself to us and declares to us his own Name 'I am who I am' – the Name that cannot be spoken by human lips for only God can speak it.[4] In the Old Testament Scriptures God is proclaimed as the mighty living God who has created heaven and earth by the command of his Word and who made himself known as God and Saviour through servants and prophets within the special covenant relation established with the people of Israel, who were specially chosen and disciplined throughout their long historical ordeal as the medium for his saving revelation to all mankind. While God revealed himself to Israel through his Word and Spirit addressing them directly as no other people in the course of his redemptive activity on their behalf, yet he was not yet made known to them familiarly and personally as he was in Jesus his incarnate Son in accordance with what he really is *in himself*.[5] In the New Testament Scriptures, however, God is proclaimed as he who in the fullness of time has drawn near to his people as *Emmanuel* (God with us), the God who has become one with them and one of them in order to act on their behalf within their actual historical existence and desperate need and thus to save them from their sins. He has come to reveal himself to them in an utterly concrete and singular way in the incarnation of his Son in the midst of Israel, in order to be the Lord and Saviour not only of Israel but of all humankind, and to bring them through the presence and power of his Spirit into cognitive union and personal communion with himself. Everything hinges here upon the personal identity between Jesus and God. Our Lord himself said to Philip 'He who has seen me has seen the Father.'[6] When we look into the face of Jesus and see there the very face of God we know that we have not seen that face elsewhere and could not see it elsehow. This relation of Jesus to God has been beautifully expressed by H. R. Mackintosh.

> The words of Jesus are the voice of God. The tears of Jesus are the pity of God. The wrath of Jesus is the judgment of God. All believers confess, with adoring praise, that in their most sacred hours, God and Christ merge in each other with morally indistinguishable identity. When in secret we look into God's face, still it is the face of Christ that rises up before us.[7]

The Christian doctrine of God is formulated not in some abstract metaphysical way apart from God's relation to us, but in strict accord with the way which God has actually taken in his self-revealing purpose, not only in naming himself ineffably to Israel and in making himself known to mankind through Israel, but also and supremely in becoming man in the midst of Israel in order to assume our human

---

[4] Exod. 3.14.
[5] Thus our Lord himself: 'Blessed are your eyes, for they see, and your ears, for they hear. Truly, I say to you, many prophets and righteous men longed to see what you see, and did not see it, and to hear what you hear, and did not hear it.' Matt. 13.15–16; Luke 10.23–24; cf. 1 Pet. 1.10–12.
[6] John 14.9.
[7] H. R. Mackintosh, *Doctrine of the Person* (Edinburgh, 1913), p. 340.

nature upon himself and become one with us in Jesus Christ, born of the Virgin Mary, the incarnate Son of God. In becoming one with us, however, and taking our nature upon himself Jesus has made our sin and death his own, in order to redeem and save us from sin and death, and thus through atoning reconciliation to break through the barrier of our enmity to God and restore us to union with him in love, and at the same time to bring about our communion with one another in Christ. In him, the Word of God made flesh, God brought his long historical interaction and revelatory dialogue with Israel to its consummation in revealing, not just something further about himself, but now his very *Self* as the God and Father of the Lord Jesus Christ, and gave specific personal content to his Name 'I am who I am / I will be who I will be' by identifying himself as the Father, the Son and the Holy Spirit. In this final revelation of himself God proclaims himself to all mankind as the one Lord God the Father Almighty, the Maker of heaven and earth, who in his overflowing love will not be without us human beings but has freely come among us to be one of us and one with us in order to reconcile us to himself and to bring us into communion with himself.

The Christian doctrine of God derives specifically from within this unique, definitive self-revelation of the one Lord God through Jesus Christ and in one Spirit – that is, from the historical self-revelation of God as God become man for us and our salvation. It is there in the Lord Jesus, the only begotten Son of the Father incarnate in history, that God 'defines' himself for us as he really is in himself, as Father, Son and Holy Spirit, and it is there that we learn that God is God precisely as he is the very Father, Son and Holy Spirit whom we come to know in the saving events of the Gospel and whom we are called to love with all our heart and mind and soul. In Christ alone, the one only-begotten Son of God, who is of one and the same Being as God the Father, is God's self-revelation perfectly identical with himself. Only in Christ, God become man for us, does he communicate his self-revelation to us by the power of his Spirit in such a redeeming and enlightening way that we may apprehend it and, human beings though we are, really know God in himself, both in his oneness as the Lord God and in his differentiation as Father, Son and Holy Spirit, one Being, three Persons. Thus to recall again the words of John Calvin:

> God designates himself in a special way by which he may be known and by which he can be peculiarly distinguished, for he proclaims himself as the One in such a way that he presents himself to be contemplated distinctly as three Persons. Unless we hold fast to these it is merely a naked and empty name of God, without the true God, that flutters about in our brain.[8]

In other words, in 'the Holy Trinity' we have to do with God himself, not just modal ways of thinking about God, for the One true God is actually and intrinsically Triune and cannot be truly conceived otherwise. There is in fact no real knowledge of God except through his revealing or naming of himself as Father, Son and Holy Spirit, for the three Persons are the One true God. The only God there is, is he who has named himself to Israel as 'I am who I am / I will be who I will be', and who as the same Lord has personally come to us as 'God with us', clothed with his triune self-revelation and self-designation as Father, Son and Holy Spirit. The transcendent God who is the free ground of his own eternal Being is none other than the very one who has shown us his face in the Jesus Christ and imparted to us his one Spirit. He is the one Lord God of heaven and earth in whom we believe and whom we worship as Father, Son and Holy Spirit.

It is the Gospel of God's revealing and saving acts in Jesus Christ that provides us with this perspective for a formulation of the Christian doctrine of God. It belongs to the essence of the Gospel that God has come among us and become one with us in such a reconciling and miraculous way as to demolish the barriers of our creaturely distance and estrangement from him, and has spoken to us directly and intimately about himself in Jesus Christ his beloved Son. In him he has made himself known to us as God the Father Almighty, the Creator of heaven and earth and of all things visible and invisible, the one Lord and Saviour of mankind. Only God can know and explain himself, so that he may be apprehended by us his human creatures only through his incarnate condescension to be one with us and through his Spirit to make us participate in the knowledge which God has of himself. As our Lord Jesus Christ himself declared:

> I thank you, Father, Lord of heaven and earth, for hiding these things from the learned and wise, and revealing them to the simple. Yes, Father, such was your choice. Everything has been entrusted to me by my Father; and no one knows the Son but the Father, and no one knows the Father but the Son and those to whom the Son chooses to reveal him.[9]

Alongside this teaching of Jesus in the Gospel should be placed the teaching of St Paul in his first Epistle to the Corinthians:

> What no eye has seen, nor ear heard, nor the heart of man conceived, what God has prepared for those who love him, God has revealed to us through the Spirit. For the Spirit searches everything, even the depths of God. For what person knows a man's thoughts except the spirit of the man which is in him? So also no one knows the things of God except the Spirit of God. And we have received this Spirit from God, not the spirit of the world, so that we may know the things which God has graciously given to us.[10]

Just as there is an exclusive relation of mutual knowing between the Father and the Son, so there is an exclusive relation of mutual knowing between God and the Spirit. The content of this self-knowing of God through the Son and the Spirit is one and the same, and so in our reception of the Spirit given to us by Christ we are enabled to share in that content, and thus know God through himself.

With the incarnation this relation in mutual knowing exclusive to the Father and the Son has been embodied among us in Jesus Christ, the Son of the Father

---

[9] Matt. 11.25-27; Luke 10.21–22.
[10] 1 Cor. 2.9–12.

become man, so that he constitutes in himself the all-important bridge between God and man and the one place in space and time where we human beings may share in God's knowledge of himself and really know him and believe in him in accordance with his own self-interpretation. It was on the ground of this mutual indwelling between himself and the Father that Jesus could say to Thomas: 'I am the way, and the truth, and the life; no one comes to the Father, but by me.'[11] In him the 'I am who I am', the Lord, has become man, yet without ceasing to be the Lord. The actualisation of that unique revelation of God the Father in Jesus Christ and its mediation to us in the Holy Spirit sent by the Father in the name of the Son,[12] tell us that God may not now be known by us in his undifferentiated and unnameable oneness, behind the back of Jesus Christ, or without the gift of the Holy Spirit, his self-witnessing presence among us. It is only through Christ and in the Spirit that we are given access to the Father,[13] and thereby may know God in his one yet three-fold self-revelation as Father, Son and Holy Spirit. While this knowledge of God is actualised in us through the Communion of the Holy Spirit, who is the Spirit of the Father and of the Son, its content is determined and informed by what has once for all taken place in Jesus Christ, the Lord and Saviour of mankind, for in him and through him, the one Word of God, all our thinking and speaking of God are brought into faithful conformity to him as the incarnate self-articulation and self-communication of God to mankind. Thus as the Word of God made flesh Jesus Christ embodies in himself not only the exclusive language of God to mankind but the faithful response in knowledge and obedience of humanity to God.

The specifically Christian doctrine of God is thus inescapably and essentially *Christocentric*, for it pivots upon God's *self*-revelation and *self*-communication in the incarnation, in an objective manifestation, an imprint of the divine *Hypostasis*, which is identical with the very Being (αὐτὸ τὸ ὄν) of God himself.[14] This does not mean that all our knowledge of God can be reduced to Christology, but that, as there is only one Mediator between God and man, who is himself both God and Man, and only one revelation of God in which he himself is its actual content, all authentic knowledge of God is derived and understood in accordance with the incarnate reality of God's self-revelation in Jesus Christ, and is formulated in doctrinal coherence with Christology. This is to say, doctrinal statements about God are possible and true only when Christologically grounded, for only in Jesus Christ do we really have to do with an objective personal self-revelation of God which bridges the distance between God and us and which is identical with the very Being of God himself. We cannot think and speak of God truly apart from his Word and his Act in the incarnation, and that means, apart from Jesus Christ.

Otherwise expressed, Jesus Christ is the one place given to us within space and time where we may know God the Father, for it is only in him, the only begotten

[11] John 14.6.
[12] John 14.26; 16.12–15; 1 Cor. 2.9–12.
[13] Eph. 2.18.
[14] Cf. Heb. 1.3. Athanasius thought of Christ the Word of God as the one Form or Εἶδος of Godhead, *Contra Arianos*, 3.6, 15–16; *De synodis*, 52; *Ad Afros*, 4.

17

Son of the Father, that the very Nature of God is revealed and that we may draw near to him through his reconciling and saving activity and know him in accordance with his Nature. Thus the Incarnation constitutes the one actual source and the one controlling centre of the Christian doctrine of God, for he who became man in Jesus Christ in order to be our Saviour is identical in Being and Nature and Act with God the Father revealed in and through him. He is not some created intermediary between God and the world but the very Word and Son of God who eternally inheres in the Being of God so that for us to know God in Jesus Christ, and to know him as the God and Father of the Lord Jesus Christ, is really to know God as he is in himself in his eternal Being as God and in the transcendent Love that God is. He is in himself not other than what he is toward us in his loving, revealing and saving presence in Christ.

It is with the same force that our knowing and worshipping of God include the Holy Spirit for, differentiated though they are in their Persons, the presence of the Spirit and the presence of the Father and the presence of Christ to us are ontically and ultimately indistinguishable. As he whom the Father sends through the Son to dwell with us and open our minds toward himself beyond ourselves, and thus to complete the circle of God's own self-revealing and self-imparting movement in us whereby he enables us to respond to him in faith and understanding, the Holy Spirit is no less divine than the Son. How could the Spirit pour the love of God into our hearts, how could the Spirit mediate Christ to us, and how could Christ be present to us in the Spirit, if the Spirit were not himself divine like the Father and the Son and of one and the same being (ὁμοούσιος) with them? Like the Son of God the Holy Spirit is no mere cosmic power intermediate between God and the world, but is the very Spirit of God who eternally dwells in him and in whom God knows himself, so that for us to know God in his Spirit is to know him in the hidden depths of his Triune Being as Holy Spirit as well as Father and Son. Apart from the Communion of the Holy Spirit we could not enjoy the Grace of the Lord Jesus Christ and the Love of God the Father.

Only because God has actually made himself known to us can we speak of him in this way. Here we leap ahead into the 'doctrine' of the Holy Trinity and anticipate something of its essential content. That is natural in view of the movement of God's trinitarian self-revelation to us in Jesus Christ and in the Holy Spirit, but before we go further several interrelated points of primary significance require our attention.

1

We must take into account the fact that this triune self-revelation of God as Father, Son and Holy Spirit, mediated to us through the Gospel, is something utterly new which we could not otherwise know or conceive. When God addresses us he tells us something about himself which we could never tell ourselves, something so radically different that it creates a new situation in human existence and history and calls for new ways of thinking and speaking about God on our part. That is why, as Jesus himself said, his contemporaries had such difficulty in understanding what he was saying, because they were unable to grasp his Word.[15] And that is why also the unique self-revelation of God in Jesus Christ gave rise among his followers to a new genre of literature, the gospels and epistles enshrined in the New Testament Scriptures, which may not be interpreted aright simply through comparison with other religious literature ancient or modern, but only in the light of the distinctive message they were divinely inspired to convey, and out of the kind of intelligibility imposed upon them by the Word and Spirit of God.

By its very nature divine revelation is what Karl Barth called 'a self-contained *novum*',[16] for it has its reality and truth wholly and in every respect within itself, and so can be known only through itself and out of itself, on its own ground and through the power of its own self-evidence and self-authentication. It is as such that revelation proceeds from God to man, breaking sovereignly into human life and thought, calling into question what people claim to know, and directing their thinking beyond themselves altogether. It creatively evokes an entirely new mode of consciousness, in faith and understanding, conditioned by a new relation to God initiated and set up, not from man's side at all, but from the other side of the boundary between man and God. The knowledge of God given in this way through divine revelation is not from the known to the unknown, but from the hitherto unknown to the known. It is a mystery so utterly strange and so radically different that it cannot be apprehended and substantiated except out of itself, and even then it infinitely exceeds what we are ever able to conceive or spell out. Far less may it be assimilated into man's familiar world of meaning and be brought into line with the framework of its commonly accepted truths, for the radically new conception of God proclaimed in the Gospel calls for a complete transformation of man's outlook in terms of a new divine order which cannot be derived from or inferred from anything conceived by man before. In point of fact it actually conflicts sharply with generally accepted beliefs and established ideas in human culture and initiates a seismic reconstruction not only of religious and intellectual belief but of the very foundations of human life and knowledge.

This was the great difficulty that confronted the Church immediately the Gospel was proclaimed in the ancient world, when Christians found that the supreme truth of God's incarnate self-revelation in salvation history could not be known on the strength of anything other than itself, but only through a primary act of cognitive assent to its compelling claims and saving impact. That is to say, the God and Father of Jesus Christ is to be known through faith creatively called forth from people in response to the thrust of its intrinsic truth upon them and in sharp antithesis to what they had believed about God before. The fathers and theologians of the Early Church reflected upon the fact that, since the proof of an unknown reality is its own evidence and the conceptual assent or basic belief it calls forth from people, the right way for people to break through into a completely new realm of meaning or truth is the way of *faith* – hence the principle widely

[15] John 8.43.
[16] Karl Barth, *Church Dogmatics* I.1 (Edinburgh, 2nd edn, 1975), p. 306.

promulgated in the Church: 'unless you believe you will not understand'.[17] This is certainly the case whenever we have to do with *ultimates* which carry their own authority calling for the intelligent commitment of belief, and provide the irreducible ground upon which rational knowledge and theological formulation take place.

Those early Christian theologians were, therefore, surely right when they insisted that we may acquire knowledge of something quite new or hitherto unknown, not through processes of explicit reasoning, important as they may be within the brackets of what is already known, but only through an ontological act of recognition and assent which cannot be further analysed, and which arises compulsorily in our minds as we allow what is new to authenticate itself to us in its own reality and to disclose itself to us in its intrinsic significance and truth.[18] Knowledge of new realities or events calls for correspondingly new ways of thinking and speaking, in which new concepts and terms have to be coined, or in which ordinary forms of thought and speech have to be stretched, adapted and refined to make them appropriate to the realities to which they are intended to refer.[19]

As we learn in the gospels, this is what had already happened to the disciples and apostles of Christ as he became disclosed to them in his revealing and saving activity and they were enabled through the gift of his Spirit, by whom God bears witness to himself, to be open to his intrinsic truth and believe in him. The mighty acts of God in the astonishingly new and utterly unique events of the birth, life, death and resurrection of Christ staked out the ground on which alone they were to be approached, apprehended and understood. No one ever spoke and acted as Jesus did with his divine self-authenticating authority. What he said and did brought about a radically new conception of God and a complete inversion and transformation of man's outlook in terms of the new divine order, the Kingdom of God that had suddenly irrupted into history with the coming and presence of Jesus Christ, and established itself finally in human existence and destiny through his Cross and resurrection. It is the same with us today, as it has been throughout the long history of the Church. Divine revelation is of such a nature that through its self-actualisation it creates within historical human existence the specific place where it anchors itself, and where through witness to it, it continues to exert its seismic and regenerating force in the life and thought of humanity. Thus the great evangelical realities and historical events to which the New Testament bears witness continue through the presence of the Holy Spirit to confront and impress themselves upon our minds in virtue of their self-evidencing force, and continue to take shape in our understanding through their intrinsic truth. It is in this way that the Gospel provides the unique perspective within which the distinctively Christian doctrine of God is continually to be shaped and expressed.

[17] See my discussion in *Divine Meaning, Studies in Patristic Hermeneutics* (T & T Clark, Edinburgh, 1995), chs 5 and 6.

[18] Refer to 'The Implications of Oikonomia for Knowledge and Speech of God in Early Christian Theology', my contribution to *Oikonomia. Heilsgeschichte als Thema der Theologie*, dedicated to Oscar Cullmann on his 65th birthday (Hamburg-Bergstedt, 1967), pp. 223-238, reprinted in *Divine Meaning*, ch. 7.

[19] Thus Athanasius, *Contra Arianos*, 1.23f; 4.27; *De synodis*, 42; *De decretis*, 12; *Ad Serapionem*, 1.8–9, 16–20.

This brings us to the all-important point that in proving itself to us and generating in us its own reception, God's self-revelation as Father, Son and Holy Spirit both creates the framework within which it is solely to be understood and generates the very forms of thought and speech with which it is to be grasped and articulated. The ultimate source of this triune self-revelation of God is God himself. There is no other point above or below God from which he may be approached, but in Jesus Christ his beloved Son God the Father has incarnated his self-revelation within our world in an utterly concrete and singular way and thus provided in the fullness of time the one place where we human beings may have access to the transcendent reality of God and may know him on the free ground of his own divine Being. Only he can reveal God who is perfectly one in Being and Nature with the One whom he reveals – this is what God in his immeasurable grace has freely provided for us in the incarnate Person of his Son and in the Person of the Holy Spirit, in and through whose oneness in Being with the Father the mystery of the Triune Nature of God, otherwise inaccessible to us, becomes disclosed.

This *incarnate* revelation of God to us as Father, Son and Holy Spirit, which derives from the ultimate ground that God himself eternally is, provides for us the immediate ground in human existence and history where God may be known as he is in his Triune Reality. It is, then, this two-fold ground in God and in Christ Jesus, in the Father and the Son, that together with the Communion of the Spirit forms the framework within which the Holy Trinity is to be known, understood and interpreted. The immediate ground on which we actually know God in his historical self-revelation is one and the same with the ultimate ground that God himself eternally is, for in Jesus Christ and in the Holy Spirit God is wholly identical with the content of his self-revelation and self-communication. God reveals himself through himself, and what God communicates to us is not something of himself but his very Self, true God from true God. In him the Revealer and the Revealed, the Giver and the Gift are of one and the same Being. In Jesus Christ God has revealed himself and given himself to us unreservedly in the fullness of his divine Reality, in such a way that what he reveals and gives to us is grounded in his ultimate Being as God. That is the central truth, the Deity of Christ, upon which the Christian conception of God and of his saving activity depends, as the great theologians and councils made clear once for all in the fourth century in their formulation of the crucial concept of the *homoousion* (ὁμοούσιος τῷ Πατρί) applied to the Son and the Spirit as the key truth they had to maintain against threats to the Gospel from every side. What God is toward us in his revealing and saving acts in the Gospel he is in himself in his own eternal Being as God. Unless that is the case, any disjunction between the self-revelation of God the Father through Christ and in the Spirit could only mean that in the last analysis the Gospel is empty of any divine reality or validity. This is why the faith of Christians rests upon the supreme truth of the Deity of Christ and the Holy Spirit, for only through God himself is saving communion with God accessible to us.

It is, then, the incarnate self-revelation of God as Father, Son and Holy Spirit anchored in human existence and proclaimed to us in the Gospel, which in complete oneness with the ultimate ground that God eternally is establishes the ground in space and time on which alone the Holy Trinity may be known by us. As such the revelation of the Holy Trinity mediated to us through the Gospel both creates the parameters within which God's Triunity may properly be apprehended, and generates the conceptual and linguistic instruments with which it may be interpreted and formulated. It was thus that the doctrine of the Holy Trinity forced itself upon the mind of the Church and transformed it in such a way that ordinary terms like 'father', 'son', 'spirit', 'word', 'being', and 'communion', were taken up and radically altered, and quite new concepts and terms, not found in the biblical revelation, like 'person' and 'consubstantial', together with quite new ways of thinking, of a dynamic, ontological and relational kind, were developed and incorporated into the articulated body of Christian dogmatics. In fact, within the framework created by the trinitarian self-revelation of God a new theological *mathesis* is required in accordance with the unique reality of God's triune self-revelation, for one can move and think properly of it only within its self-enclosed circle and strictly in accordance with the Nature of the ever-living God directly made known to us by the Father in his revealing and saving acts in Jesus Christ and the Holy Spirit.

2

It should now be clear that the self-revelation of God is necessarily exclusive both because it is only through God that God makes himself known and because he makes himself known as the one and only Lord God in the utterly singular event of the incarnation. Revelation is not the revealing of something about God, but God revealing himself out of himself in such a way that he who reveals and he who is revealed are one and the same. That is to say, God is at once the Subject and the Object of revelation, and never the Object without also being the Subject. This interlocking of the Being and the Act of God in his revelation excludes the possibility of there being any other revelation, just as the very nature of God excludes the possibility of there being any other God beside himself. This is already evident in the unique self-naming of God to his covenant people Israel as 'I am who I am' which also carries with it the sense of 'I will be who I will be', for he is the ever-living completely self-sufficient and wholly self-grounded God in all that he is and does. As such he is who he exclusively is in all his mighty acts of revelation and salvation, before whom there is and can be no other. 'I am the Lord your God: you must have no other gods beside me.'[20] That was the supreme truth which was impressed upon Israel by the Word of God through Moses once for all at the law-giving at Mount Sinai and which through the prophets was made to reverberate in the soul of Israel throughout all its long historical dialogue with God. 'I am the Lord, that is my name; my glory I give to no other.'[21] The revelation of God as One necessarily excludes not only the reality but also the possibility of there being other gods. Hence really to know God as he has revealed himself is to be totally committed to him as he who is above all gods, who cannot be confused or equated with any or be in competition with others. By its very nature the monotheism of the Old Testament revelation excludes and rejects any form of polytheism as the denial of

[20] Exod. 20.1f.
[21] Isa. 42.8.

the ultimate incomparable Godness of God – this is the point of the recurring stress in the Old Testament upon the fact that the Lord God is a 'jealous God', for the absolute oneness of his Nature is *eo ipso* intolerant of any other claim to deity. That exclusiveness of belief in God calling for unreserved commitment to him was made trenchantly clear by Moses in his final testimony to Israel before he died, which was permanently sealed upon the mind and continuing existence of Israel as the covenant people correlated to the uniqueness of God: 'Hear, O Israel: the Lord our God is one Lord; and you shall love the Lord your God with all your heart and with all your soul, and with all your might.'[22]

When we turn to the fulfilment of God's revelation as the unique and final revelation of his Self in the incarnation, we find that Jesus explicitly reiterated the Mosaic proclamation and strengthened the commitment it called for: 'You shall love the Lord your God with all your heart, and with all your soul, and with all your mind, and all your strength.'[23] 'Do not suppose', he said, 'that I have come to abolish the law and the prophets; I did not come to abolish but to complete. Truly I tell you: so long as heaven and earth endure, not a letter, not a jot, will disappear from the law until all that must happen has happened.'[24] Moreover, Jesus appropriated to himself again and again the self-designating 'I am' of *Yahweh*, as for example in identifying himself with the very Life and Light of God the Father, and was acknowledged as such by the disciples when they said of him *Jesus is Lord* ('Ιησοῦς Κύριος). In Jesus, however, we meet with the Lord who has become incarnate among us within space and time in a divinely as well as a historically unrepeatable once and for all event, so that in him the oneness of God's self-revelation as the Lord is reinforced in the most absolute way. And, as we have seen, Jesus himself personally endorsed that when he spoke of the mutual indwelling of the Son and the Father, and added: 'I am the way, the truth and the life: no one comes to the Father except by me.'[25] As the only begotten Son of the Father who is inseparably one with him Jesus Christ is the one and only self-revelation of God the Father which by its very nature excludes any other possibility – the truth which the Church was later to formulate in teaching that in the Lord Jesus Christ divine Nature and human nature are inseparably united in one Person. There is not and cannot be any other incarnation, for there is no other God than this God who has become incarnate once and for all in Christ Jesus. Nor can there be any other God-man or more than one God-man, for that would conflict sharply with the union of divine and human nature in the one Person of Christ. The absolute singularity of Jesus Christ as the only begotten Son of God become incarnate for us and our salvation, in whom God has once for all revealed and communicated his very Self to us, thus occupies the central ground on which the Christian conception of God rests. But, let it be reiterated, as such it is intrinsically and essentially exclusive. Here we have a theological form of the scientific principle in accordance with which the selection of one among other apparently possible paths in the formulation

---

[22] Deut. 6.4.
[23] Matt. 22.37; Mark 12.29ff; Luke 10.27.
[24] Matt. 5.17–18.
[25] John 14.6.

of physical law sets the others aside as unentertainable and actually impossible. It is not in principle otherwise in Christian theology. It is not arrogance but humility and obedience before the intrinsic nature of the truth which in Christ Jesus forces itself upon us that make us assent to its inherent and compelling claim to be the one and only *self*-revelation of God in accordance with his own inherent Nature and transcendent Majesty.

When we look into the trinitarian content of this self-revelation of God as Father, Son and Holy Spirit, *One Being, Three Persons* (μία οὐσία, τρεῖς ὑποστάσεις) we become even more aware of its intrinsically unique and exclusive nature, for to believe in God as a Trinity in his eternal Being, means renouncing every form of unitarianism as well as of polytheism. In fact to conceive of God as Unity and Trinity, Trinity and Unity, is the most exclusive of all possible conceptions of God, not only because there is no humanly explicable way of thinking of the Three as One and the One as Three, but because of the unique Nature of God who *is* Father, Son and Holy Spirit in his one eternal Being. However we may and surely must say that the Three Persons are integrated in the One Being and the One Being is integrated in the Three Divine Persons, such that there is no One Being apart from the Three Persons, and there are no Three Divine Persons apart from the One Being, and such that the ontological relations between the Three Divine Persons belong to what they intrinsically are both in their distinction from one another and in their union and communion with one another. *The Three Persons are God, and God is the Three Persons.*[26] Hence, for us to know God as Triune is to know the one Lord of God in his internal relations as a fullness of personal Being, and not in an undifferentiated oneness as an isolated transcendental Thou, which would be little more than a negative borderline notion of God quite unintelligible to our minds. This trinitarian self-revelation of God as three distinctive divine Persons who are indivisibly one ultimate divine Being enshrines the profoundest and the most positive conception of God's Oneness. Trinity and Unity exist in and through each other. That is why it is through the Trinity that we believe in the Unity of God, and it is through the Unity of the Father, Son and Holy Spirit that we believe in the Holy Trinity.

The Holy Trinity is categorically incomparable and non-derivable. It is not surprising, therefore, that the doctrine of the Trinity *eo ipso* involves the rejection even of theism as quite inadequate and theologically unacceptable. The one trinitarian way of thinking of God forced upon us through the incarnation calls into question and sets aside at the same time any alternative way of thinking of him, apart from the incarnation or behind the back of Jesus Christ, and without taking into account the very heart of the Gospel in the oneness in Being and Act between God the Father and his reconciling self-communication to us in his beloved Son and in his Holy Spirit. To admit any other than a trinitarian way of thinking about God is in fact not only to relativise and question the truth of the Trinity but to contradict the Trinity and to set aside the Gospel. Hence in the formulation of

---

[26] Cf. Augustine's expressions in his *Confessiones*, 1.7.7: '*una trinitas et trina unitas ... trina unitas et una trinitas Deus.*'

the doctrine of the Trinity we are committed to worshipping and obeying God unreservedly, with all our heart and soul and mind in an approach which sets aside all other religious approaches and abolishes any entertainment of alternative devotions and conceptions of God as invalid.

This does not mean that the unique revelation of God in Jesus Christ denies the fact that God has actually made himself known to people in the world from the beginning of the creation, although without revealing his own Self in the familiar personal way as he has done in Christ. Nor does it mean that this revelation of God simply extinguishes the lights of the creation or the contingent intelligibility which God has imposed upon it through his Word, but that it cuts through the twisted apprehension of them due to the alienated and self-inturned nature of the human mind whereby it eclipses the light of the creation and falsifies its truth.[27] Thus it means, as St Paul wrote to the Romans,[28] that in divine judgment upon all ungodliness and unrighteousness of the heathen, it is disclosed that what can be known of God has been wickedly suppressed, even the eternal power and deity of God manifested by him in what he has created, so that the very truth about God made known to mankind in this way becomes turned into a lie. As our Lord himself pointed out, the very light that is in people can become darkness.[29] This means that faithful Christian proclamation of the Gospel must reckon with the refracted lights and distorted conceptions of God in other religions, while nevertheless remaining true to the unique and final self-revelation of God in Jesus Christ which has the effect of calling all other approaches to the knowledge and worship of God into question. It is much the same kind of situation that obtains in justification by grace alone: by being freely put in the right with God we are thereby revealed to be in the wrong in ourselves, so that we are ashamed even of our goodness as unworthy in God's sight.

3

We have seen that God's unique self-revelation as Father, Son and Holy Spirit, effected through the sending of his only begotten Son and the mission of the Holy Spirit, stakes out the ground and establishes the parameters within which alone it is rightly to be understood. This revelation is given, not in any piecemeal way, but in a unitary way as an indivisible whole. The Holy Trinity is a Unity and the Unity is a Trinity, for God *is* Triune in himself and it is essentially in a triune way that God makes himself known to us, even though in different situations for some specific reason the immediate focus may be directed by divine revelation upon one or two and not upon all three divine Persons at the same time. For example, in the opening salutation of his Second Epistle to the Corinthians St Paul refers only to the Father and the Son, but in his benediction at the end he includes the Holy

---

[27] Refer to Karl Barth's illuminating discussion of these created lights in *Church Dogmatics* IV.3.1 (Edinburgh, 1961), pp. 135–165. See also George Hunsinger, *How to Read Karl Barth. The Shape of his Theology* (Oxford, 1991), 'Secular Parables of the Truth', pp. 234–280.

[28] Rom. 1.16ff; cf. Acts 17.22ff.

[29] Luke 11.35; Matt. 6.23.

Spirit as well.[30] Thus it may be said that the whole doctrine of the Trinity is implicit in and is unfolded from knowledge of Christ, for, as St Paul writes elsewhere, 'it is in Christ that the Godhead in all his fullness dwells embodied.'[31] This implies that in our explicit apprehension of the relation between any two divine Persons we are given in God's self-revelation an implicit apprehension of all three as a whole. It is in our knowing of the Triunity of God above all that we are engaged in a kind of knowing in which we move from the 'whole' to the 'parts', and from the 'parts' to the 'whole', understanding the 'parts' in the light of the 'whole' and the 'whole' in the light of the 'parts'. This way of speaking of the 'whole' and 'parts', however, is not strictly appropriate to God's triune self-revelation as Unity and Trinity and Trinity and Unity, for the three divine Persons may not be thought of as 'parts' of the Trinity nor may the Trinity be thought of as a 'whole' composed of 'parts'.[32] Neither is it appropriate to our apprehension of the Holy Trinity, although it may be more appropriate when we are speaking of the 'doctrine' of the Trinity as a whole and the distinct 'doctrines' of the Father, of the Son, and of the Holy Spirit.

It must also be pointed out, however, that while the Triune God reveals himself as a whole and while it is as a whole that God is the object of our knowing, this does not mean that we can know him wholly or have a comprehensive knowledge of him, for in his transcendent wholeness, God eludes our comprehension. What God does allow us to apprehend of himself breaks through the narrow confines of our grasp, so that in the very act of *apprehending* something of him we know that we are incapable of *comprehending* him. Even in his condescension to reveal himself to us God infinitely exceeds what we can grasp or conceive, so that our knowledge of the whole God cannot but be 'in part' or partial.[33] As Hilary in his work on the Trinity expressed it, in the mystery of his unfathomable Nature the God whom we know is a *Totum*, but we do not and cannot know him *in toto*, yet what God does allow us to grasp of himself is inextricably involved in his wholeness and is not just a part of him.[34] Moreover, since God in his wholeness is infinitely greater than we can ever comprehend, what we may say of him in our apprehending of him 'in part' is bound to indicate far more than we can ever express.

We have to do here with an epistemic point of quite signal importance, of which we have experience in other spheres of knowledge, in the way in which our apprehension of wholes and their constituent parts are cognised in their relation to one another. The whole is much greater and richer in its intelligibility than the sum of its parts, so that when we try to understand something through reductionist

---

[30] 2 Cor. 1.2f: 'Grace be to you and peace from God our Father, and from the Lord Jesus Christ. Blessed be the God and Father of our Lord Jesus Christ, the Father of mercies and the God of all comfort;' and 2 Cor. 13.14: 'The grace of the Lord Jesus Christ and the love of God and the communion of the Holy Spirit be with you all.'

[31] Col. 2.9; cf. also 1.19.

[32] Cf. Tertullian's subordinationist conception of the Trinity as a Unity distributed into Trinity involving an arrangement of its parts, which leads him to speak of the Son and the Spirit has having a secondary and derived status compared with the Monarchy or unique rule of the Father. *Adversus Praxean*, 2–8.

[33] 1 Cor. 13.12.

[34] Hilary, *De Trinitate*, 2.6.

analysis and consideration of its component parts we are unable to grasp it in the depths of its reality. This was an important issue for James Clerk Maxwell in his determination to move away from the traditional habit of thinking of the universe as made up of parts, when mathematicians, he said, usually begin by considering a single particle, and then proceed by conceiving its relation to other particles.

To conceive of a particle, however, requires a process of abstraction, since all our perceptions are related to extended bodies, so that the idea of the *all* that is in our consciousness at a given instant is perhaps as primitive an idea as that of any individual thing. Hence there may be a mathematical method in which we proceed from the whole to the parts instead of from the parts to the whole.[35]

Similarly Michael Polanyi pointed out in regard to the automatic perception of visual and auditory wholes, that in our cognition of the whole we are implicitly aware of the parts and in our focal cognition of the parts we are subsidiarily aware of the whole, as for example in the case of a physiognomy, a tune, or a pattern.[36] Borrowing his language, then, we may say that in our apprehension of God's trinitarian self-revelation in its intrinsic wholeness we are relying on our subsidiary awareness of the particular Persons of the Trinity and in our explicit apprehension of each particular Person we are relying on an *implicit awareness of the whole Trinity*. And using Clerk Maxwell's language we may say that the Trinitarian 'all' of God's self-revelation to us as Father, Son and Holy Spirit, must be recognised as *the* 'primitive', primordial or fundamental, conception which God gives us of himself. The 'all' is here, however, not the oneness of God as such, but his three-in-oneness as an indivisible comprehensive whole.

This being the case, we must never allow anything to downgrade or make secondary, in any account of the Christian conception of God, the trinitarian self-presentation of God to us, or correspondingly our apprehension of the Trinity, as an aboriginal comprehensive whole. Rather must we make sure that this whole is allowed to determine our formulation of the doctrine of the Trinity from end to end. There reinforces our thought here the truth, which we have already discussed, that the Holy Trinity is completely self-grounded in his own ultimate Reality, and that his self-revelation is a self-enclosed *novum* which may be known and interpreted only on its own ground and out of itself. All this means that in a faithful account of the doctrine of the Holy Trinity our thought cannot but engage in a deep circular movement from Unity to Trinity and from Trinity to Unity, for we are unable to speak of the whole Triunity without already speaking of the three particular Persons of the Trinity or to speak of any of the three Persons without presuming knowledge of the whole Triunity, for God is God only as he is Father, Son and Holy Spirit.

In this circular procedure we are not operating with a vicious circle, begging the question, or falling into the fallacy of a *petitio principii*. On the contrary, we are avoiding the grave mistake of retreating from the reality of God's trinitarian self-

---

[35] James Clerk Maxwell, *A Treatise on Electricity and Magnetism*, 3rd edn, vol. 2 (London and New York, 1954), p. 176f. See also the Preface of volume 1, p. ixf.

[36] Michael Polanyi, e.g. in *Personal Knowledge* (London, 1958), pp. 57ff.

revelation, and moving outside of it in order to argue from some starting point of our own choosing or some alleged ground above or beyond the Holy Trinity from which the truth and validity of the doctrine of the Trinity may be judged. That would be in fact to deny that God is God, that he constitutes in himself the transcendent ground which we cannot know or understand in any way except in and through himself. It would be just as fallacious as attempting to justify ultimates in terms of what is not ultimate. Let it be repeated: we cannot apprehend and interpret the Holy Trinity except upon his own ultimate ground and within the comprehensive framework of thought of which the Trinity is himself the all-decisive constituent and determinant. To say the least, what we are concerned with in theological elucidation and formulation here is the proper circular procedure inherent in any coherent system of thought operating with ultimate axioms or beliefs which cannot be justified or derived from any other ground than that which they themselves constitute. Thus in coherent conceptual systems with which we are familiar today in various fields of scientific knowledge, we are committed to certain ultimate axioms or beliefs for which we can offer no independent demonstration, but without which the scientific system concerned, together with the knowledge it yields, would not be possible at all.

Why should it be, how could it be, otherwise in the doctrine of the Holy Trinity, which is to be grasped only through a radical rethinking and structural recasting of all our prior beliefs and preconceptions about God? In the Holy Trinity we are confronted with an ultimate self-revelation of God into the truth of which there is no way of penetrating from what we already know or believe we know, far less of establishing it on grounds that are outside of it. Hence in a genuine theology, and above all in the doctrine of the Trinity, if it is only through God that we know God, and if it is only through the personal Communion which God is that we can have communion with him, then formulation of the Christian doctrine of God must be *intentionally circular*. It is constrained by the ultimate nature of its subject-matter, that is, by the very nature of the Lord God himself, to let understanding and interpretation take the internally consistent form of a proper circle in which all exposition moves from God to God, from his revelation to us back to himself, and from himself to his revelation, from what he is for us to what he is in himself, and from what he is in himself to what he is for us. Hence, as no one has pointed out more clearly than Karl Barth, 'The Church doctrine of the Trinity is a self-enclosed circle.'[37] This is to say, in giving an account of the doctrine of the Holy Trinity we cannot speak of the beginning without speaking of the end, or speak of the end without speaking of the beginning, and cannot speak of either the beginning or the end without speaking of the middle. This is why we may not properly separate knowledge of what God is toward us and for us from knowledge of what he is eternally in himself, but must consider them together in such a way that our thought moves back and forward between them, from what God is *for us* to what he is *in himself* and from what he is *in himself* to what he is *for us*: neither is properly understandable without the other within the wholeness of God's triune self-revelation.

[37] Karl Barth, *Church Dogmatics* I.1 (Edinburgh, 2nd edn, 1975), p. 380.

It was said above, with some reservation, that in our knowing of the Triunity of God we engage in a kind of knowing in which we move from the 'whole' to the 'parts' and from the 'parts' to the 'whole'. The reason for the reservation is due to the fact that the oneness of the Trinity is a three-in-oneness, that is, a wholeness which includes the three divine Persons such that each divine Person is himself whole God, so that the usual way of thinking in terms of the whole and the parts does not apply. As we will discuss fully later, the three divine Persons are related to one another and to the whole Trinity in a unique co-indwelling way. Without losing their distinctive differences they interrelate with one another and the one Being of God so that the whole Being of God belongs to each of them as it belongs to all of them, and belongs to all of them as it belongs to each of them.[38] This means that the 'whole' and the 'parts' mutually contain and interpenetrate one another in an incomparable and ineffable way. Thus we must think of the doctrine of the Holy Trinity and the doctrines of the Father, of the Son and of the Holy Spirit, as interpenetrating each other, such that the 'whole' is in each 'part', and each 'part' is in the 'whole'. Hence the doctrine of the Holy Trinity may not be expounded just by itself apart from the doctrines of the Father, the Son and the Spirit, and the doctrines of the Father, the Son, and the Spirit may not be expounded simply by themselves in isolation from one another or from the whole Trinity. The doctrines of the Father, the Son and the Holy Spirit are thus each implicitly trinitarian. This trinitarian character applies also to all the different *loci* in the body of a Christian dogmatics. As Otto Weber has written, following Karl Barth: 'Every section of dogmatics includes in its own way and from its point of view the whole of dogmatics within itself, since every dogmatic statement has in view the unity and totality of God's revelation.'[39]

The fact that God's trinitarian self-revelation confronts us as a 'primitive all', to be understood primarily and completely in terms of itself, tells us that our formulation of the doctrine of the Trinity does not start from the one God and move toward the three Persons, or start from the three Persons and move toward the one God, but takes its rise *ab initio* from God's indivisible wholeness as one Being, three Persons, and proceeds in accordance with what is revealed of God's internal *homoousial* and *hypostatic* interrelations as Father, Son and Holy Spirit. But this circular procedure does not mean that God's trinitarian self-revelation to us is without a controlling centre or that our formulation of the doctrine of the Trinity does not turn upon a central axis grounded both in the reality of God and in the realities of our world. That centre is constituted by the incarnation of God's self-revelation in Jesus Christ the Son and Word of God and by the Holy Spirit sent by the Father through the Son who are of one Being and Act with God the Father, for it is through union and communion with them that we are given to know God as he really is in the inner relations of his Triune Being, and all our

---

[38] This was Calvin's way of expressing it. See T. F. Torrance, *Trinitarian Perspectives* (Edinburgh, 1994), pp. 36 & 73f.

[39] Otto Weber, *Foundations of Dogmatics* (Grand Rapids, 1981), vol. 1, p. 349. Weber adds that, for this reason, Karl Barth has provided in his 'prolegomena' (*Church Dogmatics*, I.1 and II.1) a 'Doctrine of the Word of God' which contains a complete dogmatics.

understanding of God in his trinitarian self-revelation is governed. Of quite crucial importance here is the oneness in Being and Act between the Lord Jesus Christ and God the Father, for it is in virtue of that oneness that we know that what God is toward us in Christ he is antecedently and eternally in himself, and what he is antecedently and eternally in himself he is toward us in his revealing and saving acts in Christ. It is in the *homoousion*, therefore, distilled from the gospel presentation of the incarnate Person, life, death and resurrection of Jesus Christ as Lord and Saviour, that we have expressed the ontological and epistemological link between the economic Trinity and the ontological Trinity, or between the evangelical Trinity and the theological Trinity. Just as the *homoousion* expresses at once the distinction and the oneness between the incarnate Son and the Father, so it enables us to speak both of the distinction and of the oneness between the economic and the ontological Trinity and without detracting from the crucial significance of either.

It is ultimately the mutual coinherent relation between the Father and the incarnate Son and the incarnate Son and the Father that constitutes the ontological axis grounded both in the eternal Being of God and in the incarnation of his Son upon which through the Spirit all trinitarian formulations of Christian doctrine turn and from which they take their true configuration. Because it is the Word who eternally inheres in the Being of God, and not the Holy Spirit, who became incarnate, it is the Lord Jesus Christ who personally reveals the Father to us and speaks to us directly in our own human language of the Father, so that the Christian doctrine of God derives its truth content from him as the Word made flesh. It is as both God and man in one Person that he speaks to us directly of God his Father. The ultimate ground and controlling centre of our knowledge of God is, therefore, not simply his Being but his spoken Word, God clothed in Christ with his Word, not God without the Word nor the Word apart from God. While the Holy Spirit is not himself the Word, is not incarnate and does not speak of himself, he is the Spirit of the Father and of the Son who eternally dwells in the hidden depths of God's Being and is what Augustine spoke of as 'a kind of consubstantial communion' of the Father and the Son.[40] It is as such that he is sent by the Father in the name of the Son to dwell with us and make us capable of receiving and understanding the Word, thus fulfilling and effectuating in us the personal self-address of God to us so that it is in and through the Communion of the Spirit that we may share in the knowledge which God has of himself as Father, Son and Holy Spirit. It is, then, the two-way relation between the Father and the Son illuminated for us in the Holy Spirit that provides the frame both for our knowledge of God in his inner trinitarian relations and our knowledge of the Son in his inner hypostatic relations as God and man in one Person. The doctrines of the Trinity and of the incarnation thus form together the nucleus at the heart of the Christian conception of God and constitute the ontological and epistemological basis for the formulation of every Christian doctrine.

It should now be evident why it is not possible to speak of the doctrine of the Holy Trinity in isolation from the other doctrines of the Faith, not least the doctrine

---

[40] Augustine, *De Trinitate*, 15.27.50; cf. 5.11.12 & 6.5.7.

of redemption through the saving events of the birth, life, death, and resurrection of the Lord Jesus Christ proclaimed to us in the Gospel, for the trinitarian conception of God is *the distinctively Christian conception of God* with which every Christian doctrine and every aspect of the Christian way of life are concerned. It is not just that the doctrine of the Holy Trinity must be accorded primacy over all the other doctrines, but that properly understood it is the nerve and centre of them all, configures them all, and is so deeply integrated with them that when they are held apart from the doctrine of the Trinity they are seriously defective in truth and become malformed. Moreover, if the Christian conception of God and of all his activity toward us in creation and redemption is essentially trinitarian, then the trinitarian perspective must be allowed to pervade all Christian worship and practice, all interpretation of the Holy Scriptures, and all proclamation of the Gospel, and must be given a regulative role in the dynamic structure of all Christian thought and action. Then indeed we will live and move and have our being under the blessing of the Grace of the Lord Jesus Christ, the Love of God and the Communion of the Holy Spirit.

3

The Biblical Frame

I N the preceding chapter attention was directed to the fact that God makes himself known through himself alone, that he reveals himself in Jesus Christ and actualises his revelation through his Spirit, which implies that divine revelation is intrinsically trinitarian in its content, movement and structure. Hence, as Karl Barth expressed it, the *ratio* of the Trinity is the *ratio* of divine revelation.[1] This does not mean that the doctrine of the Trinity is a postulate of revelation, as if it could be argued that because God reveals himself in this way he must be a Trinity in himself, for that would mean that the Trinity is not itself part of divine revelation but only an inference from it. On the contrary, God's active self-revealing and the content of his self-revealing are one and the same, for, as we have previously noted, his Act and his Being inhere in one another. God is who he is in the activity of his saving love toward us, and what he is in his saving activity toward us he is in himself in his eternal Being. Within the course of this revelation God reveals himself to us in a three-fold form and a three-fold way, as he who reveals himself, as he who is the content of his revelation, and as he who enables us through his presence to understand his revelation of himself which we are incapable of doing by ourselves.

The doctrine of the Holy Trinity gives expression to the fact that through Jesus Christ and in his Spirit God has opened himself to us in such a way that in being reconciled to him we lowly sinful creatures may know him, at least in some measure, in the inner relations of his divine Being and have communion with him in his intra-trinitarian Life as Father, Son and Holy Spirit. He reveals himself to us, not only from without or from above, in the advent of his Son as the incarnate Saviour among us, but also from below, in a movement of his Spirit in which through his presence within us he meets himself from our end, thereby bringing us within the circle of his knowing of himself and his revealing of himself through himself. This movement and structure of divine revelation are to be interpreted not in abstract analytic or synthetic terms but only in the concrete soteriological terms of God's actual self-mediation and self-giving to us as the Father, the Son, and the Holy

---

[1] Karl Barth, *Christliche Dogmatik* (Munich, 1927), p. 150; see *Church Dogmatics* I.1 (Edinburgh, 2nd edn, 1975), pp. 304ff.

Spirit, for the form and content of divine revelation and salvation belong inseparably together.[2] God's self-revelation to us is actualised in the course of his saving activity for us in history, and is mediated to us in the concrete form of reconciliation through the sacrificial life and death of Christ.[3] As Karl Barth once expressed it:

> Reconciliation is not a truth which revelation makes known to us; reconciliation is the truth of God himself who grants himself freely to us in his revelation. God who is the mighty, holy, eternal God, gave himself to us who are so impotent, so unholy, and mortal. Revelation is reconciliation, as certainly as it is God himself: God with us, God beside us, and chiefly and decisively God for us.[4]

It is in this identity between revelation and reconciliation, in the oneness between what God is in the Person of Christ and what he has done for us in the atoning sacrifice of Christ, that the objective truth of the Blessed Trinity belongs to the very heart of the Gospel, for it gathers up and embraces the evangelical message of the grace of the Lord Jesus Christ, the love of God and the Communion of the Holy Spirit. It is only from this incarnate condescension of God's immeasurable love to be one with us and his unreserved self-giving in love for us that we come to know God as Father, Son and Holy Spirit toward us, but through the Communion of the Spirit our knowing of him in this evangelical or economic way is lifted up and grounded in the transcendent Life and personal Being of God as Father, Son and Holy Spirit in himself. Thomas A. Smail has expressed the essential point well:

> The doctrine of the Trinity does not lay an irreverent philosophical mystery on top of a simple scriptural gospel; it simply makes explicit what is implicit in the biblical gospel, in order to defend it against the philosophical attacks that are made upon it. The root of the doctrine of the Trinity is the same insight that in Jesus we have to do with one who is not only on our side as creature, but on God's side as Creator. He is of one being (*homoousios*) with the Father and so belongs to God's life and not only to ours, but he brings his relationship with the Father into earthly revelation and action for our salvation.[5]

While God makes himself personally known to us in this three-fold way as the Father, the Son and the Holy Spirit, it is nevertheless as an indivisible *whole* that his trinitarian self-revelation comes to us, and it is within this wholeness that we know him as Father, Son, and Holy Spirit, not just as he is toward us, but as he is

---

[2] Cf. Karl Barth, *Church Dogmatics* I.1 (2nd edn, 1975) pp. 308ff, 314ff, 363f, 450ff. When Barth sometimes speaks of his 'analysis' of the biblical concept of revelation as the root of the doctrine of the Trinity, what he intends is an implication or unfolding of its content by way of 'explicating', 'interpreting' or 'reading off' its meaning, never a logical analysis. 'The doctrine of the Trinity is simply the unfolding (*Entfaltung*) of the knowledge that Jesus is the Christ or the Lord.' *Kirchliche Dogmatik* I.1 (Munich, 1935), p. 353 (*Church Dogmatics* I.1, p. 334).
[3] For a fuller account of this see my exposition, *The Mediation of Christ* (new edition, T & T Clark, Edinburgh, 1992).
[4] Karl Barth, *God in Action, Theological Addresses* (Edinburgh, 1936), p. 17.
[5] Thomas A. Smail, *The Forgotten Father* (London, 1980), p. 105.

within himself. In the Father, the Son and the Holy Spirit, we do not have to do merely with three faces or modal self-presentations of the Godhead, but inexplicably with one God and one divine Being who is yet three Persons, and with three distinct Persons who are yet one indivisible God. Hence, as we have already seen, in our apprehension of God's trinitarian self-revelation in his intrinsic wholeness we are subsidiarily aware of the particular Persons of the Father, the Son, and the Holy Spirit, and at the same time in our explicit apprehension of each particular Person we are relying on an implicit awareness of the whole Trinity. And indeed it is the wholeness of God's triune self-revelation that is the aboriginal or primordial conception that God gives us of himself, whether the immediate focus is on the Father, or the Son, or the Holy Spirit. He reveals himself as God the Father, God the Son, and God the Holy Spirit, the one and only Lord God. His revelation of himself through himself in Christ and the Holy Spirit is at once the revelation of God as one and three and three and one, which we shall consider later as Unity and Trinity and Trinity and Unity, or as Triunity.

This is, I believe, how the trinitarian self-revealing of God to the disciples and apostles took place, and was absorbed by them in the form to which the New Testament Scriptures bear witness; this is how it is surely to be understood by us. It is to be understood, however, as in the primitive Church, on the actual historical ground which divine revelation has established for itself in the personal coming of God into our world of space and time in Jesus Christ who is the incarnation of his eternal Word within the field of human existence, speech and understanding. In the advent of the Kingdom of God embodied in Christ a new world order was inaugurated, and with the pouring out of God's Spirit upon the Church a profound revolution in knowledge of God took place, a radical reorganisation of people's consciousness and a redirection of their rational approach to God were brought about, in which far from being conformed to the pattern of this present world they were transformed through a renewal of their mind and were given new powers of discernment in the things of God.[6] It was thus that a new thought-world came into being answering to the revealing and reconciling acts of God in which he gave access to knowledge of himself as never before. This correlation of human understanding with divine revelation was not effected by the abolition of the human receiver, but brought about by revelation itself, both through God's incarnate revealing of himself in his Son and through the pouring out of his Spirit upon the disciples and apostles to actualise that revelation and reconciliation within the mind of the Church which Christ united to himself as his Body, 'the earthly-historical form of his own existence'.[7] And so through the Communion of the Holy Spirit, the eternal Spirit of the Father and of the Son, the Church was drawn within the circle of God's revealing of himself through himself and given to share in God's knowing of himself.

It was in this way that God's unique trinitarian self-revelation created the framework of thought and speech within human existence in which alone it is to be understood and interpreted by us, the Faith once for all delivered to the saints.[8]

---

[6] See Rom. 12.1f, and 1 Cor. 2.1ff.
[7] Karl Barth, *Church Dogmatics* IV.2 (Edinburgh, 1958), p. 614.
[8] Jude 3.

And it was in this way that under the creative impact of divine revelation there emerged the unique genre of literature handed down to us in the gospels and epistles of the New Testament upon which God's self-revelation as Father, Son and Holy Spirit has imprinted itself, so that they convey to us proclamation and teaching which are implicitly trinitarian. It is as such that the gospels and epistles continue under God to mediate his revelation to us in history, and to be the canonical vehicles of the living Word of God to mankind. They are to be uniquely revered and interpreted as Holy Scripture inspired by the Holy Spirit in the apostolic foundation of the Church to be the written form whereby the Word of God may be communicated to people in history through the preaching and teaching of the Church in such a way that it continues to generate faith in Jesus Christ and his Gospel. The trinitarian self-revelation of God which reaches us in this way comes to us as an internally integrated whole and not in a piecemeal or partitive way, for it was in its organic wholeness that it informed and configured the New Testament as its biblical correlate.

The Scriptures of the New Testament, accordingly, have to be treated and interpreted as a whole on the ontological ground and under the integrating force of God's reconciling self-revelation in Jesus Christ and the Holy Spirit which gave rise to them. This calls for a fully holistic approach in which the empirical and conceptual, or the historical and theological, ingredients in the New Testament are held together. In recent years, however, the New Testament has too often suffered from hermeneutical methods governed by damaging dualist and analytical epistemologies in which form and being, or structure and substance, have been torn apart, with the result that the gospels and epistles and other books that comprise it become severed from their deep roots in divine revelation and thereby lose the consistent substructure that holds them conceptually and meaningfully together. Here we have sadly breaking through the teaching of the Church once again the epistemological dualism that infected late Patristic, Medieval, and Enlightenment thought and disrupted the doctrine of the Trinity by driving a wedge between the historical and ontological factors or ingredients in God's triune self-revelation through Christ and in the Spirit, so that an understanding of what God is for us is severed from what God is in himself.

This kind of disintegration in evangelical and theological interpretation of the biblical witness to God's threefold self-revelation, is in its way not unlike what has been happening in modern culture in which the creative forces in human and social life have suffered severely from analytical forces of fragmentation and disintegration. The problems involved here have been clearly diagnosed and exposed in the arts by Erich Kahler in a seminal work in which he shows how in the realms of image, sound and language, forces of decomposition and destruction begin to be at work as soon as the arts cut loose from underlying structures or frames of being, for then the natural coherences dissolve away and a degree of disintegration sets in which is quite frightening, for what happens to artistic form happens sooner or later to man himself.[9] This fits in completely with the phenomenalist approach

---

[9] Erich Kahler, *The Disintegration of Form in the Arts* (New York, 1968).

35

to things which has so long dominated our human life and thought in the West at the hands of observationalist and instrumentalist science, in which structure is abstracted from substance and form is cut off from being, so that external organisation and mechanical connection are brought in to replace the inner organisation and natural patterns inherent in the universe. Thus the ability to think conjunctively has been eroded and displaced by disjunctive processes of analysis, so that fragmentation and decomposition of phenomena result, which have then to be clamped together by means of some artificial framework usually of a determinist kind, if they are to be handled in any coherent way. It is through constructionalist rationalism of this kind that 'laws of nature' are imposed upon nature instead of being read out of nature.

Something not unlike this has so often been taking place in biblical studies noted above in the analytical approach to Jesus as he is presented in the gospels and epistles which has been occupying scholarly attention for the last century and a half. There we find a phenomenalist bracketing off of 'the appearances of Jesus' from the frame of their natural intelligible connections in the evangelical witness, so that they inevitably become fragmented like the phenomenal particulars of observationalist natural science or philosophy, and the conclusion sometimes reached is that there are several 'Christologies' in the New Testament. The natural coherence in which the evangelical material has come down to us is explained away as an imposition upon the original appearances through the use of screen images thrown up out of the consciousness and worship of the early Christian community. But since some kind of framework is needed to interpret the books of the New Testament, artificial and unnatural frameworks are produced by scholars which derive from their own alien culture and are imposed upon the New Testament in order to make it meaningful for people today! What lies behind this approach is a sad lapse back into the obsolete analytical ways of thinking which have been comprehensively rejected and replaced by rigorous science that has learned to operate with an integrative approach in which form and being, structure and substance, intelligible and observational ingredients, instead of being torn apart, are found to be indissolubly linked together in continuous dynamic fields of relations. In this event the fragmentation of nature into discrete constituent parts fades away and the realities being investigated are grasped and interpreted in the light of their natural coherences and innate structures. Here laws of nature are once again read out of nature under the constraint of its intrinsic intelligibility, and are not imposed upon nature.

It is to a holistic approach of this kind in which we think not disjunctively but conjunctively that we must have recourse in interpreting the Holy Scriptures, on the ontological and epistemological ground on which they were produced under the power and in the light of God's unique trinitarian self-revelation. They cannot be divorced from that revelational framework, or from the form which the Word and Spirit of God created in the testimony of the disciples and apostles for the actualisation of that revelation, without serious distortion and loss of meaning. The books of the New Testament are to be understood, therefore, not as just historical documents deriving from the primitive Church which give us information about God and his reconciling love and are to be interpreted in a merely phenomenalist fashion, but as the appointed means by which God continues through his Spirit to address his living Word to us and speak to us personally and directly about himself in such a way that he is immediately present to us in his Word. Although the Word of God is communicated to us today in this indirect way through the documented witness of the Apostles in the Scriptures, it is no less his very Word that we hear directly from the mouth of God.

Before we proceed to ask what the New Testament specifically testifies of God's triune revelation of himself, we must give some attention to the distinctive kind of approach that is appropriate to the new organisation of consciousness and the new world of thought found in it. The new genre of literature in the gospels and epistles, dyed in the grain with trinitarian meaning, that arose under the creative impact of our crucified and risen Lord's revelation of the Father and his gift of the Holy Spirit, calls for a correspondingly new way of interpreting the New Testament *in depth*, in which we penetrate through the literary surface of the Scriptures, without divorcing them from their historical actuality, to the truth content of their contents, the dynamic objective reality of the living Word of God the Father, the Son and the Holy Spirit.[10]

First, we need to *indwell* the New Testament as a whole and in all its parts in such a way that we acquire the habit of looking *through* the various books and passages of the Scriptures and allowing their message to be interiorised in the depths of our mind. In this way a structural kinship becomes built up between our knowing and what we seek to know, which enables us intuitively to grasp the conjoint meaning latent in the biblical texts which we could not derive simply from the particularities and explicit features of the documents themselves. As our minds dwell in the Scriptures we find diverse passages coming together in our meditation and resonating with one another so that a spontaneous organisation of natural coherences running through them arises and a crystallisation of the truths to which they conjointly direct us takes place in our understanding of them. It is then in this light that the gospels and epistles and other texts throughout the New Testament are read and interpreted and found to provide together the means by which we may be drawn by the Word of God into the inner circle of his revelation of himself through himself. We may take our cue here from what Jesus said to his disciples when he bade them dwell in him and let his Words dwell in them.[11] Mutual indwelling of this personal kind opens the way through the Scriptures to revealed knowledge of the Father and of the Spirit as well as of the Son, for through union with him we may, like the disciples of Jesus, participate in his union with the Father, share in his gift of the Holy Spirit, and thus like them know the truth for ourselves.

This Johannine concept of *indwelling* was taken over by Michael Polanyi and applied to what he called *personal knowledge* in the process of scientific inquiry in which we interiorise what we seek to know and rely upon internal and not just

---

[10] This is the method of 'depth exegesis' which I have learned from William Manson; cf. the collection of his essays entitled *Jesus and the Christian* (London, 1967).
[11] John 15.1ff.

external evidence in our understanding and interpreting of it in its coherent structure and significance. It is through our indwelling of something that its natural integration is assimilated into our knowing of it, which then functions in a heuristic way in our inquiry by deepening and furthering our understanding of it. Thus, for example, through indwelling a conceptual framework or a musical symphony we gain comprehension of it as a whole and in the light of the joint meaning of its parts go on to understand and interpret its manifold content. By penetrating deeply inside some field of reality in this way we let it disclose to us depths of meaning which we could not have anticipated and could not otherwise obtain, far less deduce from what we already claim to know. This applies, of course, particularly to the kind of intimate knowledge we may have of other persons which, unlike conceptual systems or musical symphonies, have a living centre from which they operate. We gain knowledge of them not so much through their explicit utterances and thoughts as through the activity of mutual indwelling and the kind of cognitive kinship it yields, which enables us to appreciate and understand them consistently from the inner personal centre of their being.[12]

In seeking to interpret God's trinitarian self-revelation through the medium of the gospels and epistles we have to do with an altogether deeper dimension in knowledge. But here it holds true that it is through personal dwelling in Christ and interiorising his Word within us that we enter into a cognitive union with him as God incarnate, and are thereby admitted to an intimate knowledge of God's self-revelation in its intrinsic wholeness and are enabled to discern the truth of his self-revelation as we could not do otherwise. By indwelling the Scriptures of the New Testament and interiorising their message we become drawn into the circle of God's revelation of himself through himself. Spiritually and theologically regarded, this kind of indwelling, in Christ and his Word, involves faith, devotion, meditation, prayer and worship in and through which we are given discerning access to God in his inner Communion as Father, Son and Holy Spirit. Any faithful interpretation of the Scriptures operates on different levels, the linguistic and the conceptual level, but unless the interpreter participates in the movement of God's unique self-revelation through Christ and in the Spirit which gave rise to the Scriptures and has left its imprint upon them, he or she will fail to understand them in their deep spiritual dimension and will be blind to their essential truth content. Hence if we are to interpret the Holy Scriptures we must cultivate the habit of tuning into them as a whole in order to penetrate into their centre of meaning, so that the spiritual realities and truths of divine revelation to which they testify may be allowed to govern our knowing and shape our understanding of them. It is when we interpret different passages and statements in the light of the whole that their real meaning and force become apparent.

Second, basic consideration must be given to the fact that divine revelation is given to us not in a visual but in an *auditory* mode, that is through the *Word* to which people respond in the hearing of faith. We recall that while the original disciples and apostles, as St John recorded, had visual and tactual as well as auditory

---

[12] Michael Polanyi, see especially *Personal Knowledge* (London, 1958), pp. 279f, 344.

contact with the incarnate Word of Life,[13] it is also reported that the risen Lord said to St Thomas, 'because you have seen me you have believed. Blessed are they who have not seen and yet believe.' To which the evangelist added about his record of the things Jesus did and said, 'these are written that you may believe that Jesus is the Christ, the Son of God, and that believing you may have life in his name.'[14] We recall also what St Paul wrote to the Corinthians, 'We walk by faith and not by sight',[15] and to the Romans 'faith comes from hearing and hearing through the word of Christ.'[16]

It is significant that nowhere in the gospels or epistles of the New Testament do the eye-witnesses tell us anything of what Jesus looked like, for the divine reality they speak of was one which they knew primarily through hearing. Hence they concentrate on giving us reports of Jesus' words, and even when they tell us what they actually observed of his actions or when they describe events in the Gospel story, that is only incidental to his proclaiming and teaching the Word of God. It is right here that we can discern an outstanding element in the reorganisation of the consciousness of the disciples and apostles, when under the impact of divine revelation through the Word made flesh, there took place a shift away from optical forms of thought to *auditive* forms of thought arising from direct acts of cognition in hearing God. What is required of us, then, are ways of interpreting the New Testament appropriate to the distinctive nature of God's self-revelation through his Word, by *listening* to his *viva vox* or living voice resonating through the New Testament witness, and not just through linguistic and grammatical analysis of the New Testament documents guided by proper historico-scientific method, important as that is for rigorous exegesis.

This living Word of God is none other than the only begotten Son of the Father, the very Offspring of his divine Nature in whom the whole richness and plenitude of the Godhead dwells. It is in him, perfectly one with the Father yet distinct from him, that in the fullness of time God brought the revelation of himself through his Word, long mediated to Israel in an anticipatory discarnate form, to its incarnate consummation in the Person and Life of Jesus Christ. This is how witness is borne to him in the opening of the Epistle to the Hebrews:

> In many and various ways God spoke of old to our fathers by the prophets, but in these last days he has spoken to us by a Son, whom he appointed heir of all things, through whom also he created the world. He is the radiance of God's glory, the very expression of his being who upholds the universe by his word of power. Now after having brought about the purification of our sins, he has taken his seat at the right hand of the Majesty on high.[17]

Along with this must be placed the witness of St John in the opening of the Fourth Gospel:

[13] 1 John 1.1f.
[14] John 20.29–30.
[15] 1 Cor. 5.7.
[16] Rom. 10.17.
[17] Heb. 1.1–3. Cf. William Manson, *The Epistle to the Hebrews* (London, 1951), pp. 88ff.

In the beginning was the Word and the Word was with God, and the Word was God. He was in the beginning with God; all things were made through him, and without him was not anything made that was made ... And the Word became flesh and dwelt among us, full of grace and truth, and we beheld his glory, the glory of the only Son from the Father.[18]

The Lord Jesus Christ himself is the Word of God incarnate whose voice sounds through (*personat*, Calvin's expression) to us in the Scriptures of the New Testament, certainly in human form, for Jesus was one of us, but he was also one in Being and Act with God the Father. He himself is the living Word who meets us and addresses us in the words of Holy Scripture. Hence the Scriptures are interpreted aright only in their correlation with him the Word of life, the personal auditory self-revelation of God the Father embodied in him, as their enlightening, controlling and empowering centre.

While Jesus Christ is the Word of God made flesh dwelling among us, he remains the Word who inheres in the eternal Being of God, the Word by whom all things are created and sustained. Thus while becoming one of us and one with us in his incarnation, Jesus Christ is also very different from us, and that difference must be taken into account. In the Creator himself, Word, Person and Act are one and undivided, but in the creature this is not so. Our word is different from our act, and our act is not personal in itself. Our speech and our action do not coincide in the unity and power of our person. Act and person, word and person, word and act, while not unrelated, are all separate. With God this is not the case, for his Word and his Act belong inseparably to the self-subsistence of his Person. What he speaks takes effect of itself, for it is fulfilled in the power of his Person, the power by which he is what he is and by which he lives his personal Life in absolute self-sufficiency and freedom. His power to act is not other than the power of his Person or the power of his Word. He is in his Person identical with his Word, and his Word is identical with his Act. When the Son and Word of God became flesh in order to become Word to man, personally addressing us in the medium of human speech and physical event in space and time, he entered into the divided and finite conditions of word, person and act that characterise creaturely human beings. He came as genuine man, physically conditioned in space and time, in whom willing, speaking and doing are different. However, he did not cease to be the Word he is as the Creator, but appropriated human form within the frailty of earthly action and speech in such a way as to take up the frail and finite conditions of the creature into himself, not merely as the earthen vessel of the Word of God, but as his actual speaking to us in it. In Jesus Christ the unity in God between Person, Word, and Act was made to overlap and gather within its embrace the differences between person, word, and act in the creature, so that they are allowed wonderfully to mediate God's Word to us in time through a oneness between Christ's human utterance about God and God's self-utterance to human beings.

In the incarnation God did not just come into man but actually made our human nature his own in such a way that he came among us precisely *as Man*,

[18] John 1.1–3 and 14.

without ceasing to be God.[19] So in Jesus Christ the Word of God did not just speak to man through the instrumentality of human speech but actually assumed human speech into himself as the Word of God in such a way as to address us precisely *as human word*, without ceasing to be the Word of God. But since in his incarnation the Word and Son of God made himself one with us in all that we are in order really to be the Word of God *to us*, he also became man hearing the Word of God, thereby fulfilling in himself as God and Man the movement of God's incarnate self-revelation from the side of man in his responding to God as well as from the side of God addressing man.[20] If divine revelation is not really given until it is received, then certainly it was really given in Jesus, for it was actualised in his incarnate receiving of it, and reiterated in his human responses to the Father. It is thus that Jesus Christ is himself as God and Man, the Word of God become man in the fullest sense, for he is the Word of God not only spoken to man, but the Word of God faithfully heard by man and uttered by man in response to God. And it is as such that the living Word of God in his divine-human form actually reaches us through the faithful hearing and witnessing of the disciples and apostles of Christ, empowered as they were by the Holy Spirit in the mediation of divine revelation. This is what makes the Word of God we hear and meet in the Holy Scriptures utterly *sui generis*, God's unique Self-Word (*autologos*, αὐτολόγος[21]) who meets us and acts upon us not just from above us but from below and within us, through the active presence of his own personal reality as the living Word of God addressing us in human words in the witness of all the New Testament Scriptures.

There is another side to all this, however, which is of crucial importance. When the Word of God became man, he came to his own, but his own did not receive him, for although they had derived their being from him they had rebelled against him and fallen into darkness and enmity to God. Hence in his incarnation the Word of God penetrated into our sinful and distorted existence, into our personal darkness and mental alienation from God, even into the disintegration of human being in death. He came to share our lost and contradictory existence in order to save and reconcile us to God, and to regenerate and restore us through union with himself in his vicarious humanity as true sons and daughters of the heavenly Father who hear him, love him and obey him. Divine revelation and divine reconciliation are the obverse of each other.[22]

It is precisely in this acutely personal way that we encounter Jesus Christ, the revealing and reconciling Word of God, in the gospels and epistles of the New

---

[19] That God became incarnate in Jesus Christ precisely *as man*, not just by coming into man, was an anti-Apollinarian point stressed by Athanasius, *Contra Arianos*, 3.30ff; *Ad Antiochenos*, 7; *Ad Epictetum*, 2; *Ad Maximum*, 2, etc. See also *The Trinitarian Faith*, p. 152, and *Theology in Reconciliation* (London, 1975), pp. 156f, 227f.

[20] Hence, as Athanasius taught, in becoming Mediator between God and man to redeem mankind, the incarnate Son of God did not only act as God ministering the things of God to man but as man ministering the things of man to God: *Contra Arianos*, 3.39f; 4.7f.

[21] Athanasius, *Contra gentes*, 40, 46; *De incarnatione*, 54; *Contra Arianos*, 4.2, etc.

[22] Refer to *The Mediation of Christ.*

Testament: he calls us, as he called his disciples in the days of his flesh, to renounce ourselves and take up our cross and follow him. Since revelation and reconciliation belong together, we are unable to hear the Word of God addressed to us in the Holy Scriptures or to interpret those Scriptures aright except through reconciliation with God in Christ in which our hearing of the Word of God and our understanding of it are transformed by it and operate in the obedience of faith. Here we see further into the kind of reorganisation of the human consciousness that results from the movement of God's revealing and redeeming activity in his incarnate Son – that is, in the transformation of our hearing that we may really hear the Word of God, and in the reconciliation of our alienated minds that we may really understand the truth as it is in Christ. Only through personal meeting with Christ the Word and Son of God and being reconciled to the Father through him are we in a position properly to appreciate the semantic reference of biblical statements and discern the truth to which they direct us beyond themselves in the Holy Trinity.

In a faithful interpretation of the New Testament we may not treat the words employed in it as if they were no more than transient linguistic symbols detached from any objective content in divine revelation, and as if they were not lively oracles through which God speaks to us in Person.[23] Rather must we treat them as words which the incarnate Word of God has deliberately assimilated to himself in communicating and interpreting himself to us in the course of his reconciling activity. That is to say, in the words of the Bible through which the Word of God's trinitarian self-revelation reaches us, we have to do not with some divine Word detached from his Being and Activity, but with the very Being of God speaking to us and acting upon us in an intensely personal way. In and through them we encounter the living Word who is identical with God himself, the Word in whom we have to do with the Person and Act of God, the Son made man in Jesus Christ, and are thereby summoned to personal commitment and faith in Christ and through cognitive union with him to have knowledge of God the Father. Thus we interpret his human words as the direct personal address of God in whom he communicates to us not just some information about himself but his own divine Self, and therefore interpret them not from a centre in the man Jesus detached from his Deity, but from the organising and controlling centre of his divine-human reality. To indwell the words of Christ, therefore, is to participate in the mutual indwelling of God and man in him, or the mutual indwelling of the Father and his incarnate Son. And so through union with Jesus Christ we are drawn by the Spirit of the Father and of the Son into the Communion of the Father and the Son.

It is the mutual relation between the incarnate Son and the Father that provides us with the ground on which we are given access to knowledge of the one God in his inner relations as Father, Son and Holy Spirit. This implies that we are not to look for the biblical basis of the doctrine of the Holy Trinity in the New Testament simply in explicit statements such as the various triadic formulae found in it, significant as they are in themselves. Rather are we concerned, at least in the first place, with the apostolic witness to the series of mighty redemptive events in the

---

[23] Cf. Athanasius who thought of 'the divine Scripture as speaking to us in the person of God': ἡ θεία γραφὴ λέγουσα ἐκ προσώπου Θεοῦ (*De Incarnatione*, 3).

advent of the Kingdom of God in Jesus Christ, and with the historical manifestation in them of God as Father, Son and Holy Spirit. And so we are concerned with the whole movement of God's personal self-revealing and self-giving to us in Christ and his Spirit, from the birth and baptism of Jesus throughout his life and ministry to his death and resurrection and to Pentecost, within which we meet with the truth of the Trinity deeply embedded in a whole network of implicit indications in the gospels where we find God distinguishing himself within himself as Father, Son and Holy Spirit and yet making himself known as one Lord God.[24] That is to say, the historical and evangelical manifestations of God as Father, Son and Holy Spirit are expressions within time of distinctions that are real in the one eternal Being of God. Father, Son and Holy Spirit are not only relative to history but are relative to eternity. This passage in faith and understanding of Father, Son and Holy Spirit from history to eternity, as we shall see shortly, involves a theological as well as an empirical, or cognitive as well as an experiential, approach to the interpretation of the Holy Scriptures.

At the moment, however, let us note that since in the New Testament this revelation of the mystery of God toward us is revelation of God as Father, Son and Holy Spirit in his *wholeness*, the New Testament does not speak of the Holy Trinity in parts or in various statements, for it is his one indivisible Self that God utters in his revelation, the living Word who eternally resides in God but is now addressed to us as God speaking to us in Person. While the Word or Son of God is identical with God himself, yet he is clearly distinguished from the Father through his incarnation and crucifixion. And he is also clearly distinguished from the Holy Spirit through whom Christ was born of the Virgin Mary, by whom he fulfilled his earthly ministry, through whom he offered himself to God in atoning sacrifice for the sins of the world, and by whom he rose again from the dead, the same Spirit whom the ascended Lord poured out upon the Church at Pentecost as other than himself.

Third, another feature of the Holy Scriptures which must be taken into account in our interpreting of them is the intertwining of the empirical and conceptual, historical and theological elements in them. This means that they are to be interpreted in terms of the intrinsic intelligibility given them by divine revelation, and within the field of God's objective self-communication in Jesus Christ. The incarnation and resurrection together form the objective framework in the interaction of God and mankind within space and time, and provide us with the intelligible frame of reference within which the whole Gospel of God's revealing and reconciling activity conveyed to us in the Scriptures is to be interpreted and understood. Hence the meaning and truth of divine revelation conveyed to us through the Scriptures cannot be read off the linguistic patterns apparent in them or be deduced from the statements of the biblical authors as if they contained the truth in themselves, but may be discerned only by following through the semantic reference of biblical statements to the divine realities upon which they rest, and by thinking them out theologically within the whole organic frame of God's revealing and saving activity as Father, Son and Holy Spirit.

[24] See Karl Barth, *Church Dogmatics* I.1, p. 314.

This is to say, the Holy Scriptures are to be interpreted not in an analytical or discursive way but in terms of the integrated witness which they bear together to the fulfilment of God's eternal purpose for the salvation of the world as it has been brought to its focus and has been actualised in Jesus Christ in whom God in all his fullness has chosen to dwell. We are not concerned here, then, with thinking statements but with thinking realities through statements, and with developing an understanding of God from his self-revelation and self-interpretation mediated to us in the Holy Scriptures, in which the conceptual connections that arise compulsorily in our minds are objectively and ontologically controlled by the intrinsic connections in God's self-revelation and self-interpretation as Father, Son and Holy Spirit. Hence in our approach to the Holy Scripture we must be quite ruthless with ourselves in discarding all concepts of an *a priori* or extraneous derivation so that the truth of the Word of God may be allowed to shine through the biblical texts and generate in our minds appropriate conceptual forms with which to articulate it and bring it to doctrinal expression.

The key to this *theological* interpretation of the New Testament is found in the New Testament itself, in the way in which its presentation of the historical Jesus and its presentation of the risen Jesus are empirically and conceptually integrated with each other under the divine authority (ἐξουσία) of his self-identifying and self-authenticating reality as the incarnate Lord.[25] St Matthew recounts how in his sermon on the mount Jesus set his own word, 'but I say unto you', above that of the commandments of the decalogue, thereby claiming divine finality for his own teaching.[26] 'Heaven and earth will pass away but my words', claimed Jesus, 'will never pass away.'[27] This claim to divine finality is also apparent in the way Jesus constantly reinforced his teaching with the emphatic 'amen, amen', and called for absolute obedience to himself from all who would follow him, even to the extent of taking up their cross in complete self-renunciation. The evangelists all record events in which Jesus acted and spoke with utterly astonishing divine authority in his commands to the sick, the paralytic, the lame, the blind, evil powers and even to the dead and to the forces of nature.[28] 'No one ever spoke as this man speaks' (οὐδέποτε ἐλάλησεν οὕτως ἄνθρωπος).[29] It is thus hardly surprising that in the Fourth Gospel St John prefaced his account of the Gospel by identifying Jesus with the Word of God become flesh, the very Word who was not only in the beginning with God but was himself God.[30]

The evangelists also report statements of Jesus in which at decisive points in his ministry he identified himself and accepted identification of himself as the Son of Man and Son of God, and they record the way in which he was indirectly identified

[25] Refer to *Space, Time and Resurrection* (Edinburgh, 1976), pp. 17ff, and 159ff.
[26] Matt. 5.21f, 27f, 31f, 38f, 43f; cf. also John 5.22 & 12.44–50.
[27] Matt. 24.35.
[28] See for example Matt. 8.13 & 26; 12.13; 15.28; 17.18; Mark 1.41; 2.6, 11; 3.5; 4.39; 5.8, 41; 9.25; Luke 4.35; 5.13, 20 & 24; 7.14; 8.54; 9.42; John 8.5; 11.43.
[29] John 7.46.
[30] John 1.1f and 14.

as such in the spontaneous reaction of people.[31] However, it is clear that these direct and indirect identifications of Christ as the Son of Man and Son of God are presented in the gospels in a way that is deeply affected by what took place in the final decisive events of Jesus' messianic mission, for it was then that their real import became disclosed.[32] The disciples realised that what they had heard and witnessed in all that Jesus had said and done in the three previous years had been proleptically conditioned by his death and resurrection (although they admitted that they did not understand it at the time), so that their accounts of memories and testimonies had in all faithfulness to be given in a read-back way from the full truth that became disclosed in what Jesus said and did in the shattering events in Jerusalem: his arrest, confrontation with the high priest, trial before Pontius Pilate, his crucifixion and then his resurrection, the redemptive meaning and sacrificial purpose of which he had interpreted to them beforehand as they celebrated the Passover together on the night in which he was betrayed.

In other words, it is in the light of the startling unveiling of who Jesus Christ really is in and through his death and resurrection as the ultimate Power of God that the witness of the disciples was finally framed by the evangelists under the retroactively revealing power of the Cross and resurrection. Hence in the composition of the Gospels they allow the majestic *I am* of the crucified and risen Lord, regnant and triumphant over the forces of darkness, to provide spiritual enlightenment and objective depth to their evangelical report of the words and deeds of Jesus, which had the effect of giving their account of the life and ministry of Jesus a unifying infrastructure deriving from, and forced upon the followers of Jesus by the intrinsic nature of the Son of Man himself. That is the truth or reality of the matter which they could not but attest, for they themselves had fallen under its objective control and had suffered a profound transformation of their consciousness before God. Now they are able to present Jesus Christ in accordance with his essential nature and reality, whereas before they were able only to offer a fragmentary and relatively superficial account of him as a disturbing and enigmatic manifestation, in whom they encountered an inexplicable divine authority, *exousia* (ἐξουσία), and sovereignty, *basileia* (βασιλεία), before which the disciples and opponents of Jesus were alike turned inside out and fell back in awe, as happened at the transfiguration of Jesus which mysteriously anticipated his death and resurrection.[33]

The evangelists, however, do not erase from their accounts the way in which the mystery of the Kingdom of God embodied in Jesus was patiently disclosed by Jesus in word and deed only as they were able to hear and assimilate it, or the stumbling steps of faith taken by the disciples in responding to his teaching and preaching. St Matthew recalls the incident at Caesarea Philippi when St Peter confessed 'You are

[31] Cf. the examination of these statements by E. Hoskyns and N. Davey, *The Riddle of the New Testament* (London, 1931), especially pp. 145ff; and William Manson, *Jesus and the Christian*, especially pp. 67ff.

[32] Cf. the event of the transfiguration which adumbrated the glorification of Jesus in his death and resurrection – refer to the Lukan account, 9.28–36.

[33] Matt. 17.1ff (cf. 3.17); Mark 9.1ff.

the Christ, the Son of the living God,' and Jesus said to him, 'You did not learn that from any human being; it was revealed to you by my heavenly Father.'[34] All the evangelists recognise that in everything he had said about God and did in the name of God, Jesus confronted them in his own Person in such a way that they realised that they were face to face with the ultimate *exousia* and the very *basileia* of God himself.[35] In claiming that authority and rule as his own, Jesus was in fact putting himself in God's place. And so all that the evangelists themselves have to say of Jesus Christ, even of his life and teaching before the crucifixion, is shot through and through with deep theological and indeed Christological significance, for now they are able to see and understand what he had said and done and what he really was and indeed is, as they could not before, and thus to offer a really faithful report about him that matches his intrinsic truth and nature as the incarnate Lord. In Jesus, God himself has directly and personally intervened in the existence and plight of humanity, in accordance with the creative and redeeming purpose of his eternal love, cherished and adumbrated throughout the long history of Israel but now at last unveiled in its finality and universality.

The immediate point that interests us in our discussion here is that within the New Testament itself a definite standpoint is taken up, and a conceptual framework is adopted, such that the whole approach to Jesus, with all that was observed and heard and reported about him, is lifted up on to an altogether higher level of understanding. The resurrection discloses that *Jesus is Lord.* The Deity of Christ is the supreme truth of the Gospel, the key to the bewildering enigma of Jesus, for it provides it with a central point of reference consistent with the whole sequence of events leading up to and beyond the crucifixion. Or rather it discloses embedded in those events their own dynamic structure of significance, one that rises naturally from the very ground of Jesus' being and life, one in which the supreme purpose of God's love is seen to be operative in the life and not least the passion of Jesus. And so St Peter said on the Day of Pentecost: 'Let all the house of Israel know assuredly that God has made him both Lord and Christ, this Jesus whom you crucified.'[36] This is not to be understood as an interpretation externally imposed upon the facts but one inherent in them, belonging to the necessity of their inner reality which forced itself upon the disciples, and now continues to force itself upon our minds.

Thus, regarded in the penetrating light of the resurrection the empirical and historical data, the so-called 'observational facts' about Jesus, without in any way being undermined or discounted, assume a profound conceptual organisation in accordance with their own intrinsic significance and are found to be interpreting themselves in terms of their own coherent thrust. An important thing for us to note about the resurrection, in the evangelical accounts, is that, instead of cutting Jesus off from his historical and earthly existence before his crucifixion, it gathers it all up and confirms its concrete factuality by allowing it to be integrated on its own controlling ground, and thereby enables it to be understood in its own objective

---

[34] Matt. 16.16–17.
[35] Cf. E. Jüngel, *God as the Mystery of the World* (Grand Rapids, 1983), p. 353.
[36] Acts 2.36.

significance and intelligibility. Far from being distorted, the historical Jesus comes to his own within the dimensions of the risen Jesus, and the risen Jesus is discerned to have no other fabric than that in the life and mission of the historical Jesus. That is why, when after the resurrection Jesus is unambiguously acknowledged, glorified and worshipped as Lord, the evangelists use the designation 'Lord' of Jesus with discerning restraint, without any docetic detraction from his concrete historical actuality or human frailty. It is indeed the resurrection that really discloses and gives access to the *historical* Jesus, for it enables us, as it enabled them, to understand him in terms of his own intrinsic *logos*, and appreciate him in the light of his own inherent truth.

We return to the point that the empirical and the conceptual, the historical and the theological, factors in the New Testament presentation of Christ and the Gospel, are inseparably integrated and may not therefore be torn apart. Several analogies may help to indicate the importance of this fact. Experiments with inverting spectacles have shown us that when our visual image and our conceptual image of things are torn apart, and the semantic focus of observation is destroyed and we are thrown into disorder and we are unable to behave in accordance with the objective structure of reality around us. Rational and objective knowledge at every level requires the integration of visual and conceptual components. That is why the theologian cannot accept the results of shallow pseudo-scientific methods of exegesis which rule out from the start any theoretical component in the original witnesses to Jesus. A similar situation arises when two stereo-pictures are removed from the frame of the stereoscope which enables us to coordinate our viewing of them, for the clues to their integration are thereby effaced so that their joint significance, a three-dimensional picture, vanishes. When two separate pictures of the historical Jesus and the risen Jesus are fused into one presentation of spatio-temporal depth we are really able to see and understand Jesus Christ as he is *in reality*. But, let it be noted, it is precisely the disparities, the conflicting differences, of the stereoscopic pictures when viewed apart which, when viewed together, yield a conjoint significance that opens up for us an approach to Jesus Christ in a dimension of ontological depth. Here we have to reckon with an objective self-disclosure of Jesus Christ which is not to be read off the literary form as such, no matter how appropriate that may be, and which is not to be found in separate 'appearances' themselves. Nor is understanding of him to be derived by historico-critical analysis of, or through some process of historical deduction from, the so-called 'observational facts', but only through a process of indwelling interpretation in which we allow the natural integration deriving from the intrinsic significance of the *logos* of the living Christ himself to exercise a regulative role upon our understanding of him. Christ's self-disclosure is an intelligible revelation which requires 'depth-exegesis' (William Manson's term), and listening, intelligent and committed participation. As the Jesus of the Fourth Gospel expressed it, if people are unable to understand his language (λαλιά), it is because they are unable to understand (or cannot bear to understand) his word (λόγος).[37] Linguistic and conceptual factors have to be allowed to bear upon one another in any faithful interpretation and understanding.

[37] John 8.43ff.

47

All this demands of us a definitely *theological* and *unitary* interpretation not just of the epistles but of the gospels, in which we take our stand on the supreme truth of the Deity of Christ, and therefore interpret them in the light of the epistemic and ontological relation between the historical Jesus Christ, the incarnate Son, and God the Father. That is the evangelical truth which is brought out with such clarity in the Gospel according to St John. There, precisely where Jesus is presented to us in his earthly and fleshly reality – and no other gospel more than the Fourth Gospel stresses the humanity of Jesus so much – the eternal *I am* of the living God is irresistibly evident in Jesus' self-disclosure, above all at those points where he stands forth as the Lord of life and death.[38] 'My Father works hitherto, and I work ... As the Father raises the dead and gives them life, so also the Son gives life to whom he will. He has granted the Son to have life in himself, and has given him authority to execute judgment, because he is the Son of Man.'[39] 'I am the bread of life.'[40] 'Before Abraham was, I am.'[41] 'I and my Father are one.'[42] 'I am the resurrection and the life: he who believes in me though he were dead, yet shall he live.'[43] 'I am the way, the truth and the life; no one comes to the Father but by me ... He who has seen me has seen the Father ... I am in the Father and the Father is in me.'[44] 'I am the true vine.'[45] 'I am he.'[46] And in the Book of Revelation: 'I am Alpha and Omega, says the Lord God, who is and who was and who is to come, the Almighty.'[47]

Jesus is presented in the other Gospels in basically the same way and with much the same force. Thus we are told that on occasion he admitted frankly that he was the Messiah, the Son of God, of whom David spoke in the Psalm 110,[48] a claim that was reiterated by the apostles with reference also to the second Psalm, 'You are my Son, this day have I begotten you.'[49] While speaking of himself Jesus could say on the one hand that the Son of Man came eating and drinking, does not know where to lay his head, must suffer and be rejected and slain, but could say on the other hand that the Son of Man must rise again, will return in the clouds and with great glory, will be seen occupying the right hand of power,[50] capped by the significant *I am* spoken before the high priest, which as two evangelists tell us was in answer to the question whether he was the Son of God.[51] That is, of course, precisely how Jesus was identified at his baptism by the voice from heaven: 'This is my beloved Son, in whom I am well pleased,'[52] and again with similar words at his

[38] Cf. William Manson, 'The EGO EIMI of the Messianic Presence in the New Testament', *Jesus and the Christian*, pp. 174–183.
[39] John 5.15, 17, 21, 26f.
[40] John 6.35.
[41] John 8.58.
[42] John 10.30.
[43] John 11.15.
[44] John 14.6, 9, 11.
[45] John 15.1.
[46] John 18.6.
[47] Rev. 1.8; cf. 1.4; 21.6; 22.13.
[48] Ps. 110.1f; Matt. 22.44; Mark 12.35f.
[49] Ps. 2.7; Acts 2.34f; 13.33; Heb. 1.5; 5.5; cf. Rom. 1.4.
[50] Mark 8.31; 13.26; 14.62.
[51] Mark 14.61f; Matt. 26.63f; Luke 22.66f; cf. Matt. 27.43; John 19.7.
[52] Matt. 3.13f; Mark 1.9f; Luke 3.21f.

transfiguration.[53] Such is 'the tremendous Christology' mediated to us through the Synoptic Gospels.[54] Surely there can be no doubt in the mind of the reasonable and faithful interpreter, who does not divorce the empirical from the conceptual components in the Gospels, that although it may be found here in a lower key, it is essentially the same issue as found in the Petrine, Johannine, but especially Pauline material in the New Testament: *Jesus Christ stands revealed by the resurrection as the manifestation of God in the flesh – Jesus is Lord.*[55]

This stress on the Deity of Jesus Christ places in the very centre of God's self-revelation, and therefore of the framework of the New Testament message, the unbroken relation in being and act between the Son and the Father. And this in turn carries with it the relation of Christ to the Holy Spirit as well, as the Spirit of the Father and of the Son sent from the Father through the Son to lead those who believe in Christ into all truth and to grant them through himself participation in the Communion of the Holy Trinity. Thus the central focus of the Gospel upon the Deity of Christ is the door that opens the way to the understanding of God's triune self-revelation as Father, Son and Holy Spirit. Quite clearly a theological interpretation of the New Testament Scriptures must be at once both Christological and trinitarian. Unless Jesus Christ were the very Word of God who was in the beginning with God and was himself God through whom all things were made,[56] unless he were of one being with God the Father, he would not really be the objective content of God's self-revelation, and the Father would remain finally unrevealed and inaccessible to our knowledge. And unless the Holy Spirit were also of one being with the Father and of one being with the Son, and belonged with them in the one eternal Reality of God who is Spirit,[57] neither the revelation of the Father nor the revelation of the Son would be fulfilled and actualised among us as God's revelation of himself through himself. And unless both the Son and the Spirit were God of God, there would be no saving content or validity in the Gospel message of salvation. This means that our interpretation of the New Testament presentation of God as Father, Son and Holy Spirit must be *soteriologically* conditioned from end to end. We are thus led to hold that the evangelical Trinity and the theological Trinity, the economic Trinity and the ontological Trinity, are the obverse of one another.

This does not imply that the New Testament presents us with *explicit* teaching about the Holy Trinity, far less with a ready-made formal doctrine of the Trinity, but rather that it exhibits a coherent witness to God's trinitarian self-revelation imprinted upon its theological content in an implicit conceptual form evident in a whole complex of implicit references and indications in the gospels and epistles. In an explicit doctrine of the Trinity we move from this implicit conceptual form to definite statements we make about the objective content of divine revelation which

[53] Matt. 17.5. See also 2 Pet. 1.17f.
[54] E. Hoskyns and N. Davey, *Riddle*, p. 158.
[55] Thus, for example, Acts 1.21; 2.32; Rom. 1.2f; 4.14; 8.11; 10.9f;1 Cor. 12.3; 2 Cor. 3.15f; 4.14; Gal. 1.1; Phil. 2.9ff; Heb. 13.20.
[56] John 1.1–3.
[57] John 4.24.

are derived from it, grounded upon it and controlled by it. In such a doctrine of the Holy Trinity we are concerned to ask *who* God is who reveals himself to us in this way, through Christ and the Spirit. The formal doctrine of the Trinity arises out of the response we give to that question on the ground of God's own personal self-interpretation to us and on the ground of our interpretation of his revealing self-interpretation as our Lord and Saviour. Hence in a doctrine of the Holy Trinity we distinguish what we have to say about who God is on the ground of his trinitarian self-revelation from his revelation of himself through himself, yet with the recognition that God's direct self-revealing of himself infinitely outreaches anything that we can ever grasp or express in explicit conceptual form. In the nature of the case the doctrine of the Trinity can be no more than a limited formal interpretation of the self-revelation of God mediated to us in the Holy Scriptures. Nevertheless in so far as it is really geared into divine revelation it will indicate much more than it can truly express.

Although we have anticipated much of what follows, we must now turn to the material content of the biblical revelation of God as the Father, the Son and the Holy Spirit. We remind ourselves again of the comprehensive nature of God's trinitarian self-revelation which has an intrinsic significance as a whole that cannot be broken down and specified in terms of its constituent particulars, upon which knowledge of the whole may then be built up, for in the Holy Trinity the three divine Persons are internally interrelated in such a coinherent way that the one Being of God belongs to each of them as it belongs to all of them, and to all of them as to each of them.[58] This means that the whole Triune Being of God is known in the knowledge of each Person, and each Person is known in the knowledge of the whole Triune Being of God. However, since it is through the incarnation of his Son and Word in Jesus Christ that God has opened for us a way into the wholeness of his trinitarian self-revelation, we may consider first what is revealed to us of Jesus Christ himself, and then on that ground consider what we learn from him of the Father and of the Holy Spirit. We follow the order given in the benediction: 'The grace of the Lord Jesus Christ, and the love of God, and the communion of the Holy Spirit, be with you all.'

The Grace of the Lord Jesus Christ

In the nature of the case Jesus Christ himself is to be known as a whole, so that our knowledge of him may not be built up either from disparate statements or events, but be gained only through discipleship in which we renounce ourselves, take up

[58] As we have already noted in passing this was the way Calvin expressed the coinherent relations of the three Divine Persons in the Trinity through applying to them the Cyprianic expression *in solidum: Institutio*, 1.13.2 and 23. Cf. Cyprian, *De Unitate Ecclesiae*, 3 and 5f, and Calvin, *Institutio*, 4.2.6, 6.17. Cf. also Augustine, *De Trinitate*, 6.8.8: 'Since the Father alone, or the Son alone, or the Holy Spirit alone, is as great as is the Father and the Son and the Holy Spirit together, in no way is he to be called threefold.' And: 6.10.12: 'In the supreme Trinity one (person) is as much as the three together, nor are two anything more than one. And they are infinite in themselves. So both each are in each, and all in each, and each in all, and all are one.'

50

the cross and follow him.[59] This calls for more than a movement of thought, for it involves a personal encounter with Christ as Lord and Saviour. The heart of the matter is succinctly expressed by Jesus in the Fourth Gospel: 'God so loved the world that he gave his only Son, that everyone who has faith in him may not perish, but have eternal life. It was not to judge the world that God sent his Son into the world, but that through him the world might be saved.'[60] In Jesus Christ we meet the very embodiment of the majestic Sovereignty of God breaking into the world to claim it for himself, the coming of *Immanuel* (עִמָנוּאֵל), God himself to be with us and one of us, and specifically named *Yeshua* (יֵשׁוּעַ), meaning *Yahweh-Saviour*, for 'he shall save his people from their sins'.[61] He is the *Lord Jesus*, the divine Saviour of mankind who in his astonishing acts of forgiveness and healing is not just a sort of *locum tenens*, or a kind of 'double' for God in his absence, but the incarnate presence of *Yahweh*, the Lord God himself, although in the form of a servant who has come 'to give his life a ransom for many'[62] – the semitism 'many' being understood as 'all'.[63]

The Lord Jesus meets us, however, as the Light and the Life of God, the Word and Truth of God, in the form of personal being, whom we may know only through personal faith and commitment as we *indwell* the whole presentation of him in the gospel story and in the preaching and teaching of the apostolic witnesses, when clothed with his revealing and saving acts he comes to dwell in us through the presence of his Spirit. We come to know Christ today as the Lord and Saviour in the same way as the disciples and their converts came to know him at the very beginning, when they called upon Jesus to save them from their sins, worshipped him, and prayed to him, and glorified him, as *Jesous Kyrios* ('Ιησους Κύριος), thereby accepting the designation of him as *Yahweh*, the very Name God had given himself in his unique revelation to Israel when he delivered them redemptively out of their bondage in Egypt.[64] The relation of the disciples to Jesus was absorbed into and united with their relationship to God, for Jesus Christ was none other than the Lord himself come into the world as Saviour and Redeemer.[65] He is therefore given the Name that is above every name, the Name of *Kyrios*, and yet, as we have seen, without any docetic depreciation of his humanity.[66] This was very evident in what

---

[59] Matt. 16.24; Mark 8.34.
[60] John 3.16–17.
[61] Matt. 1.21.
[62] Matt. 20.28; Mark 10.45.
[63] 1 Tim. 2.6.
[64] Cf. Acts 2.32ff; 9.31, 11.16; Rom. 10.9ff; 1 Cor. 1.30f; 2.8, 16; 2 Cor. 3.17f; 10.17f; Eph. 6.23f; Phil. 2.9ff; 1 Thes. 3.13; 5.2; 2 Thes. 2.16; Heb. 1.10; Jas. 2.1; Rev. 1.8, etc. For a full and careful analysis of texts that identify Jesus as *Yahweh*, see C. B. Kaiser, *Theological Dialogue between Orthodox and Reformed Churches*, vol. 2 (ed. by T. F. Torrance, Edinburgh, 1993), pp. 189ff.
[65] John 1.1f; 1.18; 20.28; Rom. 9.5; Tit. 2.1ff; Heb. 1.8; 2 Pet. 1.1; 1 John 5.20. Cf. the helpful elucidation of these passages by C. B. Kaiser, *The Doctrine of God* (London, 1982), pp. 30ff; and also 'The Biblical and Patristic Doctrine of the Trinity' in *Theological Dialogue between Orthodox and Reformed Churches*, vol. 2, pp. 165f.
[66] Phil. 2.9, 11. Of course sometimes the word 'Kyrios', especially in the Gospels, is just a polite word of address, rather like our 'Sir'.

St Paul wrote to Timothy in connection with intercessory prayer: 'This is good and acceptable in the sight of God our Saviour, who wills that all men should be saved, and come to the knowledge of the truth. For there is one God, one Mediator between God and men, himself *man*, Christ Jesus, who gave himself a ransom for all.'[67]

The acknowledgement of the Deity of Christ was forced upon his followers especially by his resurrection from the dead which invested his crucifixion on the Cross with redemptive and therefore divine significance. That is very evident, for example, in the incident when the risen Jesus is greeted by the disciples on the shore of Lake Galilee with the cry 'It is the Lord', when they gave the same Name to Jesus as they used of the Father.[68] Or in the incident in the Temple after Pentecost when Peter and John were called in before the priestly authorities after the miraculous healing of a man who had been a cripple from birth. 'By what power, and by what name have you done this?' they were asked. And the answer came:

> By the name of Jesus Christ of Nazareth whom you crucified, and whom God raised from the dead, through him this man stands before you fit and well. This Jesus is the stone rejected by the builders, which has become the corner-stone. There is no salvation through anyone else; in all the world no other name has been granted to mankind by which we can be saved.[69]

That Jesus did what no one but God himself could do, in forgiving and undoing sins through the atoning sacrifice of himself upon the Cross, was immensely reinforced in the epistles of the New Testament. That is to say, the confession of the Deity of Christ was soteriologically rooted and evangelically evoked, for the death of Jesus together with his resurrection from the grave showed him to be the power of the living God over life and death and demonstrated his identity as the transcendent Lord and Saviour of the world. With the resurrection Jesus Christ was set in the very place of God who alone has the power to forgive sins.[70] In him the saving grace of God had appeared so that he was acknowledged as 'our great God and Saviour'.[71] In the background here ring words from the book of Isaiah: 'I am the Lord your God, the Holy One of Israel, your Saviour ... I even I am the Lord God, and beside me there is no saviour.'[72]

The resurrection of Jesus had the effect of illuminating the whole of his life and ministry, and, in disclosing the heart of it all, his Person as having *saving* and unqualified *divine* significance, 'he who is over all, God blessed for ever'.[73] As St John wrote: 'We know that the Son of God has come and has given us an understanding to know him who is true; and we are in him who is true, in his Son

---

[67] 1 Tim. 2.5.
[68] John 21.7.
[69] Acts 4.7–12.
[70] John 20.22f; cf. Mark 2.5f.
[71] Tit. 2. 11f; cf. 1 Tim. 4.10.
[72] Isa. 43.3 and 11; cf. 45.21f.
[73] Rom. 9.5; cf. 1 Tim. 1.17; 2 Tim. 6.15; cf. Heb. 1.8.

Jesus Christ. This is the true God and eternal Life.'[74] And so, as St John records in his Gospel, St Thomas, overwhelmed by the real presence of the crucified and risen Jesus in the midst of his disciples, could not but confess, 'My Lord and my God',[75] thereby giving voice to the faith of the other disciples but also of all who do not see Christ in the flesh and yet believe in him. In the Apocalypse it is precisely as the Lamb of God glorified and ascended that Jesus Christ is identified as the transcendent power of God;[76] and it is as the Word of God, clad in a robe dipped in blood, that Jesus is designated as 'King of Kings and Lord of Lords'.[77] It is highly significant that neither the servant form of Christ's earthly existence nor his shameful death on the Cross detracted from the acknowledgement of his Deity, for they were understood as having to do with the saving activity of the Lord God become man for our sakes, and thus even as exhibiting his exaltation and glorification.[78]

It is not, of course, merely on different incidents recorded in the Gospels, or on various statements about Christ logically analysed and strung together from different books in the New Testament, that our belief in the Deity of Christ rests, but upon the whole manifestation of 'the Christ-event' as soteriologically proclaimed and interpreted in the gospels and epistles. We rely upon the whole coherent evangelical structure of historical divine revelation given in the New Testament Scriptures. It is when we indwell it, meditate upon it, tune into it, penetrate inside it and absorb it in our ourselves, and find the very foundations of our life and thought changing under the creative and saving impact of Christ, and are saved by Christ and personally reconciled to God in Christ, that we believe in him as Lord and God. This does not come about, however, without renouncing ourselves in a repentant rethinking of all that we are and claim to know, that is, without our being crucified with Christ in heart and mind and raised to new life in him. This is poignantly indicated in what St Paul wrote to the Philippians in expressing his desire to know Christ and 'the power of his resurrection and the fellowship of his sufferings in growing conformity to his death,' which involved a radical renunciation and forgetting of what he already claimed to know in order to lay hold of that for which Christ Jesus had already laid hold of him.[79] Recognition that *Jesus is Lord* or belief in the Deity of Christ comes only with a painful reorganisation and transformation of our consciousness before God, and with a participation in the new world of thought and behaviour brought about by Christ, for it is only through Christ and in him that we may know him and through being united to him in God that we learn that the very fullness of God dwells in him. Hence like the early Christians we pray to Jesus as Lord, adore him and worship him, and sing praises *to* him as God, and not only *through* him to God.

---

[74] 1 John 5.20.
[75] John 20.28.
[76] Rev. 1.13–18; 5.6–14.
[77] Rev. 19.11–16.
[78] Gal. 4.4f; Phil. 2.1–11; John 3.14; 8.28; 12.23, 34; 13.31f.
[79] Phil. 3.7–14.

On the other hand, it is due to the crucifixion and resurrection of Christ, and perhaps particularly due to the agonised 'Abba, Father' of Jesus in the Garden of Gethsemane, and not least to the fearful cry of dereliction – 'My God, my God, why have you forsaken me?' – together with Jesus' other cry from the Cross, 'Father, into your hands I commit my spirit,'[80] that we are led to distinguish between Christ the Son of God and God the Father, while at the same time we think of Christ and worship him as our Lord and God.[81] This leads us to think of a differentiation as well as a oneness in the inner life of God between the Father and the Son, between God and God. This holds also for our understanding of the Holy Spirit in his otherness and yet oneness with the Father and the Son. It is after the accomplishment of atonement in the crucifixion and resurrection, after the lifting up and glorifying of Christ, that the power of the Holy Spirit is poured out upon the Church in his personal fullness, and so we think of the Holy Spirit also as the Lord, who with the Son, yet personally distinct from him, engages in atoning intercession for us and is the guarantee of our redemption through him. Like the Son he is also confessed and worshipped as God of God. Here then on the ground of a personal differentiation between the Son and the Father and between the Son and the Spirit, and between both and the Father, within the indivisible life of God, we have the ground on which we are led, with the apostolic Church, to consider a trinitarian differentiation within the one Being of God, yet in such a way that while the Father, the Son and the Holy Spirit are differentiated as three divine Persons from one another they nevertheless *are* in their hypostatic interrelations the one personal Being of God. Thus it may be said that it is finally in the light of what took place in the death and resurrection of Christ as Lord and Saviour and at Pentecost when the Holy Spirit promised by the Father was poured out upon the Church, that ground is given us for the discernment of God as inherently triune.[82] It is in the crucifixion and resurrection of Christ for our sakes that we really know that the God and Father of our Lord Jesus Christ is God *our* Father.[83] And it is in the power of the eternal Spirit through whom Christ offered himself in spotless sacrifice to God that we know that he who died on the Cross is the Father's own Son whom he did not spare but delivered him up for us all,[84] and it is through the same Spirit that we call upon God as *our* Father.[85]

---

[80] Matt. 26.39; 27.46; Mark 14.36; 15.34; Luke 22.42; 23.46.

[81] For Jürgen Moltmann it is particularly through the death of Christ on the cross, and his cry of godforsakenness, that our understanding is opened to the Trinity. 'If a person once feels the infinite passion of God's love which finds expression here, then he understands the mystery of the triune God. God suffers from us – God suffers for us: it is this experience of God that reveals the triune God. It has to be understood, and can only be understood, in trinitarian terms.' *The Trinity and the Kingdom of God* (London, 1981), p. 4. See further pp. 21–60; and also Eberhard Jüngel, *God as the Mystery of the World* (Grand Rapids, 1977), pp. 367–373.

[82] Consult the illuminating discussion of this by Karl Barth, *Church Dogmatics* IV.1, pp. 157–210.

[83] This knowledge is reinforced by the risen Jesus himself in his words to Mary: 'Go to my brothers and tell them that I am ascending to my Father and your Father, to my God and your God.' (John 20.17).

[84] Cf. Heb. 9.14 & Rom. 8.26–32.

[85] Rom. 8.15; Gal. 4.6.

The Love of God

Belief in the Deity of Christ does not arise alone, for it is clearly bound up with belief in God the Father whom Jesus as the incarnate Son of God makes known to us as *his* Father – belief in the Son and belief in the Father completely coincide in our belief in God, for the Father and the Son completely coincide in God's revealing of himself. By revealing himself in the Lord Jesus Christ as *his* dear Son, God reveals that Fatherhood belongs to his eternal Being, and in giving his Son to be the Saviour of the world, he reveals that he loves us to the uttermost with an eternal fatherly Love. That is the basic truth that underlies the whole Gospel of salvation from end to end, but, as St Paul reminds us, it is love which we know only through Christ dwelling in our hearts and through the Holy Spirit who sheds abroad the love of God into our hearts.[86] Thus rooted and grounded in love we are enabled to comprehend with all saints what is the breadth and length and depth and height of love, and to know the love of Christ which surpasses knowledge, that we may be filled with all the fullness of God.[87]

With Jesus himself, knowledge of God was not detached from what had been revealed in the Old Testament Scriptures but was rather an intensifying and interiorising of the Fatherhood of God in terms of his own unique relation as Son of God to the Father. In the Pentateuch, the Prophets and the Psalms to which Jesus constantly appealed in his teaching, the power and compassion of God toward his people were frequently described in colourful figurative language reflecting qualities characteristic of the parental responsibility and care of a human father or mother, but without conceptions of human fatherhood or motherhood being read back in the slightest way into the Nature of God, as was common with the heathen notions of Deity abhorred in the Old Testament.[88] The designation of God as 'Father', which is rather infrequent in the Old Testament, is found almost exclusively in contexts concerned with redemption. Thus we read of the prophet saying in prayer to God: 'You are our Father, though Abraham does not know us and Israel does not acknowledge us, you, O Lord, are our Father, our Redeemer from of old is your name.'[89] In this redemptive sense 'Father' was used frequently to speak of the special relation of God to Israel, in which he regarded his people as his 'first-born son'. 'Thus says the Lord, Israel is my son, my first-born.'[90] 'I have called my son out of Egypt.'[91]

A general conception of God as Father and Creator of all humankind was not wanting in the Old Testament. 'Have we not all one Father?' asks Malachi. 'Has not one God created us?'[92] As found in the Old Testament, however, 'Father' is not

---

[86] Rom. 5.5 and Eph. 3.17.

[87] Eph. 3.17–19.

[88] Thus rightly Thomas A. Smail, *The Forgotten Father* (London, 1980), pp. 34ff. See also the perceptive essay by Jane Williams in *The Forgotten Trinity*, ed. Alasdair I. C. Heron (London, 1991), pp. 93ff.

[89] Isa. 63.16.

[90] Exod. 4.22.

[91] Hos. 11.1; cf. 1.10.

[92] Mal. 2.10.

a proper name for God but is like the other designations of God which, as Calvin pointed out, are all strictly 'titles' or 'epithets'; the exception is *'Yahweh'*, the one ineffable substantive name with which God expressed his own unnameable self-existent Being.[93] It is rather the conception of *sonship*, applied to Israel as a whole or to one or other of its divinely recognised representatives, as in the concept of the servant-son in the Second Isaiah, which has central significance in the fulfilment of divine revelation and redemption for Israel and through Israel.

When we turn to the Scriptures of the New Testament, we find a radical change in the understanding of God, for 'Father' is now revealed to be more than an epithet – it is the personal Name of God in which the form and content of his self-revelation as Father through Jesus Christ his Son are inseparable.[94] Jesus Christ gathers up the whole filial relation of Israel to God enacted in the history and worship of Israel, embodies it in himself, and fulfils the vicarious role of the anointed servant-son in his own incarnate life and mission, all in such a way that the concepts of sonship and fatherhood are brought together to express the unique inseparable relation between Jesus Christ and God the Father. It is upon that inner relation of Love in God that the people of God in their new covenant manifestation as the Body of Christ are grounded and in it that they are granted to share through the Communion of the Spirit of the Father and of the Son.[95]

Permeating the New Testament presentation of Christ, not only in the epistles but in the gospels is the conviction that there is an uncreated and essential relation between him and God. It is on the ground of an unbroken continuity in being and act with God the Father throughout the whole life of Christ, including his death and resurrection, that we believe in him as the very Son of God, but it is also in virtue of this unbroken continuity in Being and Act between them that Christ shows us the Father precisely in showing us that God is *his* Father.[96] Knowledge of the Son and knowledge of the Father are locked into each other, so that it is in and through the unique Sonship of Christ that the Fatherhood of God is made known as the ultimate Nature and Being of God, and is thus given supreme prominence, even in relation to himself, in all that Jesus proclaimed and taught about God as the one Lord of heaven and earth whom we are bound to love unreservedly with all our heart and soul and strength and mind.

In the Gospels as in the rest of the New Testament God is spoken of as 'Father' in a two-fold way, in a general way as the Creator of mankind and the Provider for his human children, as 'our Father who art in heaven' in the Lord's prayer, and in a specific way in his unique relation to the Son, as the God and Father of Jesus

---

[93] John Calvin, *Institutio*, 1.13.9–11.

[94] Cf. Alvin F. Kimel, 'The God who likes his Name: Holy Trinity, Feminism and the language of Faith', *Speaking the Christian God. The Holy Trinity and the Challenge of Feminism*, ed. Alvin F. Kimel, Jr. (Grand Rapids and Leominster, 1992), pp. 188–208.

[95] As T. A. Smail has said, 'There is nothing sexist about the New Testament doctrine of the fatherhood of God. This is a point that has hardly needed to be made before in Christian history but certainly needs to be made today.' *The Forgotten Father*, p. 58.

[96] See especially John 5.17; 10.30, in which the oneness in Act and Being between the Son and the Father is clearly asserted. It was for this reason that the Jews sought to kill Jesus 'because by calling God his own Father, he was claiming equality with God (πατέρα ἴδιον ἔλεγεν τὸν θεόν, ἴσον ἑαυτὸν ποιῶν τῷ θεῷ).'

Christ. This two-fold way of understanding the Fatherhood of God was continued in the theology of the Early Church. It must be emphasised, however, that our Lord did not first make God known as Father and then speak of him as his own Father, but the very reverse; and likewise he did not speak of God first as Creator and therefore as Father, but of God as Father and thus as Lord of heaven and earth. Jesus Christ made God known as peculiarly his own Father, the Father of the only begotten Son, and as such revealed him through his own divine Sonship to be the one God and Father of all. This means that God is to be acknowledged as eternally Father in himself, as Father of the Son, before the foundation of the world and apart from the creation, and so is Father in a sense that is absolutely unique and transcendent.

Here in this biblical use of 'father' we have a signal instance in which a familiar human form of speech and thought is radically transformed under the power of divine revelation, for as applied to God 'father' is utterly different from its ordinary use when applied to a human being. This is why St Paul insisted that it is from the Father of our Lord Jesus Christ that all fatherhood in heaven and earth is named.[97] Of fundamental importance in this respect, therefore, is the stress in the gospels and epistles of the New Testament alike that there is a completely unique and indeed exclusive relation between the Son and the Father – there is no Father without the Son, and no Son without the Father, and no knowing of the Father apart from the Son, and no knowing of the Son apart from the Father. Hence the God and Father of Jesus Christ may not be identified with the God of whom we may think or claim to know apart from Christ, for there is no way to the Father but by him, and no God the Father Almighty Creator of heaven and earth, except him who is essentially and eternally the Father of our Lord Jesus Christ. Quite central to God's self-revelation through Christ, therefore, are the words of Jesus recorded in the Gospels:

> I thank you, Father, Lord of heaven and earth, for hiding these things from the learned and wise, and revealing them to the simple. Yes, Father, such was your choice. Everything is entrusted to me by my Father; and no one knows the Son but the Father, and no one knows the Father but the Son and those to whom the Son chooses to reveal him.[98]

H. R. Mackintosh called these words of Jesus 'the most important for Christology in the New Testament,' and added 'What is of supreme moment for us to note is the unqualified correlation of the Father and the Son.'[99]

The Synoptic Gospels do not speak directly of the Love of God the Father – in fact there is only one passing reference to 'the love of God'.[100] But they do speak powerfully of the Love of God in its concrete embodiment and manifestation in the self-giving love and compassion of Jesus for the sick and the suffering, the weary and the heavy laden, the poor and the destitute, the sinners and the outcasts,

---

[97] Eph. 3.15; cf.4.6.
[98] Matt. 11.25–27; Luke 10.21–22; cf. also Mark 13.32.
[99] H. R. Mackintosh, *Doctrine of the Person*, p. 27.
[100] Luke 11.42.

and all who hunger and thirst for righteousness. What Jesus himself is and does in life and death is the window God has provided for us through which we may discern the Love of God, for in Jesus, the Son of God who came forth from the Father to be one of us and one with us, there is disclosed the very nature of the Love of our Father in heaven for all his children. 'You have heard that it was said, "You shall love your neighbour and hate your enemy", but I say to you', taught Jesus, 'love your enemies and pray for those who persecute you, so that you may be sons of your Father who is in heaven, who makes his sun to rise upon the evil and the good, and sends rain on the just and the unjust.'[101] And where is this wonderful unconditional love of God made more evident by Jesus than in his parable of the prodigal son recorded by St Luke?[102] In Jesus the absolutely equal and infinitely holy Love of God come among us is veiled in human flesh, anonymously as it were, in the form of a servant, and proved itself to us in the life which he poured out freely in his sacrificial death for the ungodly. This is certainly how St Paul and St John looked at it. 'While we were yet helpless, at the right time, Christ died for the ungodly. Why, one will hardly die for a righteous man – though perhaps for a good man one will dare even to die. But God shows his love for us in that while we were yet sinners, Christ died for us.'[103] 'By this we know what love is, that he laid down his life for us.'[104] 'In this the love of God was made manifest among us that God sent his only Son into the world, so that we might live through him. In this is love, not that we loved God but that he loves us and sent his Son to be the propitiation for our sins.'[105]

Such is how the New Testament speaks of the manifestation of the Love of God in the activity of Jesus, above all in his self-giving for us on the Cross. In the Fourth Gospel, however, we are allowed to discern the ultimate ground for this love in the mutual relations between the Father and the Son, and the Son and the Father.[106] While in the Synoptic Gospels Jesus is reported as speaking of the mutual and exclusive relation in knowing and being between the Father and the Son, in the Fourth Gospel Jesus is reported as describing this reciprocal relation as one of loving as well as knowing between the Father and the Son. This completely mutual and exclusive relation in being, loving and knowing between the Son and the Father is singled out and stressed by Jesus: 'No one has ever seen God; God's only Son, he who is in the bosom of the Father has made him known'[107]; 'The Father knows me and I know the Father, and I lay down my life for the sheep ... Therefore the Father loves me, because I lay down my life that I may take it again';[108] 'The Father knows me and I know the Father ... I and my Father are one'[109]; 'He who has seen

---

[101] Matt. 5.43–45.
[102] Luke 15.11–32.
[103] Rom. 5.6–8.
[104] 1 John 3.16.
[105] 1 John 4.9–10.
[106] See T. A. Smail, *The Forgotten Father*, ch. 4, 'God the Father and God the Son', pp. 86ff, especially p. 104.
[107] John 1.18.
[108] John 10.15 and 17.
[109] John 10.15 and 30.

me has seen the Father.'[110] 'The Father loves the Son and shows him all that he himself is doing ... For as the Father raises the dead and gives them life, so also the Son gives life to whom he will. The Father judges no one, but has given all judgment to the Son, that all may honour the Son, even as they honour the Father. He who does not honour the Son does not honour the Father who sent him.'[111] This inseparable bond between the Father and the Son is further emphasised in the First Epistle of John: 'No one who denies the Son has the Father. He who confesses the Son has the Father also.'[112] St Paul too makes the point that faith in the Son and faith in God the Father coincide: 'For us', he wrote to the Corinthians, 'there is one God, the Father, from whom are all things, and we exist for him; there is one Lord Jesus Christ through whom are all things, and we exist through him.'[113]

The profound theological import of all this is that the Father/Son, Son/Father relation belongs to the innermost Being of God as God – in fact the flow of Love from the Father to the Son and from the Son to the Father reveals that God *is* the ever-living and ever-loving God precisely as this dynamic Communion of loving and being loved within himself. At the same time this reveals both that God is not undifferentiated within the absolute oneness of his eternal Being, and that this differentiation between the Father and the Son in their loving of one another and in their being loved by one another belongs to the sublime fact that God *is* Love.[114] It must be added that this self-originating Love is not only the ground of all God's loving within himself but the ground of all his self-giving in unconditional love toward us. It is then to this dynamic fullness of the Love of God which he is in himself before the very foundation of the world that all the ways and works of God in creation and redemption go back. Since God is Love, in that he loves within himself and in that he loves us in Christ, he can no more cease loving, or cease to love us, than he can cease to be God or go back upon the incarnation and death of his only Son. 'Who shall separate us from the love of Christ?' asks St Paul. 'I am persuaded that neither death nor life, nor angels, nor principalities, nor powers, nor things present, nor things to come, nor height, nor depth, nor anything in all creation shall be able to separate us from the love of God in Christ Jesus our Lord.'[115]

The Communion of the Holy Spirit

Since it is only through himself that God reveals himself, God himself is the personal content of his revelation to us embodied in Jesus Christ his incarnate Son. Since it is only through himself that communion with God is accessible to us, God himself is the personal reality of that communion granted to us in the Holy Spirit. That is

---

[110] John 14.9.
[111] John 5.20–23; cf. also John 5.37; 6.46; 8.19; 17.25; and 1 John 2.23; 2 John 9.
[112] 1 John 2.23.
[113] 1 Cor. 8.6.
[114] The differentiation as well as the unique bond between the Father and the Son is clearly brought out in the words of the Lord to Mary Magdalene on the morning of his resurrection: 'Do not hold me, for I have not yet ascended to the Father; but go to my brethren and say to them, I am ascending to my Father and your Father, to my God and your God' (John 20.17).
[115] Rom. 8.1,38–39.

to say God's self-revelation to us is actualised in the Communion of the Holy Spirit through whom God brings his divine Reality to bear personally, and indeed experientially, upon us, both in the address of his Word to us and in our hearing and understanding of that Word. It is through his own presence to us in his Spirit that God establishes the relation between us and himself which we need in order to know him. God creates that relation by the presence of his Spirit within us as a relation of himself to himself. Hence, as Karl Barth has expressed it:

> The Spirit of God is God in his freedom to be present to the creature, and so to create this relation and thereby to be the life of the creature. And God's Spirit, the Holy Spirit, especially in revelation, is God himself in that he can not only come to man but also be in man, and thus open up man and make him capable and ready for himself, and thus to complete his revelation in him.[116]

This is, I believe, how we are led to think of the Holy Spirit as we indwell the New Testament Scriptures and listen to the incarnate Word of God speaking to us in Christ, and through the holy presence of God in his Spirit find Christ himself coming to dwell in us in such a way that we are enabled to receive and apprehend God's revelation of himself. This understanding of the Spirit is one we gain, therefore, not just through exegetical study of relevant passages of Scripture, but through non-analytical intuitive acts of knowledge such as arise in our meditating upon them in worship and prayer in the course of which their underlying coherence becomes imprinted on our minds and integrates our response to the whole tenor of the New Testament teaching about the Spirit. As the Holy Spirit makes the revelation of the Father through the Son, mediated to us in the New Testament Scriptures, to resonate in our hearts, we learn that as the Spirit of the Father and of the Son he is no less God than the Father and the Son while nevertheless personally distinct from them.

The Spirit is intrinsically holy, divine and personal as his very designation the *Holy Spirit* indicates,[117] for it implies the identification of the Spirit with him whom Isaiah spoke of as 'the Holy One of Israel.'[118] It is significant that this expression is also applied to the Father and to the Son,[119] recalling the liturgical *Trisagion* of Isaiah's vision: 'Holy, holy, holy is the Lord of hosts, the whole earth is full of his glory.'[120] 'Holy' in this use refers to the utterly transcendent Nature, and the unapproachable Glory and Majesty of God. This divine Nature and Majesty of the Holy Spirit are reflected not least in our Lord's severe condemnation of blasphemy

---

[116] Karl Barth, *Church Dogmatics* 1.1 (Edinburgh, 1975), p. 450. Thus also Colin Gunton, *The One, The Three and The Many* (Cambridge, 1993), p. 185. He also links 'the unqualified openness of the triune persons to each other' to the fact that God *is* Spirit, p. 188.

[117] Cf. the Old Testament references to 'Holy Spirit', Ps. 51.11; Isa. 31.3; 63.10; and Torrance, *The Trinitarian Faith*, pp. 192–3.

[118] See again *The Trinitarian Faith*, ch. 6 on 'The Eternal Spirit', p. 192f; and Isa. 1.4; 5.19, 24; 10.17, 20; 12.6; 7.7; 29.19, 23; 30.11f; 31.1; 37.23; 40.25; 41.14, 16, 20; 43.3, 14f, 11; 45.11; 47.4; 48.17; 49.7; 54.5; 60.9, 15. Cf. Mark 1.24; Luke 4.34; John 6.69; Acts 3.14; 1 John 2.20.

[119] As for example in John 17.11; Mark 1.24; John 6.69.

[120] Isa. 63.

against the Holy Spirit as unforgivable sin.[121] And they are clearly acknowledged in St Paul's reference to the Spirit as *Kyrios* in the same way in which he refers to Christ as *Kyrios* or *Yahweh*.[122] Like Christ and like the Father the Spirit is himself the Lord (ὁ Κύριος),[123] and is called the Spirit of God and the Spirit of Christ, but he is clearly distinguished from Christ as he is from the Father. This is very evident in the teaching of Jesus as recorded by St John about the Person of the Spirit as the Paraclete sent by the Father in the Name of Christ, and about his activity as the Spirit of truth in bearing witness to Christ.[124] While the Spirit is personally other than Christ, he nevertheless shares with him divine Lordship and is inseparably related to him in his incarnate mission from the Father. Thus it is by the crucified, risen and ascended Lord that his presence and power are bestowed.[125]

It seems clear, then, that within the orbit of God's revealing and reconciling activity proclaimed in the Gospel, belief in the Deity of the Holy Spirit stands or falls with belief in the Deity of Christ. To be 'in the Spirit' is to be 'in Christ', and to be in Christ is to be in God, for the operation of the Holy Spirit in us like the work of Christ for us is empty of evangelical substance or saving validity unless it is grounded in God and flows from God. To have to do with the Holy Spirit is to have to do directly with Christ and with God himself, as is evident in the association of the Spirit with the Son and with the Father in the triadic statements we are to consider below in which the Holy Spirit is spoken of on the same sublime level as the Father and the Son.

In a very important passage for our understanding of the Holy Spirit St Paul tells us that it is through the Spirit who dwells in the depths of God's Being that we are given access to the hidden wisdom of God which is otherwise quite unknowable.

> Scripture speaks of things beyond our seeing, things beyond our hearing, things beyond our imagination, all prepared by God for those who love him; and these things are what God has revealed to us through the Spirit. For the Spirit explores everything, even the depths of God's own nature. Who knows what a human being is but the human spirit within him? In the same way, only the Spirit of God knows the things of God. And we have received this Spirit from God, not the spirit of the world, so that we may know all that God has graciously bestowed upon us; and because we are interpreting spiritual truths to those who have the Spirit, we speak of these gifts of God in words taught us not by our human wisdom but by the Spirit.[126]

The significance of this teaching can be brought out by linking it to the words of Jesus, to which reference has already been made more than once:

> At that moment Jesus exulted in the Holy Spirit and said, 'I thank you, Father, Lord of heaven and earth, for hiding these things from the learned

---

[121] Matt. 12.31; Mark 3.29; Luke 12.10.

[122] 2 Cor. 3.17–18.

[123] 2 Cor. 3.17.

[124] John 14.16f, 26; 15.26; 16.13–15.

[125] John 20.21–23.

[126] 1 Cor. 2.9–13.

61

and wise, and revealing them to the simple. Yes, Father, such was your choice. Everything is entrusted to me by my Father; and no one knows the Son but the Father; and no one knows the Father but the Son and those to whom the Son chooses to reveal them.'[127]

Just as no one knows the Father but the Son, so no one knows the depths of God but the Spirit; and just as Jesus made this revelation in the Holy Spirit, so it is through the same Spirit freely given to us that by the grace of God we may really know the deep things of God through sharing in the mutual knowing of the Father and the Son. As we learn from Jesus and Paul, it is only the Spirit of God who dwells within God and knows the immanent depths of his eternal being, and shares in the inner Communion of knowing between the Father and the Son, who can reveal them to us. If the Holy Spirit were not himself personally God, this would be quite impossible, for only God himself can reveal the secrets of his own internal relations. God the Father, God the Son, and God the Holy Spirit, revealed to us through himself in this profound way, are the transcendent Communion of personal Being which God is in himself, and it is through the Communion of the Holy Spirit, who is the Spirit of the Father and of the Son, that we may know God in his Triune Reality.

According to the New Testament, Jesus was conceived by the Holy Spirit and born of the Virgin Mary, baptised by the Spirit as the Lamb of God to bear and bear away the sins of the world, anointed by the Spirit for his messianic mission of redemption, endowed with the Spirit of God by whose power he healed the sick and raised the dead, offered himself in atoning sacrifice through the eternal Spirit, was declared to be the Son of God with power, according to the Holy Spirit, through his resurrection from the dead. And then with his ascension to the right hand of God the Lord Jesus poured out the Holy Spirit in fullness and power upon the Church at Pentecost, uniting the Church to himself as his Body and realising within the faith, understanding and teaching of the apostles the truth about himself in such a way that through the Communion of the Spirit they were given participation in the very mind of Christ himself. It was thus that God's revelation of himself through himself, and our fellowship with God through himself, were fulfilled in the foundation of the Church with an essentially trinitarian content.

As St Paul tells us, it is only through the Holy Spirit that we may know and believe in Jesus Christ: 'No one says Jesus is Lord (or *Kyrios*) but by the Holy Spirit,'[128] for it is only through the Spirit that we are made free to receive and apprehend God's self-revelation and believe in the Lord Jesus Christ. It is only through God's own Spirit that we can believe in the utterly astonishing truth announced to us, that in Jesus Christ God himself, the Creator of heaven and earth has become one of us and one with us creaturely beings in space and time. How could we ever come to believe, by means of our believing, that which we cannot

[127] Luke 10.21–22 & Matt. 11.25–27.
[128] 1 Cor. 12.3. See also the words of Jesus in Mark 12.36: 'David himself, inspired by the Holy Spirit, declared, "The Lord said to my Lord, Sit at my right hand, till I put your enemies under your feet."'

believe at all by ourselves? It can take place and actually does take place only through the Lord the Spirit that God himself is. Moreover, it is through the agency and power of the same Holy Spirit speaking in us and through us that the Word of God can be and continues to be communicated as living dynamic Reality to mankind in the proclamation and the teaching of the Church. This holds good in the most difficult circumstances, for it is the coming of the Kingdom of God in Christ and the Lordship of the Holy Spirit on earth that are at stake in the mission of the Church. Just as when Jesus cast out demons by the Spirit (or 'finger') of God, the Kingdom of God or his sovereign Presence and Power came among people,[129] so when the Church proclaims the victory of Christ over all the forces of evil and darkness, it is God himself in the sovereign Presence and Power of his Spirit who is at work bringing redemption and freedom to captive humanity. Hence Jesus said to his disciples with regard to the troublous days ahead, not to worry beforehand what they will say: 'When the time comes say whatever is given you to say, for it is not you who will be speaking, but the Holy Spirit.'[130]

It should now be evident, then, that far from being some kind of potency or impersonal influence, the Holy Spirit is fully and intensely personal. The New Testament makes this very clear when it refers to the Spirit as speaking, witnessing, crying, grieving, interceding, intervening, creating, rebuking, judging, etc. Although the Greek word used in the New Testament for the Spirit is linguistically neuter, Jesus referred to him in distinctly personal terms as 'he' and 'Paraclete'.[131] The Holy Spirit is God himself speaking although he is not himself the Word of God. It was not of course the Spirit but the Word who became incarnate, and so the Spirit does not bring us any revelation other than or independent of the Word who became incarnate in Jesus Christ. The Holy Spirit has no 'Face', but it is through the Spirit that we see the Face of Christ and in the Face of Christ we see the Face of the Father. The Holy Spirit does not manifest himself or focus attention upon himself, for it is his mission from the Father to declare the Son and focus attention upon him. It is through the speaking of the Spirit that the Word of God incarnate in Christ is communicated to us in words that are Spirit and Life and not flesh.[132] They are spiritual realities which may be discerned only in a correspondingly spiritual way.[133] Only as God in Christ meets us and speaks to us personally through the presence and power of his Spirit do his self-revealing and self-imparting to us strike into the depths of our being and liberate us for communion with himself, making us capable of responding to him as Lord and Saviour with faith and love and understanding beyond our natural capacities altogether. Thus in the gift of his Holy Spirit God gives us *himself* – the Gift and the Giver are one – thereby pledging and guaranteeing to us inclusion within the saving and reconciling embrace of the transcendent Love that God himself is. That is the wonderful import of the Grace of the Lord Jesus Christ, and the Love of God, and the Communion of the Holy

---

[129] Matt. 12.28 & Luke 11.20.
[130] Mark 13.11.
[131] Thus John 15.26; 16.13f.
[132] John 6.63.
[133] 1 Cor. 2.14f.

Spirit: God's revealing and saving activity is the work of the whole Trinity. As we read St Paul's epistles we learn that it was out of his basic experience of the Spirit and understanding of atoning reconciliation with God in Jesus Christ that the apostle could not but speak of the Spirit as Lord in the same way that he spoke of the Father as Lord and of the Son as Lord, yet without implying that there are three Lords, for there was for him only one saving activity of the Lord God through Christ and in the Spirit that had transformed his life.

We cannot forget that apart from the fulfilment of the atoning sacrifice of Christ on the Cross, the Holy Spirit, the immediate presence of God in unreserved self-giving to his people, would not have been poured out at Pentecost, and we sinful human beings would be unable to draw near to God and enter into personal communion with him, for without being reconciled to him we could not endure his transcendent purity and holiness. Pentecost and Calvary belong inseparably together, for the outpouring of the Holy Spirit upon us, and the actualising of God's personal presence within us through the Spirit, belong to the fulfilment of God's reconciling of the world to himself. It is only through the Holy Spirit, St Paul wrote to the Galatians, that the crucifixion of Jesus Christ placarded before them could be effectual in their lives.[134] This inner soteriological connection between the self-giving of God in the Cross and his self-giving in the Holy Spirit, is pointed out by the evangelist in explanation of the teaching of Jesus: 'He was speaking of the Spirit whom believers in him would receive; for the Spirit had not yet been given, because Jesus had not yet been glorified.'[135] It was to this glorifying of himself by the Holy Spirit that Jesus pointed again and again in anticipation of his death on the Cross when his own divine glory which he shared with the Father would be manifest.[136] It is because of this relation between the vicarious work of Christ, the Lamb of God who bears away the sin of the world, and the Holy Spirit that St Paul could speak of the Holy Spirit as sharing in the vicarious intercession of Christ, and making it inarticulately to echo in our prayer.[137]

Behind St Paul's thought here there appears to lie an Isaianic passage in which the prophet spoke of the Lord as sending his glorious power to be with his servant Moses and endowing his people with his Holy Spirit: 'In all their affliction he was afflicted and the angel of his presence saved them; in his love and in his pity he redeemed them; and he bare them and carried them all the days of old. But they rebelled, and grieved his Holy Spirit; therefore he became hostile to them and fought against them.'[138] Neither in the Old Testament nor in the New Testament is the Spirit of God regarded as the emission of some divine force detachable from God, but as the confrontation of human beings and their affairs with the immediate presence of God who in the dynamic outreach of his own Self brings the saving impact of his divine power and holiness to bear directly and personally upon the lives of people in judgment and salvation alike. It is above all as *Holy* Spirit, that the Spirit of God acts in this way.

---

[134] Gal. 3.1ff; 5.1ff.
[135] John 7.39; cf. 17.1ff.
[136] John 11.4; 12.16, 23, 28, 31f; 13.31f; 14.13; 15.5; 16.14; 17.1, 4, 5, 10.
[137] Rom. 8.26f and 34.
[138] Isa. 63.9–11; cf. Exod. 23.20; 33.14.

It is the mission of the Holy Spirit, as we have already noted, to be the *Paraclete* (Παράκλητος) personally and subsistently distinct from Christ and from the Father while remaining one with them in Being.[139] He is specifically named by Christ, however, as '*another* Paraclete',[140] that is, another Advocate of men and women in the presence of God, who is not a substitute for Christ but who is sent in his name to dwell in the Church on earth uniting it with the risen and ascended Lord, and whose presence and activity in the life and mission of the Church on earth answer to the presence and activity of the Paraclete above.[141] As the other Paraclete the Holy Spirit has a distinctively vicarious function reflecting and mediating the advocacy and priestly intercession of Christ.[142] With the coming of the Spirit the Lord fulfilled his promise not to leave his disciples orphaned but to come himself among them in such a way that they would know that he is in the Father and that they are in him and he is in them.[143] As Jesus himself shows us the Father, the Spirit shows us Christ, and makes us know the Father in the Son.[144]

This trinitarian revelation of God the Father through the Spirit in Christ is at once the glorifying of Christ and the glorifying of the Father with a glory within which we also are embraced. 'God, who commanded the light to shine out of darkness, has shined in our hearts, to give the light of the glory of God in the face of Jesus Christ.'[145] It was with this truth that St John prefaced his Gospel: 'The Word was made flesh, and dwelt among us (and we beheld his glory, the glory as of the only begotten of the Father) full of grace and truth.... No one has seen God at any time, the only begotten Son, who is in the bosom of the Father, has declared him.'[146] Jesus Christ is therefore presented in the Gospel as himself the one Way and the one Truth, apart from whom there is no way to the Father, and it is the mission of the Spirit in glorifying Christ in God and glorifying God in Christ to guide the disciples in the Way and to lead them into knowledge of the Truth. He is the living personal Agent of Christ sent by him from the Father as the Spirit of truth who will guide the disciples into all truth, and convince the world of sin and of righteousness and of judgment. Jesus made it clear that he did not speak from himself, but spoke only what he received from the Father.[147] He spoke in similar terms of the Holy Spirit: in his coming the Holy Spirit does not glorify himself or speak from himself but speaks whatever he hears and makes known what is still to come. 'He will glorify me, for he will take what is mine and make it known unto

---

[139] John 14.16f.
[140] John 14.16: 'I will ask the Father, and he will give you another Paraclete that he may abide with you for ever.'
[141] For a fuller account of this mission of the Spirit, see T. F. Torrance, *Theology in Reconstruction* (London, 1965), pp. 245ff and 251ff.
[142] Rom. 8.26ff.
[143] John 14.16–20 and 28.
[144] John 14.7ff, 19f; 15.26f; 16.13ff; 17.24ff.
[145] 2 Cor. 4.6; cf. also 2 Cor. 3.18 and Eph. 1.17f.
[146] John 1.14 and 18.
[147] John 7.16ff.

you. All that the Father has is mine, and that is why I said "he will take what is mine and make it known unto you."'[148]

It is not the function of the Spirit, then, to bear witness to himself in his distinctive personal Being, but to bear witness to Christ and glorify him as Lord and Saviour, whereby God the Father also is glorified in the revelation of his divine Being in the Son. For the Spirit to glorify Christ is to radiate his Life as the incarnate Son with divine Light in such a way as to make his intrinsic Deity, *the Glory of Yahweh*, to shine forth, and thereby also to make the Face of the Father radiant in the Face of the Son.[149] Thus through the Son and in the Spirit the divine *Shekinah*, the glory of God's personal Presence, shines in gracious blessing and peace upon all who draw near to him in adoration and worship, and bears transformingly upon them.[150] We recall here what St Paul wrote to the Corinthians with reference to what happened to Moses under the radiance of the divine Shekinah: 'And we all, with unveiled face, beholding the glory of the Lord, are changed into his likeness from one degree of glory to another; for this comes from the Lord who is the Spirit.'[151]

Like Christ the Holy Spirit is one in being and of the same being as the Father, but unlike Christ the Holy Spirit is not one in being and of the same being as we are, for he incarnated the Son but does not incarnate himself, he utters the Word but does not utter himself. He directs us through himself to the one Word and Face of God in Jesus Christ in accordance with whom all our knowledge of God is formed in our minds, knowledge of the Spirit as well as of the Father and of the Son. This is the diaphanous self-effacing nature of the Holy Spirit who hides himself, as it were, behind the Father in the Son and behind the Son in the Father, but also the enlightening transparence of the Spirit who by throwing his eternal Light upon the Father through the Son and upon the Son in the Father, brings the radiance of God's Glory to bear upon us. We do not know the Holy Spirit directly in his own personal Reality or Glory. We know him only in his unique spiritual mode of activity and transparent presence in virtue of which God's self-revelation shines through to us in Christ, and we are made through the Spirit to see the Father in the Son and the Son in the Father. While the Holy Spirit thereby guards the transcendence of God who infinitely exceeds what finite minds can grasp, nevertheless through his personal presence to us he brings the ineffable Being and Reality of God out of his unapproachable Light to bear upon us, and brings us out of our distance and darkness to have communion with himself and through himself with the Father and the Son. Because through him the Word of God continues to sound forth and is heard and believed, because in his light we see light and by his

---

[148] John 16.14–15. See also John 13.31f; 17.1ff. Wolfhardt Pannenberg points out that in the glorifying of Christ by the Spirit 'we have a self-distinction which constitutes the Spirit a separate person from the Father and the Son and relates him to both.' *Systematic Theology* (tr. by G. W. Bromiley, Grand Rapids, 1991), vol. 1, p. 315.

[149] Cf. Hebrews 1.3 where the Son is spoken of as 'the radiance of God's glory and the express image of his hypostasis'.

[150] Cf. the three-fold high-priestly benediction through which the Name of Yahweh is put upon his people: 'The Lord bless you and keep you; the Lord make his face to shine upon you, and be gracious unto you; the Lord lift up his countenance upon you, and give you peace' (Num. 6.24f).

[151] 2 Cor. 3.18. Cf. 1 Pet. 4.14: 'The Spirit of glory and of God rests upon us.'

creative operation we come to know the unknowable and eternal God, we know the Holy Spirit, although personally distinct from the Father and the Son, to be no less Lord God than the Father and the Son, both as he is toward us and as he is antecedently in the undivided oneness of God's eternal Being.

How does this three-fold revelation of God as Father, Son and Holy Spirit given to us in the New Testament square with the revelation of God given in the Old Testament who is the one Lord God apart from whom there is no other? These Hebrew Scriptures, of course, were the Scriptures and the only Scriptures which Jesus had and reverenced as utterly holy and inviolable. He had no hesitation in referring faith to the self-revelation of God to Moses at the burning bush, 'I am the God of Abraham, the God of Isaac, and the God of Jacob;' and took upon his own lips the *Shema Israel*: 'Hear, O Israel, the Lord our God is the one Lord.'[152] But he could also say 'Before Abraham was, *I am*,'[153] and in face of divine revelation in the Old Testament Scriptures he could say 'but *I say* unto you'.[154] He could accept the designation of himself as *Kyrios*,[155] but without infringing the Oneness of God. The same holds good of our Lord's claim that God 'our heavenly Father' is peculiarly *his* Father, which brought on him the accusation of blasphemy.[156] According to St John, Jesus claimed, as we have noted, that he and the Father are One and inexist in one another.[157] This was not a rejection of the one Lord God but a radically new revelation of his divine Being and Nature as the God and Father of Jesus Christ. Nowhere in the New Testament Scriptures is there any suggestion that the confession 'Jesus is Lord' conflicts with or competes with belief in the One Lord God of divine revelation in the Old Testament Scriptures who could also be addressed as 'Father' where the main stress is upon divine care and redemption.[158] But nowhere is there any suggestion either that this new revelation of God as Father, through Jesus Christ his Son and the Communion of the Holy Spirit, is given or received apart from God's revelation of himself through the medium of Israel. Jesus himself was a Jew, and insisted that salvation is from the Jews, and that Jews know whom they worship while Gentiles do not.[159]

How the knowledge of God revealed in Jesus Christ is related to the knowledge of God mediated to Israel is a question with which St Paul was personally concerned, as an Israelite and a Hebrew of the Hebrews. Like Jesus he held that Gentiles do not know what they worship,[160] and are indeed 'without hope and without God in the world' – theirs is an unrevealed God.[161] Knowledge of the true God is to be found only in Israel, the people whom God elected and bound into a covenant

---

[152] Deut. 6.4; Mark 12.28–29.
[153] John 8.58.
[154] Matt. 5.22.
[155] Matt. 6.21; Mark 12.35f; Luke 6.46; 11.17; John 20.28, etc.
[156] John 5.17f; 10.30ff.
[157] John 10.38; 14.10, etc.
[158] Isa. 63.16; 64.8; Mal. 2.10.
[159] John 4.22.
[160] Acts 17.23.
[161] Eph. 1.12.

relation with himself as the medium of his unique revelation to mankind destined to be brought to its fulfilment in the advent of Christ. It is to the people of Israel that the oracles of God were committed, the adoption, the divine worship, the promises, the patriarchs, and the Christ;[162] but the Gentiles are without Christ, excluded from the community of Israel, strangers to God's covenants and the promises that go with them, and are in fact without hope and without God in the world.[163]

Paul clearly had in mind here the barrier erected around the Temple in Jerusalem to separate the believing people of God from unbelievers, those who might 'draw near' to God and those who were 'far off'. But he went on to tell his Ephesian converts

> now in Christ Jesus you who used to be far off have been brought near by the blood of Christ. For he is our peace, who has made us both one, and has broken down the middle wall of partition between us … By his cross Christ has reconciled both Jews and Gentiles in one body to God, putting an end in himself to all enmity between them. And so Christ came and proclaimed that Gospel of peace, to you who were far off and to you who were near, for through him we both have access in one Spirit to the Father. Hence you Gentiles are no longer strangers and exiles but fellow-citizens with the holy people and members of the family of God. You are built upon the foundation of the apostles and prophets, with Jesus Christ himself as its cornerstone; in him the whole building is joined together and becomes a holy temple in the Lord, and in him you are built into a home where God dwells through his Spirit.[164]

Paul believed that the covenant made by God with Israel is irrevocable, and of permanent significance for the salvation of Gentiles as well as Jews, for through it God prepared the special interpretative framework, handed on in the Hebrew Scriptures, within which alone the fulfilment of his self-revelation in the advent of Christ is to be understood. Hence he tells us in this passage that the Christian understanding of God is grounded in the revelation of the one Lord God given to Israel and mediated to us in the Old Testament Scriptures. In these Scriptures it is very clear that through his presence and power God was accessible to his people within the covenant relations he had graciously established with them, nowhere more evident than in his personal interaction with Abraham, Moses, or Samuel. Nevertheless it is also clear that he did not make *himself* personally accessible to them but remained hidden behind his mighty acts of revelation and salvation. St Paul tells us here, however, that access to knowledge of God as he is in himself has now been provided for us through the reconciliation with God brought about by the Cross of Christ. By his blood Christ has reconciled us to God and thereby opened the way for all who believe in his name to enter with him into the holy

---

[162] Rom. 3.2; 9.4f.
[163] Eph. 2.11–12.
[164] Eph. 2.13–22. Cf. Heb. 10.19–22.

presence of God and share in the gift of the Holy Spirit which he received from the Father. Thus through the Grace of the Lord Jesus Christ and the Communion of the Spirit we sinful human beings have access to the Love of the Father, and know him not from afar but intimately as he is in himself, yet without intruding upon the inner sanctum of his transcendent holiness. The proper understanding of God as Father, Son and Holy Spirit takes place only within the movement of atoning propitiation whereby God draws near to us in the world and draws us near to himself in believing response and brings us into union with himself through the gift of his Spirit. In the incarnation and the Cross God the Father opens his innermost heart and mind to us in the self-revelation of his redeeming love, and through the Communion of the Spirit makes himself present to us within the conditions of our creaturely existence in such a healing and creative way as to open our hearts and minds to receive and understand his self-revelation as Father, Son and Holy Spirit, beyond anything that we could ever be capable of by ourselves.

St Paul's teaching also implies that Jews for their part cannot have access to knowledge of God as he really is in himself except through Christ and the Holy Spirit on the ground of the atoning reconciliation effected in the Cross. This does not mean, however, that Christians for their part can bypass the Old Testament Scriptures for, as we have just noted, they provide the framework of divine meaning within which the New Testament Scriptures are to be interpreted, and it is upon the foundation of the revealed knowledge of the one Lord God which they mediate to Israel that Christian knowledge of God rests and takes shape. This interconnection between Jewish and Christian knowledge of God must not be left out of account either by Jews or by Christians. For Jews it is finally only in the light of what has taken place in God's incarnate self-revelation in Christ in fulfilment of his covenant promises to Israel that distinctive features in the knowledge of God given in the Old Testament itself unfold their full significance. This applies above all to the Word and the Spirit of the living God which are not created intermediaries between God and mankind but are immediate emanations and agencies of his personal presence and power, and as such point to real distinctions within the indivisible oneness and fullness of God in his regular designation in the Hebrew Scriptures as *Elohim*. But if Christians are properly to grasp the trinitarian understanding of God within the unitary structure of his self-revelation they must also take seriously what the Old Testament Scriptures have to say about the Word and the Spirit of God which figure alongside of the one Lord God as hypostatic extensions of his presence and agency and yet clearly belong to what God is in himself, and sometimes like 'the Name' or 'the Face' of God take on the role of a 'double' for God. This is true also of what is said of the personalised role of Wisdom in creation which is another designation for the mighty Word of God.[165]

Some attention should also be directed to the 'theophanies', and not least to those relating to the mysterious figure designated 'the angel of the Lord' who can even be identified with *Yahweh* himself, the heavenly form in which God acts at decisive points in the history of his covenant people Israel, in the announcing of a

---

[165] See Prov. 8, especially 22–31, and cf. also Wisd. 9.1ff; 10.1ff; and Ecclus. (Sirach) 24ff.

heavenly message or in the heralding of a divine act of salvation.[166] As we look back upon these theophanies and angelic messengers from within the perspective of God's self-revelation in Christ, they appear to reflect a revelation of the Being of God which is not an absolutely undifferentiated oneness. The prophet Isaiah could even speak in a well-known passage about the promised Messiah as 'Son of God' and 'Mighty God'.[167] It is quite otherwise with traditional Rabbinic Judaism. In spite of the strange plurality with which God (*Elohim*) speaks of himself in the Old Testament,[168] he is regarded as a God of absolutely unfigured undifferentiated oneness who cannot be apprehended in himself at all, or even named by human beings. What may be known of God, it was explained, does not have to do with what he is in himself but only with his moral and metaphysical attributes as they are manifested in his historical interaction with Israel, his covenant people, and in his external relations to the world which he has created.

For St Paul, however, an immense change has now come about, which is decisive for Jews as well as Christians. Through Christ and in one Spirit we are *both* given access to the Father and know him, the God of Abraham, Isaac and Jacob, the God of Moses and Isaiah and Jesus, the one Lord God of the Old Testament Scriptures, in an altogether profounder way, within the inner relations of his one Being, only of course as 'clothed' with his self-revelation to us. He is not undifferentiated in himself, but is a Triunity, indivisible in his Unity and inseparable in his Trinity, who has identified and designated himself to us as Father, Son and Holy Spirit. Reconciled to God in this way Christians and Jews are fellow-citizens with one another in one people of God, members of God's household, built upon the foundation of both apostles and prophets, or the New and Old Testament revelations, crowned by Christ himself, and indwelt by God through his Spirit. They are thus bonded together in a community conditioned and informed by the self-revelation and reconciling presence of the Holy Trinity which in the purpose of God have been actualised in the world through the medium of his covenanted relations with the people of Israel.

This trinitarian revelation of God is deeply imprinted in the Scriptures of the New Testament implicitly informing their witness, so that it is hardly surprising that it crops up on the surface here and there in more explicit form in *triadic formulae* to which our attention must be directed. There are not a few passages in which the Father, the Son and the Holy Spirit are somewhat loosely associated with one another but without evidence of there being any deliberate coordination of the three divine Persons in a three-fold pattern.[169]

---

[166] See Genesis 16.17f; 17.1f; 22.11, 15; 31.11f; Exod. 3.2 & 14; Judges 2.1, etc. The angel of the Lord also appears at decisive points in the Gospel story as recorded in Matt. 1.20; 2.9; Acts 5.19; 12.7; 27.23, etc. Refer to Karl Barth, *Church Dogmatics* III.3 (Edinburgh, 1961), pp. 369ff, 459ff, 477ff.

[167] Isa. 9.6; cf. Pss. 2.7; 89.26f.

[168] Cf. for example Gen. 1.20; 3.22; 11.7; or Isa. 6.8.

[169] See Matt. 11.25–27; Luke 10.21f; Acts 2.32f & 38f; 11.17; Rom. 1.3f; 5.5, 8; 8.3, 4, 8f, 11, 16f; 15.16 & 30; 1 Cor. 6.11; 12.4ff; 2 Cor. 1.21f; 3.3; Gal. 3.13f; 4.4–6; Eph. 2.18, 20–22; 3.14–16; 4.4–6; Phil. 3.3; Col. 1.6–8; 2 Thess. 2.13f; Tit. 3.4–6; Heb. 6.4f; 10.29; 1 Pet. 1.2; 4.14; 1 John 5, 6–12; Jude 20f.

This is very apparent, for example, in those accounts of the Gospels which speak of the birth and the baptism of Jesus,[170] but it is in the Fourth Gospel particularly that Father, Son and Holy Spirit are spoken of together in ways which indicate a trinitarian correlation in their personal relations.[171] This is sometimes implied when not all three Persons are explicitly mentioned.[172] There are, however, more explicit triadic formulations in the New Testament which came to have special theological importance in the developing tradition of the early Church:[173]

(1) Of primary importance is the dominical baptismal formula, Matt. 28.19: 'In the name of the Father, and of the Son, and of the Holy Spirit.'

(2) The Pauline benediction from 2 Cor. 13.14: 'The grace of the Lord Jesus Christ, and the love of God, and the communion of the Holy Spirit, be with you all.'

(3) The influential text 1 Cor. 12.4–6: 'There are varieties of gifts, but the same Spirit. There are varieties of service, but the same Lord. There are varieties of activity, but it is the same God who is active in all of them and in everyone.'

(4) The economic formulation in Gal. 4.4–6: 'When the time had fully come, God sent forth his Son, made of woman, made under the law, to redeem those who were under the law, so that we might receive adoption as sons. And because you are sons, God has sent the Spirit of his Son into our hearts, crying "Abba, Father".'

(5) The verses that were so important for the Nicene-Constantinopolitan Creed, Eph. 4.4–6: 'There is one body and one Spirit, just as there is one hope held out in God's call to you, one Lord, one faith, one baptism; one God and Father of all, who is over all and through all and in all.'

While these formulations do not give us an explicit *doctrine* of the Holy Trinity, they do more than pave the way for it, for they give expression to the three-fold structure of God's astonishing revelation of himself through himself, and disclose something of the inscrutable judgments and unsearchable ways of the mind of the Lord: 'from him, through him, and to him are all things, to him be glory for ever and ever.'[174] Thus in the *kerygma* and *didache* of the Gospel as handed on in the apostolic deposit of Faith, the Father, the Son, and the Holy Spirit are intimately linked together in the essential devotion and worship of the Church in Christ. It is significant that in these formulations reference to the Father, to the Son, and to the Holy Spirit is not always made in the same order, which suggests that already in the apostolic mind there was lodged an implicit belief in the equality of the three divine Persons. Entry into the knowledge of God as Father, Son and Holy Spirit in himself, was certainly given through faith in Jesus Christ as Lord and Saviour, which had the effect of giving a strong Christological and soteriological slant to

---

[170] Matt. 1.18–23; 3.16f; 28.19; Mark 1.8ff; Luke 1.35; 3.22; cf.4.1ff; John 1.32f.
[171] John 5.19–14.16, 26; 16.15; 20.21f.
[172] Especially in John chapters 1, 5, 6, 8, 10, 14–17.
[173] Refer to *The Trinitarian Faith*, pp. 196ff.
[174] Rom. 11.36. Cf. Augustine, *De Trinitate*, 2.15.25; 5.8.9.

the earliest Christian confessions of the Church.[175] However, it was the institution and administration of Baptism in the Name of the Father, the Son, and the Holy Spirit, which, in accordance with the irreversible relation of the Father to the Son, established the trinitarian order regularly used in the Church's proclamation, worship and tradition. It was thus that the understanding of God's three-fold self-revelation expressed in the trinitarian formulae of the New Testament, developed with reference to the apostolic deposit of Faith and the canon of truth, played a significant role in the unfolding and explicit formulation of the doctrine of the Holy Trinity.[176]

It was, of course, with the unequivocal recognition of the Holy Spirit as Lord, along with the Father and the Son, that it became clear that the differentiation within the Godhead is not a binity but a trinity, and that in turn formally brought into the open the triadic pattern of divine revelation as grounded in the one Being of God. This had the effect of forcing the Church to reflect on the nature of God's triune self-revelation and to face the question of the relation between the threeness and the oneness of God in his revealing and saving acts in the Gospel. Does this threeness derive from a threeness in the one eternal Being of God or does it have to do only with a transient form of his revelation to mankind in space and time? The answer to be given to this question, and was in fact given by the great Nicene theologians, rests on the recognition of the unbroken relation in Being and Act between Jesus Christ and God the Father, upon which the whole substance of the Gospel finally depends, and along with it the reality and validity of God's saving activity through the Holy Spirit in us. The nerve of this conviction was given decisive expression in the doctrine of the *homoousion* (ὁμοούσιος τῷ Πατρί) first applied to the Son and then to the Spirit, on the ground of which a positive answer of ontological oneness was given to the relation between what God is toward us as the Father, the Son and the Holy Spirit in his revealing and saving acts in history, and what he is antecedently and inherently in himself as the Father, the Son and the Holy Spirit, *One Being, Three Persons.*

---

[175] See Oscar Cullmann, *The Earliest Christian Confessions*, tr. by J. K. S. Reid (London, 1949).
[176] See *The Trinitarian Faith*, pp. 31ff, 195ff.

4

The Trinitarian Mind

WHENEVER we seek to define the meaning of something in precise terms we have to make use of other terms which for this purpose must themselves remain undefined. This is very obvious in looking up the meaning of any word in a dictionary, but it applies to all acts of knowledge whether in everyday life or in rigorous scientific inquiry, for any formal account of what we know rests upon a base of informal undefined knowledge, from which it cannot be cut off without becoming empty of significance and useless. This means that a complete formalisation of knowledge in explicit terms is impossible. A cognate reason for this is to be discerned in the fact that in objective knowledge the realities we seek to know in any field inevitably break through the frame of concepts and statements which we use to describe them, even though they are developed under the constraint of those realities. Concepts and statements of this kind do not have their truth in themselves but in the realities to which they refer. Thus in all authentic knowledge we have to take into account an informal and undefined knowledge grounded in the inherent intelligibility of what we know, and must constantly look for appropriate ways of letting it exercise a regulative force in all our explicit formulations. This is what happens in normal scientific inquiry in which we seek to reduce to rational order knowledge in any particular field, through relying on an ultimate belief in order, or an inarticulate intuition of an ultimate ground of order, which we are unable to prove or bring to explicit knowledge and expression. It is only through relying implicitly on such an inarticulate ingredient in knowledge, the content of which cannot be made fully explicit, that the most rigorous scientific operations are possible.

This applies not least but above all to theological inquiry in which we operate with an implicit understanding of God through his self-revelation but which we are unable fully to reduce to explicit understanding and conceptual expression, for the transcendent intelligibility of God infinitely exceeds all that we can ever grasp or bring to articulate form. God remains utterly inscrutable to us in the essence of his divine Being.[1] This is why the New Testament speaks of divine revelation as

[1] Karl Barth, *Church Dogmatics* I.1, p. 321 : 'It is of the very nature of God to be inscrutable to man. In saying this we naturally mean that in his revealed nature he is inscrutable. It is the *Deus*

mystery (μυστήριον), for even when God reveals himself to us, as in Christ or in the Cross, he does not surrender his transcendence or reduce knowledge of himself or of his activity to what we are able completely to grasp or articulate. It is in this sense also that the term 'mystery' is applied, for example, to the Kingdom of God, to Christ, to the Gospel, and of course to God himself.[2] God's self-revelation is a profound inexhaustible mystery in which he continues both to reveal himself and yet to hide himself, for while in his self-revelation the Word of God became visible man in Jesus Christ, he did not cease to be the eternal invisible God. Access to the mystery of God, then, to knowledge of him as he is in himself, is given through Christ and in the Spirit, for the Word of God incarnate in Christ is the objective content of God's self-revelation in whom we know the Father, and the Spirit is the unobjectifiable transparent Presence of God by whose power the Word and Truth of God in Christ are realised in our faith and understanding. As God may be known only through himself, through his self-revelation, so the Holy Trinity may be known only through the Trinity, in God's trinitarian self-revelation of himself. Here we must think of the informal undefined mystery of the Trinity as operating along with the explicit Word and Truth of God incarnate in Christ in pressing for an understanding of itself in explicit form in the mind and teaching of the Church and regulating its theological formulation. It is thus that the original *datum* or μυστήριον of God's self-revelation in the triadic pattern of Father, Son and Holy Spirit found in the New Testament Scriptures came to take formal doctrinal shape in the mind of the Church, yet in such a way that it was revered as the great mystery of God which is more to be adored than expressed, and which may therefore be expounded only in the use of statements of a marginal kind that have an open range reaching far beyond themselves into the unfathomable depths of the riches and wisdom of God.

'Great beyond all question', St Paul wrote to Timothy, 'is the mystery of godliness (τὸ τῆς εὐσεβίας μυστήριον), he who was manifested in the flesh, vindicated in Spirit, seen of angels, proclaimed among the nations, believed on throughout the world, raised to glory.'[3] That was a passage that came to play a central and important role in formulating the doctrine of the Trinity. Understood in the light of the overarching framework of God's self-revelation as Father, Son and Holy Spirit, this mystery of godliness or godly worship came to mean thinking of God in an essentially *trinitarian* way, so that the equation theology = godliness, or θεολογία = εὐσέβεια , was identified with trinitarian thinking or simply with the worship and doctrine of the Holy Trinity, as with Origen and the great Athanasius.[4] The worship and doctrine of the Trinity belong together, for it is godly thinking of God in unrestrained awe and adoration of his unfathomable Triune Nature that

---

revelatus who is the *Deus absconditus*, the God to whom there is neither path nor bridge, concerning whom we could neither say nor have to say a single word if he did not of his own initiative meet us as the *Deus revelatus*.'

[2] Mark 4.11; Matt. 13.11; Luke 8.10; Rom. 16.25; 1 Cor. 2.7; Eph. 1.9f; 3.3f; 6.19; Col. 1.26; 4.3; 1 Tim. 3.9,16.

[3] 1 Tim. 3.16.

[4] E.g., Origen, *In Luc.* 14.28, and Athanasius, *Con. Arianos*, 1.18; see *The Trinitarian Faith*, pp. 17ff, and 302ff.

must guide any move toward formulating a doctrine of the Trinity in terms worthy of him.

This was how 'the mystery of the faith'[5] or 'the faith once delivered to the saints',[6] or the truth-content of the Gospel, was understood in the second and third centuries. It is particularly with Irenaeus in the middle of the second century that we find the most enlightening account of how the trinitarian pattern in the evangelical and apostolic tradition of the Faith began to be unfolded under the guidance of 'the rule of faith' (*regula fidei*) or 'the canon of truth'(κανὼν τῆς ἀληθείας), given with the ordinance of Baptism in the context of the trinitarian worship of God, meditation upon the Holy Scriptures and instruction of catechumens.[7] The canon of truth, as we learn from Irenaeus, gave an essentially trinitarian account of the Gospel and the whole mind of the apostles, and guided inquiry into 'the mystery and economic activity of the living God'.[8] He himself was particularly concerned with inquiring into the theological content of 'the deposit of the Faith' (ἡ παραθήκη τῆς πίστεως) handed down from the apostles,[9] and its intrinsic order or structure reflecting the economic design of God's redemptive action in Jesus Christ.[10] Irenaeus held that it is by uncovering this internal structure and bringing into clear relief the essential arrangement of 'the body of truth and the harmonious adaptation of its members', that the sacred deposit of the Faith enshrining the truth of the Gospel can be used both as an instrument of inquiry in the interpretation of the Holy Scriptures and as a canon of truth enabling the Church to offer a clear demonstration of the apostolic *kerygma* (κήρυγμα) of God's self-revelation as Father, Son and Holy Spirit, whereby its truth can be distinguished from all heretical deviations and distortions and be allowed to shine forth in of its own self-evidence.

It was characteristic of Irenaeus' understanding of the Gospel and his presentation of the Faith that the primary focus should be on Jesus Christ himself as Lord and Saviour within the overarching framework of God's self-revelation as Father, Son and Holy Spirit. It is only through Christ the incarnate Son of God that true knowledge of God is possible, so that his trinitarian understanding of God was Christologically and soteriologically conditioned through and through. However, the effect of this was greatly to strengthen his belief in the Deity and Majesty of the Lord Jesus Christ and to reinforce its centrality in the confession, worship and mission of the Church in the world. This is very evident in the way in which two-membered confessions of faith in the Father and the Son and three-membered confessions of faith in the Father, the Son and the Holy Spirit, are found placed together by Irenaeus.[11] His understanding of Christ and of the Trinity profoundly

---

[5] 1 Tim. 3.9.

[6] Jude 3.

[7] Irenaeus, *Adv. haer.* 1.1.20; cf. *Epideixis* 6.

[8] Irenaeus, *Adv. haer.* 2.11.1.

[9] For the biblical sources of this concept see 1 Tim. 4.6; 6.20; 2 Tim. 1.12–14; 2.2, 4; 4.3; Titus 1.9,13; cf. 2 Thess. 2.15; 3.6; Gal. 1.9; 2.2, 9; 1 Cor. 11.23; 15.3; 2 Cor. 11.3–4; Rom. 6.7; Heb. 3.1; 4.14; 10.23.

[10] Refer to my essay 'The Deposit of Faith', *SJT*, Edinburgh, 1983, vol. 36, pp. 1–28, and to *The Trinitarian Faith*, pp. 31ff.

[11] Thus Oscar Cullmann, *The Earliest Christian Confessions*, pp. 36f, 42f.

affected each other, and were so deeply intertwined in his whole outlook that he could even speak in a trinitarian way of the threefold nature of Christ's divine Saviourhood, and of his threefold anointing as 'Christ'.[12]

Irenaeus claims that confession of belief in God as Father, Son and Holy Spirit was already embedded in the canon of truth, but his vigorous defence of the Faith shows us that when the Church was engaged in clarifying its grasp of the doctrinal substance of the Gospel in the light of its objectively grounded structure, there emerged the incipient formulations of belief in God the Father, the Son and the Holy Spirit, which were eventually to take explicit form in the early creeds.[13] From the way in which Irenaeus handled these confessional formulae, it would seem clear that they were not sets of doctrinal propositions logically deduced from the original deposit of the Faith but were coherent convictions in the process of taking definite form in the mind of the Church through a general consensus arising spontaneously out of the apostolic *kerygmata* (κηρύγματα) and controlled by the implicit structure embodied in them.[14] This incipient credal formulation of belief was not a 'hypothetical system' of ideas excogitated out of the inner religious consciousness of the Church – such as the Gnostics kept dreaming up and putting forward as an alleged 'body of truth' – and then arbitrarily and distortingly imposed upon the interpretation of the Gospel.[15] Rather was it a disclosure of the internal unity and harmony of the Gospel through a representation of the way in which different 'members of the truth' are conjoined within the organic structure of 'the body of the truth'. The various beliefs are formulated in such a way that each is given its appropriate place within the coherent whole much like the limbs of a living body which cannot be severed from the body without dismemberment and destruction of the whole.[16]

In other words, the credal statements thus formulated by the Church cannot be abstracted from the objective substance of the whole coherent structure of the evangelical Faith, for they are what they are only through their conjoint embodiment in it and their service of it. They are not statements that are connected with one another through some sort of logico-deductive system, but statements that are ordered and integrated from beyond themselves by their common ground in the apostolic deposit of Faith, and in the final analysis in the objective self-revelation of God in Jesus Christ as Father, Son and Holy Spirit. They are to be treated, therefore, not as closed but as open formulations of belief, locked into the truth of divine revelation that exceeds their capacity adequately to express. Although they fall short of what they intend, they are not for that reason false, since they do not have their truth in themselves but in that to which they refer independent of themselves, and are true in so far as they are rightly related to it. Credal formulations of this kind that arise under the constraint of and in response to the objective self-

[12] Irenaeus, *Adv. haer.* 3.11.2, 19.3.
[13] Irenaeus, *Adv. haer.* 1.2; 3.1f,4; 4.1f; 4.53.1; 5.20.1f; *Epideixis*, 6.
[14] See the *Epideixis*, or *Demonstration of the Apostolic Preaching*, by Irenaeus, in which κηρύγματα refers to *doctrines* in kerygmatic, not dogmatic, form.
[15] Irenaeus, *Adv. haer.* 1.18; 2.37–43.
[16] Irenaeus, *Adv. haer.* 1.15.

revelation of God express sure and firm convictions, for they are sustained from beyond themselves, but on the other hand they have an open range which answers to the fact that even while God condescends to make himself known within the lowly conditions of human existence in space and time, as he has done in the incarnation of his Word and Truth in Jesus Christ, nevertheless by his very nature he transcends the range of all human knowledge and speech. That is to say, we have to reckon with the fact, as Irenaeus rightly insisted, that all theological knowledge and certainly all credal formulations of the Truth are only 'in part' (in St Paul's sense of the expression ἐκ μέρους[17]), since there is much that belongs to God which we must frankly leave to him, for it would be impious to think of intruding into it.[18]

At this point theologians of the Church like Irenaeus were faced with a fundamental question bearing upon the ultimate validity of the truth content of the Gospel. This was the question as to how the self-revelation of God to man within the range of human comprehension in this visible, tangible world is related to the invisible, intangible, and incomprehensible Reality of God in the mystery of his own ultimate Being. Unless there is a substantial bridge between the visible and the invisible, the tangible and the intangible, the comprehensible and the incomprehensible, there can be no sure or firm ground, it was argued, for authentic human knowledge of God as he really is in himself. In fact, if there were no such bridge, the Gospel would be finally detached from reality, empty of truth and validity and its account of the saving acts of God would be no more than a mythological projection out of human fancy, similar to that of the Gnostics who separated the Redeemer from the Creator and even Jesus from Christ.[19] If the revelation of God presented to us in Jesus Christ is what the Gospel claims about it, the revelation of God himself to us, then it must be anchored in the very Being and Reality of God through a bridge, and indeed a oneness in being, between the incarnate Son and the Father. This was precisely what Irenaeus found to be the central issue of the Gospel, in the incarnation of the very Word, Mind and Truth of God himself in Jesus Christ. 'Since it is impossible, without God, to come to knowledge of God, he teaches men through his Word to know God.' 'No one can see God except God.' 'The Lord has taught us that no one can know God unless God himself is the Teacher, that is to say, without God, God is not to be known.'[20] A real revelation of God to us must be one which God brings about through himself. This is precisely what we find in the evangelical account of the relation of mutual knowing between the Son and the Father,[21] which implies, Irenaeus points out, that there is a mutual relation or proportion in being as well as in knowing between them.[22] With the incarnation, however, that relation in mutual knowing and being exclusive to the Father and the Son applies to Jesus Christ the Son of the Father

---

[17] 1 Cor. 13.12.
[18] Irenaeus, *Adv. haer.* 2.15 – 3,4; 2.41.1–3.
[19] Irenaeus, *Adv. haer.* 2.7.1f; 3.11.10.
[20] Irenaeus, *Adv. haer.* 4.8.1 & 11.3.
[21] Matt. 11.27; Luke 10.22.
[22] Irenaeus, *Adv. haer.* 2.37.1–4; 3.6.2; 4.11.1–5.

become man, so that he constitutes in himself the incarnate Son of God the all-important mediation between God and man, and thus between the invisible and the visible, the intangible and the tangible, and between the incomprehensible and the comprehensible.[23] It may even be said, according to Irenaeus, that 'the immeasurable Father is measured in the Son, for the Son is the measure (*mensura* / μέτρον) of the Father seeing that he comprehends him.'[24]

All this signifies to us that the 'gap' between God's knowing of himself as only God can know himself and man's knowing of God, between what God has made known to man of himself in Jesus Christ and what he is inherently in his own being, has been bridged in Jesus Christ, for he is in himself what he reveals of the Father and what the Father reveals of himself in the Son he is in himself as Father. In fact 'the Father is the invisible of the Son and the Son is the visible of the Father.'[25] More concretely, 'the Son is the knowledge of the Father, but the knowledge of the Son is in the Father and has been revealed through the Son.'[26] That is to say, as Mediator between God and man and man and God, who is both God and man himself,[27] Jesus Christ imparts to us something of the knowledge of God which he has in the intimate and mutual relation between the Father and himself. He does this, Irenaeus argues, in a two-fold movement of his Word who 'became man and dwells in man in order to accustom man to receive God and God to dwell in man'. God acts from both sides of the relation between himself and man through a movement in which 'he reveals God to man and presents man to God', and yet in such a way that 'he preserves the invisibility of the Father' or the sanctity of his ultimate incomprehensibility.[28]

While Irenaeus was faithful to the biblical way of speaking of Christ as the 'Son of God' and 'Son of Man', he was concerned not merely to build up understanding of divine revelation by adducing biblical testimonies, but rather to give a theological account of the truth to which they referred, and of what he himself had to think and say about Christ as the incarnate Lord and Saviour on the ground of what was attested in the Holy Scriptures. Nor was he just an apologist for the faith, but was essentially a biblical theologian, committed to give firm and clear formulation to the unchanging evangelical truth upon which the Church rests. Thus he gave unambiguous expression to the supreme truth of the Deity of Christ as he who 'in his own right (*ipse proprie*) is God and Lord and King eternal and the incarnate Word.'[29] In his incarnation 'God has become man and the Lord himself has saved us.'[30] It is the fact that Jesus Christ is the incarnate Reality of God which, as he rightly discerned, gives substance, finality and ultimate validity to all his acts of

---

[23] Irenaeus, *Adv. haer.* 3.11f; 3.17.6; 4.11.1–5; 4.34.1, 4–5.

[24] Irenaeus, *Adv. haer.* 4.6.

[25] Irenaeus, *Adv. haer.* 4.14.4. This applies, Irenaeus held, to the relation between the Son or Word and the Father even before the incarnation.

[26] Irenaeus, *Adv. haer.* 4.14.5.

[27] Irenaeus, *Adv. haer.* 5.17, 1–2.

[28] Irenaeus, *Adv. haer.* 3.19.6, 21.2; and 4.34.7.

[29] Irenaeus, *Adv. haer.* 3.20.2.

[30] Irenaeus, *Adv. haer.* 3.23.1.

revelation and salvation. What God reveals to us of himself in Jesus Christ and the Gospel he has done with all the power and authority of his own Reality as God the Father Almighty, Creator of all things visible and invisible. While Jesus Christ is himself God who has condescended to be one with us in our human being and made himself known to us within the limited range of what we may comprehend, he does so as the eternal Word and Son of God from beyond that range in the eternal and incomprehensible God. As such he guarantees that what we are granted to know of God the Father through the condescension of his immeasurable love in Jesus Christ, is entirely consistent with what God retains hidden from us in the greatness and mystery of his own Being which transcends the range of what we can know altogether.[31] What God is toward us in his immense love and infinite kindness, what he is in his all revealing and saving acts in the Gospel, he is inherently and always was in himself.

The incipient credal formulations which we find emerging in Irenaeus' theological interpretation of the truth of the Gospel and his elucidation of the order implicit in the fundamental deposit of the Faith, already manifest the essential trinitarian features of the Church's understanding of God's self-revelation as it eventually came to formal expression in the Nicene Creed.[32] However, in the place and preponderance given to the Christological formulae by Irenaeus, it is evident that it was at this point, in the indivisible union between God and man in the Person of the Mediator and in the oneness in being and agency between the incarnate Son and the Father, that Irenaeus found the central connection in the inner structure of God's self-revelation upon which faith in God the Father, and in the Holy Spirit hinged, for in a significant sense they are presented as functions of faith in Jesus Christ the incarnate Word and Truth of God through whom and in whom we have access to the Father in one Spirit.[33] That was clearly a feature that left its mark upon the developed organisation of the credal articles in which most of the clauses were devoted to Christ and his saving work, although that was due, of course, not simply to Irenaeus but to the general biblical tradition and the consensus of the Church in the full unfolding of the baptismal creed – particularly in the East – into the Creed of Nicaea and Constantinople. So far as Irenaeus himself was concerned, however, what was particularly needed was an appropriate conception and form of speech to give the key connection between God and man embodied in the person and work of the Mediator appropriate theological expression. Quite clearly he was groping for adequate terms with which to express what came to be called 'the hypostatic union' between divine and human natures in Christ.[34] So far as the oneness between the incarnate Son and God the Father is concerned, however, he did not put forward any formal expression for it, doubtless because he felt that here we have to do with an ineffable relation in God which he retains in the unfathomable mystery of his

---

[31] Irenaeus, *Adv. haer.* 2.15.3; 2.39.1; 4.34.4.

[32] Irenaeus, *Adv. haer.*1.2; 3.1.2; 3.4.1–2; 3.16.6.

[33] Thus Oscar Cullmann, *The Earliest Christian Confessions*, p. 39.

[34] Irenaeus, *Adv. haer.* 4.34.4; 5.1.2; cf. also 3.19.6; 3.20.1; *Epideixis* 5 & 31; and the fragment cited by W. W. Harvey, *Sancti Irenaei Libros quinque adversus Haereses* (Cambridge, 1871), vol. II, p. 493.

own eternal Being.[35] Like Clement of Alexandria and Origen,[36] Irenaeus was familiar with the expression 'of the same being' (ὁμοούσιος, *eiusdem substantiae*)[37] which was later appropriated by the Nicene Fathers to express the key concept in the Christological heart of the Creed, but he himself did not use it to give expression to the mediating bridge between God and man in Jesus Christ.[38]

Clearly, the non-biblical term ὁμοούσιος could only be employed, and was actually employed, as Hilary tells us, along with a scrupulous reinterpretation of it.[39] In that event ὁμοούσιος came to be used as a theological instrument to make indubitably clear the fundamental sense of the Holy Scriptures in their many statements about the relation of Christ the incarnate Son to God the Father, and to give expression to the ontological substructure upon which the meaning of these biblical statements rested and through which they were integrated in the understanding and teaching of the Gospel by the Church. Thus the term was of immense help to the Church in the doctrinal formulation of the material content of God's triune self-revelation in the Gospel, for it provided a careful form of thought expressing the oneness in being between Christ and God as the all-important hinge between the statements of the Creed about God the Father, the Son and the Holy Spirit. Far from being an explicit definition, ὁμοούσιος τῷ Πατρί in the context of the Nicene declaration of faith was primarily an exegetical and clarificatory expression to be understood under the control of the objective relation to God which it was forged to signify.

Nevertheless, once ὁμοούσιος became employed by the Church in this way to bring to light the decisive relation between the incarnate Son and the Father, with which the very core of the Gospel and its ultimate validity were discerned to be bound up, it took on the role of an interpretative instrument of thought through which the Church's general understanding of the evangelical and apostolic deposit of the Faith was given more exact guidance in its mission to guard, defend, and transmit the Faith in its essential truth and integrity. What the ὁμοούσιος did was to give decisive expression to the truth that God's revelation of himself as Father, Son and Holy Spirit in the incarnate economy of salvation was grounded in and derived from God as he is in own eternal Being and Nature. It was thus at once *evangelical and ontological* in its purpose and import in asserting firmly that Jesus Christ the incarnate Lord and Saviour who constitutes the very heart of the Gospel is of one and the same Being as God the Father, and thereby it settled and established

---

[35] Irenaeus, *Adv. haer.* 2.15–17; 2.42–3; *Epid.* 43 & 47.

[36] Cf. Clement of Alexandria, *Strom.* 2.16f; Origen, *In Jn.* 13.25; 20.20; see also Pamphilius on Origen's use of the term, *Apol. pro Or., MPG,* 14.1308D.

[37] Irenaeus' rejection of this expression to speak of the oneness in being between Christ and the Father is doubtless due to its use by the Gnostics, *Adv. haer.* 1.1.9f; 2.18.4; 2.21.2 & 4. However, he did use it to speak of the substantial oneness of the old and new covenants in the economy of divine grace, *Adv. haer.* 4.18.1 & 19.1.

[38] For the pre-Nicene use of ὁμοούσιος see G. L. Prestige, *God in Patristic Thought* (London, 1952), pp. 197ff; Archbishop Methodios G. Fouyas, *The Person of Jesus Christ in the Decisions of the Ecumenical Councils* (Addis Ababa, 1976), p. 28f; and his essay, 'The Homoousion', in *The Incarnation. Ecumenical Studies in the Nicene-Constantinopolitan Creed,* ed. T. F. Torrance (Edinburgh, 1981), p. 5f.

[39] Hilary, *De syn.* 70, 91; *De Trin.* 4.4–7.

the confidence of the faithful in the central truth of the Gospel in the face of hostile deviations and harmful misconstructions. Moreover, as such, the ὁμοούσιος supplied the Church with the very theological key it needed to unlock the implicit doctrine of the Holy Trinity in the New Testament, and to bring it to explicit formulation, as far as that is possible, in respect of both the distinction and the identity between what God is and has done for sinful men and women in his historical self-communication in the Gospel and what he really is and ever is in himself. The enshrining of the ὁμοούσιος in the organic structure of the Nicene Creed, thereby bringing into sharp relief the inherent trinitarian structure of the Gospel, had the effect of making the Nicene Creed the operative canon of truth with reference to which the Church could continue to instruct the faithful, protect the Gospel from heretical distortion and provide further doctrinal formulation as it might be needed.

Let us return at this point to the biblical conception of divine revelation as *mystery.* God reveals himself to us in such a way as still to be veiled from us in the infinite depths of his ultimate Being, for he does not surrender his transcendence or sovereign freedom but remains the absolute Lord of what he reveals and of our knowing of him. Thus in a strange way God is known by us in not being known, or known in such a way that our knowing of him rebounds back from the Holiness and Majesty of his Being, for what we may know of him through Christ and in the Spirit we cannot master and capture within the brackets of our explicit theological constructs. While it is in his Light that we see light, the very splendour of God's Light finally hides him from us. In the mystery of his self-revelation God reserves the innermost secret of his eternal Being as God into which, as Irenaeus insisted, we cannot intrude. As Athanasius used to express it: 'Thus far human knowledge goes. Here the cherubim spread the covering of their wings.'[40] To use another Old Testament analogy, God reveals himself to us only under the cover of his hand, and in such a way that we are unable to get behind the back of his revelation to see him face to face in his unveiled Glory. Hence even when God draws near to us and draws us near to himself on the ground of the atoning sacrifice of Christ, and gives us access to himself through Christ and in his Spirit to know him, in some real measure, as he is in the inner relations of his eternal Being as Father, Son and Holy Spirit, he does not surrender (in Irenaean terms) his invisibility in the visibility, his incomprehensibility in the comprehensibility, of the incarnation, or therefore reduce knowledge of himself to what we can completely grasp or articulate. This is to say, in the mystery of God's self-revealing there is an inarticulate as well as an articulate ingredient, an unspecifiable as well as a specifiable factor, such that in our knowing God in his self-revelation it is the inarticulate or unspecifiable element that governs what is articulated and specified in the incarnation of his Son in Jesus Christ: we know of him more than we can ever tell. This is what St Paul, as we have seen, called the 'great mystery of godliness', for the incarnate self-revelation of God is more to be worshipped in sheer wonder and praise than conceived and expressed, and as such regulates all sound doctrine.

[40] Athanasius, *Ad Ser.* 1.17; also *In ill. om.* 6.

It was *mystery* in this sense that came to be applied supremely to the Holy Trinity, while *godliness* was identified in a special way with the doctrine of the Holy Trinity. Thus it may be said that under the control of the informal undefined mystery of the Trinity imprinted upon the New Testament Scriptures and upon the mind of the worshipping Church, the formulation of the doctrine of the Holy Trinity in explicit terms, as far as that was possible, had to be done in such a godly way as to guard the great mystery of God's self-revelation, 'God manifest in the flesh'. It was with this godly or trinitarian way of thinking, then, that the Church sought to clarify and confess its faith in God the Father, God the Son and God the Holy Spirit, and to give devout but firm credal expression to the saving truths of the Gospel. In and through the doctrine of the Holy Trinity the doctrine of the incarnation of God in Jesus Christ, and with it the very essence of the Gospel of divine salvation, was formulated in such a way as not to surrender the transcendence of God, and the doctrine of the Holy Spirit was formulated in such a way as not to surrender the ineffability or incomprehensibility of God.[41] At the same time the doctrine of the Holy Trinity had the effect of grounding the doctrine of the incarnation in the very centre of faith in God in such a way as to establish the absolute centrality of Jesus Christ the one Mediator between God and man in the triune movement of God's self-revelation, from the Father *through* the Son *in* the Spirit, and correspondingly in the trinitarian movement of faith and devotion in the Church, *in* the Spirit *through* the Son to the Father. It is thus that trinitarian thinking enters into the inner fabric of all our Christian worship and knowledge of the one God, and the doctrine of the Trinity is recognised to constitute the fundamental grammar of Christian dogmatic theology.

Our concern in the rest of this chapter is not so much with the detailed content of the doctrine of the Holy Trinity, but with how we are to formulate it on the ground of the biblical witness to God's self-revelation as Father, Son and Holy Spirit in the saving events of the Gospel, not without help from the great Nicene and post-Nicene fathers of the Church, and how we are to coordinate the different conceptual levels which careful theological formulation involves. In this task we have to reckon with the fact that God reveals himself to us in Jesus Christ within the field of our human existence in space and time, but in such a way that the content of his self-revelation does not become netted within the spatial-temporal processes of our world. Nevertheless, under the creative impact of his self-revelation the trinitarian pattern of his internal relations becomes imprinted upon the series of saving events proclaimed to us in the Gospel, and upon our knowing and speaking of him under the constraint of his three-fold manifestation in those events as Father, Son and Holy Spirit.

Through the incarnation of God's Word and Truth in Jesus Christ, empirical correlates have an ineradicable place both in the mediation of divine revelation to us and in the theological concepts and statements we are bound to employ in any faithful interpretation of it. These concepts and statements point indefinitely beyond themselves to the ultimate mystery of the Triune God, and must do so if they are to

---

[41] Cf. F. W. Camfield, *Revelation and the Holy Spirit* (London, 1933), pp. 242, 248ff.

have divine significance and validity, but unless they are correlated with empirical reality in our creaturely world they can have no meaning for us. This is not to say, of course, that every theological concept and statement must have a specific empirical correlate, but that, in so far as they are true, theological concepts and statements are integrated within a coherent system which at certain essential points must be correlated with the empirical world if divine revelation is to get through to us and have its way in our mind. In this situation theological formulation of the doctrine of the Trinity cannot but involve a stratified structure comprising several coordinate levels concerned with God as he is in himself, with the incarnation of his self-revelation in Jesus Christ, and with our receiving and articulating of that revelation. To express it the other way round, formulation of the doctrine of the Trinity develops a stratified structure arising on the ground of our evangelical experience, knowledge and worship of God in the life of the Church, deriving from the historical revelation of God as Father, Son and Holy Spirit mediated to us in the incarnate life and work of Jesus Christ, and directed to the transcendent mystery of God the Father, the Son and the Holy Spirit as he is in his one eternal Being.

This way of describing the formulation of the doctrine of the Trinity is of considerable merit, in that it sets out the different levels of truth in their cross-level coordination with one another. This helps us to check and clarify the precision of the theological concepts and terms we use and the nuanced changes that are involved as they are employed in the movement of thought from one level to the other. The ground level where we are concerned with evangelical apprehension and experience is open to the level of the revealing and saving acts of Christ in his incarnate economy, and is dependent upon it in order to be what it is; while the level of the revealing and saving acts of Christ is found to be open to the transcendent level of the trinitarian relations in God himself and is dependent on it in order to be what it is. Thus there becomes disclosed the multi-levelled organic structure that characterises our Christian apprehension of God in which our thought moves from its fundamental base in what God is toward us and has done for us in the Gospel as Father, Son and Holy Spirit, to what he is antecedently and eternally in himself as Father, Son and Holy Spirit, that is, from the economic Trinity to the ontological Trinity, or the evangelical Trinity to the theological Trinity. However, this account of the stratified structure in the formulation of the doctrine of the Trinity is but a posterior reconstruction of the way in which our knowing is coordinated with the reality of God's self-revelation, and does not take into account the actualisation of that knowledge through the reconciling condescension of God to communicate himself to us in Jesus Christ and to lift us up in the Communion of the Spirit out of ourselves, as it were, into God, thereby enabling us to know him and love him and enjoy him as he is in himself, in his eternal reality as Father, Son and Holy Spirit. Such an *a posteriori* reconstruction of theological formalisation serves to bring into open and sharp relief the objective grounds of our evangelical knowledge of God in the incarnation and the Trinity; but it must be emphasised that the conceptual structure thus exposed cannot be disengaged from the dynamic and cognitive union with God that we are given through Christ and in the Spirit, as if it could have a validity of its own quite irrespective of any objective reference or content, for then it could be no more than a merely formal, empty theoretic shell. The significance of this theological formulation will be brought home to us as we turn in the following chapters to look fully at the detailed content of God's self-revelation as Father, Son and Holy Spirit.

Now since this stratified structure is not, formally at any rate, unlike the multi-levelled structure that we develop in a rigorous scientific account of knowledge in any field of investigation, it will be helpful to take a side-glance at it first.[42] As Einstein, Polanyi, and others have shown us,[43] the stratified structure of scientific knowledge usually comprises three levels of thought coordinated with one another: the primary or basic level, which is the level of our ordinary day-to-day experience and the loosely organised natural cognitions it involves; the secondary level of scientific theory with its search for a rigorous logical unity of empirical and conceptual factors; and the tertiary level where we develop a more refined and higher logical unity with a minimum of refined concepts and relations. Theoretically this process of raising our thought from one level to higher level is indefinite: it goes on until we reach a level where we can operate with a set of ultimate concepts and relations as few as possible, but with the greatest conceivable unity. In actual practice, however, three levels are normally sufficient to enable us to reach a unified conceptual grasp of the reality in the field of our investigation.

At the ground or primary level of daily life, our experiences and cognitions are naturally and inseparably combined together. Here (as Pascal used to point out with reference to mathematics) the intuitive mind takes in its first principles at once as a whole, not through analytical and deductive processes of thought but naturally and tacitly, and thereby gains the primitive informal cognition on which it afterwards relies in analytical and demonstrative operations.[44] Our basic concepts are thus intuitively derived and are directly correlated with the complex of our experience. When we move from this realm of ordinary thought close to experience to the secondary or scientific level, we seek to order the basic concepts in our understanding of the real world by connecting them together into an explanatory theory, in the process of which we shed what we judge to be unnecessary, merely temporal or peripheral cognitions and ideas, in the aid of economic simplicity. The purpose of such a theory is to enable us to penetrate into the intelligible connections latent in reality that ground and control our basic experiences and cognitions, and illuminate them for us. Although the concepts and relations that we deploy at this secondary level may not appear to be immediately connected with common experience, they arise out of it and are epistemically correlated with it as refinements and extensions of the basic cognitions bound up with it, and are therefore subject to testing through reference to it; their function is to enable us to grasp and to understand common experience from the intelligible relations intrinsic to it, but

---

[42] For a fuller discussion of the following see my works *The Ground and Grammar of Theology* (Charlottesville, 1980), pp. 155ff; *Reality and Evangelical Theology* (Philadelphia, 1982), pp. 34ff; and *Reality and Scientific Theology* (Edinburgh, 1985), chs 5 & 6, pp. 131ff & 160ff.

[43] E.g., A. Einstein, 'Physics and Reality', *Ideas and Opinions* (London, 1973), pp. 290–323; and M. Polanyi, *The Study of Man* (London, 1959), pp. 46ff, 93ff.

[44] Blaise Pascal, *Pensées de Pascal* (ed. L. Lafuma), 110, 188, 298, 511f, 821. See especially *De l'Esprit Géométrique*, part 1 of *De l'Art de persuader* – Jacques Chevalier, *Pascal* (Paris, 1922), pp. 373–386.

which are not themselves directly experienced. The concepts and relations we develop at this level are no more than useless abstractions unless they are compatible with and testable by reference to our ground experiences and cognitions, so that empirical correlation with them at least indirectly is essential. In the effort to organise our basic concepts and relations at this level into a proper theory, we bring in certain ideas that we have creatively thought up under the constraint of reality, and that are therefore intuitively correlated with reality, and we deploy them as freely chosen fluid axioms through which we develop the theorems needed for coherent and consistent formulation of the theory. These theorems turn the set of basic concepts and relations thus organised into a problematic theoretic structure or heuristic instrument through which we may question reality and grasp it in its intrinsic structures more effectively than we could without it, but which by its very nature is revisable in the light of what becomes disclosed through it. If the theory is consistent it is open to the disclosure of further and deeper truth; it is thus completed beyond itself, for its consistency depends on cross-level reference to relations on a higher, or meta-scientific, level where again we must seek to order our thoughts round the basic concepts and relations within it into a tighter and more rigorous formulation.

As we move from the scientific level to the meta-scientific (or second scientific) level, we seek to deepen and simplify the organisation of basic concepts and relations developed at the scientific level. This will involve the revision and clarification of the theorems already used, to test their compatibility with experience, and the formalisation of a higher and more rigorously ordered theory, in which theoretical connections that played a significant and useful role at the lower level may well have to be discarded as having served a significant *ad hoc* role but as now no longer necessary. The higher-order theory will also have to be put as a question to reality and be clarified, revised, and simplified accordingly. Thus we reach the ultimate theoretic structures characterised by logical economy and simplicity (i.e., with a minimum of conceptual relations), through which we grasp reality in its depth as faithfully as we can, and which we use as the unitary basis for simplifying and unifying the whole body of our knowledge in the field in question, in the course of which not a little of it will disappear, after having served their purpose, as of only a temporary nature and as finally irrelevant.

Relativity theory is the most striking example of a higher-order theory of this kind characterised by a honed down economy or logical simplicity and comprehensiveness. In reaching the idea of relativistic invariance, Einstein devised a mathematical form of invariance as a theoretic structure or conceptual instrument through which he could discern and grasp an inherent relatedness in the universe. This mathematical invariance is not to be identified with the objective invariance in the universe, but is relativised (in the other sense of the term) by it and is revisable in the light of it. Thus in relativity theory we have to do with one of those top level structures in nature and in science that constitute a rational basis for the unification and simplification of knowledge, but which are what they are through transfinite reference to an ultimate ground of rational order. Regarded in this light the stratified structure of a scientific system appears like a sort of 'hierarchy of truths' (to transpose to science a theological expression) which is pyramidal in shape – for from a broad basis, scientific theory advances through levels of increasing rigour and simplicity until it reaches the ultimate set of a minimum of intelligible relations in terms of which, as its ultimate conceptual grammar, the whole theoretic structure is to be revised and construed. While each level within the structure is the limiting case of the one above it, it is in reference to the one above it that it reaches its own consistency and truth – which cannot but apply, of course, to the top level although only in some informal or non-formalisable way with reference to the ultimate ground of rational order upon which all rational order in the universe is finally contingent.

It should be noted that the concepts organised at the tertiary level are coordinated with those at the secondary level, not through a one-to-one relation between them, but as the level by which each is organised and defined is coordinated with the lower level, where it is left open to it at its boundary conditions, and where the higher level constitutes the controlling meta-level. Similarly, the concepts organised and defined at the secondary level are coordinated with the concepts at the primary level, which arises directly out of our experience as we interact with the world around us. Thus the concepts of the higher level are coordinated with those at the empirical level through cross-level relations, but without being grounded in that way in our actual experience and intuitively derived knowledge they are ultimately no more than speculative forms of thought lacking in material content. The hierarchical system of truths formed in this way is open upward but not reducible downward. Reductionist thinking is thus ruled completely out of court.

At this point it is worth reinforcing the idea noted above that even the tertiary or top level in the scientific structure is what it is through open undefined reference to the mysterious reality of the universe which, as Einstein used to point out with unabated awe, manifests an unlimited range of intelligibility or *Verständlichkeit*: we can apprehend it only at comparatively elementary levels.[45] This means that in so far as the concepts and theories of natural science have their truth in their reference to the inexhaustible intelligibility, the miraculous unlimited comprehensibility, of the universe, they can never be final, for they are thereby revealed to be ultimately inadequate, although that does not detract from their truth. It is well to recall here the undecidability theorem of Kurt Gödel: to be consistent, no logico-deductive or logico-syntactic system, at least of sufficient richness, can be complete in itself, but at significant points must be open for reference beyond itself to a wider and higher system.[46] This means that any meaningful rational system must have indeterminate areas where its formalisations break off and retain their consistency only through controlling organisation from a higher frame of reference.

There are interesting formal similarities between this scientific structure and the kind of theological structure that arises in Christian dogmatics which it is helpful for us to consider. This shows us that no doctrinal formulation can be elaborated into a consistent and significant body of truths through the organisation

[45] A. Einstein, 'The Religious Spirit of Science', *Ideas and Opinions*, p. 40; 'Science and Religion', ibid, pp. 41–49; 'Physics and Reality', ibid. pp. 290ff, etc.

[46] Kurt Gödel, *On Formally Undecidable Propositions of Principia Mathematica and Related Systems*, tr. by B. Meltzer (Edinburgh, 1962).

of their conceptual interrelations on one and the same epistemological level, for they require cross-level reference to a higher level in order to be ontologically significant as well as theologically consistent. Thus in the articulation and formulation of its material content derived from the history of salvation, dogmatic theology must reckon with boundary conditions over which it has no control. These are basic truths or axioms which are not decidable or logically accountable within the dogmatic system but which derive their intelligibility and force through an informal intuitive apprehension of God who, even in his self-revelation, infinitely exceeds what we can comprehend within the bounds of our conceptual structures and dogmas. In short, no dogmatic system contains its own truth-reference. *Mutatis mutandis,* Gödel's theorem clearly holds good for our formulation of the doctrine of the Holy Trinity. However, there are very important differences between theological formulation and the kind of formalisation that is appropriate in physics or mathematics. These are all-important differences that must be taken into account if we are to appreciate the dynamic way in which the different strata are organised in our knowledge of the Holy Trinity.

These differences have to do with the fact that in theology we are up against the sheer Mystery and Majesty of the living God and his unbeginning uncreated Word, and are summoned to respond to him in a way quite foreign to anything found in natural science. In the hierarchy of theological truths it is the living God himself who is the supreme Truth who retains his own authority over all our inquiry and understanding. This means that the stratified structure must finally and properly be understood the other way round, not from the bottom upward but from the top downward in accordance with God's self-revelation to us, for that is actually how its truth-content is ontologically constituted, although it is empirically derived from below where God's self-revelation is actually mediated to us in the history of salvation. This transcendent origin must not be forgotten even when (as we will do here) we may begin from below with our basic experience and knowledge of God in the Church, for that is where divine revelation reaches us, and build up the edifice of theological knowledge. While in scientific knowledge we tend to speak of nature disclosing itself to us in reaction to our experimental questioning, in actual fact nature is dumb and does not actively reveal or declare itself to us as God does. The Lord God opens himself to us through his Word and Spirit, and informs us of himself in a way that no created reality or being can. He is not dumb but supremely eloquent in his divine Being, characterised by what St Anselm used to speak of as *intima locutio apud Summam Substantiam.*[47] Even though God retains behind a veil of ineffability the infinite Mystery of his uncreated Being, he nevertheless unveils himself to us as far as we are able to apprehend him, addresses us in his Word and acts upon us by his Spirit in making himself known to us. God's Word and God's Act inhere in his Being, and it is as such that he actively reveals himself and identifies himself to us in Jesus Christ and in the Holy Spirit. This radically affects the way in which we have to think of the different levels and the interrelations between them that arise in doctrinal formulation of God's triune self-revelation to us.

---

[47] Anselm, *Monologion,* 10–12, *Opera Omnia,* ed. F. S. Schmitt, vol. II (Edinburgh, 1946), pp. 24ff.

Moreover, since as Father, Son and Holy Spirit God is a fullness of personal Being in himself and the transcendent Source of all personal being, all his actions toward us in making himself known are intensely personal. We will have to consider the nature of personal Being in God and in ourselves later, but at this juncture we must think of the different levels in our knowledge of the Holy Trinity as of a distinctively personal as well as of an epistemic nature. God interacts personally and intelligibly with us and communicates himself to us in such a personalising way or person-constituting way that he establishes relations of intimate reciprocity between us and himself, within which our knowing of God becomes interlocked with God's knowing of himself. Thus, unlike anything that is found in natural science, there is a two-way relation between the different levels that obtain in theological knowledge, initiated by God, informed by his personal address to us in his Word, and sustained through the presence of his Spirit in our personal response to his Word. Hence we pass theologically from one level to another in our knowledge of the Holy Trinity not just through a movement of thought but through a movement of personal response and commitment in worship, obedience and love in which a transformation of our mind or a spiritual reorganisation of our consciousness of God takes place.[48] How are we, then, in this light to describe the stratified structure that arises in a careful formulation of the doctrine of the Trinity?

1

First there is the ground level of religious experience and worship in which we have to do with God's revealing and saving activity in the Gospel, and are committed to faith in Jesus Christ whom God in his love has given to the world as its Saviour so that whoever believes in him should not perish but have everlasting life. It is in him and through him that God fulfils his supreme purpose and design to effect the reconciliation of mankind with himself. The experience we are concerned with at this primary level takes place, not just privately, but within the context of the daily life and activity of the Church: that is, along with others who share with us this common experience and faith. Its focal point is personal encounter with Jesus Christ within the structures of our historical existence in space and time – and therefore within the structures and rationalities of our subject–subject and subject–object experiences in this world – where we are summoned to live and act, certainly as intelligent beings who are members of the intelligible creation in which God has placed us, yet in such a way as to live and think not out of a centre in ourselves but out of a centre in the Lord Jesus. This basic level may be called *the evangelical and doxological level*, for it is the level of our day-to-day worship and meeting with God in response to the proclamation of the Gospel and the interpretation of the Holy Scriptures within the fellowship of the Church.

This is the level on which the focus of our attention is directly and primarily on the New Testament presentation of Jesus Christ as Lord and Saviour and the evangelical narrative provided by the four evangelists of his saving words and deeds

---

[48] This is the transformation of our minds of which St Paul speaks in Romans 12.1–2, and calls λογικὴ λατρεία or 'rational worship'.

throughout his life from his birth to his crucifixion and resurrection. But our attention is also focused on the missionary activity of the Church recounted in the Acts of the Apostles in which the saving power of God in the Cross of Christ, as interpreted by the apostles, was proclaimed throughout the Mediterranean world, with such effect in the conversion of multitudes of people to belief in Christ as their Lord and Saviour. Here we are concerned with the historical facts and events of divine redemption through which there took place a revelation of the Father through the Son and in the Holy Spirit in such a way that they formed indivisibly together the sublime Object of the faith and worship of the apostolic Church.

It is on this evangelical and doxological level where we have to do with the *kerygma* and *didache* of the New Testament, with the Lord Jesus Christ clothed with his Gospel, and with the mediation in his vicarious human life of the redeeming Love that flows to mankind from God the Father, together with the gift of the Holy Spirit sent from the Father through his Son, that our faith and worship take on the imprint of the three-fold self-revelation of God as Father, Son and Holy Spirit. Our minds apprehend this evangelical Trinity intuitively, and as a whole, without engaging in analytical or logical process of thought, which we are constrained through faith in Christ to relate to the Mystery of God's inmost Life and Being. Thereby we gain the basic undefined cognition which informally shapes our faith and regulates our trinitarian understanding of God.

We may speak of this level as that of *incipient theology* on which, as we would expect, empirical and conceptual, historical and theological, factors are naturally and spontaneously interwoven with one another. From the very start of our believing experience and knowledge of the incarnate economy of redemption undertaken by Jesus Christ for our sakes, form and content are found fused together both in what we are given to know and in our experience and knowing of it. A child by the age of five has learned, we are told, an astonishing amount about the physical world to which he or she has become spontaneously and intuitively adapted – far more than the child could ever understand if he or she turned out to be the most brilliant of physicists.[49] Likewise, I believe, we learn far more about God as Father, Son and Holy Spirit, into whose Name we have been baptised, within the family and fellowship and living tradition of the Church than we can ever say: it becomes built into the structure of our souls and minds, and we know much more than we can ever tell. This is what happens evangelically and personally to us within the membership of the Church, the Body of Christ in the world, when through the transforming power of his Word and Spirit our minds become inwardly and intuitively adapted to know the living God. We become spiritually and intellectually implicated in patterns of divine order that are beyond our powers fully to articulate in explicit terms, but we are aware of being apprehended by divine Truth as it is in Jesus which steadily presses for increasing realisation in our understanding, articulation and confession of faith. That is how Christian theology gains its initial impetus, and is then reinforced through constant reading and study of the Bible within the community of the faithful.

---

[49] Cf. H. Bondi, *Assumption and Myth in Physical Theory* (Cambridge, 1967), pp. 12ff.

It must be emphasised that there is no way through logical analysis or rational speculation to gain a grasp of the distinctive kind of order which divine revelation embodies. This is not to discount the role of the reason in theological understanding of divine truth, for only rational beings are capable of appreciating and responding to divine revelation, but rather to call for a mode of rational activity in which the human reason allows itself to be adapted in ways that are appropriate to the distinctive nature and intelligibility of its object, in this case, the distinctive kind of order immanent in the incarnate economy of God's revealing and saving acts in Jesus Christ made known to us in the Gospel. Disclosure of that divine order takes place only as we live in personal union and communion with Christ and find our minds under the impact of his Spirit becoming at home, as it were, in the field of God's self-revelation and self-communication. It is as we tune in to God's eternal purpose of love and grace embodied in the humanity of the Lord Jesus Christ that under the enlightenment of the Holy Spirit we are given the anticipatory insights or basic clues we need in developing formal cognition of that divine order, and so apprehend something of the trinitarian structure of God's self-revelation and self-communication to mankind. Appropriate understanding of this kind arises only within the sphere of evangelical experience in the on-going mission of the Church where the proclamation and instruction of the Gospel of salvation are carried out. And it develops within the sphere of Christian fellowship and love, within the sacramental life of the people of God and within the matrix of eucharistic communion and the worship of the Father through the Son and in the Holy Spirit. It is through the imprinting of divine truth upon our hearts in these ways that we become inwardly so adapted to God's triune interaction with us that we learn to think in a godly and worthy way of him appropriate to his divine Nature – in the Spirit the great mystery of godliness becomes stamped upon our souls and spirits.

It is understandable that at this basic level of our personal faith in God and our worship of him, empirical and theological components in our knowledge of God become fused together, in a kind of stereoscopic coordination of the perceptual and auditive images, which yields the cognitive instruments we need for explicit theological understanding of God's interaction with us. It is as we indwell the Scriptures of the New Testament that the trinitarian pattern of God's self-revelation implicit in them becomes stamped on our minds, and begins to take a more defined conceptual form in our grasp of the Faith. What is being described at this ground level corresponds to the confession of faith and the incipient formalisation of trinitarian belief which, as we learn from Irenaeus, took its initial guidance in the early Church from the unfolding of the baptismal creed or rule of faith as it had been handed down from the apostles along with Baptism in the Name of the Father, the Son and the Holy Spirit.

Before we pass on it must be stated very emphatically that this ground level of evangelical experience and apprehension remains the necessary basis, the *sine qua non*, of the other levels of doctrinal formulation developed from it. They depend entirely upon it, for it is here that we are concerned with our actual knowledge and experience of divine redemption centering in the historical life, death and resurrection of Jesus, and it is only within the frame of this salvation history that we meet with the real self-communication of God himself to us through himself, and share in the inner fellowship of God through the fellowship which he establishes with us. It is on this Christological and soteriological basis that the truth of the Gospel rests, and it is from the evangelical pattern or economy of the redeeming acts of God in Jesus Christ and the gift of the Spirit sent to us from the Father in the name of his Son, that the information content of God's self-revelation as Father, Son and Holy Spirit is mediated to us. In other words, here we have to do with the foundational disclosures in the Gospel of redemption, upon which the evangelical or economic Trinity rests and apart from which no trinitarian theology can have objective epistemic content or even arise. Thus it may be said that at this primary level we are concerned with an implicit or incipient form of the evangelical or economic Trinity. The second and third levels of trinitarian understanding, which we shall go on to discuss, probe into this implicit pattern of God's three-fold self-revelation in the Gospel and seek to clarify and express its intrinsic relation to the ultimate source and ground of revelation in the eternal Mystery of God's Triune Being. Unless that is done we are unable to relate Jesus Christ and our redemption in and through him intelligibly to the inner Life of God, and faith withers away. On the other hand, however, the inner Life of God, as H. R. Mackintosh once said, 'is apprehended by us for the sake of its redemptive expression, not for the internal analysis of its content.'[50]

2

Then we come to *the theological level*. At the fundamental level of our evangelical and experiential apprehension and worship of God arising out of the incarnate economy of his saving love in Jesus Christ, we learn that the Person of Christ as Lord and Saviour, his saving acts and his message of salvation are ultimately one and the same.[51] It is as such that Christ constitutes the focal point in God's saving self-revelation to us as Father, Son and Holy Spirit in a unitary and comprehensive movement of God's redeeming love for the world. It is through the common tradition of shared spiritual experience and insight in the Church that theologians make cognitive contact with the truths of divine revelation into which they inquire, and then through following up the clues thus mediated to them they seek to evoke depths of knowledge not discerned hitherto. This is further developed at the secondary or theological level. By forming appropriate intellectual instruments with which to lay bare the underlying epistemological patterns of thought, and by tracing the chains of connection throughout the coherent body of theological truths, they feel their way forward to a deeper and more precise knowledge of what God has revealed of himself, even to the extent of reaching a reverent and humble insight into the inner personal relations of his Being. Our concern at this secondary level, however, while distinctly theological, is not primarily with the organic body of theological knowledge, but with penetrating through it to apprehend more fully the economic and ontological and trinitarian structure of God's revealing and saving acts in Jesus Christ as they are presented to us in the Gospel.

[50] H. R. Mackintosh, *Doctrine of the Person*, p. 526.
[51] Cf. Irenaeus, *Adv. haer.* 3.11.2 where he speaks of Christ as *salus, Salvator et salutare*, identifying his Person with the message and activity of salvation.

As we direct our inquiries in the field of evangelical and doxological experience, we reflect on the fact that God reveals his one Being to us as God the Father, God the Son, and God the Holy Spirit, in a three-fold *self*-giving in which revelatory and ontological factors are indivisibly integrated. Our relations to Jesus Christ and to the Holy Spirit while different and distinctive are relations in which we have to do immediately with God the Father himself. We do not know the Father except as the Father of the Son, and do not know the Son except as the Son of the Father, and do not know the Holy Spirit except as the Spirit of the Father and of the Son. The Son and the Spirit are not just intermediaries between God and mankind external to his Being, but are themselves of God and very God, for it is the one Lord God the Father Almighty the Creator of heaven and earth who communicates himself to us with, in and through them. What God is toward us in his saving condescension to be with us in Jesus Christ, he is in himself, and what he is in his real presence with us and in us as the Holy Spirit, he is in himself. Hence 'Father', 'Son' and 'Holy Spirit' are found to refer not just to three interrelated forms in which divine revelation functions, but to three distinctly hypostatic or personal Realities, or objective self-identifying Subsistences of God's Being and Activity. They are more than modes, aspects, faces, names or relations in God's manifestation of himself to us, for they are inseparable from the hypostatic Realities of which they are the distinctive self-presentations of divine Being – the three divine Hypostases or Persons, Father, Son and Holy Spirit who in their differentiation from one another and in their communion with one another *are* the one eternal God.

It is at this level that the inchoate form of the doctrine of the Holy Trinity latent in the triadic structure of God's redemptive revelation of himself through himself, and in the trinitarian understanding of God implicit in the mind and worship of the God's people, evident in the various New Testament formulae which bring the Father, the Son and the Holy Spirit together in the Name of God, is given explicit formulation as the doctrine of the Holy Trinity that underlies and gives coherent structure to all Christian dogmatics. This, then, is the first definitely *theological* level in which we are concerned with expressing doctrinal knowledge of the Holy Trinity in which our thought moves on from the intuitive incipient form of an understanding of the Trinity to conceptions of what is called the economic Trinity, the level in which the dynamic reality of God's triune Being is being brought into clearer and more explicit formulation in terms of his differentiated yet unitary personal self-presentations and acts as Father, Son and Holy Spirit. The word 'economy' (in its theological sense) is the patristic expression, developed from St Paul, for the orderly movement in which God actively makes himself known to us in his incarnate condescension and his redemptive activity within the structures of space and time, through Christ and in one Spirit, in such a way as to identify and name himself to us as the Father, the Son and the Holy Spirit. However, through the oneness in Being and Act of the Son and the Spirit with the one eternal God, the economic Trinity cannot but point beyond itself to the theological or ontological Trinity, otherwise the economic Trinity would not be a faithful and true revelation of the transcendent Communion of Father, Son and Holy Spirit which the eternal Being of God is in himself.

The conceptual clarification of the relation between what God is economically toward us and what he is ontically in himself is the task with which the Fathers at the Council of Nicaea were mainly concerned, that is, in moving from the evangelical and doxological level to the theological level where the conceptual content of the Faith could be given definite credal form, without of course abandoning their evangelical and doxological approach. Here a number of basic relations and concepts disclosed in the Gospel and found operating in the understanding and appropriation of salvation were selected and collated in order to work out their intelligible interconnections, so that they might be organised into a form to be used as a conceptual instrument enabling us to get a more accurate grasp of the ontological structure underlying the Gospel message of salvation and its teaching about God. Here we operate with forms of thought and speech taken from our ordinary discourse but refined and redefined under the creative impact of divine revelation, terms such as 'father', 'son', 'spirit', 'being'. Here too, however, quite new terms are brought in from outside biblical discourse, such as 'trinity' or τριάς, but are reminted and correlated with biblical forms of thought and speech to give their theological meaning sharper focus and precision, and to prevent them from being interpreted by heretics in accordance with their pre-Christian use. The cardinal issue here was found by the Nicene theologians to be the unbroken relation in being and agency between Jesus Christ and God the Father, to which they gave decisive expression by a carefully defined non-biblical term, ὁμοούσιος, to speak of his oneness with the Father: ὁμοούσιος τῷ Πατρί. This is the kind of theological term for which Irenaeus had been groping in order to describe the nature of the substantial bridge across the gap between the Creator and the creature, anchored both in God and in man, which is needed to secure for us objective and authentic knowledge of the invisible God and of our salvation in Christ.

The *homoousion* (to refer to it in this abstract form) was thus identified as the all-important hinge in the centre of the Nicene Creed upon which the whole Confession of Faith, and indeed the whole Christian conception of God and of the salvation of mankind, turns. In the *homoousion* the Council of Nicaea, and later of Constantinople, unambiguously affirmed the Deity of Christ, thereby identifying him with the unique objective content of God's saving self-revelation and self-communication to mankind, and affirming the oneness in Being and Act between Christ and the Father upon which the reality and validity of the Gospel of God's revealing and saving acts in Christ depend – for apart from it the inner core of the Gospel of divine forgiveness and salvation from sin and the essential message of redemption through the Cross of Christ would die away and disappear. The supreme truth of the Deity of Christ, the only begotten Son of God, true God from true God, one in being and of the same being with the Father, was undoubtedly the great concern that occupied the mind of the bishops and theologians at the Council of Nicaea when the credal formulation it produced, in spite of heated discussion, clearly arose out of a profound evangelical and doxological orientation. It was composed by the Fathers, so to speak, on their knees. Face to face with Jesus Christ their Lord and Saviour they knew that they had to do immediately with God, who had communicated *himself* to them in Jesus Christ so unreservedly that they knew him to be the very incarnation of God; they not only worshipped God through and with Christ but *in* Christ, worshipping God face to face in Christ as himself the Face of God the Father turned toward them. Jesus Christ the incarnate Son *is* the God whom they worshipped and loved in the ontological and soteriological mode of his personal *self*-communicating in the flesh, so that in their union and communion with Christ they knew themselves to be in union and communion with the eternal God. They knew that if there were no bond in Being and Act between Jesus Christ and God, the bottom would drop out of the Gospel and the Church would simply disappear or degenerate into no more than a social and moral form of human existence.

As we have noted, the Nicene term ὁμοούσιος was not a biblical term, but it was appropriated by the fathers of Nicaea and recoined through believing commitment to God's self-revelation in Jesus Christ and careful interpretation of the biblical witness in order to give unequivocal expression to the Deity of Christ, the incarnate Lord and Saviour. Thus they confessed their faith 'in one Lord Jesus Christ, the only begotten Son of God, begotten from his Father before all ages, Light from Light, God of God, true God from true God, begotten not made, of one and the same being with the Father, through whom all things were made.' The *homoousios* here represents a faithful distillation of the fundamental sense of the New Testament Scriptures in many statements about the unique relation between the incarnate Son and the Father in order to describe it in as definite and precise a sense as possible. It is important to note that this confession of the Deity of Christ was set in a *soteriological context:*

> who for us men and our salvation, came down from heaven, and was made flesh from the Holy Spirit and the Virgin Mary, and was made man, and was crucified for us under Pontius Pilate. He suffered and was buried, and the third day he rose again according to the Scriptures and ascended into heaven and sits at the right hand of God the Father. And he shall come again in glory to judge both the living and the dead: his kingdom shall have no end.

That is to say, the *homoousios* was harnessed to the Gospel of salvation proclaimed in the New Testament and linked it to their belief 'in one God the Father Almighty, Maker of heaven and earth and of all things visible and invisible.' It was through this two-way reference that it acquired increasing spiritual authority for it supplied the Church with a firm conceptual grasp of the central truth of the incarnate economy of redemption which Christ undertook for our sake. Apart from such a oneness in Being there is no Mediator between God and man, and the identity of Jesus Christ has nothing to do with any *self*-revealing and *self*-giving on the part of the eternal God for the salvation of mankind.

The *homoousion*, however, is to be taken along with a cognate conception about the indissoluble union of God and man in the one Person of Christ, to which the Church later gave theological formulation as the hypostatic union (ἕνωσις ὑποστατική). This conception considerably reinforces our movement of thought when we advance from the evangelical and doxological level of intuitive knowing to the explicitly theological level in which we understand the self-revelation of God as Father, Son and Holy Spirit not just in terms of his economic relations toward us but in terms of what he is antecedently and eternally in himself. The *homoousion* is thus seen to have immense significance, for it enables us to deepen and refine our grasp of the self-revealing and self-communicating of God to us as Father, Son and Holy Spirit, in such a way that our thought has to move from the secondary level in which we have to do with the economic Trinity to the tertiary or higher theological level where we have to do with the ontological Trinity, that is, in patristic language, the move from οἰκονομία to θεολογία. The *homoousion* crystallises the conviction that while the incarnation falls within the structures of our spatio-temporal humanity in this world, it also falls within the Life and Being of God – that is its astounding implication which needs to be thought out very carefully. Jesus Christ is not a mere symbol, some functional representation of God detached from God, but God in his own Being and Act come among us, exhibiting and expressing in our human form the very Word which he is eternally in himself. Hence in our relation with Jesus Christ, the Son of God incarnate in history, crucified and risen, now taken up into God and invested 'at his right hand' with full divine authority and power, we have to do directly with the ultimate Reality of God.

As the epitomised expression of this truth, the *homoousion* is the ontological and epistemological linchpin of Christian theology. It gives expression to the truth with which everything hangs together, and without which everything ultimately falls apart. The decisive point for Christian theology, and not least for the doctrine of the Holy Trinity, lies here, where we move from one level to another: from the basic evangelical and doxological level to the theological level, and from that level to the high theological level of ontological relations in God. In that movement a radical shift in the basic fabric of theological thought takes place along with a reconstruction in the foundations of our prior knowledge. This is evident not least in the fact that in formulating the *homoousion* of Christ in connection with both his creative and redemptive activity, Nicene theology laid the axe to the epistemological dualism latent in Greek philosophy and religion that threatened the very heart of the Gospel; and as such it gave powerful expression to the indissoluble connection in Act and Being between the economic Trinity and the ontological Trinity, between οἰκονομία and θεολογία, which secured the Church in its belief that in the Lord Jesus Christ and his Gospel they had to do directly with the ultimate Presence and downright Reality of God himself. *Jesus Christ the incarnate Son is one in Being and Act with God the Father. What Jesus Christ does for us and to us, and what the Holy Spirit does in us, is what God himself does for us, to us and in us.*

This sanctifying and renewing act of God upon us is the theological and salvific import of the terms *theopoiesis* and *theosis* (θεοποίησις and θέωσις) and the reason for their wide appeal in the early Church.[52] They were used to carry in a succinct

---

[52] The original source for this concept is John 10.35 – see Athanasius, *Con. Ar.* 1.39; *Ad Afr.* 7, and consult *The Trinitarian Faith*, pp. 139f. The Platonising translation of θέωσις as 'deification' is rather misleading, for there can be no suggestion that the *nature* of human being is deified through what might be called *theotic* activity in the renewing and sanctifying presence of God. 2 Pet. 1.4: θείας κοινωνοὶ φύσεως may be translated 'partners of the Deity', not 'partakers of divine nature' – A. Wolters, "'Partners of Deity': A Covenantal Reading of 2 Peter 1:4', *Calvin Theological Journal*, 25 (Grand Rapids, 1990), pp. 28–44. θεία φύσις would then be a periphrasis like 'heaven' for God.

form the evangelical promise that, while God alone has immortality, through communion with him we human beings are admitted into an intimate sharing of what is divine. Nevertheless they are rather unfortunate even in the form to which Athanasius gave expression in his often cited statement: 'He became man in order to make us divine,'[53] as Georges Florovsky frankly admitted.

The term *theosis* is indeed embarrassing, if we would think of it in 'ontological categories'. Indeed, man simply cannot become 'god'. But the Fathers were thinking in 'personal' terms, and the mystery of personal communion was involved at this point. Theosis means a personal encounter. It is the ultimate intercourse with God, in which the whole of human existence is, as it were, permeated by the Divine Presence.[54]

That was well said.

To return to the concept of the *homoousion* itself, it should be pointed out that it was not restricted to the Son, but was applied, and had to be applied also, and very significantly, to the Holy Spirit. At the Council of Nicaea itself very little was said about the Holy Spirit beyond confession of faith in him within the trinitarian framework of the Creed, which carried with it belief in his Deity. Belief in the Deity of the Holy Spirit belonged to the received tradition of the Church, as we have noted in the teaching of Irenaeus. But when controversy broke out over the doctrine of the Holy Spirit after the Council, as it had broken out over the doctrine of the Son before the Council, it became clear that a revision or an extension of the Creed of Nicaea was needed. This was undertaken at the Council of Constantinople half a century later, when the fathers and bishops confessed faith 'in the Holy Spirit, the Lord and Giver of Life, who proceeds from the Father, who with the Father and the Son together is worshipped and glorified, who spoke by the prophets.' That had the effect of affirming full belief in the unqualified Deity of the Holy Spirit along with the Father and the Son. And so the Council wrote in its explanatory Epistle: 'According to the Faith there is one Godhead, Power and Being of the Father, of the Son, and of the Holy Spirit, equal in Honour, Majesty and eternal Sovereignty in three most perfect Subsistences, that is, in three perfect Persons.'[55] Although the term ὁμοούσιος was not employed in the Creed itself, the intention was to offer definitive clauses about the Holy Spirit parallel to those about the Son, as in the expression 'from the Father' (ἐκ τοῦ Πατρός) which was held to be equivalent to 'of one being with the Father'. However, the Encyclical issued by the Council of Constantinople, as we learn from Damasus and Theodoret, contained the full expression 'of one and the same being (μιᾶς καὶ τῆς αὐτῆς οὐσίας) with the Father and the Son'.[56] The specific application of the *homoousion* to the Holy Spirit had already been given decisive and authoritative backing by Athanasius,

---

[53] Athanasius, *De Incarnatione*, 54; *Ad Adelphium*, 4.
[54] Georges Florovsky, 'St Gregory Palamas and the Tradition of the Fathers', in *Bible, Church, Tradition: An Eastern Orthodox View* (Collected Works, vol.2, Belmont, 1972), p. 115.
[55] *Ep. Constantinopolitanae*, AD 392.
[56] Theodoret, *Ecclesiae Historia*, 5.11; cf. Denzinger-Schönmetzer, *Enc. Symb.* (Freibourg, 1965), 144f.

Gregory Nazianzen, Epiphanius and others. And so belief in the Holy Spirit who is of one and the same being as the Father and the Son became permanently incorporated into the orthodox doctrine of Spirit as Church dogma alongside that of the Son.[57]

The coordination of the *homoousion* of the Son and the *homoousion* of the Spirit was of considerable importance in the formulation of the doctrine of the Holy Trinity, for it reaffirmed in strict theological terms the recognition embedded in the New Testament Scriptures that Holy Spirit is *Lord* or *Kyrios* as well as the Son and the Father, and declared that the Spirit is to be worshipped together with them, equal with them in Honour, Majesty and Sovereignty. Emphasis was laid also upon the redemptive mission and the saving efficacy of the Holy Spirit as the Lord and Giver of Life, whose renewing and sanctifying operation in the faithful was identical with the direct act of God himself, that is as θέωσις. Moreover, for our purpose here, the *homoousion* of the Holy Spirit, together with that of the Son, has much to tell us about how our thought moves from the first to the second theological levels, for it has an important contribution to make in determining how we are to think of the dynamic and spiritual nature of the ontological relation that obtains between the economic Trinity and the ontological Trinity. The *homoousion* of the Spirit with God who, as our Lord taught, *is* Spirit,[58] and the *homoousion* of the Son together mean that we must think of the relation between the economic Trinity and the ontological Trinity in an essentially spiritual way appropriate to the Nature of the Holy Spirit and the Nature of the incarnate Son. In this way the *homoousion* is found to have a critical significance in regard to what may and what may not be read back from God's revealing and saving activity in history to what he is antecedently, eternally and inherently in himself. It does tell us that what God is antecedently, eternally and inherently in himself he is indeed toward us in the incarnate economy of his saving action in Jesus Christ on our behalf, but it relates that economy ontologically to God in the ineffable Mystery of his Being who remains transcendent over all space and time, so that a significant distinction and delimitation between the economic Trinity and the ontological Trinity must be recognised as well as their essential oneness. That is the all-important double reference of the *homoousion*. Thus, for example, we may not read back into the eternal Life and Being of God the kind of temporal and causal connections that obtain in our creaturely existence in time and space, and yet the *homoousion* carries with it the recognition that the incarnation and the atoning mediation of the Son of God, together with the mission of the Spirit from the Father through the incarnate Son, have an essential place within the very Life of God. This is a point of crucial importance on which we must reflect later, although admittedly there is much here that we cannot, and will never, understand.

It should now be clear that the theological activity involved at this second level in our formulation of the doctrine of the Holy Trinity, governed by the key concept

---

[57] See particularly Athanasius, *Ad Serapionem*, 1.27; Gregory Nazianzen, *Orationes*, 31.10; Epiphanius, *Haereses*, 74; Theodoret, *Ecclesiae Historia*, 5.11. For a fuller account refer to *The Trinitarian Faith*, pp. 199ff.

[58] John 4.14.

of the *homoousion*, does not take off in a speculative movement of thought that leaves behind the primary level of evangelical and doxological experience concerned with the manifestation of God as Father, Son and Holy Spirit in the history of redemption. On the contrary, in its affirmation of the oneness in Being and Act between Jesus Christ and God the Father, and between the Holy Spirit and God the Father, the *homoousion* gives careful expression to the ontological and dynamic substructure upon which there rests the meaning of many biblical passages about the saving activity of God proclaimed in the Gospel, and thereby enables their interpretation to be conceptually integrated in the New Testament revelation. In rendering this service, the Nicene *homoousion* has proved to be one of those supremely important movements of thought from a preconceptual to a conceptual understanding which the committed mind takes under the compelling claims of the reality into which it inquires, in this instance, the Truth as it is in Jesus Christ. Far from being a rigid and alien imposition upon the Gospel, therefore, the *homoousion* has proved, through its bearing upon the ontic nexus in the relations of Christ, and of the Spirit, to God the Father to be one of the most fertile interpretative and elucidatory instruments serving the Gospel in its continuing disclosure of ever deeper truth, that Christian theology has seen in the whole of its history.

This is not to claim for the word *homoousios* that it is somehow sacrosanct and beyond reconsideration, for all authentic theological terms and concepts fall short of the realities they intend. Like any other creative 'definition' of this kind employed in the formulation of Christian doctrine, owing to its fundamentally semantic function, this also must be continually tested and revised in the light of what it was originally coined to signify, as well as in the light of its fertility in the subsequent history of theology. The all-important test to which the *homoousion* is to be put, is whether it really serves our understanding of the Gospel of God's redeeming Love, in giving decisive expression to the unbroken oneness in Being and Act between Jesus Christ, the incarnate Saviour, and God the Father, upon which the very essence of the Gospel rests. In my judgment, it does this superbly well. And in this context of doctrinal formulation which concerns us here, the test must be whether it serves theological clarification and deeper understanding in the movement of our thought from the primary level of evangelical and doxological experience to the second level of theological articulation of the doctrine of the Holy Trinity, when the judgment must be that it does so very well indeed. That is to say, *homoousion*, as the central organising truth upon which the second or first theological level hinges, far from promoting or encouraging a split between the economic Trinity and the ontological Trinity, serves to bind them firmly and indissolubly together in the supreme interest of the Gospel of God's saving and redeeming Love.

3

We come now to the *third or higher theological level*, in which our thinking enters more deeply into the self-communication of God in the saving and revealing activity of Christ and in his one Spirit. At this level we are explicitly concerned with the epistemological and ontological structure of our knowledge of the Holy Trinity, moving from a level of economic trinitarian relations in all that God is toward us in his self-revealing and self-giving activity to the level in which we discern the trinitarian relations immanent in God himself which lie behind, and are the sustaining ground of, the relations of the economic Trinity. Here too the *homoousion* is of primary significance: it stands for the basic insight deriving from God's self-communication to us, that what God is toward us in his saving economic activity in space and time through Christ and the Holy Spirit, he is antecedently and inherently in himself. The focal point is the Lord Jesus Christ. In the cross-level reference from the basic level to the theological level, the insight takes the form that what *Jesus Christ* is toward us in love and grace, in redemption and sanctification, in the mediation of divine Life, he is inherently in himself in his own divine Being. He is not different in himself from what he manifests toward us in his life and work. But in the cross-level reference from the second to the third level, the insight takes the form that what *God* is toward us in Christ Jesus, he is inherently and eternally in himself in his own Being. He is not different in himself from what he manifests toward us in Jesus Christ – there is a relation of perfect oneness between them. This means that our evangelical experience of God in Christ is not somehow truncated so that it finally falls short of God, but is grounded in the very Being of God himself; it means that our knowing of God is not somehow refracted or turned back on itself in its ultimate reference to God, but that it actually terminates on the Reality of God, even although in the mystery of his self-revelation God sets boundaries to our knowing of him. In actual fact, of course, this movement of reference on our part is grounded in the movement of God himself in the free outpouring of his love and grace to be one with us in the incarnation of his beloved Son, and in and through him to raise us up to share in his own divine Life and Love which he eternally is in himself. This is the inner core of the Christian Faith which the *homoousion* expresses so succinctly and decisively, and with the greatest 'economic simplicity' (in the scientific sense of this expression).

It must be pointed out here again, however, that the *homoousion* does not allow us indiscriminately to read back into God what is human and finite – far from it. A critical edge enters into the *homoousial reference*, especially from the second to the third level, in the movement of our thought from the economic activity of God toward us in space and time to what he is ontically or immanently in himself. Here our thinking operates with appropriate objectivity in much the same way as in all rigorous scientific thinking and activity, when we develop devices with which to obstruct ourselves from projecting our own subjective notions or fantasies into the object or reality we seek to know. This is what we are bound to do in scientific theology, in order to cut away any mythological projection of ideas of our own devising into God, and to prevent us from confounding God known by us with our deficient knowing of him. It belongs, of course, to the essence of our ordinary rational behaviour that we distinguish objective states of affairs from subjective states of affairs, and thus constantly distinguish what we know from our knowing of it. This is not always easy, for in our self-centredness we constantly tend to eclipse the object which we seek to know from ourselves by getting ourselves in the way. In some ways the situation is rather more difficult in theology than in natural science, for due to our deep-rooted sin and selfishness we are alienated from God in our minds,[59] and need to be reconciled to him. Hence, as we have seen, a repentant rethinking of what we have already claimed to know and a profound reorganisation of our consciousness are required of us in knowing God, as was made clear by Jesus when calling for disciples he insisted that they must renounce themselves and take up their cross in following him.

Since God makes himself known to us within the modalities of our creaturely and human reality (as in the incarnation), there is an inevitable and proper element of anthropomorphism in our human knowledge of God.[60] This makes it all the more imperative for us, however, to distinguish what is properly anthropomorphic from what is improperly anthropomorphic in our knowledge of him. God reveals himself to us through establishing a relation of reciprocity between himself and us in which he condescends to address us in our *human* forms of thought and speech, but in this reciprocity God relates himself to us as Lord and Saviour, the Judge of our wrong and the Forgiver of our sins, so that there is a continuous critical moment throughout his relations with us in which he distinguishes himself from us, his ways from our ways, his thoughts from our thoughts, and his truth from our error.[61] This is the context in which we must undertake a rigorous criticism of all anthropomorphic forms of thought, submitting them to the judgment of the divine Majesty, so that we may discern and reject what is improperly anthropomorphic. This applies above all, of course, to our use of the terms 'father' and 'son' which we will discuss shortly.

Here we revert to the point discussed above that the Nicene *homoousion* also applies to the Holy Spirit, whom we believe to be of the Holy Trinity no less than the Father and the Son. The *homoousion* applies to the Spirit, however, in a different way from that in which it applies to the Son, for it applies to the Spirit in a manner appropriate to his distinctive personal reality and nature as Holy Spirit. What the Holy Spirit is toward us in his divine acts of renewal and sanctification in Christ, he is inherently in himself in God. He is so inwardly and essentially related to the very Self of God in his personal self-giving and self-communicating that the Holy Spirit is revealed to be of one and the same Being as the divine Giver and not some impersonal gift detached from God or some created emanation from him. The Communion with God that the Holy Spirit is toward us – as through Christ he gives us access in himself to God – he is in his own Being as God. He also is God of God, of one and the same Being with the Father. But there is a further difference in our use of the *homoousion* of the Spirit from our use of it of the Son. The Son is, as the Word, the distinctive *hypostasis* or Person in whom God utters or expresses himself; and it is in the incarnation of the Word in space and time that God's self-revelation is fulfilled. This takes place within the structured objectivities of our created world in such a way that an epistemic bridge is established in Christ between

---

[59] Thus St Paul, Col. 1.21.

[60] I have discussed this in 'The Christian Apprehension of God the Father', my contribution to *Speaking the Christian God. The Holy Trinity and the Challenge of Feminism*, ed. Alvin F. Kimel, Jr (Grand Rapids, 1992), pp. 123ff.

[61] Thus Isa. 55.6–9.

man and God that is grounded in the Being of God and anchored in the being of man. Hence in Christ the *homoousion* is inseparably bound up with the *hypostatic union*. This is why the incarnation of the Son or Word constitutes the epistemological centre, as well as the ontological centre, in all our knowledge of God, with a centre in our world of space and time and a centre in God himself. It is in and through that Word that we have cognitive access to God and may have real knowledge of him in himself, for the Word precisely as Word as well as Son belongs to the innermost Being of God.[62]

It is by reference to this epistemological centre in the incarnate Son or Word made flesh – that is, to the *homoousion* of the Son and the hypostatic union of divine Nature and human nature in him – that we also clarify our knowledge of the Spirit. He is not knowable in his own distinctive Person or *hypostasis* in the same way, for he is not embodied, like the incarnate Son, in the concrete modalities and structured objectivities of our world of space-time, or, like him, therefore, brought within the range of our human knowing at our lowly creaturely level.[63] The Holy Spirit is God of God but not man of man, so that our knowledge of the Holy Spirit rests directly on the ultimate objectivity of God as God, unmediated by the secondary objectivities of space and time, and it rests only indirectly on those objectivities through relation to the Son with whom he is of one being as he is with the Father. Throughout all God's self-revelation to us in the incarnate Son, the Holy Spirit is the creative Agent in mediating knowledge of God to us in himself and the creative Agent in our reception and understanding of that revelation, although he is not himself the Word (λόγος) of that revelation or the Form (εἶδος) which that revelation assumes in Jesus Christ as it comes from the Father and is appropriated by us. But because it is in the Spirit as the immediate presence and power of God's revelation to us that we know God in this way, the Father through the Son and the Son from the Father, we know the Spirit in himself as Lord God no less than the Father and the Son, who therefore with the Father and the Son together is worshipped and glorified. It is through holding constantly in our thought the inseparable unity between the economic activity of God in the Spirit and the economic activity of God in the Son that we may be prevented from reading back into God himself the material or creaturely images (e.g. latent in human father-son relations) that rise out of the reciprocity he has established with us through the incarnation of his Son in space and time as one with us and one of us. Through the oneness of the Son and the Spirit the imaging of God in Jesus the incarnate Son or the Word made flesh is *signitive*, not mimetic. Thus the creaturely images naturally latent in the forms of thought and speech employed by divine revelation to us are made to refer transparently or in a diaphanous way to God without being projected into his divine Nature.[64]

---

[62] According to Athanasius, since both the Act of God and the Word of God are internal to his Being (ἐνούσιος ἐνέργεια, ἐνούσιος λόγος), we may know God through the Act and Word in the inner reality of his own Being – *Con. Ar.* 1.9ff, 14ff, 24f; 2.1f, 22, 31ff; 3.1ff, 15ff, 24f; 4.1, 5, 9; *Ad Ser.* 1.14, 19ff, 25; 3.5f.

[63] See 'The Epistemological Relevance of the Spirit' in *God and Rationality* (London, 1971), pp. 165–192.

[64] Refer again to 'The Christian Apprehension of God the Father', loc. cit., p. 138f.

Through the application of the *homoousion* in these ways, then, appropriate to the Spirit as well as to the Son, our thought is lifted up from the level of the economic Trinity to the level of the ontological Trinity (although without leaving the economic Trinity behind), and we reach the supreme point in the knowledge of God in his internal intelligible personal relations. In this process we have to bring in a new concept to be used along with the *homoousion* and the hypostatic union. This is what is known as *perichoresis* (περιχώρησις), a refined form of thought which helps us to develop a careful theological way of interpreting the biblical teaching about the mutual indwelling of the Father and the Son and the Spirit and thus about the Communion of the Spirit. *Perichoresis* derives from *chora* (χώρα), the Greek for word 'space' or 'room', or from *chorein* (χώρειν), meaning 'to contain', 'to make room', or 'to go forward'. It indicates a sort of mutual containing or enveloping of realities, which we also speak of as *coinherence* or *coindwelling*. This concept in a verbal form was first used by Gregory Nazianzen to help express the way in which the divine and the human natures in the one Person of Christ coinhere in one another without the integrity of either being diminished by the presence of the other.[65] It was then applied to speak of the way in which the three divine Persons mutually dwell in one another and coinhere or inexist in one another while nevertheless remaining other than one another and distinct from one another.[66] With this application the notion of *perichoresis* is refined and changed to refer to the complete mutual containing or interpenetration of the three divine Persons, Father, Son and Holy Spirit, in one God.[67] But this had the effect of defining it in such a way that it may not be applied to the hypostatic union of divine and human natures in Christ, without serious damage to the doctrine of Christ. Whenever that has been attempted in ancient or modern times, without qualification, it has resulted in some form of docetic rationalising and depreciating of the humanity of Christ. Its application to the doctrine of the Trinity, on the other hand, enables us to recognise that the coinherent relations of the Father, the Son and the Holy Spirit, revealed in the saving acts of God through Christ and in the Spirit, are not temporary manifestations of God's Nature, but are eternally grounded in the intrinsic and completely reciprocal relations of the Holy Trinity. In this way the concept of *perichoresis* serves to hold powerfully together in the doctrine of the Trinity the identity of the divine Being and the intrinsic unity of the three divine Persons.

It was in connection with this refined conception of *perichoresis* in its employment to speak of the intra-trinitarian relations in God, that Christian theology developed what I have long called its *onto-relational* concept of the divine Persons, or an understanding of the three divine Persons in the one God in which the ontic relations between them belong to what they essentially are in themselves in their distinctive *hypostases*. Along with this there developed out of the doctrine of the Trinity the new *concept of person*, unknown in human thought until then, according to which the relations between persons belong to what persons are. Just as the differentiating

[65] See *The Trinitarian Faith*, p. 234.
[66] See Hilary, *De Trin.* 3.1–4.
[67] Consult again *The Trinitarian Faith*, pp. 305f, 311f, 326ff.

102

relations between the Father, the Son and the Holy Spirit belong to what they are as Father, Son and Holy Spirit, so the homoousial relations between the three divine Persons belong to what they are in themselves as Persons and in their Communion with one another. This onto-relational concept of 'person', generated through the doctrines of Christ and the Holy Trinity, is one that is also applicable to inter-human relations, but in a created way reflecting the uncreated way in which it applies to the Trinitarian relations in God.

In the course of this movement of thought, described here as from the secondary and tertiary theological levels in the formulation of the doctrine of the Trinity, *perichoresis* and *person* were introduced as new forms of relational thought and speech developed and refined under the impact of divine revelation upon the mind of the Church, and other terms such as 'spirit' and 'being' (πνεῦμα and οὐσία) were radically changed from having an impersonal to having an intensely *personal* meaning. It is within the same movement in theological understanding that we find the familiar concepts of 'father', 'son', 'spirit', 'being', undergoing refinement and redefinition from level to level for their special theological use. This is the movement from the evangelical and doxological level close to experience, to the second (or the first theological) level concerned with bringing to light the intrinsic intelligibility of God's incarnate self-revelation through Christ and in the Spirit, and then from it to the third (or higher theological) level leading us to the supreme point in our knowing of God in the inner perichoretic relations of his triune Being. These concepts, 'father', 'son', 'spirit', and 'being', are all rooted in the reciprocity which God has established with us in the incarnation of his Word in Jesus Christ through whom he addresses us in the creaturely forms of our own *human* thought and speech, in order to make himself known to *us*. They thus belong to the very ground level of our knowledge of God with which we are concerned in the first or basic level of Christian experience and worship. As words and concepts taken from our human existence they carry a natural and primitive sense which they have apart altogether from God's self-revelation to us, but when they are taken up by God and employed in his self-revelation to us as Father, Son and Holy Spirit, they suffer a fundamental change in being adapted to be vehicles of his Word.

Of particular importance here was the radical transformation of the Greek concept of *being* (οὐσία), when used of God, from a pre-Christian impersonal to a profoundly personal sense. That transformation was rooted in God's *self*-revelation and *self*-naming to Israel as 'I am' which was applied by Christ to himself in his 'I am' ('Εγώ εἰμι) sayings.[68] This had a very important effect in the economic self-revelation and self-communication of God manifested in the incarnation of God's beloved Son in Jesus Christ within the subject-subject, interpersonal relations of human existence. It not only revealed the profound personal nature of God's Being, but considerably strengthened and intensified the personal relation to God in the understanding, faith and worship of his people, which enabled them to appreciate as never before the personal Nature of God. Of course neither in the Old Testament nor in the New Testament Scriptures was the Nature or Being of God ever regarded

---

[68] See the illuminating essay by William Manson, 'The EGO EIMI of the Messianic Presence in the New Testament', in *Jesus and the Christian* (London, 1967), pp. 174–183.

as impersonal, while orthodox Christian theology, faithful to 'the great mystery of godliness manifest in the flesh'[69] and thus operating κατ' εὐσέβειαν, declined to use the term οὐσία in the impersonal sense it had in secular Greek thought.[70] However, with the three-fold self-revelation of God as Father, Son and the Spirit, in the Gospel, and with the move from an implicit to an explicit understanding of the Holy Trinity, together with the onto-relational concept of the 'person' to which it gave rise, the evangelical and theological understanding of the personal Being of God deepened and developed very considerably. The distinctively Christian conceptions of 'person' and of 'being' in the doctrine of God (applied to divine Being in a unique way and to human being in a creaturely way) arose together, each bearing decisively on the other. God was now known and worshipped and glorified as a fullness of Personal Being in himself, indeed as himself a transcendent *Communion of Persons*, for the three divine Persons, Father, the Son and the Holy Spirit *are* the One God. With God, Being and Communion are one and the same. The theological concept of the Being of God as used, for example, in the formula 'One Being, Three Persons' (μία οὐσία, τρεῖς ὑποστάσεις) agreed at the Council of Alexandria presided over by Athanasius in AD362, is not to be understood as referring to three Persons *in* God's Being as if the three Persons were other than and not identical with the one Being of God, but precisely as the One Being of God. Hence the Being of God was not understood in terms of any preconceived idea or definition of divine Being, but exclusively in the light of God's naming of himself as 'I am who I am' in the Old Testament revelation[71] and as the Father, the Son and the Holy Spirit in the New Testament revelation, as in the dominical formula for Holy Baptism. Within this New Testament revelation the Old Testament self-naming of God as 'I am' was taken up in the 'I am' of the Lord Jesus Christ in whom as the very offspring of God's Nature and in his Spirit God has made himself more fully known to us in the personal Communion which his own Being is.[72] Thus in the doctrine of the Holy Trinity the one Being of God who is three Persons, does not refer to some abstract essence, but, as noted above, to the intensely personal 'I am' of God, the eternal living Being that God is of himself as the Father, the Son and the Holy Spirit, and so as intrinsically triune and intrinsically personal. The divine Being and the divine Communion are to be understood wholly in terms of one another.

Theological formulation is deeply concerned, especially in moving from the first to the second and third levels, with the *changed sense* of these theological

---

[69] 1 Tim. 3.16.

[70] The translation of οὐσία by the Latin terms *substantia* or *essentia*, however, did tend to give rise to an impersonal and somewhat abstract conception of God's Being that has damaged Western notions of the Trinity.

[71] While the Hebrew for 'I am who I am' (Exod. 3.14), אהיה אשר אהיה, may mean 'I will be who I will be', only the Greek text as found in the LXX, Ἐγώ εἰμι ὁ ὤν, meaning 'I am who I am', was used by the fathers and theologians of the Church in formulating their doctrine of God.

[72] Cf. Athanasius, *Con. Ar.* 3.6; 4.1; *De syn.* 34–35; *De decr.* 22. See the 'Agreed Statement on the Holy Trinity between the Orthodox Church and the World Alliance of Reformed Churches' in *Theological Dialogue Between Orthodox and Reformed Churches*, vol.2 (Edinburgh, 1993); and my discussion of this in *Trinitarian Perspectives, Toward Doctrinal Agreement* (Edinburgh, 1994).

terms. However, we must not forget the original connection of these terms with their ordinary pre-theological significance. In handling them we have to resist the temptation to interpret them through the spectacles of their old-established creaturely meanings, and so we have to fight against the inertial drag of their natural or secular use. This is the problem that constantly crops up in our having to use terms such as 'father' and 'son' in their new theologically transformed sense, as in the doctrine of the Trinity, as also in doctrinal use of the term 'being' which too frequently but disastrously tends to be drawn back into the abstract and impersonal philosophical notion of 'substance', not least when interpreted in terms of Aristotle's primary and secondary substance. We have to remember, however, that our doctrinal formulation can be valid for us only in so far as it remains coordinated with our fundamental experience of God and controlled by his redeeming self-revelation to us in Jesus Christ the Son of the Father incarnate within our creaturely modes of existence in this world. We can no more get away from using our fragile human expressions 'father' and 'son' than we can do without or by-pass God's *self*-revelation *to us* as Father through the Son and in the Spirit. But the use of these expressions 'Father' and 'Son' in speaking of God can be of genuine theological significance for us *if and as* they direct us away from themselves even in their transformed sense to the ineffable Reality of God, to the transcendent mystery of his Triune Being. Considered in themselves they are quite inadequate for they fall far short of the Nature of God; but in spite of their fragility and inadequacy they do fulfil a God-given function in revelation when they enable us to grasp something of the inner relations in the Life of God on which our knowledge and experience of God are grounded, and which are quite independent of our concepts and expressions referring to them. Thus the fragility of our theological terms and the inadequacy in our use of them in a faithful formulation of the doctrine of the Trinity, paradoxically, play a significant role in the truth and precision of their semantic reference to the Truth of God beyond themselves.

Hence it may be said that the concepts 'Father' and 'Son' as they are adapted and employed in divine revelation do not build some kind of image of God with a point to point correspondence between it and God, but constitute, as it were, a divinely forged *lens* through which we may discern God's personal self-revelation as it shines into our minds, while discriminating itself from the creaturely representations necessarily employed in the terms 'father' and 'son'. In other words, in addressing his Word to us in our human words God uses the notions of 'father' and 'son' taken from us to reveal something of himself to us in the interrelations of his own inner Communion, yet in such a way as to reject any mythological projection by us into God of the creaturely relations and images latent in the natural and pre-theological significance of these concepts. Within the sphere of divine revelation an *epistemological inversion* takes place in our knowing of God, for what is primary is his knowing of us, not our knowing of him.[73] This is precisely how we are to understand God's Fatherhood, for all other fatherhood is properly to be understood from its relation to his Fatherhood and not the other way round.[74]

[73] Gal. 4.9.
[74] Eph. 3.15.

Let us reflect further upon what is involved in this process, for it is of pressing importance today. While we know God only through God and not apart from him, we know him only as he enters into a reciprocal personal relation with us, in which he reveals himself to us within the range of our human knowing and at the same time empowers and sustains our knowing of him. God turns himself toward us and at the same time turns us toward himself, and therein adapts his revealing to us and adapts our knowing to him, so that our knowing of him is humanly as well as divinely conditioned. Thus there compulsively arises, as we have already noted, a significant anthropomorphic ingredient in our knowledge of God, but this is properly not one defined by what we human beings are and read back into God: it is one that derives from the reciprocal relation that God establishes between us and himself.[75] This is not to be understood without reference to the biblical teaching that God has created man (i.e. man and woman) for fellowship with himself in such a way that, in spite of our utter difference from God, we are made after the image and likeness of God. We are thus specifically destined to live in faithful response to the movement and purpose of God's love toward us and therein to reflect God in our creaturely partnership with him. Hence far from God being conceived in the image of man, man is conceived in the image of God. It is this biblical *theomorphism* that must be taken into account in assessing the place of any *anthropomorphism* in our thinking and speaking of God, for since God has made man in his own image all authentic knowing of God by man is grounded in and points back to God's relation to man.[76] Our knowledge of God arises, accordingly, by way of response to God's initiative in addressing us and in revealing himself to us. In establishing reciprocal relations with his human creature God not only posits and sustains a God-manward relation between them, but a man-Godward relation as well, so that any independent man-Godward relation is ruled out, and yet in such a way that a proper man-Godward relation, and thus an anthropomorphic ingredient, is given by God himself an integral place in the fulfilment of his self-revelation to man. Expressed otherwise, God's incarnate self-revelation to man incorporates into itself as part of its concrete actualisation a human coefficient through which it realises itself in human understanding and thus, as it were, 'earths' God's revealing of himself to man in man's knowing of God.

That God makes himself known to us in this way is not without real difficulty for theological clarification and formulation, since, as we have seen, in our interpretation of divine revelation we have to learn how to use common human forms of thought and speech without carrying over into our understanding of God the primitive images that cling to them along with the pre-established interpretations they bear. Quite clearly we cannot shed their anthropomorphic elements entirely without retracting out of the intimate personal encounter at the root of the very knowledge of God which he mediates to us human beings. We may not forget, however, that the Mystery of God sets limits to the reciprocity which he establishes

---

[75] Refer to the discussion by Martin Buber, *The Eclipse of God* (New York, 1957), pp. 14–17.

[76] For the term 'theomorphism' see Oliver C. Quick, *Doctrines of the Creed* (London, 1947), pp. 29–31.

between us, and thereby sets boundaries to our knowledge of him, which interdicts the projection of our human subjectivities and creaturely relations into him. Thus while God appropriates our human words and conceptions, along with their anthropomorphic elements embedded in them, and uses them in the mediating of his reconciling revelation to us, he nevertheless remains transcendent over them all and makes his Truth marvellously to shine through them at the same time, and thereby reveals himself to us in spite of the infinite difference between the creature and the Creator.

It must be noted here that the primacy and centrality of the Incarnation in all our relations with God implies that the proper anthropomorphic elements inevitably involved in the reciprocity he establishes with us, far from being eliminated, are actually reinforced although radically transformed and refined through the incarnation. As the one and only Form and Image of God given to us, Jesus Christ constitutes the crucial point of reference to which we have constantly to appeal in putting all spatial and temporal and creaturely ingredients in our thought to the test, in order to filter away from our conceiving of God all that is inappropriate or foreign to him such as, for example, sexual relations or distinctions in gender which by their nature belong only to creaturely beings. This is the kind of critical discrimination and refinement that takes place when we move from the first to the second levels in our formulation of the doctrine of the Holy Trinity, but especially when we move from the second to the third level in which we have to do with the supreme truth that what God is toward us in his revealing and saving acts in Jesus Christ he is antecedently and inherently in his eternal Being, and what he is antecedently and inherently in his eternal Being he is in his concrete self-revelation to us in Jesus Christ. As we have seen the coordination of the *homoousion* of the incarnate Son and the *homoousion* of the Holy Spirit helps us to discern what may and what may not be traced back properly into God. But it is in the recognition of the homoousial oneness between the economic Trinity and the transcendent Trinity, together with the doctrine of the perichoretic relations within the eternal Communion of the Father, the Son and the Holy Spirit, that a thorough refinement of all our theological beliefs and truths takes place. This is what we are concerned with in the formulation of the doctrine of the Holy Trinity and in clarifying the stratified structure which that formulation involves.

In bringing the discussion in this chapter to an end, it may not be amiss to offer some comments by way of emphasising several decisive issues.

First, the movement from economic to ontological relations in our formulation of the doctrine of the Holy Trinity must be taken seriously, for only in the Lord Jesus Christ, the Incarnation of God's eternal Word, in whom there dwells embodied all the fullness of the Godhead, are we really in touch with God, and through him with the trinitarian relations of love immanent in God. Even though by their ineffable nature they defy anything like a complete formalisation, they are the ultimate constitutive relations in God, which by their internal perfection are the ground upon which the intelligibility and objectivity of all our knowledge of God finally repose, so that our apprehension of them plays an important clarificatory role of unifying simplicity in all theological formulation. Of particular note here is the feed-back of doctrine of the Trinity of God upon the evangelical conviction that there is one unifying divine activity at work issuing from the Father through the Son and in the Holy Spirit as they are made known to us in the history of salvation and in our evangelical experience of it through faith. There is for us no activity of God behind the back of Jesus Christ or apart from the mission of the Spirit, for there is only one movement of God's Love, one movement of his Grace, and one movement of divine Sanctification, which freely flows to us from the Father through the Son and in the Holy Spirit, which took concrete form in our human existence in space and time in the incarnate economy of redemption.[77] It cannot be sufficiently emphasised, that the theological or ontological Trinity remains *evangelical*, not only because it is coordinated with the evangelical revelation of God as Father, Son and Holy Spirit, but because it is essentially and intrinsically evangelical. This should be clear even from an examination of the structure of the Nicene-Constantinopolitan Creed, in which the clauses devoted to the incarnate Son and his saving activity are placed in the very centre of confession of faith in the Father, the Son and the Holy Spirit.

It was, of course, not the Godhead or the Being of God as such who became incarnate, but the Son of God, not the Father or the Spirit, who came among us, certainly from the Being of the Father and as completely *homoousios* with him, yet because in him the whole fullness of the Godhead dwells, the whole undivided Trinity must be recognised as participating in the incarnate Life and Work of Christ. However, a reservation in our thought must be registered here. The incarnation must not be understood as involving any surrender of God's transcendence, or any compromising of his eternal freedom, or any renouncing of what he ever was before the foundation of the world, or any imprisoning of his eternal trinitarian relations within the space-time processes of our creaturely world. The incarnation was not necessary for God to be God and live as God: it flowed freely, unreservedly and unconditionally from the eternal movement of Love in God, the very Love which God is and in which God lives his Life as God; it took place in the sovereign ontological freedom of God to be other in his external relations than he eternally was, and is, and to do what he had never done before.[78] Thus in his freedom God chose not to live alone entirely in and by himself, but to create others for fellowship with himself, and in his wisdom chose to become incarnate, condescending in sheer love and grace to be one with us and one of us in our world, in order to realise his saving love for us in our lost existence, yet in such a way that he remains undiminished in the transcendent Freedom, Nature and Mystery of his eternal Being. Hence, as Athanasius used to insist, since God was not always incarnate any more than he was always Creator, the incarnation and the creation are to be regarded as new even for God, although they result from the eternal outgoing movement of his Love.[79] All this warns us that we cannot think of the ontological Trinity as if it

---

[77] This point was given fundamental place in *The Letters of Saint Athanasius on the Spirit to Serapion*, and was taken up and developed by St Basil in his widely acclaimed work *On the Holy Spirit*.

[78] I have in mind here Karl Barth's account of 'The Being of God in his Freedom', *Church Dogmatics* II.1, pp. 297ff.

[79] See my account of this in *The Trinitarian Faith*, pp. 84ff, and 89ff.

were constituted by or dependent on the economic Trinity, but must rather think of the economic Trinity as the freely predetermined manifestation in the history of salvation of the eternal Trinity which God himself was before the foundation of the world, and eternally is. Hence when we rightly speak of the oneness between the ontological Trinity and the economic Trinity, we may not speak of that oneness without distinguishing and delimiting it from the ontological Trinity – there are in any case, as we have already noted, elements in the incarnate economy such as the time pattern of human life in this world which we may not read back into the eternal Life of God. On the other hand, the fact that the ontological Trinity has ontological priority over the economic Trinity, does not preclude us from saying that the ontological Trinity is essentially and intrinsically evangelical, for it is precisely the ontological Trinity that God has made known to us in his self-giving and self-revealing as Father, Son and Holy Spirit in salvation history, and it is on the ontological Trinity that the evangelical nature of the economic Trinity entirely depends.

Second, in advancing from the second to the third epistemological level, we move from an ordered account of the economic activity of God toward us as Father, Son and Holy Spirit, to an ultimate set of fundamental concepts and relations whereby we seek to formulate in forms of thought and speech the hypostatic, homoousial and perichoretic relations in the eternal dynamic Communion in loving and being loved of the three Divine Persons which God is. This is done, however, through the employment of highly refined and attenuated relations for the concrete relations of God's self-revealing and self-giving through Christ and in the Spirit of which we learn in the Gospel, enabling us to discern the oneness between the economic Trinity and the ontological Trinity. Hence we must keep a constant check on these refined theological concepts and relations to make sure that they are in definite touch with the ground level of God's actual self-revelation to us and our evangelical experience of his saving activity in history, and that they remain empirically correlated with the saving truths and events of the Gospel, otherwise they tend to pass over into mythological projections of our own rationalisations into Deity. Hence it is of the utmost importance for us to keep our feet on the concrete ground of God's actual revelation to us in the incarnation and atonement, and to keep in mind the twofold truth that he who reveals himself to us in the incarnate life and death of Jesus is really God himself, and that the immanent relations in God on which his self-revelation to us is grounded do not detract from the economic relations in which God has actually made himself known to us in the historical life and saving activity of Jesus Christ.

The Lord Jesus Christ, in whom human nature and divine Nature while not confused are indissolubly united in his one Person, is taken up in his ascension into the very heart of the Godhead.[80] Hence the incarnate Truth of Jesus Christ as

---

[80] While in the New Testament Christ is spoken of as he by whom all things in heaven and earth are made (Col. 1.6) and as the Lamb slain from the foundation of the world (Rev. 13.8), that is surely to be understood as *proleptically conditioned* by his incarnation as the Creator Word, and by his atoning sacrifice on the Cross. See H. R. Mackintosh, *Doctrine of the Person,* p. 70. On the other hand, neither the incarnation nor the atonement can be regarded as a divine afterthought. Cf. Athanasius, *Con. Ar.* 2.73–77.

our Lord and Saviour now belongs for ever to the ultimate Truth of the one Triune God – and that includes the whole of his atoning mediation on our behalf from his birth to his crucifixion and resurrection. It is in and through him in whom we believe, and whom we worship as true God of true God, that the doctrine of the Blessed and Undivided Trinity has its material content – the crucified Jesus, risen again, is now for ever lodged in the heart of the Triune Being of God.

Third, the formulation of the doctrine of the Trinity through the unfolding of its stratified structure reinforces our basic evangelical conviction that theological understanding and doctrinal formulation are properly grounded in God's unique self-giving to us in the Lord Jesus Christ through whom we have access to the Father in one Spirit. Moreover, under the constraint of the semantic focus constituted by the hierarchical coordination of different levels of truth, theological knowledge is progressively concentrated upon the one objective centre and content of God's self-revelation in Christ, which is identical with the Truth which God eternally is in the mystery of his Triune Being. This is to say, to give revelatory and controlling priority to the oneness of God's self-revelation through the Son and in the Spirit, the one comprehensive Truth from which all other truths derive and to which they all finally refer, cannot but have the economic effect of purifying and simplifying all theological doctrines, if only by disclosing that, while relatively few have really central significance, others have but an off-centre or peripheral significance. As the different levels coordinated in this stratified way become narrower and narrower, they focus our thought more and more sharply upon the fundamental truths of the Gospel of divine salvation through Jesus Christ and in the Spirit with which we are concerned in the ground level. If they did not, let it be repeated, they would cut themselves off from any saving reality in the Gospel and would show themselves to be no more than empty theoretical speculations. But if they do focus our faith and understanding on those fundamental truths they have the effect of reinforcing and clarifying our understanding of their ultimate foundation in the Triune Communion and Nature of the Living God.

With the aid of the *homoousion* and the *perichoresis* our understanding of God's self-revelation to us is lifted up from the economic Trinity to the ontological Trinity, yet, paradoxically, without leaving the economic Trinity behind. In the course of the movement of our thought from level to level we acquire the refined theological concepts and relations by which we seek to express, as far as we may, the ultimate constitutive relations in God, in virtue of which he is who he is as the Triune God. Let us be quite frank. To speak like this of God's inner Being, we cannot but feel to be a sacrilegious intrusion into the inner holy of holies of God's incomprehensible Mystery, before which we ought rather to cover our faces and clap our hands upon our mouths, for God is utterly ineffable in the transcendence and majesty of his eternal Being. The God whom we have come to know through his infinite condescension in Jesus Christ, we know to be infinitely greater than we can ever conceive, so that it would be sheer presumption and theological sin on our part to identify the trinitarian structures in *our* thinking and speaking of God with the *real* constitutive relations in the triune Being-in-Communion of the Godhead. All true theological concepts and statements inevitably fall short of the God to whom they refer, so that, as we have already noted, their fragility and their inadequacy, as concepts and as human statements about God must be regarded as part of the correctness and truthfulness of their reference to God.

This does not mean that when we reach this point, at the threshold of the Trinity *ad intra*, theological activity simply breaks off, perhaps in favour of some kind of merely apophatic or negative contemplation. While the Triune God is certainly more to be adored than expressed, the ultimate Rationality, as well as the sheer Majesty of God's self-revelation, and above all the Love of God, will not allow us to desist. They summon us instead to respond to him in committed rational worship and praise through godly ways of thought and speech that are *worthy* of God. As Athanasius once wrote: 'There is one eternal Godhead in Trinity and there is one Glory of the Holy Trinity ... If theological truth is now perfect in Trinity, this is the true and only divine worship, and this is its beauty and truth, it must have been always so.'[81] Again:

> There is one Form of Godhead, which is also in the Word and one God the Father, existing in himself as he transcends all things, and in the Spirit as in him he acts in all things through the Word. Thus we confess God to be one through the Trinity, and claim that our understanding of the one Godhead in Trinity is much more godly than the heretics' conception of Godhead with its many forms and its many parts.[82]

For the great Athanasius, however, godly contemplation and humble worship of the Holy Trinity, and the reverent formulation of the doctrine of the Trinity, which he found so necessary if only in order to defend the evangelical and apostolic Faith from the impiety of heretical deviations that undermined the Gospel, had the effect of making him concentrate his personal faith all the more squarely upon the vicarious humanity of Christ who identified himself with us in our lost and corrupt existence in order to heal and redeem us, and restore us to participation through the Communion of the Spirit in the eternal Life and Love of God.[83]

> The Word was made flesh, and dwelt among us, and we beheld his glory, the glory of the only begotten of the Father, full of grace and truth ... No one has seen God at any time; the only Son who is in the bosom of the Father, he has made him known.[84]

---

[81] Athanasius, *Con. Ar.* 1.18.
[82] Athanasius, *Con. Ar.* 3.15.
[83] This is particularly clear in Athanasius' expositions of the priesthood and atoning mediation of the Incarnate Son embedded in his *Orations against the Arians* which greatly influenced the soteriological approach to the Trinity by Gregory of Nazianzus and Cyril of Alexandria.
[84] John 1.14 & 18.

5

One Being, Three Persons

UNDER this title we are following the way in which the agreement between Athanasian and Cappadocian approaches were brought together at the Council of Alexandria in AD 362 under the presidency of Athanasius: *one Being, three Persons* (μία οὐσία τρεῖς ὑποστάσεις).[1] Hence we will not be lapsing into what Karl Rahner called 'the Augustinian-Western conception of the Trinity ... which begins with the one God, the one divine essence as a whole, and only *afterwards* does it see God in three persons.'[2] The 'whole' with which we are concerned is that of the divine Triunity in which 'the One and the Three' and 'the Three and the One' are the obverse of one another. We will take our cue mainly from Gregory Nazianzen who stood rather closer to Athanasius than the other Cappadocians, Basil, his brother Gregory Nyssen, and Amphilochius, Gregory Nazianzen's cousin,[3] and recall several well-known passages from his *Orations* to which we have already drawn attention.

> No sooner do I consider the One than I am enlightened by the radiance of the Three; no sooner do I distinguish them than I am carried back to the One. When I bring any One of the Three before my mind I think of him as a Whole, and my vision is filled, and the most of the Whole escapes me. I cannot grasp the greatness of that One in such a way as to attribute more greatness to the rest. When I contemplate the Three together, I see but one Torch, and cannot divide or measure out the undivided Light.[4]

> To us there is one God, for the Godhead is One, and all that proceeds from him is referred to One, though we believe in Three Persons. For One is not more and another less God; nor is One before and Another after; nor are they parted in will or divided in power; nor can you find here any of the features that obtain in divisible things; but the Godhead is, to speak concisely, undivided in being divided; and there is one mingling of Light, as it were of three suns joined to each other.[5]

---

[1] Athanasius, *Ad Antiochenos*, 6; see also *Ad Serapionem*, 1, 2, 10.
[2] Karl Rahner, *The Trinity* (London, 1970), p. 17.
[3] Refer here to Nazianzen's *Oration on the Great Athanasius*, *Orationes*, 21.
[4] Gregory Nazianzen, *Orationes*, 40.41; cited by John Calvin several times, *Institutio*, 1.13.17; *Commentary on John*, 1.1; *Epistles*, 607.
[5] Gregory Nazianzen, *Or.* 31.14.

These citations from Saint Gregory Nazianzen, designated in the Early Church 'Gregory the Theologian', give impressive expression to the way in which we apprehend the self-revelation of God to us in his indivisible wholeness as *one Being, three Persons, three Persons, one Being.* Our concern in this chapter is to concentrate our thought on the one Being, although not apart from the three Persons, and in the following chapter entitled, 'Three Persons, One Being', we shall concentrate on the three Persons, but not apart from the one Being. While the discussion is presented in this way for elucidatory purposes and in order to amplify the account of the doctrine of the Holy Trinity already given, there can be no question, in this further discussion of the doctrine of the Triune God, of separating the Trinity from the Unity, or the Unity from the Trinity.

In the previous chapter we sought to clarify the way in which the unfolding of the doctrine of the Trinity takes place as it moves from its implicit biblical form to an explicit theological form. We found that doctrinal formulation involves here, as in all areas of scientific knowledge, a stratified structure of several coordinated levels of understanding in which the conceptual content and structure of basic knowledge becomes progressively disclosed to inquiry. We moved from the ground level of evangelical or biblical knowledge of God as he is revealed to us in the saving activity of his incarnate Son, to a distinctly theological level in an attempt to grasp and give intelligible expression to the unbroken relation in Being and Act between Christ and the Holy Spirit to God the Father, which belongs to the very heart of the Gospel message of God's redeeming love. This involved a decisive movement of thought, under the guidance of the key insight of the Nicene Creed expressed in the *homoousion,* from a preconceptual to a conceptual level of understanding which Christian faith takes under the compelling claims of God's self-revelation and self-communication in the incarnation. We then moved to a higher theological level devoted to a deepening and refining of the theological concepts and relations operating at the second level, this time with particular help from the notion of *perichoresis,* in terms of which the doctrine of the Holy Trinity as one Being, three Persons comes to its fullest formulation, yet in such a way that it serves understanding and appreciation of the saving and redemptive message of the Gospel upon which the whole Christian faith is grounded. In this stratified structure of different epistemological levels, we noted that each level is open to consistent and deeper understanding in the light of the theological concepts and relations operating at the next level, and that the top level, and indeed the whole coordinated structure with it, while open-ended and incomplete in itself, points indefinitely beyond itself to the ineffable, tránscendent Mystery of the Holy Trinity. Thus each level serves deeper and fuller understanding of the ground level of evangelical experience and cognition and relates the Trinity to God's redemptive mission in Christ and in the Holy Spirit, inspiring worship and calling forth from us wonder, thanksgiving, adoration and praise.

In earlier chapters we reflected upon the Irenaean principle, taken up and developed in our day by Karl Barth, that *God reveals himself through himself,* and discussed the historical actualisation of that self-revelation in the saving events of the Gospel in which we learn that God has drawn near to us by the atoning blood of Christ in such a reconciling way that through Christ and in one Spirit we are brought near to him and given access to knowledge of God as Father, Son and Holy Spirit. In our recognition of the Deity and saving power of Christ and of the Holy Spirit we are led to believe that what God is toward us and has done for us in this way he really is in himself, for it is his own divine *Self*, nothing less, whom he has communicated to us in the Son and imparts to us in the Spirit. We also reflected upon the fact that God reveals himself to us as Triune, and that he makes himself known to us as a whole and not in partitive ways, so that we need to think in conjunctive and not in analytical ways of his trinitarian self-communication to us. This also applies to our formulation of the doctrine of the Holy Trinity considered in the foregoing chapter in which we moved from an understanding of the economic Trinity to an understanding of the ontological Trinity, and then through its all-important bearing upon the Gospel of redemption back again to the economic Trinity. However, while for elucidatory purposes we traced the epistemic steps taken in moving from the economic to the ontological Trinity and back again, that is, from below upward and from above downward again, strictly speaking we must think of the economic Trinity and the ontological Trinity together or conjunctively as a whole.

This is not unlike the proper theological procedure we adopt in Christology, in which we do not seek to understand the Person and work of Jesus Christ by approaching him either from below or from above, but from below and from above at the same time, for it is in the light of what we learn from below that we appreciate what derives from above, and in the light of what derives from above that we really understand what we learn from below. In a faithful and rigorously theological approach, therefore, we apprehend both together. It was when the dualist ways of thinking endemic in the Mediterranean culture and its prevailing framework of knowledge were allowed to affect people's approach to the mystery of Christ, that conflicting attempts were made to interpret him, operating not only from contrasting Hellenistic and Judaistic starting-points, but from the sharp antithesis in the prevailing framework of knowledge between the conception of God and the empirical world. Thus there arose the so-called 'ebionite' and 'docetic' types of Christology which had the effect in different ways of breaking up the wholeness of the New Testament presentation of Jesus Christ as God and man by separating the human Jesus from the divine Christ. The ebionite approach to Christ was from below, and the docetic approach to Christ was from above. However to be successful in commending the Christian Gospel of divine revelation and redemption, ebionite Christology had in some way to present Jesus Christ as a divine Saviour and thereby tended to cut itself loose from its starting point in the humanity of Christ. The docetic approach to Christ, on the other hand, in seeking to commend the relevance of the Christian message to mankind tended to cut itself off from its starting point in the Deity of Christ and thus to transmute itself into human speculation or mythological constructs projected into God from below. Thus a strange dialectic was at work in ebionite and docetic approaches to Christ, for owing to the similar dualisms which they each presupposed, an antithesis between the creature and the Creator, and between physical event and divine idea, they tended inevitably to pass over into each other.[6] However, the fact that each approach ended up on the other side of the wide gulf between God and man where the other began, showed that neither had really started from the fundamental datum of the Gospel that in Jesus Christ, who was born of Mary and suffered under Pontius, God himself had come into the world in order to be one of us and one with us and reveal himself to us, and that in the one Person of Jesus Christ God and man are inseparably united for us and our salvation. The New Testament does not present Christ in contrast to God or alongside of God, or argue from one to the other, as in ebionite and docetic Christologies, but presents him in the unbroken relationship of his incarnate life and work to God to the Father, and thus in the undivided wholeness of his divine-human reality as the Son of God become man.[7] It is as such that Jesus Christ is our Lord and Saviour apart from whom there is no way to knowledge of the Father. If Jesus Christ were not God, he would not reveal God to us for only through God may we know God, and if he were not man, he would not be our Saviour, for only as one with us would God be savingly at work within our actual human existence.

That Jesus Christ *is* the Son of God and that the Son of God *is* Jesus Christ was the supreme evangelical truth that the Council of Nicaea reaffirmed in their inclusion of the *homoousion* in the heart of the Creed. They were convinced that they had to do that in order to set aside any disjunction between the humanity and the Deity of Christ, not only in ebionite and docetic Christologies, but also in their heretical successors, the Arian and Sabellian approaches to the doctrine of the Holy Trinity, which no less than ebionite and docetic Christologies threatened the integrity of the Faith, and which like them tended dialectically to pass over into one another. What was at stake here was the essential oneness in Being and Act between the economic Trinity and the ontological Trinity, which after the Council Athanasius and the Neo-Nicene theologians upheld with great vigour, explaining and developing the profound import of the *homoousion* for our salvation and sanctification through Christ and in the Holy Spirit in the face of disjunctive thinking that in different ways gave rise to the damaging heresies of Arianism, subordinationism and Sabellianism. Against all tritheist and modalist conceptions of the Trinity, they insisted that God really is indivisibly and eternally in himself the *one indivisible Being, three coequal Persons* which he is toward us in the redemptive missions of his Son and his Spirit.[8]

This tells us that as in the doctrine of Christ so in the doctrine of the Holy Trinity we must take care to think conjunctively of God's trinitarian self-revelation

---

[6] Cf. Athanasius, *Contra Arianos*, 1.18; 2.12, 14; *De decretis*, 12, 32; *De synodis*, 45; *Ad Afros*, 11.

[7] Note the stress of Athanasius on 'the whole man and God together' (ὅλον αὐτὸν ἀνθρωπόν τε καὶ Θεὸν ὁμοῦ), *Contra Arianos*, 4.35, which was both anti-ebionite and anti-docetic. See also 3.41: 'He was true God in the flesh and true flesh in the Word' ('Αληθινὸς γὰρ Θεὸς ἦν ἐν τῇ σαρκί, καὶ ἀληθὴς σάρξ ἦν ἐν τῷ Λόγῳ).

[8] See Gregory Nazianzen's 'Athanasian' account of *one Being, three Persons* which avoids both a Sabellian confusion of the three Persons in the One Being, and an Arianising division of the One Being into three Persons, *Oration on the Great Athanasius, Orationes*, 21.13 & 35; cf. also 1.36f; 18.16; 34.8f; 39.11f.

from below and from above, of what God is toward us and of what he is in himself, and thus think of the Trinity in his Unity and of his Unity in his Trinity, and consider the economic Trinity and the ontological Trinity inseparably together, for it is as an undivided whole and not partitively that God makes himself known to us from below and from above in a movement to which we respond in a unified act of apprehension. That is the revelatory perspective in which we must seek to understand, as far as it is given to us, the one Being of God.

The word that the Greek Fathers used to speak of the Being of God was *ousia* (οὐσία), a term familiar in the schools of Greek philosophy, but used in Christian theology in a very different way governed by the revelation of God's redemptive activity in history as recorded in the Scriptures of the Old and New Testaments, that is, not as static but as *living being* and not as dumb but as *speaking being*, and hence as *personal being*. If we turn to Athanasius we find that from the very start he thought of God the Creator of the universe as 'beyond all being and human conception of being', 'beyond all created being',[9] whom he identifies with 'the all-holy Father of Christ beyond all created being'.[10] That is to say, Athanasius did not operate with a preconceived idea or definition of being in speaking of God's Being, but drew his understanding of the Being of God from the ever-living God himself as he speaks to us personally in his Word and reveals himself in his creative and saving activity. God's Being and his revealed Being are one and the same. When Athanasius applied the term *ousia* to speak of the Being of God the Creator and of God the Father of Christ in this dynamic way he used it, as Sellers pointed out, in its simple meaning of 'being', but as transformed through the biblical revelation of God's intervention in history in order to effect man's redemption.[11] Moreover it is 'being' understood in light of the truth that the Son and the Spirit are each of one and the same being or *homoousios* with God the Father; or expressed the other way round, in light of the truth that the fullness of the Father's Being is the Being of the Son and of the Spirit. It is in view of the identity of Being (ταυτότης τῆς οὐσίας) between the Father, the Son and the Holy Spirit, that 'being' or οὐσία is used throughout this book, not in the metaphysical and static sense of being, ὄν / οὐσία, as in Aristotle's *Metaphysics*,[12] variously translated by Western theologians as *essentia* and *substantia* in Latin.[13]

This is not to say that the conception of 'being' as that which is and subsists by itself was entirely rejected by Patristic theology, for it was used in an appropriate way to speak of the truth that God's transcendent Being is infinite, unlimited,

---

[9] Athanasius, *Contra Gentes*, 2: ὁ ὑπερέκεινα πάσης οὐσίας καὶ ἀνθρωπίνης ἐπινοίας, & 35: ἀόρατος καὶ ἀκατάληπτός ἐστι τὴν φύσιν, ἐπέκεινα πάσης γενητῆς οὐσίας. Contrast the ἐπέκεινα τῆς οὐσίας of Plato, *Republic*, VI.509b.

[10] Athanasius, *Contra Gentes*, 40: ὁ πανάγιος καὶ ὑπερέκεινα γενητῆς οὐσίας, ὁ τοῦ Χριστοῦ Πατήρ.

[11] R. V. Sellers, *Two Ancient Christologies. A Study in the Christological Thought of the Schools of Alexandria and Antioch in the Early History of Christian Doctrine* (London, 1940), p. 6.

[12] E.g. Aristotle, *Metaphysics*, 1028b.

[13] Although he himself wrote in Latin, Hilary once remarked about Latin translations of the decisions of Eastern Bishops: 'Much obscurity is caused by translation from Greek to Latin, and to be quite literal is sometimes to be partly unintelligible.' *De synodis*, 9.

unoriginated and wholly grounded in himself, for God and his Being are one and the same.[14] However, it became adapted and transformed in the theological activity of the Church in seeking to understand the nature of God's Being, not speculatively from some point outside of God, but from within the actual definite self-revelation of God in Jesus Christ as Lord and Saviour in the economy of redemption. It is in and through him the only begotten Son of the Father, the very Offspring of the Divine Nature, that the Nature of God is alone to be known. It is then strictly by reference to the Father-Son, Son-Father relation that the Nature of God's Being is to be defined, or rather that God defines his own Nature for us. Thus as Athanasius used to say: 'It would be more godly and true to signify God from the Son and call him Father, than to name God from his works alone and call him Unoriginate.'[15] It belongs to the epistemological significance of the incarnation that it has opened up for us knowledge of God in accordance with what he is in himself, but to know God in himself through the relation of the Son and the Father in the Godhead, that is, in his internal relations, makes the doctrine of the Trinity essential to the Christian understanding of God. This applies of course equally to the epistemological relevance of the Spirit who proceeds from the Father and is sent by the Son, and who as the Spirit of the Father and of the Son imparted to us enables us in communion with himself to participate in God's knowing of himself.

Athanasius much preferred to use verbs rather than nouns when speaking of God as the mighty living and acting God,[16] for abstract terms or substantives seemed to him (as indeed to the biblical writers) to be inappropriate in speaking about the dynamic Nature of God, or in expressing *who* God is who makes himself known to us in his mighty acts of deliverance and salvation. For Athanasius, here as elsewhere, the precise meaning of theological terms is to be found in their actual use under the transforming impact of divine revelation. This is how he believed that the words *ousia* and *hypostasis* were used at the Council of Nicaea, not in the abstract Greek sense but in a concrete personal sense governed by God's self-revelation in the incarnation.[17] He preferred a functional and flexible use of language in which the meaning of words varied in accordance with the nature of the realities intended and with the general scope of thought or discourse at the time.[18] Hence he retained the freedom to vary the sense of the words he used in different contexts, and declined to be committed to a fixed formalisation of any specific theological term for all contexts which might have violated his semantic principle that terms are not prior to realities but realities come first and terms second.[19] This intention is nowhere

---

[14] Thus Gregory Nazianzen with reference to God's naming of himself to Moses, *Orationes*, 28.5, 9; 30.18; 45.3.

[15] Athanasius, *Contra Arianos*, 1.34; *De decretis*, 31.

[16] Thus when speaking of three distinct but undivided subsistences in the one Being of God, he preferred to use verbs like ὑφιστάναι, ὑπάρχειν together with the personal pronoun αὐτός. See Torrance, *Theology in Reconciliation* (London, 1975), p. 246f.

[17] See Athanasius, *Ad Antiochenos*, 5–11.

[18] Cf. my discussion of Athanasius' use of terms in 'Athanasius: A Study in the Foundations of Classical Theology', *Theology in Reconciliation* pp. 242ff; republished in *Divine Meaning. Studies in Patristic Hermeneutics*, ch. 8 (Edinburgh, 1995).

[19] Athanasius, *Contra Arianos*, 2.3: καὶ γὰρ οὐ πρότεραι τῶν οὐσιῶν αἱ λέξεις, ἀλλ' αἱ οὐσίαι πρῶται, καὶ δεύτεραι τούτων αἱ λέξεις. While the word οὐσία here simply means

more evident than in his cautious and differential use of human terms to speak of the Being of God or the Subsistence of Persons in the doctrine of the Holy Trinity.[20]

However, when Athanasius did refer directly to the Being of God, as in the agreed formula, 'one Being, three Persons', he took his guidance from the answer God gave to the question as to his name: 'Say this to the people of Israel "*I am who I am*".' The Name of God and the 'I am' of God are identical – the Name of God signifies his very Being, for the Being of God *is* God himself. While Athanasius cited this in the Greek form of the LXX, Ἐγώ εἰμι ὁ ὤν, he understood it and used it in a concrete and Hebraic personal way, not in an abstract and impersonal way. This is clear, for example, in Athanasius' argument in the *De synodis* for the truth that Jesus Christ is from the Being of the Father and of one and the same being or *homoousios* with God.

> When you hear it said 'I am who I am', and 'In the beginning God created the heaven and the earth', and 'Hear, O Israel, the Lord our God is one Lord', and 'Thus says the Lord Almighty',[21] we understand nothing else than the very simple and blessed and incomprehensible Being of him who is (αὐτὴν τὴν ἁπλῆν καὶ μακαρίαν καὶ ἀκατάληπτον τοῦ ὄντος οὐσίαν νοοῦμεν), for although we are unable to grasp what he is (ὅ, τι ποτέ ἐστιν), yet on hearing 'Father' and 'God' and 'Almighty' we understand nothing else to be signified than the very Being of him who is (αὐτὴν τὴν τοῦ ὄντος οὐσίαν). And if you have said of Christ that 'he is the Son of God', you have thereby said that 'he is from the Being of the Father (ἐκ τῆς οὐσίας τοῦ Πατρός)'. And since the Scriptures have anticipated you in declaring that the Lord is the Son of the Father, and the Father himself has already said 'This is my beloved Son'[22] – and a son is no other than the offspring of his father – is it not evident that the Fathers of Nicaea were right to have said that the Son is from the Being of the Father (ἐκ τῆς οὐσίας τοῦ Πατρός)?[23]

That is to say, it is the *Fatherhood* of God as revealed in Jesus Christ that determines for us precisely how we are to understand the nature of his divine Being. 'To name God Father is to signify his very Being.'[24]

This is a particularly significant argument for our immediate concern here, since in it Athanasius shows that the word *ousia* (οὐσία), derived from the verb εἶναι, to be, with the quite straightforward meaning of *be-ing* (ὤν), is to be

---

'reality', Athanasius goes on to indicate that its meaning is changed when it is used to refer to the reality of God, e.g. under the impact of his self-manifestation as Father. For this semantic principle cf. also *De decretis*, 10–11; *De sententia Dionysii*, 9; Gregory Nazianzen, *Orationes*, 42.16; Gregory Nyssen, *Contra Eunomium*, 1.37; Hilary, *De Trinitate*, 4.14.

[20] Cf. Athanasius, *Ad Antiochenos*, 6ff; *Ad Afros*, 4f.

[21] Exod. 3.14; Gen. 1.1; Deut. 6.4; 2 Sam. 7.8.

[22] Matt. 3.17.

[23] Athanasius, *De synodis*, 34; cf. *De decretis*, 22; *Ad Afros*, 8.

[24] Athanasius, *De synodis*, 35; also 34. Similarly Gregory Nazianzen speaks of the ὁ ὤν concept of God as applicable to the unoriginate Father, but of the Nature of the Father as perfectly exhibited by the Son in his identity with the Father in Being, κατ' οὐσίαν, and as ὁμοούσιος with him – *Orationes*, 30. 19f.

understood in terms of the divine 'I am' (Ἐγώ εἰμι); and at the same time he relates it to the fact that Jesus Christ is of one and the same being as God the Father. Moreover, he follows this up with another passage in which he points out that the 'I am' sayings of Christ can be understood only in terms of his being *homoousios* with God.[25] Thus the 'I am' of God and the 'I am' of Christ in their bearing upon one another determined for Athanasius, as they must surely do for us, the Christian understanding of the divine Being or οὐσία as living self-revealing and self-affirming personal Being. The repeated 'I am' of Christ in the Gospel confirms the intensely personal nature of the 'I am who I am' of *Yahweh*, while the 'I am who I am' of *Yahweh* discloses the ontological ground of the 'I am' of Christ in God. As we noted at an earlier point, the concept of person and of the personal actually arose only along with the doctrines of Christ and of the Holy Trinity, so that it is not surprising that the personal nature of God's Being should become clearly manifest among us in the acutely personalised form of Jesus Christ his incarnate Son in whom we believe and whom we love as our Lord and Saviour.

In corroboration of this point it is worth recalling what Karl Barth has written with reference to this conception of the personal Nature of God as a derivation from the doctrine of the Trinity. 'It follows from the trinitarian understanding of God revealed in the Scripture that this one God is to be understood not just as impersonal lordship, that is as power, but as the Lord; not just as absolute Spirit but as Person, that is as an I existing in and for himself with his own thought and will. This is how he meets us in his revelation. This is how he is thrice God as Father, Son and Holy Spirit.'[26]

It is at this very point, then, in the bearing of the 'I am' of God and the 'I am' of Christ upon one another, that we may discern how profound and intensely personal the ontological interrelation between the economic Trinity and the ontological Trinity is. If God were ontically other in his eternal Being than the Father, the Son and the Holy Spirit whom we encounter and know in the economy of redemption proclaimed to us in the Gospel, there would be no objective basis for God's revelation of *himself* to us or for any divine truth in the soteriological message of the Gospel, or, therefore, in the Christian doctrine of the Holy Trinity.

We must now take a closer look at what the Old Testament Scripture has to say about *Yahweh* as 'I am who I am',[27] for it is rather fuller in meaning than it may at first appear. The Hebrew for this, אהיה אשר אהיה, means as much 'I will be who I will be' as 'I am who I am', for the verb 'to be', היה, has a dynamic sense which comes out more clearly in a preceding verse in which the Lord said to Moses 'I will be with you'.[28]

---

[25] Athanasius, *De synodis*, 41. John 14.6 & 9 were favourite passages for Athanasius.

[26] Karl Barth, *Church Dogmatics* I.1 (Edinburgh, 2nd edn, 1975), p. 349f.

[27] Exod. 3.14. See the whole chapter. Consult the discussion of George A. F. Knight, *A Christian Theology of the Old Testament* (London, 1959), pp. 40ff; and also *A Biblical Approach to the Doctrine of the Trinity*, Scottish Journal of Theology Occasional Papers, No.1 (Edinburgh, 1953), pp. 77, 60f.

[28] Exod. 3.12. See Gerhard von Rad, *Old Testament Theology*, vol.1 (London, 1962), pp. 179ff. And cf. also Gregory Nazianzen, *Orationes*, 45.3: 'God ever was and is and will be (Θεὸς ἦν μὲν ἀεὶ καὶ ἔστι καὶ ἔσται), or rather God ever is... He is the eternal Be-ing (ὁ δὲ ὤν ἀεί), and names himself so when speaking oracularly to Moses on the Mount.'

'I am the Lord, and will bring you out from under the burden of the Egyptians, and I will deliver you from their bondage, and I will redeem you with an outstretched arm and with great acts of judgment, and I will take you for my people, and I will be your God, and you shall know that I am the Lord your God, who has brought you out from under the burden of the Egyptians. And will bring you into the land which I swore to give to Abraham, Isaac, and to Jacob; I will give it to you for a possession. I am the Lord.'[29]

This dynamic sense of the divine 'I am who I am / I will be who I will be' is thus in line with the whole context which is concerned with what God has already done in taking Israel for his people and with what he will do for them in delivering them from bondage. It is in accordance with this primary constitutive event in Israel's history that God is presented throughout the Old Testament revelation as Saviour and Redeemer. Who God really is, is to be understood not primarily in the light of his creation of heaven and earth, but in the light of his covenant purpose for the community of Israel and of his concrete saving activity on their behalf in history – beside him there is no other Saviour and therefore no other God. In other words, we are to understand by the divine 'I am' or 'I will be' the Being of the mighty living and active Lord God, Being in respect of which who God is and what he does interpret one another, for his Being and his Act are not separable from one another.

This is why, as we have seen, Karl Barth used to speak of God's Being as his Being-in-his-Act, and his Act as his Act-in-his-Being.[30] That is indeed rather like how Athanasius understood the Being of God in the light of his saving and redemptive activity in history, particularly as it is embodied in the incarnate Person of the Son of God, who is one in being and agency with God the Father.[31] Hence he could speak of the activity of God as inherent in his Being (ἐνούσιος ἐνέργεια) in precisely the same way in which he could speak of the Word of God as inherent in his Being (ἐνούσιος λόγος).[32]

It is significant that the self-revelation of God as 'I am who I am / I will be who I will be', was spoken by the Lord in the first person singular, which tells us that even when we think of the Being and the Act of God as inhering in one another, that Being and Act are the very Being and Act of God's transcendent *I*, for he the Lord God is the Subject (יהוה, Κύριος) and the sole Subject of all he is and will be, and of all his ways and works. 'I am the Lord (אני יהוה) your God, the Holy One of Israel, your Saviour.' 'I, I am the Lord (אנכי אנכי יהוה), and besides me there is no Saviour.'[33] This emphatic reiteration of the 'I am' of *Yahweh* found not only in

[29] Exod. 6.6–8.
[30] Karl Barth, *Church Dogmatics* II.1 (Edinburgh, 1957), pp. 257ff.
[31] R. V. Sellers was very much to the point when he spoke of Athanasius as having a Hebraic mind in his doctrines of God and salvation – *Two Ancient Christologies*, pp. 15, 34, 70, 243. This may help to explain why the thought of Epiphanius, the Jewish Bishop of Salamis, was so close to that of Athanasius, e.g. in respect of the personal nature of God's Being revealed in his self-naming as Ἐγώ εἰμι.
[32] See for example, Athanasius, *Contra Arianos*, 2.1ff.
[33] Isa. 43.3 & 11.

120

these citations from Isaiah but throughout the Old Testament Scriptures, reinforces for us the fact that the one Being (μία οὐσία) of God must be understood as intrinsically and intensely personal – even, it may be said, apart from the 'I am' of the Lord Jesus, although the oneness between the 'I am' of Yahweh and the 'I am' of the Lord Jesus makes it quite impossible for us to think otherwise of the Christian use of ousia than as essentially personal. The Being or 'I am' (οὐσία or Ἐγώ εἰμι) of the Lord God is the ultimate divine Source of all his personal and personalising activity through Jesus Christ and in the Spirit, God himself acting personally in the Lord Jesus and God himself acting personally in the Lord the Spirit.[34] As we have seen, in God's revelation of himself through himself, Christ and the Spirit in their oneness in Being and Act with the Father are both acknowledged and reverenced as Lord, together with the Father. Hence in addressing us through the Son and in the Spirit the one Lord God speaks to us as 'the irreducible Subject' of his revelation,[35] and reveals himself in the power of his 'monarchical' Person.[36] It is thus that the one Being, the lordly 'I am', of the ever-living God is made known to us as one Being (μία οὐσία) as well as three Persons (τρεῖς ὑποστάσεις), that is, in the Unity of the Trinity, as well as in the Trinity of the Unity.

Before we proceed further we must draw out the import of the 'I am who I am / I will be who I will be' of the Old Testament revelation in respect of the special relation between God and Israel which it involved and promised. With Abraham, Isaac and Jacob God had established his covenant and promised to give them an inheritance in the land of Canaan, but had not made himself known to them by the Name of Yahweh. Now, however, with the revelation of his Name, God promises to realise that purpose by delivering Israel from its oppression in the Land of Egypt, and to redeem them with an outstretched arm and with great acts of judgment.

> I will take you for my people, and I will be your God, and you shall know that *I am Yahweh* (אני יהוה) your God who has brought you from under the burden of the Egyptians, and I will bring you into the land which I swore to Abraham, Isaac and Jacob, and I will give it to you for a possession. *I am the Lord* (אני יהוה).[37]

That is what took place in the historic exodus of Israel from Egyptian slavery when its redemption as a covenanted community was sealed with the Passover sacrifice and finalised in the tremendous event of the promulgation of the Law at Mt Sinai when God proclaimed his Name: 'The Lord, the Lord (יהוה, יהוה), a God merciful

---

[34] Far from needing to be personalised through the ὑπόστασις of the Father (as some misguided people hold, which presupposes that the Being of God is impersonal) the very opposite is the case, cf. Athanasius, *De synodis*, 51. The οὐσία and the ὑπόστασις, the Being and the Person, of the Father are one.

[35] Thus Karl Barth, *Christliche Dogmatik* (Munich, 1927), compare pp. 143ff, and 214ff.

[36] Cf. again Karl Barth, *Christliche Dogmatik*, p. 135: 'Gott allein offenbart sich oder er offenbart sich gar nicht. Nur in der Kraft seiner monarchischen Person und in ihrer Tat gibt es Offenbarung.' This 'monarchical Person' is to be understood not in a Sabellian or modalist sense, but in the sense of Gregory Nazianzen's remark that the divine Monarchy is not to be limited to one Person, *Orationes*, 29.2.

[37] Exod. 6.2–8.

and gracious, slow to anger, and abounding in steadfast love and faithfulness, keeping steadfast love for thousands, forgiving iniquity and transgression and sin, but who will by no means clear the guilty…'[38] This is an awesome revealing of the Name of God to Israel in which his self-naming, self-affirming and self-giving as *Yahweh* are intertwined with one another. He gives himself to his chosen people in steadfast love and faithfulness as the Lord who affirms himself to be the Lord who in his holiness cannot pass over evil but who affirms himself precisely as he who gives himself to them in abounding love and grace, so that his merciful compassion and his righteous judgment involve one another. The same revelation was granted to Moses personally when he asked God to show him his glory.

> And the Lord said, I will make all my goodness to pass before you, and will proclaim before you my name, 'the Lord (יהוה)'; and I will be gracious to whom I will be gracious and will shew mercy on whom I will shew mercy. But you cannot see my face; for no man shall see me, and live.[39]

Moses is taught that while God reveals his Name, he does not thereby resign his transcendence or glory, but makes himself known nevertheless in the utter freedom of his grace, within the covenant fellowship he has established with his people.

The significant point to be emphasised here is that the self-naming of God as *Yahweh* is bound up with the covenant of steadfast love and truth he made with Israel. The divine pronouncement 'I am who I am / I will be who I will be,' is not isolated from the establishing of a holy fellowship between *Yahweh* and Israel which he backs up with his own Being: 'I am the Lord', and reinforces with his promise 'I will be with you'. The Being of *Yahweh* is his Being-in-union with his people. God is revealed as he who freely chooses Israel for fellowship with himself and even adopts Israel as his first-born son,[40] and as he who in his covenant love commits himself to this people in fellowship and pledges himself in the fulfilment of their redemption in virtue of a bond of kinship or community which he establishes between them and himself.[41]

Within this covenant fellowship God names himself and puts his ineffable Name *Yahweh* upon Israel so that Israel is committed to him and becomes called by his Name. 'Fear not', the Lord says, 'for I have redeemed you and called you by my name – you are mine.'[42] Israel was thus constituted by God's redeeming, fellowship-seeking, communion-creating activity as the people of *Yahweh* (יהוה עם) in whose midst he has placed his Name and within which he dwells so intimately that, as the prophet said, 'in all the affliction of his people he was afflicted … and in his love and in his pity he redeemed them.'[43] The covenant was certainly established with

---

[38] Exod. 34.6–7.
[39] Exod. 33.18–20.
[40] Exod. 4.22f: 'Thus says the Lord, Israel is my first-born son.' Cf. also Hos. 11.1: 'When Israel was a child, I loved him, and out of Egypt I called my son.'
[41] In this activity *Yahweh* is spoken of in the Old Testament Scriptures as the גאל or 'kinsman-redeemer', he who stands in for others and makes their cause his own at cost to himself.
[42] Isa. 43.1.
[43] Isa. 63.9.

Israel unilaterally by God out of his inexplicable love,[44] but it was a covenant with a two-sided relation within which *Yahweh* gives himself to Israel and gives Israel to himself at one and the same time, thereby binding them within a holy fellowship which is governed by what the Old Testament calls 'mercy and truth' or 'steadfast love and faithfulness' (חסד ואמת). Within that fellowship God keeps faith with his people and summons them to keep faith with him as the distinctive people of *Yahweh*, for through his living Word or Voice he calls them to be the congregation, community or church of *Yahweh* (קהל יהוה).

An enlightening account of this covenant relation between the 'I am who I am / I will be who I will be' of *Yahweh* and Israel is given by the prophet Hosea through the analogy of his marriage relation to the unfaithful Gomer.[45] According to the prophet the names given to her children speak of the adulterous way that Israel has behaved in its covenant relation to *Yahweh*: 'And the Lord said call his name "not my people" (לא עמי), for you are not my people and I am not your God.'[46] In spite of being chosen as the people of *Yahweh* and named with his Name, Israel has turned the name of *Yahweh* into *not-Yahweh*, יהוה into לא יהוה, so that the divine 'I am' has become for them 'not I am', לא אהיה. That is to say, the essential significance of the 'I am who I am / I will be who I will be' in the loving determination of the Lord *to be with and to act for* his people was deflected into its opposite, which allowed Israel to create and follow its own idols, and thereby destroy itself as the people of *Yahweh*, by detaching itself from the covenant- and community-constituting 'I am who I am, I will be who I will be.' Nevertheless the message of the book of Hosea is that in spite of the unfaithfulness of his people, God insists on holding on to them through the unswerving fidelity of his covenant love in order at last to heal them of their unfaithfulness and restore them to true fellowship with him in his love.[47]

I have been directing considerable attention to the Hebraic way of understanding the *I am* or Ἐγώ εἰμι of God to which the Early Church so often appealed in seeking to understand the Being or οὐσία of God, for it is very different from the static metaphysical notion of essence or substance found in the Greek philosophical tradition. The Being of God, known only in the fellowship created through his personal self-naming, self-affirming and self-giving to his people, is the living dynamic Being (ζῶσα καὶ ἐνεργητικὴ οὐσία) of God's redeeming presence *to* them, *with* them and *for* them. It is to be understood not simply in terms of the self-grounded Being of God, but as *the Being of God for others* with whom he seeks and creates fellowship, although that is to be regarded as flowing freely from the ground and will of his own transcendent Self-Being. While the Being of God is not to be understood as constituted by his relation to others, that free outward flowing of his Being in gratuitous love toward and for others reveals to us something of the inmost nature of God's Being, as at once transcendent and immanent – God in the highest and God with us and for us, the divine *ousia* being understood as *parousia*

[44] Deut. 4.37; 7.6ff; 10.15, etc.
[45] Hos. 1.1ff. I owe this point to John Mackenna, physicist and Hebraist, Pasadena, California.
[46] Hos. 1.9. Cf. Ps. 50.21: 'Because I was silent you likened the existence of *Yahweh* to your own.'
[47] Cf. Rom. 9.25–26, where this is applied also to Gentiles.

and the divine *parousia* being understood as *ousia*. Hence it may be said that the Being of God is to be understood as essentially *personal, dynamic and relational Being*. The real meaning of the Being or *I am* of God becomes clear in the two-way fellowship he freely establishes with his people as their Lord and Saviour, for it has to do with the saving will or self-determination of God in his love and grace to be with them as their God as well as his determination of them to be with him as his redeemed children.

The Being of God is to be understood, therefore, as living and dynamic Being, fellowship-creating or communion-constituting Being, but if it is communion-constituting Being toward us it is surely to be understood also as ever-living, ever-dynamic *Communion* (κοινωνία) in the Godhead. By his very Nature he is a Communion in himself,[48] which is the ground in the Being of God for his communion with his people. Hence God's Being, as J. B. Torrance has expressed it, is his Being-in-Communion.[49] This is surely an essential aspect of God's self-revealing and self-naming as *I am* proclaimed in the Old Testament which was appropriated by Jesus Christ and identified with his own *I am* proclaimed to us in the Gospel of the saving love and grace of God the Father. The full significance of this 'I am' on the lips of Jesus ('I am the Light of the World', ' I am the bread of life', 'I am the Resurrection and the Life', 'I am the Vine', ' I am the Way, the Truth and the Life', 'I am with you', etc.) becomes disclosed in what Jesus said to his disciples, 'I am in the Father and the Father is in me,'[50] for he thereby showed them that his own 'I am' is grounded in the indwelling of the Father and the Son in one another, in the eternal Communion which belongs to the inner Life of God as Father, Son and Holy Spirit. And so, as St John reports, Jesus prayed that the Father would give to the disciples the Holy Spirit who proceeds from the Father and is given in the name of the Son, and he prayed that the disciples themselves might be made perfect (or consecrated) in one as the Father and the Son are one.[51] Although the specific concept of 'person' and of the 'personal' had not yet arisen, the coupling of the 'I am' of *Yahweh* and the 'I am' of our Lord together gave rise, as we have seen, during the formulation of the doctrine of the Trinity, to an onto-relational and fully personal conception of the Being of God, and indeed to the understanding of the Being of God as Communion, for the three divine Persons in their Communion with one another *are* the Triune Being of God, and there is no other God but he who is Father, Son and Holy Spirit.

The communion-constituting activity of the divine *ousia* and its source in the mutual dwelling of the Father and the Son in one another, together with the oneness

---

[48] G. A. F. Knight relates this to the mysterious unity in diversity and diversity in unity which he finds in the Old Testament statements about God. *A Biblical Approach to the Doctrine of the Trinity* (Edinburgh, 1953), pp. 11ff & 28. Certainly the intensive plural of the words used so frequently throughout the Old Testament Scriptures for 'God' and 'Lord', *Elohim* and *Adonai*, seems to point in this direction. Cf. also Hilary's interpretation of Isa. 44.6: 'I am the first God and I am the last God, and beside me there is no God.' *De synodis*, 38 & 56.

[49] James B. Torrance, 'Contemplating the Trinitarian Mystery of Christ', in *Alive to God. Studies in Spirituality, Presented to James Houston*, ed. J. I. Packer and L. Wilkinson (Downers Grove, Illinois, 1992), p. 141f.

[50] John 14.10.

[51] John 14.10f, 20, and 17.21ff.

between the 'I am' of *Yahweh* and the 'I am' of the Lord Jesus, tell us that the Being of God is not undifferentiated in his oneness, but comprises a Triunity of relations internal to the Godhead. As Athanasius discerned, this was already evident in the Nicene concept of the *homoousion* which implied a distinction as well as a oneness in being between the Son and the Father, and, as he and Gregory Nazianzen also showed, between the Holy Spirit and the Father and the Son as well. The *homoousion*, with its rejection of any notion of undifferentiated or of partitive relations between the three divine Persons or ὑποστάσεις, carried with it the conception of eternal distinctions and internal relations in the Godhead wholly and mutually interpenetrating one another in the one identical Being of the Father, the Son, and the Holy Spirit.

How then are we to understand the *one Being, three Persons*, (μία οὐσία, τρεῖς ὑποστάσεις) of the Holy Trinity? It certainly means that the οὐσία or Being of God cannot be understood in a generic sense as seems implied in some statements of the Cappadocian theologians to the effect that the *ousia* has the same relation to the *hypostasis* as the general or the common to the particular, with recourse to the dangerous analogy of three different people having a common nature.[52] The absolute identity of being (ἡ ταυτότης τῆς οὐσίας) between the Father, the Son, and the Holy Spirit promulgated at Nicaea, rules that out entirely, but it does not rule out the idea that internal differentiation characterises the one Being of God in the form of an eternal Communion in Being between the three divine Persons. And that is surely how we are to think of the *one Being, three Persons* of the Holy Trinity:

> not as three disparate hypostases estranged from one another, alienated in being, and individually separated from one another like created things...
> but as a Holy Trinity, not Trinity in name only, but really existing and subsisting, a Father really existing and subsisting, and a Son really existing and subsisting, and a Holy Spirit really existing and subsisting.[53]

It was when the concept of the *homoousion* was resolutely applied to the understanding of the Holy Spirit, as well of the Son, by St Athanasius in his epoch-making *Letters on the Holy Spirit to Serapion*, that the doctrine of the Holy Trinity was brought to its full measure in respect of the mutual inexisting, coindwelling and coactivity of the three Divine Persons who are completely homoousial with one another and have in common the one indivisible Being of the Godhead. It is only through the Communion of the Spirit, he insisted, that we may have union and communion with the Father and the Son, for God *is* Spirit: the *Communion* of the Holy Spirit belongs to the mutual relation between the Father and the Son.[54]

[52] For references see *The Trinitarian Faith*, pp. 236f and 313ff.
[53] See Athanasius, *Ad Antiochenos*, 5, from the Confession of Sardica. The context makes clear that this was intended to convey a rejection of any generic conception of the relation between οὐσία and ὑπόστασις and any tritheistic conception of the three divine Persons as three ἀρχαί. Cf. Cyril of Alexandria, *De Trinitate, Dialogus*, II, PG 76, 753d, where he tells us that 'the term οὐσία (*ousia*) indicates to those who hear it neither genus, nor species, nor any additional qualification or differentia at all, but only being' - τὸ δὲ τῆς οὐσίας ὄνομα μήτε γένους, μήτε εἴδους, μήτε μὴν διαφορᾶς ἢ διαφορῶν ἐπεινηγμένων, ὑποφανεῖ τοῖς ἀκρουμένοις τὸ σύμπαν οὐδέν, πλὴν ὅτε μόνον οὐσία .
[54] Athanasius, *Ad Serapionem*, especially 1.20, 31; 3.5-7.

This Athanasian teaching, together with the agreed formulation, 'one Being, three Persons',[55] was taken up and developed by Epiphanius, the Jewish Christian Bishop of Salamis, who with a distinctly Hebraic slant linked together the *I am* (or Ἐγώ εἰμι) of the Lord God with his one Being, and with the help of the Nicene *homoousios* thought out the coinherent 'enhypostatic' relations of the three Divine Persons which they cannot but have with one another, for one Person cannot be *homoousios* with himself.[56] Moreover he understood the *homoousion* to apply not only to each Person but to the inner relations of the Trinity as a whole, and thereby deepened the conception of the coinherence of the Father, Son and Holy Spirit in their enhypostatic relations with one another. In this context he spoke of the Holy Spirit as 'in the midst (ἐν μέσῳ) of the Father and the Son', or as 'the bond of the Trinity (σύνδεσμος τῆς Τριάδος)'.[57] In other words, as the Spirit of the Father and the Spirit of the Son, and yet as personally distinct from them, the Holy Spirit is to be understood in his oneness in Being and coequality with the Father and the Son as being in himself the homoousial Communion of the Father and the Son with one another.

It was with Basil's celebrated book *On the Holy Spirit* that the conception of the Trinity as κοινωνία or Communion was given prominence. While he was strangely hesitant in speaking of the Holy Spirit as *homoousios* with the Father and the Son, he held in accordance with the liturgy of the Church that the Spirit is glorified and adored equally with the Father and the Son in the indivisible oneness of the Holy Trinity. While the Father, Son and Holy Spirit are hypostatically or personally distinct they are inseparably united in the 'I am' of God, in the uncompounded Nature and Communion of the Godhead, and in one three-fold activity toward the world created through them and sustained by them.[58] Moreover he thought of 'the Spirit as living Being (οὐσία ζῶσα), Lord of sanctification, from which his kinship (οἰκειότης) with God becomes disclosed, while his ineffable mode of existence is preserved (τοῦ δὲ τρόπου τῆς ὑπάρξεως ἀρρήτου φυλασσομένου).'[59] If God *is* Spirit, if Spirit is the specific Nature of God's living Being (ζῶσα οὐσία), whether as Father, Son or Holy Spirit, and if, in St Basil's words, 'the Spirit is glorified through his Communion with the Father and Son (διὰ τῆς πρὸς Πατέρα καὶ Υἱὸν κοινωνίας)', then the Holy Spirit himself is to be thought of as the ever-living two-way Communion between the Father and the Son in which he is no less fully God than the Father and the Son. Through sharing equally in the one living Being of God, in an essentially *spiritual and onto-relational way*, the Father, the Son and the Holy Spirit form and constitute together in their distinctive

[55] Athanasius, *Ad Antiochenos*, 6; *In illud, omnia*, 6; *Expositio fidei*, 2; Basil, *De Spiritu Sancto*, 7; *Epistulae*, 52, 69, 125, 214, 230, 258; Gregory Nazianzen, *Orationes*, 21.35; 31.7–16; 43.40; Epiphanius, *Anchoratus*, 81; *Haereses*, 73.16, 34.
[56] Epiphanius, *Anchoratus*, 6, 8; *Haereses*, 57,10; 62.3–8; 63.7; 65.12–8, etc.
[57] Epiphanius, *Anchoratus*, 4.7f, 10; *Haereses*, 62.4; 74.11. Gregory Nazianzen also spoke of the Holy Spirit as 'between (μέσον)' the Son and the Father, the Unbegotten and the Begotten of God, *Orationes*, 31.8.
[58] Basil, *De Spiritu Sancto*, 37–47.
[59] Basil, *De Spiritu Sancto*, 46; *Contra Sabellianos*, 6.

properties in relation to one another the natural Communion (ἡ κατὰ φύσιν κοινωνία) and indivisible Unity of the Holy Trinity. And so St Basil emphatically declared, 'Their oneness consists in the Communion of the Godhead.'[60] This is precisely what 'One Being, Three Persons' advocated by the Post-Nicene Fathers intends, and indeed succinctly expresses in a way that excludes any unipersonal view of God or any tritheistic conception of the Holy Trinity.[61]

It was Gregory Nazianzen, especially in his famous 'Five Theological Orations' and his Presidential Oration delivered at the Council of Constantinople in 381, who, following his theological hero Athanasius,[62] provided Christian theology with the most influential teaching about the Holy Trinity. Unlike Basil he had no hesitation in applying the *homoousion* to the Holy Spirit,[63] and would have nothing do with his fellow Cappadocians' description of the divine Persons as 'modes of Being' (τρόποι ὑπάρξεως). Moreover, he dissociated himself from the element of subordinationism or 'degrees of Deity' implied in the way they related the Son and the Spirit to the Father as the 'Principle' (ἀρχή) or 'Cause' (αἰτία) of their Deity.[64] Through his alternative conception of the divine Persons as timeless, beginningless, uncaused relations subsisting ineffably in the Blessed and Adorable Trinity he gave us the most powerful account of the inseparable oneness of the divine Persons, and indeed the identity between the one ever living Being of God and the three coequal divine Persons – citations from which were given at the beginning of this chapter.[65]

We now return to the fact that we apprehend God's trinitarian self-revelation from below and from above holistically through a unifying act of cognition. This has far-reaching implications, as we have seen, for the formulation of the doctrine of the Holy Trinity and the formation of the theological terms it deploys. It rules out any speculative or metaphysical approach through logico-deductive operations for one governed by the Nature of God as he is made known to us through the incarnation of his Son and the emission of his Spirit. It is, to borrow words from Irenaeus, through personal union and communion (ἕνωσις καὶ κοινωνία) with Christ and in the Spirit that our minds become adapted to a knowing of God in accordance with his Triune Nature as Father, Son and Holy Spirit. It is in the course of the two-way activity of God's revelation of himself through himself from below and from above, in the unity of his economic and ontological self-communication as the undivided and ever-blessed Trinity, that our theological concepts and terms are generated out of ordinary human forms of thought and speech. Thus while the early theologians of the Church, like the evangelists and the apostles, made considerable use of Greek terms and ideas in seeking to articulate the conceptual content of the Gospel, they reshaped them in a very basic way

---

[60] Basil, *De Spiritu Sancto*, 45: ἐν τῇ κοινωνίᾳ τῆς Θεότητός ἐστιν ἡ ἕνωσις.
[61] Refer again to Athanasius, *Ad Antiochenos*, 5–6.
[62] See Gregory Nazianzen's *Oration On the Great Athanasius, Orationes*, 21.
[63] See for example Gregory Nazianzen, *Orationes*, 31.10.
[64] Gregory Nazianzen, *Orationes*, 29.15; 40.43.
[65] See my account of 'The Doctrine of the Holy Trinity in Gregory Nazianzen and John Calvin', reprinted from *Sobornost*, vol. 12.1 (London, 1990) in *Trinitarian Perspectives. Toward Doctrinal Agreement* (Edinburgh, 1994), ch. 2, pp. 21ff.

under the impact of the Holy Scripture. As we have seen, 'being', 'word', 'act', and other common words in Greek patristic theology came to mean something very different from what they meant in Platonic, Aristotelian, or Stoic thought: they are in fact radically 'un-Greek'. Hence, far from Nicene theology resulting from a Hellenisation of biblical Christianity, there took place in it a Christian recasting of familiar Hellenic thought-forms in order to make them vehicles of the saving truth of the Gospel, and to enable the Church to clarify and give consistent expression to the trinitarian structure inherent in evangelical knowledge of God. It was above all in their service to the adoration and apprehension of the Holy Trinity in the Church that the thought-forms appropriated from Greek culture received their indelible stamp. It was thus that godliness and accuracy, worship and precision, were allied inseparably together in the theological activity of the bishops and theologians who gave us the Nicene-Constantinopolitan Confession of Faith upon which all Christendom has rested ever since.

Of decisive importance for our concern in this chapter is the way in which the Greek terms *ousia* and *hypostasis* used at the Council of Nicaea in AD 325 were shaped and developed toward the formulation of the μία οὐσία, τρεῖς ὑποστάσεις, or *one Being, three Persons*, agreed at the Council of Alexandria in 362, and finalised at the Council of Constantinople in 381. We have looked in detail at the community-constituting activity of God's self-revelation to Israel as 'I am who I am / I will be who I will be' and the effect of that in the understanding of the biblical conception of God's Being as God determining himself for fellowship with his people. And we related that to the community-constituting activity of God's concrete self-revelation in Jesus Christ as the incarnate 'I am' of God, through whom and the Holy Spirit we have access to knowledge of God the Father, the Son and the Holy Spirit both as he is in communion with us and as he is in his intra-trinitarian relations as Father, Son and Holy Spirit. The effect of this was to disclose the nature of God's Being as a Communion of divine Persons, who in and through their distinctive properties and their indivisible relations with and for one another are the triune Being of God. This brings us to the point where we must consider more specifically the relation of God's one Being to the three divine Persons.

In the original text of the Creed of Nicaea there was added a statement to reinforce the clause that the second Person of the Trinity was begotten from the Being of the Father (ἐκ τῆς οὐσίας τοῦ Πατρός) by way of rejecting the Arian allegation that he was from another being (ἐξ ἑτέρας ὑποστάσεως ἢ οὐσίας) than the Being of the Father. In it the two words commonly signifying being, *hypostasis* and *ousia*, were used together in a cognate way, carrying an ambiguity which gave rise in some quarters to misinterpretation. In certain contexts Athanasius himself when speaking of the Being of God used *ousia* in its ordinary sense as that which is and subsists by itself, which in this use was more or less equivalent to *hypostasis*.[66] His variational handling of the words at these points was in line with the requirement of his semantic principle. Here as elsewhere he retained his freedom to vary the

[66] Athanasius, *Contra Arianos*, 1.11; 2.10; 3.63; *De decretis*, 22.27; *De synodis*, 35, 41; *Ad Afros*, 4.8; *Ad Serapionem*, 2.5.

sense of these words in accordance with the nature of the realities which they were intended to signify so that they might be allowed to show through the language being used. That is why Athanasius hesitated to commit himself to a fixed formalisation of the terms οὐσία and ὑπόστασις for all contexts which would have gone against his conviction that it is not the words themselves that mattered so much as the truths of divine revelation which they were meant to serve and indicate.

However, it became evident that some people treated these terms as regular equivalents in such a way as to imply that the three divine Persons or ὑποστάσεις are separate divine Beings or οὐσίαι, thereby advocating a tritheist heresy. A change clearly had to be made, as the Cappadocian theologians argued, in drawing a clear distinction betwee *ousia* and *hypostasis* in order to bring more sharply into focus the Persons of the Father, the Son and the Holy Spirit, but in such a way as to avoid the twin errors of tritheism and modalism, although that led, but not with Gregory Nazianzen, to a withdrawal from the concrete personal sense of οὐσία in Nicene and Athanasian theology. In order to avoid error, however, Athanasius agreed that *ousia* in the strict sense should be used properly of the one Being of God, while *hypostasis* should be used to speak strictly of the distinct objective reality of each of the three divine Persons in their onto-relations with one another. Thus when associated with God's self-revelation as the Father, the Son and the Holy Spirit, *ousia* was used, in distinction from *hypostasis*, to signify the one eternal Being of God in the indivisible reality and fullness of his intrinsic coinherent personal relations as the Holy Trinity. Far from being an abstract or general notion, therefore, *ousia* applied to God had an intensely personal and concrete meaning, as was the case in the Nicene conception of the relation between Jesus Christ and God Father. This is very clear in Athanasius' rather distinctive conceptions of the Word and Act of God inhering in his Being,[67] for they indicate that God is as fully personal in his ultimate Being as he is in his *self*-revealing, *self*-affirming and *self*-giving to us through the Son and in the Spirit. What God is toward us in the Word and Activity of Christ and the Spirit he is in his ultimate Being or οὐσία from which, or rather from whom, they issue and to whom they direct us. That is to say, the one Being of God is intrinsically personal, and indeed as intensely personal as God is in the manifestation of himself to us in the Gospel as Father, Son and Holy Spirit.[68]

It was this understanding of the one Being of God that Athanasius upheld in his acceptance with the Cappadocians of the formula *one Being, three Persons*, μία οὐσία, τρεῖς ὑποστάσεις. As he understood it, this was already implied in the concept of the *homoousion*, when taken strictly, for while on the one hand it implied a distinction between the Persons of the Son and the Father and the Holy Spirit, on the other hand it implied an indivisible and continuous relation of personal being between them as well, so that the Being of the Godhead was recognised as whole and complete not in the Father alone, but also in the Son and in the Spirit.[69]

---

[67] Cf. here again Athanasius' conception of the *enousios logos* and *enousios energeia*, *De synodis*, 34, 41; *Contra Arianos*, 2.2; 4.1; *Ad Antiochenos*, 5.

[68] Athanasius, *Expositio fidei*, 1–4; *In illud, omnia*, 1–6; *Contra Arianos*, 3.1ff.

[69] Athanasius, *De decretis*, 16ff, 22ff; *Ad episcopos*, 17f; *Contra Arianos*, 1.16, 28; 2.33; 3.1ff; *Ad Afros*, 4f. See also Gregory Nazianzen, *Orationes*, 14–16.

The *homoousion* of the Son and the Spirit stood for the indivisible unity of the Being of the Godhead in three co-equal Persons – hence Athanasius' constant emphasis upon the simple, uncompounded and undivided nature of the Being of God, in sharp opposition to the Arian separation of the Son from the Father, and to the semi-Arian separation of the Spirit from the Godhead.[70] For Athanasius, then, *ousia* refers to the Being of God in the inner reality and unity of his coinherent trinitarian relations. It was in entire consistency with this view that he spoke of the three distinct but undivided Persons, Subsistences or ὑποστάσεις in the one Being of God – although, as we have seen, he preferred to use verbs rather than nouns to speak of this, for the three divine Persons are inseparably interrelated in being and act through a mutual indwelling and a mutual movement toward and for one another in the homoousial Communion of the Holy Trinity which they constitute.

It should now be clear that owing to the concept of the Nicene *homoousion* a profound reconstruction in the basic concepts of Greek thought took place. On the one hand, it put an end to the menace of the dualist structure of thought that in different ways lay behind the modalist and tritheist conceptions of God, and on the other hand it related the economic Trinity to the ontological Trinity in such a dynamic and unifying way that a radical change was brought about in the understanding of *ousia* and *hypostasis* as theological terms. Through their use the conceptual content of the Gospel and the redemptive import of the Holy Trinity could be given consistent exposition and be brought along with the liturgy to bear effectively on the daily life of the faithful. The doctrine of the *homoousion* was as decisive as it was revolutionary: it expressed the evangelical truth that what God is toward us and has freely done for us in his love and grace, and continues to do in the midst of us through his Word and Spirit, he really is *in himself,* and that he really is *in the internal relations and personal properties* of his transcendent Being as the Holy Trinity the very same Father Son, and Holy Spirit, that he is in his revealing and saving activity in time and space toward mankind, and ever will be.

In precise theological usage *ousia* now refers to 'being' not simply as that which is but as what it is in respect of its internal reality, while *hypostasis* refers to 'being' not just in its independent subsistence but in its objective otherness. This is a distinction that has been expressed by G. L. Prestige, not in accordance with the relation between the general and the particular, so much as in accordance with the relation between subject and object. According to him, *ousia* denotes being in its 'inward reference', while *hypostasis* denotes being in its 'outward reference'.[71] Again:

> When the stumbling block had been cleared away by Athanasius, the formula of three hypostaseis and one ousia (substance) was generally accepted. Ousia also means 'object', but with a difference. While hypostasis lays stress on concrete independence, ousia lays it on intrinsic constitution. Hypostasis means 'a reality *ad alios*', ousia 'a reality *in se*'; the one word denotes God as

---

[70] Athanasius, *Contra Arianos,* 1.15, 28: 2.34, 38; 3.3f, 15, 36; 4.2; *De decretis,* 11; *De synodis,* 34f; *Ad Serapionem,* 1.2f, 14, 28; 2.2.
[71] G. L. Prestige, *Fathers and Heretics* (London, 1954), p. 88.

manifest, the other connotes God's being. Athanasius taught that in God one and the same identical 'substance' or object, without any division, substitution or differentiation of content, is permanently presented in three distinct objective forms. It is one in content and consciousness, but three to contact and apprehension. Humanly speaking, this is a paradox. But it has the justification that any human thought about the infinite must of necessity be paradoxical. It does not pretend to be the formula by which God veritably lives, but it does provide a concept by which he can be presented to human understanding, according to its capacity to receive a measure of genuine enlightenment.[72]

The main point that should be taken from this account is that while both *ousia* and *hypostasis* describe 'being' as such, in the trinitarian formulation 'one Being, three Persons', Being or οὐσία is being considered in its internal relations, and Person or ὑπόστασις is being considered in its otherness, i.e. in the objective relations between the Persons. In the case of the Father, this would amount to a distinction between the Father considered absolutely, as he is in himself, and the Father considered relatively to the Son, although of course it is one and the same Fatherly Being that is being considered absolutely *in se* as *ousia* and relatively *ad alium* as *hypostasis*. We shall consider the three divine Persons relatively or in relation to one another in the following chapter with the help of Gregory Nazianzen's concept of relations (σχέσεις), but here the focus of our thought has been on the one Being of God which all three divine Persons have in common: *ousia* is, in fact, identical with the personal Being or intrinsic Communion that the one God is in himself.

However, there is a fundamental and very important sense, as we have seen, in which we must think also of the one Being of God, not as isolated in himself (*in se*), but as *Being for others (ad alios)*, and this means that we must think of his Being for others as grounded in the transcendent freedom of his own Being. While we live, and move and have our being in God, God lives and moves and has his Being *for us* as well as for himself. For God to *be*, is to be for himself in himself, that is, for the three Divine Persons which God is to be *for one another* in the onto-personal relations of the Holy Trinity. As such God's Being is, so to speak, inherently altruistic, *Being for others, Being who loves*.

This is what we learn from the Old Testament revelation of God as the God who freely created the world and human beings within it for personal relations with himself, who in his redeeming purpose for all mankind made a covenant with the people of Israel for fellowship with himself which he backed up by his own Being: 'I am the Lord.' In this covenant the Lord promised to keep faith with his people even when they were unfaithful – he refused to retract his promises or abandon his purpose for them. 'I have loved you with an everlasting love; therefore have I continued my faithfulness toward you.'[73] As we noted earlier in this chapter,

---

[72] G. L. Prestige, *God in Patristic Thought* (London, 1952), p. xxix. See also pp. 168ff & 188. For Prestige's word 'object' in this citation I would prefer the word 'reality'.

[73] Jer. 31.3.

who God is and what the nature of his Being is, become disclosed only within a fellowship with God grounded in his personal self-naming, self-affirming and self-giving to Israel. The Being of God is the living dynamic Being of *Yahweh* who has set his Name upon his people and who blesses them with his holy and redeeming Presence. It is to be understood not simply in terms of the self-grounded Being of God, but as the Being of God *for others* with whom he seeks and creates communion, although that is to be regarded, not as something necessary for his existence as God, but as flowing freely from the ground and will of his transcendent Self-being.

The Being of God is the personal, living and active Being, fellowship-seeking and communion-constituting Being, but if it is fellowship-seeking and communion-constituting toward his human children, it is so as the fruit among men of the ever-living and productive Communion which God's Being is *ad intra*. While it is not to be regarded as constituted or determined in any way by God's relation to others, any more than God himself is, the outward flowing of his Being freely in love toward and for others reveals the innermost nature of God's Being, as at once transcendent and immanent: God in the highest and God with us. What God is in his *parousia* with us he is in his *ousia* in the highest, and what he is in his *parousia* with himself he is in his *ousia* among us. Thus the real meaning of the Being or the 'I am / I will be' of God for us is conditioned by the two-way fellowship which he freely establishes with us as our Saviour, for it has to do with the saving self-determination of God in his love and grace to be with us as our God as well as his determination of us to be with him as his redeemed children.

This is what we learn above all from the message of the Gospel in the New Testament revelation of God who so loved the world that he gave his only-begotten Son to be our Saviour. The Gospel tells us that God does not choose to live for himself alone, for he has become man in order to seek and save the lost, to bring human beings into reconciling relation with himself and to share his own divine fellowship with them. And so we learn that the one Being of God *is* the Being of the Father who did not spare his only Son but freely gave him up in atoning sacrifice for us, and *is* the Being of the Son who loved us and gave himself for us, and *is* the Being of the Holy Spirit who for our sakes brings us through himself into communion with the Father and the Son. God's whole Being as three divine Persons is his Being for others, but to his Being for others beyond himself, his Being with us in our human existence in time and space, there corresponds his Being for others within himself, for that is the eternal ground in God for what he is and promises in the Gospel to be for others beyond himself.

The eternal ground in God from which there flows his communion-seeking love and grace toward us, is the Communion which the Father, Son and Holy Spirit have among themselves, and, let it be repeated, really are. In the Holy Trinity himself, in the mutual indwelling of the three divine Persons, each Person is who he is as Father, Son, or Holy Spirit, in hypostatic and homoousial relation to the Others, and indeed through their one Being, in being who he is for the Others. The Father is not properly (κυρίως) Father apart from the Son and the Spirit, and the Son is not properly Son apart from the Father and the Spirit, and the Spirit is not properly Spirit apart from the Father and the Son, for by their individual characteristics or distinctive properties as Father, Son and Holy Spirit, they exist in and through one Another and belong to and ever live for each Other. Each Person is intrinsically who he is for the other two. They coinhere in one Another by virtue of their one Being for one Another and by virtue of the dynamic Communion which they constitute in their belonging to one Another. Hence in establishing communion with us through his Son and in his Spirit God wants us to participate in this living Communion which as Father, Son and Holy Spirit he eternally is, and it is thus that the nature of his divine Being is disclosed to us as Communion, οὐσία as κοινωνία.

The one triune Being of God is to be thought of, then, as essentially and intrinsically a mutual movement of loving self-communication between the Father, the Son and the Holy Spirit, an intensely personal Communion, an ever-living ever-loving Being, the *Being for Others* which the three divine Persons have in common. To say that God is intensely or inherently personal does not mean, of course, that he is *a* Person in the relational sense of the three particular divine Persons in their otherness or objective relations to one another, but rather that God is a fullness of personal Being within himself, just as he is full of Love within himself. He is not less personal, any more than he is less loving, in his one indivisible Being as whole God (ὅλος Θεός, Athanasius' expression) than he is in each Person who is true God of true God and is in himself as the Son or the Spirit whole God (ὅλος Θεός) as well as the Father. He is perfectly One in Three and Three in One. That is the one transcendent personal Being of God who is the creative source of the personal communion which in his outgoing love for others he wants to establish between himself and us. Due to its inherently reciprocal nature, however, we cannot have communion with the Father, or with the Son, or with the Holy Spirit, without having communion with all three, for they are who they are precisely as one indivisible Being, three inseparable Persons / three inseparable Persons, one indivisible Being.

We must remind ourselves again of the oneness between the majestic 'I am' of *Yahweh*, and the gracious 'I am' of the Lord Jesus, between the Being of God and the Being of Christ. 'No one has ever seen God; the only Son who is in the bosom of the Father has made him known.'[74] Everything hinges, then, upon the ontological and dynamic oneness between the economic Trinity and the ontological Trinity. It is through the loving, saving self-revelation of God to us in his incarnate Son, in the unity of his Person, Word, and Work, that the glory and nature of the One Being of God become disclosed to us. It is in seeing Jesus that we see the Father, and it is the Being of Jesus, the incarnate Love of God, who defines for us the Being of God, the one dynamic, personal Being which the Father, the Son and the Holy Spirit have in common, and which each of them equally and perfectly is. Since the one Being is three Persons, and God *is* Love, and by its nature love involves reciprocal personal relations, we must go on to consider rather fully the reciprocal perichoretic relations between the Persons of the Father, the Son and the Holy Spirit which are the onto-relations of their mutual love for one another. This movement of our thought is designated in the following chapter as 'Three Persons,

---

[74] John 1.18.

One Being', corresponding to the 'One Being, Three Persons' of this chapter, but there too we shall be concerned with the one Being of God as well as with the three Persons, for the three Persons constitute the Communion which the one Being of God is.

As we close this chapter let us recall, like St Basil in his *De Spiritu Sancto*, the traditional doxologies of the Church which are uniformly trinitarian, and which are expressed in such a way that there is no division in the adoration and worship and glory offered to the Father, the Son and the Holy Spirit, for they are homogeneous and indivisible in their Being and Nature and are worshipped and glorified together as One God. While each divine Person is Lord and each is God, there are not three Lords or three Gods; while Father, Son and Holy Spirit are three active Persons, they are not worshipped as a trio of divine Objects or Beings, but as intrinsically and eternally triune. They are worshipped and glorified as One, for each of them and all of them together are accorded the same glory, the same honour, and the same worship.[75]

The principle involved here later came to be known as *lex orandi, lex credendi*, but it had a powerful place in the thought of the apostolic and early Catholic Church, as we see it reflected in the writings of Origen, Athanasius, Hilary, Cyril of Jerusalem and Cyril of Alexandria, as well as Basil and in the eucharistic liturgy attributed to him: it is reverence, adoration and worship that shape and determine belief. However, the reverse is also true, *lex credendi, lex orandi*, for true belief informs worship – belief and worship are inextricably intertwined, as in the theological use of *doxologia*, which refers both to worship and doctrine.[76] This is supremely evident in the early liturgies of the Church and their trinitarian character, as in the *Gloria in excelsis*, and the *Gloria Patri*, and in the doxologies which were appended to the Psalms during the fourth century.[77] It is not, however, the general implications of this principle that concerns us at the moment, so much as the fact that our worship of the Father, the Son and the Holy Spirit, worship of the Father, through the Son and in the Holy Spirit, is the worship of *one* Lord God. It is an adoration that will not allow us when we pray specifically to the Father, or to the Son or to the Holy Spirit, to divide our prayer between them, or to direct our devotion separately to the three Persons, for in worshipping and praying to each Person we worship and pray to the whole undivided Godhead, *one Being, three Persons.*

As we have noted several times, belief in the Holy Trinity reinforces and deepens belief in the Unity, but this is due in large measure to the unifying nature of the worship that the Father, the Son and the Holy Spirit in their indivisible oneness call forth from us. Our belief in the one Being of God is not something that we

---

[75] Basil, *De Spiritu Sancto*, 3, 13, 16f, 45f, 58, 63f, 71f.

[76] Thus, for example, Epiphanius declared that the Scriptures acknowledge 'the same Godhead in Trinity and the same Trinity in one Godhead, and glorify the Father in the Son and the Son in the Father with the Holy Spirit, one Sanctity, one Worship, one Deity, one Glory.' *Ancoratus*, 24.

[77] Following this Nicene practice Trinitarian doxologies were appended to the Psalms in the Scottish Reformation, 'The Psalmes of David' published with *John Knox's Liturgy* (1560–1638); and see Robert Edward, *The Doxology Approven, or The Singing Glory to the Father, Son and Holy Ghost, in the worship of God* (Edinburgh, 1683 and 1731).

think out for ourselves through reflecting on the perichoretic relations and properties of the three divine Persons with one another or on their common Nature. Worship is primarily the act of God upon us and arises in us as an echo of his own transcendent Nature which we offer back to the Father through the Son and in the Spirit, and takes place as in the Spirit we are given to share through Christ in the inter-personal Communion of love and self-giving in the Life of God.[78] It arises compulsively in our spirits under the impact of the one Lord God upon our consciousness and faith, which we do not trace to a coordination of three distributed divine effects upon our souls. This does not mean that the personal distinctions between the Father, the Son and the Holy Spirit are blurred in our minds, but that while they remain distinct in our thought they arise as distinctions discerned within the one undivided whole of God's revelation of himself through himself to us. The Lord our God is one Lord, and we cannot but worship him with all our heart, and with all our soul and with all our mind.[79]

It is understandable, therefore, that Didymus the Blind of Alexandria, while resolutely affirming *one Being three Persons*, should nevertheless have said that the three divine Persons of the Holy Trinity are to be heard, known, worshipped and glorified 'as one Person (πρόσωπον)'.[80] Gregory Nazianzen made the same point, rather paradoxically but more circumspectly, when with reference to the Names of the Father, the Son and the Holy Spirit, he pointed out that in our worship we distinguish them before conjoining them, and conjoin them before distinguishing them, but in so doing we do not regard the Three as one Person – they are neither impersonal nor one in hypostasis – but we do regard the Three as one Reality.

They are One not in hypostasis but in Godhead, Unity worshipped in Trinity and Trinity summed up in Unity, all adorable, all royal, one in sovereignty, one in glory, beyond the cosmos, beyond time, uncreated, invisible, impalpable, unbounded, completely incomparable and known only to himself, but to us equally venerable and adorable, dwelling Alone in the Holy of Holies.[81] *One Being, three Persons.*

---

[78] This is strongly emphasisd by James. B. Torrance who points out that properly speaking worship is not what we do but what Christ does, and as such is essentially trinitarian in character. 'Worship is rather the gift of participating through the Spirit in the (incarnate) Son's communication with the Father – the gift of participating, in union with Christ, in what *he* has done for us once for all by his self-offering to the Father in his life and death on the cross, and what *he* is continuing to do for us in the presence of the Father, and in his mission from the Father to the world.' 'Contemplating the Trinitarian Mystery', op. cit., p. 142.

[79] Matt. 22.37.

[80] Didymus, *De Trinitate*, 2.36. This was not meant, of course, in any unipersonalist Sabellian way, as *mia hypostasis*. See also Cyril of Alexandria, *In Joannis Evangelium*, 15.1.

[81] Gregory Nazianzen, *Orationes*, 6.22; cf. 38.8; 45.4 where he refers to the Holy Trinity as 'the Holy of Holies' the innermost Sanctum of the divine Mystery hidden even from the seraphim who glorify the Lord God as 'Holy, Holy, Holy'.

6

Three Persons, One Being

'ONE Being, Three Persons', and 'Three Persons, One Being' are the obverse of one another, or the mirror image of one another. In the previous chapter we found that the one Being of God is to be understood in his interior relations as the Communion of the three divine Persons with one another: to the communion which God establishes with us in the incarnate economy of his redeeming and revealing acts in history there corresponds a transcendent Communion in himself. These may not be held apart, for while God may be known by us only out of himself, we may not have knowledge of him except at a point of access which is both in our creaturely existence and in God himself. This is precisely what we have in the incarnation, where God's self-revelation as Father takes place through his self-giving to us in Jesus Christ his Son and in the Holy Spirit who, as the Spirit of the Father and of the Son, constitutes with them the Communion of the Holy Trinity. In this chapter we focus attention more particularly on the Communion of the three divine Persons who in their perichoretic interrelations are the one Being of God. It is only in knowledge of the economic Trinity that by divine grace we have access within the space and time of our earthly existence to knowledge of the ontological Trinity, for what God has revealed of himself in his activity toward us and on our behalf as Father, Son and Holy Spirit he assures us that he really and eternally is in himself. He is in himself the content of his self-communication to us. Our knowledge of the economic Trinity, in the *ordo cognoscendi*, and our knowledge of the ontological Trinity, in the *ordo essendi*, may not be separated from one another, for they arise together, interpenetrate each other and regulate each other.

In looking at the biblical basis of our knowledge of the Trinity at an earlier point we considered various formulations in which there was evident an implicit trinitarian pattern, but it is worth recalling that mention of the Father, the Son and the Holy Spirit in the New Testament was not always made in the same order. The fact that each of the divine Persons could be mentioned first indicates that the order used did not detract from belief in their full equality. In the actual mission of the Church, however, in which the Gospel of God's saving activity was being proclaimed, the spotlight naturally fell on Jesus Christ himself, for it was through him as the one Mediator between God and man that human conceptions of God were critically transformed and Christian belief in God the

Father and in God the Holy Spirit became grounded. It was in line with this approach that in our consideration of the biblical frame of the doctrine of the Trinity we followed the evangelical or economic order presented in the benediction, 'the Grace of the Lord Jesus Christ and the Love of God and the Communion of the Holy Spirit'.

Now, however, without moving off the ground of that economic self-revelation of God through the Lord Jesus Christ his incarnate Son, we will follow the order given in the ordinance of Baptism in the Name of the Father, the Son and the Holy Spirit. In this dominical statement, which is of primary importance in the Church's formulation of the doctrine of the Holy Trinity, the Father comes first: it is to him that the Lord Jesus Christ directs us through himself as the Son of the Father. Moreover, although in the order of our knowing the Son comes first, in the order of God's triune Being it is the Father who comes first precisely in virtue of his being the Father of the Son. The relation of the Son and the Father is irreversible, for 'the Son is from the Father, not the Father from the Son'.[1] The Father comes first because he is the Father, although the Son is not less divine because he is the Son of the Father for there is no difference in Being or Nature between them. It is to be remembered, of course, that God the Father is not Father without the Son, for the Sonship of the Son belongs to the very Being of the Father and the Nature of his Fatherhood.

GOD THE ETERNAL FATHER

In the New Testament Scriptures and in the theology of the Early Church 'Father' was evidently used in a two-fold way, of God the heavenly Father as the Creator and Lord of all that is, and of the Father of our Lord Jesus Christ, although they were never thought of as separate from one another. This two-fold use is apparent in the words spoken by the crucified and risen Jesus to Mary on the morning of his resurrection: 'Go to my brethren, and say unto them, I ascend to my Father and your Father, to my God and your God.'[2] This implies a distinction, as Gregory Nyssen pointed out, between 'Father' as the unbegotten or unoriginate Source and Lord of all that is, and 'Father' as the Father of his only begotten Son through whose incarnation humanity is restored and united to God.[3] Thus with Athanasius, as we have seen, to name God Father in this way signifies his very Being as God the Creator, but this very Being is identified with the Father of Jesus Christ his Son.[4]

---

[1] Augustine, *De Trinitate*, 4.20.27.

[2] John 20.17.

[3] Gregory Nyssen, *Contra Eunomium*, 1.37f, where he shows that other names, e.g. 'emperor' with the double sense of 'masterless' and 'ruler over his subjects', may have two meanings with a mutual relation between them, but are not confined in their use to only one or other meaning. See also 2,8 and 13.1; and Hilary, *De Trinitate*, 2.6.

[4] Athanasius, *Contra Gentes*, 2 & 40; *De decretis*, 22; *De synodis*, 34–35; *Ad Afros*, 8.

This duality is found throughout the New Testament witness to Jesus Christ in respect of the Lord-Servant and the Father-Son relation in which in his self-designation as the Son of Man he fulfilled his incarnate ministry of revelation and salvation.

On the one hand, then, we think of God the Father as the eternal Creator and Lord of all being and existence, he to whom our Lord referred as 'the heavenly Father' and to whom he taught us to pray. He is the Father who cares for all his creatures in such a personal and detailed way that, as he taught in the sermon on the Mount, not a sparrow falls to the ground without him, the very hairs of our head are all numbered, and his divine provision for people's needs is extended equally to the just and the unjust. This fatherly conception of God was given definitive expression in the opening clause of the Nicene Creed, 'We believe in God the Father Almighty, the Maker of heaven and earth and of all things visible and invisible.' The Almighty is Father, and the Father is Almighty. There the omnipotence of the Creator, his power over all existents and realities whether visible or invisible, is not defined in some abstract metaphysical way, but is defined quite concretely with reference to God precisely as *Father* – it is as such that he is the one eternal self-grounded personal Being who is the Source and Lord of all that was, is and ever will be. Nevertheless, as the Father Almighty, God does not exist for himself alone. While he is the ungrudging creative Source of all being distinct from himself, he has given his creatures a reality and a rationality of their own in continuous dependence on himself but delights to maintain them throughout all time and space in unceasing relation to himself and his providential purpose for them. This means that God directs us in our knowledge of him not to some superessential realm beyond the space-time universe which he has brought into being out of nothing but to his unceasing interaction with us in the midst of our creaturely and historical existence where in his loving purpose he makes himself known to us as our God and Father. And this means that our knowledge of God the Father is through his revealing and reconciling activity in the incarnate *oikonomia* and *parousia* of his Word by whom all things that are made were made, the Word who was with God and was God, but who in the fulfilment of God's eternal purpose became flesh and dwelt among us full of grace and truth.

On the other hand, we think of God the Father as the Father of Jesus Christ our Lord and Saviour, for it is through his unique filial relation to the Father that the nature of the Father is revealed to us, Father precisely and peculiarly as Father of the Son, hence Father eternally in himself and irrespective of his being Creator. Fatherhood and Sonship belong inseparably together in the one eternal Being of God. It is as the Father of the Son that in his love God has freely condescended to be *our* Father, and to make us his sons and daughters by grace. It is this Son/Father, Father/Son relationship, that constitutes, along with the Holy Spirit, the inner ontological framework of the Gospel message, and it is by reference to it that all our knowledge of God the Father, undefined before, now becomes defined, so that all our prior conceptions of God and of his Fatherhood however reached are now critically sifted and replaced. As the eternal Father of his only begotten Son, God is the only one who is properly and really (κυρίως καὶ μόνον ἀληθῶς) Father, for when men are called fathers of their own children that is ultimately with respect to

God's eternal originating Fatherhood.[5] Apart from this relation to the eternal Fatherhood of God, all presentation of divine Fatherhood in the Gospel hangs in the air.

Our knowledge of God as Father and Creator, then, is derived from and regulated through the mutual relation of exclusive knowing between the Son and the Father, as Jesus indicated.

> I thank you, Father, Lord of heaven and earth, that you have hidden these things from the wise and understanding and revealed them unto babes; yes, Father, for such was your gracious will. All things have been delivered to me by my Father; and no one knows the Son except the Father, and no one knows the Father except the Son and anyone to whom the Son chooses to reveal him.[6]

This revelation of the eternal Father through his Son incarnate in our midst is nowhere more clear than in our Lord's high-priestly prayer which we are allowed through St John to overhear: 'Father ... I have finished the work which you gave me to do ... I have manifested your Name unto men.'[7]

With reference to this prayer of Jesus, Hilary of Poitiers argued that it was the primary purpose of the Son to enable us to know the one true God as *Father*. This was a theme to which he gave considerable theological reflection in view of the Nicene *homoousion* and what it implied for our two-fold belief in God the Father Almighty and in God the Son of the Father. 'All who have God for their Father through faith have him for Father through the same faith whereby we confess that Jesus Christ is the Son of God.'[8] Again: 'The very centre of saving faith is the belief not merely in God but in God as Father; not merely in Christ, but in Christ as the Son of God; in him, not as a creature, but as God the Creator, born of God.'[9] 'The work which the Lord came to do was not to enable you to recognise the omnipotence of God as Creator of all things, but to enable you to know him as the Father of the Son who addresses you ... The end and aim of this revelation of the Son is that you should know the Father ... Remember that the revelation is not of the Father manifested as God, but of God manifested as the Father.'[10]

It is only in the light of the unsparing self-giving and the intimate self-revelation of God to us in Jesus Christ his beloved Son that we come to know the Nature of God the Father as Love, the transcendent Love with which he loves himself and which is the inner movement of his eternal Being, the Love with which he loves the Son and the Son loves the Father, out of which his love flows freely and unstintingly toward us. We do not think of God as the eternal Being who also loves, but of God's very Being as Being who loves and of God as he who is Love. It is in terms of that eternal unoriginated fatherly Love that we are taught to think of God the Father as the Almighty or Omnipotent Creator. And, what is more, it is only in the

---

[5] Athanasius, *Contra Arianos*, 1.23; *De decretis*, 31, with reference to Eph. 3.15.
[6] Matt. 11.25–27; Luke 10.21–22.
[7] John 17.1ff. Cf. also the Lord's Prayer, 'Our *Father* who art in heaven, hallowed be thy *Name*.'
[8] Hilary, *De Trinitate*, 6.30.
[9] Hilary, *De Trinitate*, 1.17.
[10] Hilary, *De Trinitate*, 3.22.

light of the atoning sacrifice of Christ on the Cross and of his triumphant resurrection from the dead for our sakes, that we may really begin to understand what it means for God to be Lord of our existence, as the Lord over life and death, over being and non-being, and over the future as well as over the past and the present. The one eternal God and Father of our Lord Jesus Christ, is *our* God and *our* Father through him.

It is in and through this revelation of God the Creator as the Father of Christ Jesus, and also as our loving Father in virtue of our adoption in Christ and our union with him, that we may discern the wonderful truth that God does not exist for himself alone, that he will not be without us but has made us for himself and has actually given himself for us so that, without ceasing to be creaturely beings utterly different from him, we may nevertheless be one with him, as the Father and the Son are one in the Holy Trinity. Hence nothing in all creation will ever be able to separate us from his love, any more than anything can separate the Father and the Son from one another.[11] And here too in the light of the Fatherhood of God revealed to us in the Son we may discern something of the ultimate meaning of the creation and the mystery of its contingent rational order as it is locked into the mystery of the Holy Trinity. This has been given bold, and nowhere better, expression than by Karl Barth in his *Dogmatics in Outline*.

> Only when we keep before us what the triune God has done for us men in Jesus Christ can we realise what is involved in God the Creator and his work. Creation is the temporal analogue taking place outside of God, of that event in God himself by which God is Father of the Son. The world is not God's Son, is not 'begotten' of God, but is *created*. But what God does as the Creator can in the Christian sense only be seen and understood as a reflection, as a shadowing forth of the inner divine relationship between God the Father and the Son. And that is why the work of creation is ascribed in the Confession to the *Father*.[12]

A similar duality in the concept of the Fatherhood of God becomes apparent in the formulation of the doctrine of the Holy Trinity, in which we speak of the Father along with the Son and the Spirit as constituting in their otherness and in their homoousial Communion with one another the one Being of God. When the Father is considered relatively, that is *ad alios* in relation to the Son and the Holy Spirit, he is thought of as the Father of the Son, but when the Father is thought of absolutely, that is *in se*, as God himself (Αὐτοθεός), the name 'Father' is often applied to God (Θεός) or the Godhead (Θεότης).[13] The name 'Father', then, may refer to the one Being or οὐσία of God, but it may also refer to the Person or ὑπόστασις of the Father. In this particular sense and use, as Gregory Nazianzen held, 'Father' is to be understood as the name for the relation or *schesis* (σχέσις) the Father bears

---

[11] Rom. 8.31–38; Eph. 1.3ff; 3.14ff.

[12] Karl Barth, *Dogmatics in Outline*, tr. by G. T. Thomson (Edinburgh, 1949), p. 52.

[13] This was the way of thinking taken from Gregory Nazianzen by Augustine and Calvin – see 'The Doctrine of the Holy Trinity in Gregory Nazianzen and John Calvin', in *Trinitarian Perspectives*, ch. 2, pp. 21–40.

to the Son, and is not a name for being or *ousia*.[14] This does not mean, however, that the Son is to be thought of as proceeding from the *Person* of the Father (ἐκ τῆς ὑποστάσεως τοῦ Πατρός), but from the *Being* of the Father (ἐκ τῆς οὐσίας τοῦ Πατρός), as in the pronouncement of the Council of Nicaea. In this event it is understandable that Epiphanius declined to restrict the name 'Father' merely to the *hypostasis* of the Father, for when considered absolutely, as we have just noted, it does signify *ousia*.[15] It is not always easy to distinguish the two senses, for they cannot be separated and always overlap, for God the Father is both *ousia* and *hypostasis*. When considered absolutely God the eternal Father is the one Principle of Godhead, the μόνη Ἀρχή, Μοναρχία, or the Monarchy, but when the Father is considered in his inseparable oneness in Being with the Son and the Spirit, as One Being (μία οὐσία), then the Monarchy, as we shall see, is to be thought of as identical with the Holy Trinity, for it is not limited to one Person, since each divine Person is the whole God.[16]

In this two-fold presentation of God in divine revelation as God the eternal Father and as the God and Father of Jesus Christ his incarnate Son we have embodied the ontic and the epistemic link between the evangelical revelation of God as Father mediated to us in the incarnate economy of his saving acts in the Son and the Spirit, and the revelation of God as the eternal Father of the eternal Son. We are not given to know the one Fatherhood without the other Fatherhood, for they are one and the same Fatherhood whether God is considered as he is in himself in eternity or whether he is considered as he is toward us in time. It is because he is God the eternal Father apart from his relation to us, that his relation to us as taught by Christ Jesus and as exhibited in his own unique relation to the Father, is a relation of utterly free unsparing love and completely unconditional grace, and that in turn discloses to us the transcendent Nature of God the Father as he is inherently and eternally in himself. This means that the relation of the economic Trinity and the ontological Trinity is not an identity that can be expressed in terms of a logical 'is', but is one of infinite love and grace that is found in the immanent depths of what took place at Calvary to which Jesus himself gave expression in his anguished cries of 'Father' in the Garden of Gethsemane and of 'my God, my God' on the Cross, and then one of sublime tranquillity: 'Father, into your hands I commit my Spirit.'[17]

GOD THE ETERNAL SON

We have been considering the truth that no one knows the Father except the Son and those to whom he reveals him; now we turn to consider the other side of that

---

[14] Gregory Nazianzen, *Orationes*, 23.8, 11; 29.2ff, 16; 30.11, 19f; 31.9, 14, 16, 32; 42.15ff.
[15] Epiphanius, *Haereses*, 73.21; *Expositio fidei*, 14.
[16] Cf. Athanasius, *Contra Arianos*, 1.14; 3.1f, 15; 4.1ff; *Ad Antiochenos*, 5; *Ad Serapionem*, 1.16, 20, 28; 3.1,6; and Gregory Nazianzen, *Orationes*, 29.2; 31.14; 40.41; 42.15–16. See also the 'Agreed Statement on the Holy Trinity' in *Theological Dialogue between Orthodox and Reformed Churches*, vol. 2 (Edinburgh, 1993), p. 223f.
[17] Luke 23.46.

truth, that no one knows the Son except the Father who makes him known to us in Jesus Christ: 'This is my beloved Son, in whom I am well pleased, hear him.'[18] And so in the Nicene-Constantinopolitan Creed we confess our belief in God the Father and in his incarnate Son together.

(1) 'We believe in one God the Father Almighty, Maker of heaven and earth, and of all things visible and invisible'; and

(2) we believe 'in one Lord Jesus Christ, the only-begotten Son of God, begotten from his Father before all time, Light from Light, true God from true God, begotten, not made, of one and the same being with the Father, through whom all things were made, who for us men and for our salvation, came down from heaven, and was made flesh from the Holy Spirit and the Virgin Mary, and was made man, and was crucified for us under Pontius Pilate. He suffered and was buried and the third day he rose again according to the Scriptures and ascended into heaven, and sits on the right hand of God the Father. And he shall come again in glory to judge both the living and the dead: his kingdom shall have no end.'

We believe in Jesus Christ as our Lord and Saviour with the very same faith with which we believe in God the Father Almighty, and we believe that what he is toward us, with us and for us in his incarnate mission from the Father he is antecedently and eternally in himself, the eternal Son of the eternal Father. Everything hinges on the unqualified oneness of the Father and the Son who are with the Holy Spirit the One Lord in whom we believe and whom we love and worship. We believe that if the Lord God *himself* had not actually come among us and become one with us and acted for us in the life and work of Jesus Christ, the Gospel of the Love of God, the Grace of Lord Jesus Christ and the Communion of the Holy Spirit, would be utterly wanting in any divine validity in its message of reconciliation, salvation, and redemption. It would therefore be quite empty of any real hope for mankind in their desperate plight in guilt and judgment, and in their alienation from God and subjection to the forces of evil and darkness. How abysmal and desperate the lost condition of man is, may be discerned in the fact that it needed nothing short of the Lord God himself to become one with us in our sin and death in order to redeem and save mankind. Far from the Gospel being empty of reality the fact that Jesus Christ is the incarnation within our alienated human being and perishing existence of the eternal Son of the eternal Father means that the message of reconciliation, salvation and redemption does indeed have divine content and eternal validity.

This basic truth is what the Nicene Creed asserts so decisively in its affirmation that the one Lord Jesus Christ, the only begotten Son of God, begotten of the Father before all time, is true God of true God, of one and the same Being with the Father.[19] In the incarnation God has communicated *his divine Self* to us in Jesus

---

[18] Matt. 3.17; Mark 1.11; Luke 3.33; Matt. 17.5; Mark 9.7; 2 Pet. 1.17.

[19] 'Revelation has eternal content and eternal validity. Down to the very depth of Deity, not as something penultimate but as the ultimate thing that is to be said about God, God is God the Son as he is God the Father. Jesus Christ, the Son of God, is God himself as God his Father is God himself.' Karl Barth, *Church Dogmatics* I.1, p. 414.

Christ,[20] and done that in such a triune way in the revealing and saving activity of Christ among us that God the Father and God the Holy Spirit are directly present and personally operative with him, the Father as his and our God and Father, and the Holy Spirit as the one Spirit of the Father and the Son through whom we are given to share in the Communion of Love which the Father, the Son and the Holy Spirit eternally are.[21] The knowledge of Jesus Christ as the eternal Son of God is given to us only in the trinitarian structure of God's revealing of himself through himself, that is, as Father, Son and Holy Spirit. The pivotal issue here, as we have already seen in our discussion of the *homoousion*, is the identity (the ταυτότης as Athanasius expressed it[22]) between God and the revelation of himself, between what he reveals of himself and of his activity in Jesus Christ and what he really is in himself in his own ever-living and dynamic Being. In Jesus Christ, as St Paul wrote, there dwells the very 'fullness of the Godhead bodily' (τὸ πλήρωμα τῆς Θεότητος σωματικῶς).[23]

This incarnate embodiment of the fullness of God in Christ has opened up for us an astonishing way of knowing God personally in himself, which was not available to the chosen people of God within the covenant relation which God established with them even when he made himself known to them as *Yahweh*, as he who he really is and will be as their Lord and Saviour. While this grace was not yet present to Israel in very person (αὐτοπροσώπως, as Cyril once expressed it[24]), that is precisely what took place through God's personal self-communication and self-donation in 'the concrete Jesus'.[25] By taking our human nature upon himself and coming to us in Jesus Christ as Man, by uniting himself to us in our human nature and by living his divine Life within our human life as real human life and addressing us within it, God has revealed to us something of the innermost secret of his own divine personal life not otherwise possible. Thus Jesus Christ revealed God both by *word*, by teaching us about God the heavenly Father through himself as the eternal Word who inheres in God and is now made flesh, and by *being*, by manifesting the Father as his own Father through himself as the only Begotten Son who eternally indwells the Father and is now become man for our sakes. His revelation of God was made through embodying God's self-revelation and self-giving to mankind in himself as the Son of Man, in the form of his personal Being as the one Mediator between God and man. In the language of the Nicene Fathers it is he who came down from heaven and was made man for us and our salvation who is acknowledged to be of one and the same Being as God the Father, that is of the same equal Being

---

[20] Cf. the stress laid by Athanasius upon 'God *himself*', αὐτὸς ὁ Θεός, in the incarnation and his relating of this to the '*I am*', Ἐγώ εἰμι, of Christ which has eternal significance. *Contra Arianos*, 1.11–12 – see further 1.60; 2.9, 11f, 45f, 51f.

[21] Cf. Karl Barth: 'The work of the Son of God includes in itself the work of the Father as its presupposition and the work of the Holy Spirit as its consequence.' *Dogmatics in Outline* (London, 1949), pp. 65 & 71.

[22] Athanasius, *De synodis*, 53.

[23] Col. 1.19; 2.9.

[24] Cyril of Alexandria, *In Joannis Evangelium*, 7.32f, *Patrologia Graeca* 73, 509.

[25] Karl Rahner, 'The Scriptural Doctrine of the Trinity', *Sacramentum Mundi* (London, 1970), vol. 6, p. 295.

as the eternal Father, while nevertheless distinct (ἄλλος) from him as his only begotten Son. The incarnate Son, Jesus who was born of the Virgin Mary and crucified under Pontius Pilate, is none other than the eternal Son of God – the eternal Son of God, he who was begotten of the Father before all time, is none other than the incarnate Son, Jesus who was born of the Virgin Mary and crucified under Pontius Pilate.

We have to do here with a two-fold movement of mediation, from above to below and from below to above, in God's gracious condescension to be one with us, and his saving assumption of us to be one with himself, for as God and Man, the one Mediator between God and man, Jesus Christ ministers to us both the things of God to man, and the things of man to God.[26] This has to be understood as the self-giving movement of God in Christ to us in our sinful and alienated existence where we live at enmity to God, and therefore as a movement in which the revealing of God to us takes place only through a reconciling of us to God. The incarnation of the eternal Word and Son of God is to be understood, therefore, in an essentially soteriological way. Divine revelation and atoning reconciliation take place inseparably together in the life and work of the incarnate Son of God in whose one Person the hypostatic union between his divine and human natures is actualised through an atoning union between God and man that reaches from his birth of the Virgin Mary throughout his vicarious human life and ministry to his death and resurrection. It was of this intervening activity of Christ in our place that St Paul wrote to the Corinthians: 'You know the grace of the Lord Jesus Christ who though he was rich yet for your sakes became poor that you through his poverty might be rich.'[27]

We may express this two-fold movement of revelation and reconciliation in another way by saying two things.

a) Since the Father-Son relation subsists eternally within the Communion of the Holy Trinity we must think of the incarnation of the Son as falling within the eternal Life and Being of God, although, of course, the incarnation was not a timeless event like the generation of the Son from the Being of the Father, but must be regarded as new even for God, for the Son of God was not eternally Man any more than the Father was eternally Creator.

b) Correspondingly, since in Jesus Christ the eternal Son of God became man without ceasing to be God, the atoning reconciliation of man to God must be regarded as falling within the incarnate life of the Mediator in whose one Person the hypostatic union and the atoning union interpenetrate one another. We shall consider the nature of the Person of Christ later in terms of the patristic couplet *anhypostasis* and *enhypostasis*, but at the moment, let us think of the relation of the Lord Jesus Christ the incarnate Son of God within the Holy Trinity absolutely and relatively.

---

[26] See further the chapter on 'The Incarnate Saviour' in *The Trinitarian Faith*, pp. 146ff.
[27] 2 Cor. 8.9.

Considered absolutely *in se*, he is true God of true God and indeed, as we have noted above, there resides in him the fullness of the Father, that is, as Athanasius expressed it, 'the whole Godhead' (ὁλόκληρος ἡ Θεότης). He is 'whole God of whole God' (ὅλος ὅλου), for everything that God the Father is, the Son is, except his being 'Father'.[28] 'The whole Being of the Son is proper to the Being of the Father', and 'the Being of the Son is the fullness of the Father's Godhead.'[29] Hence Athanasius could say repeatedly that the Son shares perfectly and fully in the one Being of the Godhead. When considered in himself, he is himself very God, and has his divine Life from himself. 'For as the Father has life in himself, so he has given to the Son to have life in himself.'[30] Considered relatively, however, *ad alium*, in relation to the eternal Persons of the Father and the Holy Spirit, the Son in his own particular Person is distinct from the Father and the Spirit, yet of the same equal being with them so that he constitutes hypostatically with them the eternal Communion of the Father, the Son and the Holy Spirit, three Persons, one Being. Each divine Person retains his unique characteristics as Father, Son, or Holy Spirit, in a union without confusion, for the individual characteristics of each of the three Persons do not separate them, but constitute their deep mutual belonging together.[31] There is no Son apart from the Father, and the Holy Spirit, and no Father, apart from the Son and the Holy Spirit, and no Holy Spirit apart from the Father and the Son. Homoousially and hypostatically they interpenetrate each other in such a way that each Person is distinctively who he is in relation to the other two.

Since the incarnation falls within the Life of the Holy Trinity, and the atonement falls within the life of the Mediator, we must think of this mutual interpenetration of the Father, the Son and the Holy Spirit as obtaining in the *oikonomia* as well as in the *theologia*, and in the *theologia* as well as in the *oikonomia*. Although the grace manifested in the economy appeared in history with the incarnate advent (ἔνσαρκος παρουσία) of Christ, it derives from and is to be traced back to the eternal outgoing love of God that antedates the creation. It is surely in this way that we may interpret the biblical statements that God has 'chosen us in Christ before the foundation of the world' and that 'the Lamb was slain from the foundation of the world'.[32] This is what St Paul called 'the economy of the mystery hid from the ages in God (ἡ οἰκονομία τοῦ μυστηρίου τοῦ ἀποκεκρυμμένου ἀπὸ τῶν αἰώνων ἐν τῷ Θεῷ).'[33] We may turn here once more to Athanasius who with reference to the purpose and grace of God toward us in Christ before the world began, interpreted his predestination of us for adoption in Christ to mean that he the eternal Son himself constitutes the foundation before the world began on to which the economy

---

[28] Athanasius, *Ad Serapionem*, 1.16 & 24; *De synodis*, 49; *Ad Afros* 8; *Contra Arianos*, 3.4, 16, etc. See G. D. Dragas, *Athanasiana*, 1 (London, 1980), p. 69ff.

[29] Athanasius, *Contra Arianos*, 3.3, 6; 4.1ff.

[30] John 5.26. See Athanasius, *In illud, omnia*, 6; *Contra Arianos*, 4.1; and *Expositio fidei*, 1 & 4.

[31] For this way of expressing the oneness and threeness of the three Divine Persons, see Nikos A. Nissiotis, 'The Importance of the Doctrine of the Holy Trinity for Church Life and Theology', in *The Orthodox Ethos*, ed. by A. J. Philippou (Oxford, 1964), pp. 41 and 42; and also my discussion, 'The Trinitarian Theology of Nicolas Nissiotis', in *Trinitarian Perspectives*, ch. 5, pp. 103–109.

[32] Eph. 1.4; Rev. 13.8.

[33] Eph. 3.9.

of salvation effected in the flesh for our sakes was taken up.[34] Apart from that transcendent ground in *theologia* the incarnate *oikonomia* cannot but be of transient or merely ephemeral significance, and therefore without saving power. It is in Christ himself the eternal Son incarnate among us that the *theologia* and the *oikonomia* are inseparably united, for in him they are anchored in the one Being of the Holy Trinity. This is to say, unless God himself were directly involved in the saving work of Christ in the depths of our human existence and in the heights of his eternal Being, what took place on the Cross would have been in vain. 'God crucified'! That is what Gregory Nazianzen in an Easter oration once declaimed as a 'miracle'. 'We needed an incarnate God, a God put to death, that we might live. We were put to death together with him, that we might be cleansed; we rose again with him, because we were put to death with him; we were glorified with him, because we rose again with him.'[35] Since *theologia* and *oikonomia* interweave with one another, the doctrine of the atonement and the doctrine of God, and therefore the doctrine of the Trinity, may not be separated from one another.

We need to take into account here also the doctrine of the Spirit which we shall consider more fully later. It is when we consider this movement from God toward man and from man toward God in Christ, together with the movement of the Holy Spirit in his mission from the Father through the Son and in his advocacy of us before the Father, that we may discern how intimately and completely the Father, the Son and the Spirit are coordinated both in the economic fulfilment of God's revealing and saving acts on our behalf, and in their inner union and Communion with one another. The oneness of the Father and the Son and the oneness of the Son and the Spirit are inseparable from one another in themselves as they are in their economic manifestation toward us. God the Father communicates himself to us in his Son and imparts himself to us in his Spirit in such a way as to enable us to receive his revelation and participate in the movement of mutual knowing and loving between the Father and the Son. This reinforces for us the truth that the doctrines of the Son and of the Spirit may be formulated properly only within the compass of the doctrine of Holy Trinity. While the immediate centre of our knowledge of the Holy Trinity is lodged in the divine-human Person of Christ, for it was he the Son and Word of God, and not the Holy Spirit, who became incarnate as the self-communication of God to us within the bounds of our human existence and knowledge, nevertheless it is only by the Spirit that we are enabled to recognise Jesus as Lord, and it is only through him, who was anointed with the Spirit and endowed with the Spirit without measure for our sakes, that the Holy Spirit is mediated to us. It is through the self-imparting of God to us in the Spirit along with his self-communication to us through the Son, that we may really know God in Christ Jesus.

In this event we are unable to offer a proper formulation of the doctrine of Christ himself without taking into account the essential relation between the work of incarnate Son on our behalf and the activity of the Holy Spirit who is sent by

---

[34] Athanasius, *Contra Arianos*, 2.74–76.
[35] Gregory Nazianzen, *Orationes*, 45.28.

Christ to dwell in us and be with us as his 'Other Self', the Paraclete.[36] Nor indeed may we do so without taking into account the mutual indwelling of the Person of the eternal Son and the Person of the eternal Spirit, within the Life of the Triune God which he lives not only for himself but also for us whom he loves and seeks to bring through his Son and his Spirit into communion with himself. All the revealing and saving acts of God come to us from the Father, through the Son and in the Holy Spirit, and all our corresponding relations to God in faith, love and knowledge are effected in the Spirit through the Son and to the Father.

GOD THE ETERNAL SPIRIT

Our approach to the doctrine of the Holy Spirit must be fully in line with our approach to the doctrine of the Son, for it is through the Son and in the Spirit that God reveals and gives himself to us. The Holy Spirit is no less than the Son the self-giving of God, for in him the divine Gift and the divine Giver are identical. This is why the *homoousion* was applied to the understanding of the nature and identity of the Holy Spirit, for like the Son he is of one and the same being as God the Father and belongs to the inner Life of the Triune God. However, the controlling point of reference for our knowledge of the Spirit is the inner relation of the Spirit to the Son, for it is in the Son or Word of God, as we have just noted, that the informational content of God's self-revelation is given. This is why in the Early Church controlled doctrine of the Holy Spirit followed upon and was taken from knowledge of the Son and of the Father through the Son.[37] The Holy Spirit does not bring to us any independent knowledge of God or add any new content to God's self-revelation, but while the knowledge of the Spirit himself as well as of the Father is derived through the Son, it is mediated and actualised within us through the presence and activity of the Holy Spirit. He is 'the Spirit of truth', as Jesus called him, sent to us by the Son from the Father to lead us into all truth,[38] who as the Spirit of the Father and of the Son reveals to us the Father in the Son and the Son in the Father, and is recognised accordingly as himself *God*, true God of true God.[39] The doctrine of the Holy Spirit, therefore, develops out of the inner structure of knowledge of the one God grounded in his *self*-revealing and *self*-imparting as the Father, the Son and the Holy Spirit, *three Persons, one Being*.

A distinction must be drawn between thinking of the Spirit absolutely and thinking of him relatively. Absolutely considered the Spirit is God of God, and like the Son whole God of whole God, so that the Being of the Spirit is the Being or

---

[36] John 14.16–18; 16.7; 1 John 2.1.

[37] This was how, for example, Athanasius formulated the doctrine of the Spirit in his *Letters on the Spirit to Serapion*, written between AD 356 and 361. This was a development of his teaching in the *Orations against the Arians*, cf. 1.47ff, 56; 2.18; 3.15, 24f, 44.

[38] John 14.17 & 16.13f.

[39] For the following see *Theology in Reconciliation* (London, 1975), pp. 231–239; and *The Trinitarian Faith*, pp. 191–251.

οὐσία of the Godhead. 'God is Spirit', as Jesus said to the woman of Samaria.[40] In this absolute sense 'Spirit' refers to the Deity, without distinction of Persons, and is equally applicable to the Father, the Son and the Holy Spirit. Considered relatively, however, the Spirit is Person or ὑπόστασις who in distinction from and together with the Persons of the Father and the Son belongs with them to the one Being of God. The Holy Spirit is, then, like the Father and the Son, both *ousia* and *hypostasis*, and with the Persons of the Father and the Son is eternally in God and inseparable from him who is *one Being, three Persons*. This means that when the New Testament speaks of us as being 'in the Spirit (ἐν Πνεύματι)' or of the Spirit being 'in us (ἐν ἡμῖν)', as St Paul does so frequently, this is to be understood not in a subjective but in a profoundly *objective* sense, not least because of the homoousial relation between the Spirit and the Son and their mutual indwelling of one another. A proper understanding of the Holy Spirit, therefore, does not carry with it a concept of psychological inwardness in our experience of him or a concept of a subjectification of the Spirit in the life of the Church. While corresponding to the mutual indwelling of the Spirit and the Son in the Holy Trinity there arises through the two-fold mission of the Son and the Spirit an indwelling of the Spirit and the Son in us, and an indwelling of us in the Father through union with them, this is essentially an 'objective inwardness'.

Our receiving of the Spirit is objectively grounded in and derives from Christ who as the incarnate Son was anointed by the Spirit in his humanity and endowed with the Spirit without measure, not for his own sake (for he was eternally one in being with the Spirit in God) but for our sakes, and who then mediates the Spirit to us through himself. As one of us and one with us he sanctified himself in the Spirit that we might be sanctified in him and thus be sanctified in the truth.[41] Our receiving of the Spirit, therefore, is not independent of or different from the vicarious receiving of the Spirit by Christ himself but is a sharing in it. Since he received the Spirit in the humanity he took from us, we on our part receive the Spirit through union with him and through him with the Father. This was the point Athanasius had in mind when he wrote: 'Our being in the Father is not ours, but is the Spirit's who is in us and dwells in us ... It is the Spirit who is in God, and not we viewed in ourselves.'[42]

Crucial to this experience of ours in the Spirit is the inherent relation in Being and Act between the Spirit and the Son: for us to be in the Spirit or to have the Spirit dwelling within us means that we are united to Christ the incarnate Son of the Father, and are made through this union with him in the Spirit to participate, human creatures though we are, in the Communion which the Father, the Son and the Holy Spirit have among themselves and are in themselves. In other words, we must think of our being *in the Spirit* in the incarnate economy of God's saving acts

---

[40] John 4.24: Πνεῦμα ὁ Θεός.

[41] John 17.17–19. In an unusual comment on the self-sanctification of Christ Athanasius put this internal utterance into his mouth: 'I, being the Word of the Father, personally give myself, become man, the Spirit; and sanctify myself become man in him, in order that henceforth in me who am truth (for 'your word is truth') all may be sanctified.' *Contra Arianos*, 1.46. See G. D. Dragas, 'The Eternal Son', in *Athanasiana* I, 1980, pp. 62f, and in *The Incarnation. Ecumenical Studies in the Nicaeno-Constantinopolitan Creed*, which I edited in 1981, p. 36f.

[42] Athanasius, *Contra Arianos*, 3.24 & 25. Cf. *Theology in Reconciliation*, p. 234f.

in Jesus Christ as deriving from and grounded objectively in the homoousial Communion of the eternal Spirit and the eternal Son in the Holy Trinity. In this two-fold movement of the Holy Spirit from above and from below, along with the two-fold movement of the incarnate Son in receiving the Holy Spirit and giving him to us, we must think once more of the *theologia* and the *oikonomia* as bearing internally and reciprocally upon one another.

Regarded in this way, from his internal enhypostatic relation to the Trinity, the Holy Spirit is to be understood as the presence to us and with us of the Lord God in the ever-living and ever-active reality of his divine Being. The fact that God is Spirit and that the Holy Spirit is God means that far from being static the Being of God is essentially and eternally *dynamic*. Hence the presence among us of the Holy Spirit is the immediate *parousia* (παρουσία) of the dynamic Being (οὐσία) of God in his sublime Holiness and Majesty as the Lord God Almighty, the transcendent Creator and Lord of all existence from whom and in whom we live and move and have our being. It must be emphasised, therefore, that in the Spirit we have to do with God in the *unity of his Being and his Act*. While God is the Holy Trinity of three Persons, there is yet *one* divine activity (ἐνέργεια) and *one* divine Being in the Father, the Son and the Holy Spirit. It is this unity of Activity, and unity of Being, and the unity of the Trinity, which force themselves upon our faith and understanding when we know God in the Spirit, and know the Spirit himself as the divine Person who in his oneness with the Father and the Son realises and actualises among us the presence and power of God's eternal Being. When the Holy Spirit is in us, God is in us and the Son is in us also. Thus it is particularly as we move from the doctrine of the Son to the doctrine of the Spirit that we have to think of the one Being of God in his Acts, and of the one Activity of God in his Being. That was true both of the theology of Athanasius in his conception of the Activity of God as inhering in the very Being of God as ἐνούσιος ἐνέργεια,[43] and of the theology of Karl Barth in his conception of the Being of God in Act and of the Act of God in his Being.[44] Any separation between the Being and the Activity of God would imply that God is not after all *in himself* always and reliably what he is toward us through his Son and in his Spirit, and that, so far as the Spirit is concerned, it would imply that God is not really by Nature what he imparts to us through his Son and in his Spirit.

The inherent unity of Being and Act in God forces upon us an understanding of God in which movement belongs to his eternal Being. If God is who he is in his activity toward us through the Son and in the Spirit, then it belongs to the essential Nature of his eternal Being to move and energise and act. When it is said of the Word of God who inheres in his eternal Being that he *became* man or *became* flesh, that *becoming* must be regarded not as a movement on the way toward 'being', a becoming that is eventually swallowed up in 'being', far less something adventitious or accidental to God, but as being-in-movement or being-in-action.[45] The divine

[43] Athanasius, *Contra Arianos*, 2.2; cf.2.28; 3.65; 4.1f.
[44] Karl Barth, *Church Dogmatics* II.1, pp. 257ff.
[45] See S. Kierkegaard, *Philosophical Fragments* (Princeton, 1936), p. 60; Karl Barth, *Church Dogmatics* I.2, pp. 182ff, 215ff; E. Jüngel, *The Doctrine of the Trinity. God's Being is in Becoming* (Edinburgh, 1976), pp. 1ff; and T. F. Torrance, *Karl Barth, Biblical and Evangelical Theologian* (Edinburgh, 1990), pp. 95ff.

Becoming disclosed in the incarnation is the outgoing movement of the divine Being in condescension and love; it is the coming-and-presence, the presence-and-coming of God, the Being of God with us, the παρ-ουσία of the οὐσία of the ever-living God himself among us in Jesus Christ and in the Holy Spirit. It is essentially a *dynamic* or *operative presence* in which God himself is freely and lovingly at work in and through the Son, and an activity in which he is immediately and personally present with us in the Spirit.

Let it be repeated that the God who has revealed himself to us in the Gospel as Father, Son and Holy Spirit is not a God who lives for himself alone, but who lives his all self-sufficient divine Life in love for others and has poured out his love without reserve in the gift of his only begotten Son to us as our Saviour, and in the Holy Spirit who sheds abroad that very love in our hearts. This does not imply, as we have taken care to show, that God is conditioned by, far less constituted through, his relation to us who are quite other than he is, for he is already concerned with Others eternally and inherently in himself, in the three-fold otherness of the Father, the Son and the Holy Spirit in their Love for one another and Communion with another. It is from the free ground of that transcendent otherness in himself in his Triune Being, that God freely and spontaneously creates others outwith himself for fellowship with himself and brings them into actual communion with himself. This free-flowing unconditioned outgoing movement of his Being means that God refuses to be shut off from us in his unapproachable Majesty, infinite otherness and incomprehensibility. He makes himself really accessible to us, and does so not only in communicating himself to us in the incarnation of his Son, but in imparting to us his Holy Spirit in such an utterly astonishing way as to actualise among us his self-giving to us as the Lord and at the same time to effect our receiving of him in his self-giving.

The impartation of the Holy Spirit to us as specifically the *Holy* Spirit confronts us with God himself in his unlimited Godness and Majesty, God in his utter Sublimity and Lordship. This was brought sharply home to people by Jesus himself when he told them that while evil-speaking against himself might be forgiven, blasphemy against the Holy Spirit will never be forgiven.[46] This stress on the inviolable Majesty of the Person of the Spirit had the effect of filling the Church with an overwhelming sense of awe at the pouring out of the Holy Spirit upon it at Pentecost, and of calling forth from it unceasing thanksgiving, veneration and adoration. Liturgical expression was given to this doxological worship in the *Trisagion*, taken over by the Church from Isaiah of Jerusalem in his vision of the enthroned Lord God before whom the Seraphim covered their faces as they called to one another, 'Holy, Holy, Holy is the Lord of Hosts, the whole earth is filled with his glory.'[47] In his coming and presence to us, supervening upon the awesome atoning self-sacrifice of Christ on the Cross in whom the Father reconciles us to himself, the Holy Spirit guards the ultimate mystery and ineffability of God in the very heart of his self-revelation and self-communication to us, precisely through his own invisibility and transcendent holiness.

---

[46] Matt. 12.31f; Mark 3.28f; Luke 12.10.
[47] Isa. 6.1ff.

While God the Father and God the Son are revealed to us in their distinctive personal subsistences or ὑποστάσεις, as through the Spirit we are given to share in the knowing of the Son by the Father and of the Father by the Son, God the Holy Spirit is not directly known in his own Person or ὑπόστασις for he remains hidden behind the very revelation of the Father and the Son which he mediates *through* himself. He is the invisible Spirit of Truth who is sent from the Father in the name of the Son, but not in his own personal name as the Holy Spirit, and thus does not speak of himself, but declares of the Father and the Son what he receives from them, while effacing himself before them.[48] He does not show us himself, which is the reason why, as Jesus explained, the world cannot receive him or know him.[49] In virtue of the distinctive nature of his Person and Mission the Holy Spirit hides himself from us behind the Father in the Son and behind the Son in the Father, so that we do not know him face to face in his own ὑπόστασις. Through him the Son of God became incarnate, but he did not incarnate himself among us. He is the one Spirit in whom the Father communicates himself to us through the Son and in whom we have access to the Father. He is the invisible Light in whose shining we see the uncreated Light of God manifest in Jesus Christ, but he is known himself only in that he lights up for us the Face of God in the Face of Jesus Christ. The Holy Spirit is indeed personally present among us as a result of what took place at Pentecost, but is known in his own distinctive, transparent and translucent *hypostasis*, through whom as of one and the same being (ὁμοούσιος) with the Father and the Son the eternal Light of God radiates across to us in the world from the Father and the Son. In this way the Father, the Son and the Holy Spirit in their Triune Being shine through him to us in their three-fold Light.

It is in virtue of the mysterious ineffability of his own personal Being, then, that the Holy Spirit confronts us with the sheer mystery, unnameability and ultimate incomprehensibility of the Lord God, for through him what God reveals of himself in the economy of salvation is directed back ineffably to its eternal Source and Ground in the Holy Trinity. Through the presence of the Holy Spirit we are certainly put in sanctifying and enlightening touch with the dynamic Being and Act of the All-Holy and Almighty God resulting in a transcendental determination of our own being *for God* – the experience which the Greek Fathers spoke of as *theosis* (θέωσις) – and are thereby enabled to apprehend him, yet only in such a way that what he is as God (τί ἐστι Θεός) is completely veiled from us. Even in his self-revelation to us God reserves the hiddenness of his Being and does not come under the control of our knowing of him – before him all our human forms of thought and speech break off in wonder and adoration. In and through the presence of the Holy Spirit supervening upon the revealing and saving events of his incarnate Son, God really does impart himself to us and actually makes himself known to us within the conditions of our creaturely forms of thought and speech, but without any compromise of his sheer Godness or any diminution of the Mystery of his transcendent Being. 'Thus far human knowledge goes. Here the cherubim spread the covering of their wings.'[50]

---

[48] John 14.16f, 25f; 15.26f; 16.13f.
[49] John 14.17.
[50] Athanasius, *Ad Serapionem*, 1.17.

We must not forget, however, the other side of this truth, for while the Holy Spirit guards the ultimate unknowableness of God, he is the outgoing movement of God's Triune Being whereby he takes us into communion with himself, making himself open to our knowing of him and making us open to him and receptive of his self-revealing to us.[51] If the Act which God directs towards us is other than or detached from his Being, then he does not give *himself* to us in his activity and cannot therefore be known by us as he is in himself; but if his Act and his Being instead of being separate from one another inhere in each other, then in giving us his Spirit God actively makes himself open to us and known by us. That is precisely what God does in giving us his Holy Spirit, for the Spirit is the outgoing movement of God in which his Being and Act belong inseparably together, but since the Spirit is the Gift of God who is identical with God the Giver, it is God himself who is the living dynamic content of his self-revelation and self-communication in the Holy Spirit.

What is of paramount importance here is the *unlimited freedom* of God, not only to become man in Jesus Christ without ceasing to be God, but really to impart himself to us in the Spirit while remaining the transcendent Lord over all our creaturely being and knowing.[52] 'The Lord is the Spirit; and where the Spirit of the Lord is, there is freedom.'[53] This freedom of the Spirit may well be understood in a two-fold way, as the freedom of God to actualise his relation with us and the freedom of God to actualise our relation with himself. This is evident in the activity of the Spirit in creation. Although infinitely exalted above and beyond all creatures, the Spirit of God is free to be present to the creature and to realise and bring to its completion the creative purpose of God for the creature. He does this not only from the side of the Creator to the creature but from the side of the creature toward the Creator by bringing its relations to the Creator to their proper end in him, and thereby establishing the creature in an enduring ontological relation to God. While the creature does not have any continuity in relation to God that belongs to the creature in itself, it does have a relation to God which is continuously given and unceasingly sustained by the presence of the Holy Spirit. This two-way activity of the Holy Spirit is particularly evident in reconciliation and recreation.

As in the incarnation God became one of us and one with us as the one Mediator between God and man who acts both from the side of God toward man and from the side of man toward God in the saving life and the work of the Lord Jesus, so in God's impartation of the Holy Spirit to us he acts on both sides of the relation, in making himself open for our knowing of him in his revelation and in making us open for him in receiving and understanding his revelation. Through the imparting of his Spirit to us God gathers us into a two-way relation with himself, in which he activates his relation toward us and at the same time activates our relation toward himself. He does this, for example, when we pray in the Spirit, through a relation

---

[51] Refer here to Colin E. Gunton's perceptive account of 'The Lord who is the Spirit', in his Bampton Lectures, *The One, The Three and The Many* (Cambridge, 1993), pp. 180–209.

[52] See the account given by Karl Barth of 'The Being of God in his Freedom', *Church Dogmatics* II.1, pp. 297–321.

[53] 2 Cor. 3.17: ὁ δὲ Κύριος τὸ Πνεῦμά ἐστιν· οὐ δὲ τὸ Πνεῦμα Κυρίου, ἐλευθερία.

of the Spirit to himself[54] – that is, from himself above to us below and from us below to himself above. Thus in establishing his relations with us in the Spirit, God upholds us from below and sustains us within, and brings us as people whom he has made for himself to our true end in communion with himself, and thereby makes us participate in his own eternal life.[55]

On the one hand, the indwelling of the Holy Spirit along with the Father and the Son in the Holy Trinity imports an openness on the part of God in which in virtue of the inherent movement of his own eternal Being he is free to relate himself to what is not himself and to become open to created realities beyond himself. On the other hand, the presence of the Holy Spirit to the creation imports an openness on the part of God's creation toward himself, for through the Spirit God is able to take possession of his creatures, to sustain them from below, and to be present within them in such a way as to lift them up to the level of participation in God where they are opened out for union and communion with God far beyond the limits of their creaturely existence. To be 'in the Spirit' is to be in God, for the Spirit is not external but internal to the Godhead. But since it is only the Spirit of God who knows what is in God and it is he who unites us to the Son of God in his oneness with the Father, through the Communion of the Spirit we are exalted to know God in his inner trinitarian relations as Father, Son and Holy Spirit. When this actually takes place, however, we are restrained by the sheer Holiness and Majesty of the divine Being from transgressing the bounds of our creaturely being by inquiring beyond what is given through the Son and received in the Spirit, and therefore from intruding upon the mystery of God or thinking presumptuously and illegitimately of him. When God is present to us in his Holy Spirit we are on holy ground like Moses at the Burning Bush where he was bidden to take the shoes off his feet. Before the Face of God we are constrained by the Holy Spirit to think of him only in a reverent and godly way worthy of him, in which worship, wonder and silence inform the movement of our creaturely spirits to the Father, through the Son and in the Spirit, answering to the movement on God's part from the Father, through the Son and in the Spirit.

The holiness of the Spirit imports a critical element into the two-way activity of the Spirit, from God toward man and from man toward God, which must be taken into account. As our Lord taught his disciples, when the Holy Spirit comes he will come not only as Advocate but as Judge, for he will prove the world wrong about sin, righteousness and judgment.[56] When we consider this two-way activity of the Spirit in its coordination with the two-way activity of Christ, as we are bound to do in view of their oneness in Being and Act, we must think of the Spirit as participating in the vicarious and intercessory activity of Christ. Thus we must think of the presence of the Spirit as actualising within us the intervening and reconciling work of Christ when as the Son of God he assumed our wayward and

---

[54] Cf. Gregory Nazianzen, *Orationes*, 31.12, in a comment on Rom. 8.26.

[55] Cf. the powerful discussion of this two-way relation by Karl Barth, *Church Dogmatics* I.1, p. 450f & 471f, behind which may be traced the influence of Basil and Gregory Nazianzen on the doctrine of the Holy Spirit.

[56] John 16.8f.

disobedient humanity and through his own obedient life and atoning sacrifice offered himself to the Father in our place and in our stead, and thereby restored it in obedient sonship to the Father as our Father as well as his Father. Hence when the Holy Spirit is sent to us by the crucified, risen and ascended Lord to dwell in us, he unites us so intimately to Christ that he not only makes the intercessions of Christ to echo inaudibly in our hearts, but as the Spirit of the Son makes us cry with him 'Abba Father' as those who are adopted in Christ to be joint-heirs with him. Thereby 'the Spirit himself bears witness with our spirits that we are the children of God.'[57]

It is as the two-sided reconciliation (καταλλαγή) of man with God and God with man effected by God in Christ becomes actualised in us through the Spirit, whereby we are translated out of darkness into light, from enmity to peace, from judgment to grace, and from death to life, that we are really made open to divine revelation and made free to respond to the saving Gift of God's Love. We are unable to respond to this mighty act of God for us in Christ unless we are internally reconciled to him, and in being reconciled to him we are assumed by his Spirit into union with Christ who died in our place and rose again for us, and unless we are incorporated into his incarnate life and assimilated into what he has done in our place and on our behalf and continues to do in such a way that what we do in our response of faith and love to God is what he does by his Spirit within us. Hence in the paradoxical language used by St Paul, the life which we live as those who have been crucified with Christ we do not live out of ourselves but out of Christ, for it is not we who live but Christ who lives in us, and the life which we now live in the flesh we live through the faithfulness of the Son of God who loved us and gave himself for us.[58] However this two-sided reconciled life is viewed, wrote Otto Weber, 'it is God himself at work on both sides, God over against himself, and yet in such a way that he is as God completely with man and stands in man's place.'[59] Through this saving identification of Christ with us in which he acts within us on our behalf, and through our union with him actualised in us by the Holy Spirit, there is imparted to us an openness and a freedom toward God and toward others which is the divinely given counterpart in us to the transcendent openness and freedom of God in his love for all mankind. We must think of this astonishing work of the Holy Spirit within us also as deriving from and belonging to the very heart of the divinely forged bond between the economic Trinity and the ontological Trinity.

We must now think of the interrelations between the eternal Father, the eternal Son, and the eternal Spirit, who are three distinct Persons and yet one God, and take up again our discussion of the theological concepts and terms with which we formulate their interrelations. In the foregoing chapter we considered the relations between the three divine Persons in respect of their Unity in Trinity, but now we turn to consider them in respect of their Trinity in Unity, although these considerations inevitably overlap with one another for their Unity is a Trinity, and

[57] Rom. 8.15ff & Gal. 4.5f.
[58] Gal. 2.20.
[59] Otto Weber, *Foundations of Dogmatics* (Grand Rapids, 1981), vol. 1, p. 383.

their Trinity is a Unity. It is through the divine Trinity that we believe in the divine Unity, and through the divine Unity that we believe in the divine Trinity.[60] We will direct our attention first to the concept of 'Person' as it arose out of the doctrine of the Trinity, and then go on to elucidate the mutual indwelling of the Father, the Son and the Holy Spirit personally in each other and their homoousial Communion with one another which they constitute together as *three Persons, one Being.*

1) THE PERSONS OF THE FATHER, THE SON AND THE HOLY SPIRIT

In our understanding of the New Testament witness to God's revelation of himself, 'the Father', 'the Son', and 'the Holy Spirit' are unique and proper names denoting three distinct Persons or real Hypostases who are neither exchangeable nor interchangeable while nevertheless of one and the same divine Being. There is one Person of the Father who is always the Father, distinct from the Son and the Spirit; and there is another Person of the Son who is always the Son, distinct from the Father and the Spirit; and another Person of the Holy Spirit who is always the Holy Spirit, distinct from the Father and the Son. In this three-fold tri-personal self-revelation of God one Person is not more or less God, for all three Persons are coeternal and coequal. They are all perfectly one in the identity of their Nature and perfectly homoousial or consubstantial in their Being. Each of the three Persons is himself Lord and God, and yet there are not three Lords or Gods, but only one Lord God, and there is only one and the same eternal Being of the Father, the Son and the Holy Spirit. The Holy Trinity of three divine Persons is thus perfectly homogeneous and unitary, both in the threeness and oneness of God's personal activity, and in the threeness and oneness of his eternal unchangeable personal Being. *Three Persons, one Being.*

However, in the biblical tradition itself, in the Old and New Testaments, there is no explicit concept of 'person', although we find emphasis upon the Name, the Presence, the Face and the Glory of God associated with the self-revelation of God through his Word and Spirit in such a way that the Name, the Presence, and the Face and the Glory of God were regarded as a kind of doubling for God in a dynamic and quasi-hypostatic way which clearly correspond to what we would think of as the personal presence and self-presentation of God in creating fellowship with his people in revelation and salvation. This left an indelible imprint upon the Old Testament understanding of the worship of God and of reconciliation with God highlighted both in the Pentateuchal literature and in the prophetic realisation that the redemption of Israel called for a concretisation of covenant relations with

---

[60] For this and what follows consult 'Agreed Statement on the Holy Trinity' in vol. 2 of *Theological Dialogue between Orthodox and Reformed Churches*, edited by me (Edinburgh, 1993), ch. 10, pp. 219ff; and my presentation and discussion of it in *Trinitarian Perspectives. Toward Doctrinal Agreement* (Edinburgh, 1994), chs. 6 & 9, pp. 110ff & 127ff.

God in the actual existence of Israel.[61] All this is found also in the New Testament Scriptures, but it was specifically the understanding of the incarnation of the Word and Son of God in Jesus Christ in which the 'I am' of *Yahweh* and the 'I am' of the Lord Jesus were brought together within the three-fold manifestation of God as Father, Son and Holy Spirit, that not only deepened the Old Testament understanding of the Being of God as profoundly 'personal', but forced the Church in giving explicit expression to the implicitly trinitarian self-revelation of God to develop the theological concept of the 'person'.

The basic term used in this development was the word *hypostasis* (ὑπόστασις) taken over from the New Testament reference to Christ the Son of God as 'the express image of his being (χαρακτὴρ τῆς ὑποστάσεως αὐτοῦ)'.[62] Then within the context of the Church's deepening understanding of the Gospel the word *hypostasis* was adapted to express the objective self-revelation of the Son and Word of God made flesh in Jesus Christ full of grace and truth who encounters us and speaks to us face to face as the incarnate 'I am' of the living God. But it was only when this was further thought out in the light of the three-fold self-revelation of God as Father, Son and Holy Spirit that the specific concept of 'Person' took shape, and then only within the inter-personal relations of the Holy Trinity as one Being, three Persons. In the course of this development the term *hypostasis* was filled out through association with 'name' or ὄνομα used in its concrete sense, 'oneself' or αὐτός and especially 'face' or πρόσωπον, to refer to self-subsistent self-identifying subject-being in objective relations with others. In its theological deployment, therefore, the term *hypostasis* was not taken over from Greek thought unchanged, but was stretched and transformed under the impact of God's trinitarian self-revelation through Christ and in the Spirit to such an extent that it became suitable to express the identifiable self-manifestation of God in the incarnate economy of divine salvation as Father, Son and Holy Spirit – that is, as three distinctive hypostatic Realities or Persons. This change from a Hellenistic impersonal to a Christian personal way of thinking is very evident in the penchant of early Church theologians to qualify words for 'God', 'Word', 'being', 'life', 'authority' etc., by attaching to them the expression for 'oneself' or αὐτός, as for example, αὐτόθεος, αὐτολόγος, αὐτουσία, αὐτοζωή, αὐτοεξουσία, in order to stress the intensely personal nature of God's interaction with us through the presence and power of his Word and Spirit. Thus *Logos*, far from being some impersonal cosmological principle, is identified with the Son or Word of God, the divine Αὐτολόγος incarnate in Jesus Christ who reveals himself to us face to face, πρόσωπον κατὰ πρόσωπον, and speaks to us in the Holy Scriptures directly in person, ἐκ προσώπου, or αὐτοπροσώπως.

When the Church Fathers thought out the homoousial and hypostatic interrelations of the three divine Persons (ὑποστάσεις) within the one Being (οὐσία understood in its internal relations) or Communion (κοινωνία) of the Holy Trinity, it became clear to them that the ontic relations between the divine Persons belong

---

[61] Refer to my account of this in 'The Hope of Israel. Israel and the Incarnation', *Conflict and Agreement in the Church*, vol. 1 (London, 1959), pp. 284–303; and also in *Royal Priesthood*, SJT Occasional Papers, No. 3 (Edinburgh, 1955; second edn, T&T Clark, Edinburgh, 1993).
[62] Heb. 1.3.

to what they are as Persons. No divine Person is who he is without essential relation to the other two, and yet each divine Person is other than and distinct from the other two. They are intrinsically interrelated not only through the fact that they have one Being in common so that each of them is in himself whole God, but also in virtue of their differentiating characteristics as Father, Son, or Holy Spirit which hypostatically intertwine with one another and belong constitutively to their indivisible unity within the Trinity. There is an indivisible and continuous relation of being between the Father, the Son and the Holy Spirit so that the Being of the Godhead is understood to be whole or complete not in the Father only but in the Son and in the Holy Spirit as well. These ontic and holistic interrelations between the three divine Persons in virtue of which they are what and who they are as Persons are substantive relations (οὐσιώδεις σχέσεις) or 'onto-relations'.

This concept of Persons as substantive relations was put forward by Gregory Nazianzen in preference to the concept of 'modes of being (τρόποι ὑπάρξεως)' developed by the other Cappadocians and Didymus the Blind.[63] He took over and adapted the Greek notion of πρός τι to express the kind of 'for to' relations (σχέσεις) that subsist eternally and essentially in God which are beyond all time (ἀχρόνως), beyond all origin (ἀνάρχως) and beyond all causality (ἀναιτίως). The relations between the divine Persons are not just modes of existence but hypostatic interrelations which belong intrinsically to what Father, Son and Holy Spirit are coinherently in themselves and in their mutual objective relations with and for one another. These relations subsisting between them are just as substantial as what they are unchangeably in themselves and by themselves. Thus the Father *is* Father precisely in his indivisible ontic relation to the Son and the Spirit, and the Son and the Spirit *are* what they are as Son and Spirit precisely in their indivisible ontic relations to the Father and to One Another. That is to say, the relations between the divine Persons belong to what they are as Persons – they are constitutive onto-relations. 'Person' is an onto-relational concept.

What then does it mean to think of the three divine Persons specifically as 'Father', 'Son' and 'Holy Spirit'? This was a question that had kept cropping up in the Church since the Arian controversy when attempts were made to speak of divine Fatherhood and Sonship on the analogy of human fatherhood and sonship. While there is certainly a figurative or metaphorical ingredient in the human terms 'father' and 'son' as they are used in divine revelation, they are to be understood in ways that point utterly beyond what we mean by 'father' and 'son' among ourselves and thus utterly beyond all sexist connotations and implications. Both the generation of the Son and the procession of the Spirit are incomprehensible mysteries which are not explicable through recourse to human modes of thought. Hence, as Athanasius and Gregory Nazianzen insisted,[64] we must set aside all analogies drawn from the visible world in speaking of God, helpful as they may be up to a point, for they are theologically unsatisfactory and even objectionable, and must think of 'Father' and 'Son' when used of God as *imageless relations*. 'Father', Gregory pointed

[63] For references see Torrance, *The Trinitarian Faith*, pp. 239ff; 318ff.
[64] Cf. Athanasius, *In illud, omnia*, 3; Gregory Nazianzen, *Orationes*, 31.7ff, 33.

out,[65] 'is the name of the *relation* in which the Father stands to the Son, and the Son to the Father,' but as such it is an ineffable relation which exceeds and transcends human powers of imagination and conception, so that we may not read the creaturely content of our human expressions of 'father' and 'son' analogically into what God discloses of his own inner divine relations. Hence Gregory Nazianzen like Athanasius insisted that they must be treated as referring *imagelessly*, that is in a diaphanous or 'see through' way, to the Father and the Son without the intrusion of creaturely forms or sensual images into God. Thus we may not think of God as having gender nor think of the Father as begetting the Son or of the Son as begotten after the analogy of generation or giving birth with which we are familiar among creaturely beings.[66]

If 'God is Spirit', then Spirit is the specific Nature of God's eternal Being, as the Father and the Son as well as the Holy Spirit – hence he is rightly known in accordance with his Nature, and must be understood, in an essentially spiritual way, and of course in a completely genderless way. The effect of this on the doctrine of God may be discerned in the statement of Athanasius that while Christ is the one Ἐῖδος, the 'Form' or 'Image' of Godhead, the Spirit is the Ἐῖδος of the Son.[67] The idea that the Spirit is the 'Image' of the Son may be rather puzzling until it is realised that the Spirit himself is *imageless*. This implies that since the Father and the Son and the Holy Spirit are of one and the same Nature, it must be in an ineffable, imageless and wholly spiritual way that we are to think of them in their relations with one another in the Holy Trinity. This ineffability of God, however, is not negative but positive, for it is precisely in making himself known to us through the Son and in the Spirit that God reveals himself as infinitely greater than we can conceive. As Basil once said, 'We confess that we know what is knowable of God and yet what we know reaches beyond our comprehension.'[68]

Let us recall further here the fact that classical Christian theology placed the *homoousion* of the Spirit alongside the *homoousion* of the incarnate Son. While the *homoousion* of the Son expresses the truth that what God is in Christ Jesus he is antecedently and eternally in himself, the bracketing with it of the *homoousion* of the Spirit has the effect of excising from our thought any projection into God of the creaturely, corporeal or sexist ingredients in the terms 'father', 'son', 'offspring', or 'generation' into God. Much the same role was played by the statement inserted in the Nicene Creed that the incarnate Son is 'Light of Light' as well as God of God, for that was specifically intended to clarify the unique nature of the inexpressible relation of the only begotten Son to the Father and may help us to grasp some aspects of the truth to which they refer. The image of light given us in the Holy Scripture is one analogy which Athanasius and Gregory Nazianzen felt they could use carefully without going wrong. Thus they referred to the Epistle to the Hebrews which speaks of Christ as 'the brightness of God's glory and the

[65] Gregory Nazianzen, *Orationes*, 29.16.
[66] See Gregory Nazianzen, *Orationes*, 31.7f, 31ff.
[67] See Athanasius, *Contra Arianos*, 3.6, 10 16; *De synodis*, 52; *Ad Serapionem*, 1.19f.; cf. Didymus, *De Trinitate*, 2.5, 11; and John of Damascus, *De fide orthodoxa*, 1.13.
[68] Basil, *Epistulae*, 235.2.

expression of his hypostasis';[69] and to the Psalmist who says: 'With you is the fountain of life and in your light we see light.'[70] God who dwells in unapproachable Light is nevertheless revealed to us through the shining of his Light upon the face of Jesus Christ and through the enlightening presence of his Spirit who leads us into the truth as it is in Jesus, to whom we are directed through his transparent and translucent mode of being.

When in this approach we think and speak of God as 'Father', and of Jesus Christ as his 'Son', our minds are directed by the Spirit to consider the truth that divine revelation conveys to us through and beyond the actual language employed, namely, the *relation* in which the Father stands to the Son and the Son stands to the Father. That was, to a large extent, the point of the *homoousion* in the Nicene Creed which was added to the clauses about Jesus Christ as the only begotten Son of God, begotten of his Father from all ages, begotten, not made, in order to give a precise statement about the relation between the Son to the Father as one of *identity of nature*. The *homoousion* thus regarded and used enables us to affirm the real and intimate relation between the Father and the Son while allowing us to exercise a measure of apophatic reserve in our use and understanding of the words 'father' and 'son' as applied to God, for the truth they signify even in divine revelation lies beyond the limits of the terms used to signify it. They are intended to denote God in the inner relation of his Being as Father and Son in ways that elude our imagination and conceptual grasp. This does not mean that God is in himself, in the depths of his eternal Being, other than what he has revealed of himself in the Gospel as the Father of the Son, but rather that we are unable to pierce behind what God has revealed of himself as he addresses us in the language of the Holy Scriptures to what he is in himself apart from his self-revelation to us. In response to his Word we cannot help but use human language in speaking of God, but in itself it is far from adequate or proper.[71] The ultimate truth to which we seek to give theological expression when, following Holy Scripture, we call God 'Father and Son', is hidden in the mystery of God's transcendent Being. That is holy ground upon which we dare not try to intrude through human speculation. Karl Barth went so far as to write about this: 'We do not know what we are saying when we call God Father and Son. We can say it only in such a way that on our lips and in our concepts it is an untruth. For us the truth we are expressing when we call God Father and Son is hidden and unsearchable.'[72]

We return to the point that the technical theological concept of *hypostasis* or 'person' was formed as a direct product of the doctrine of the Holy Trinity as three Persons, one Being. It is important to note, however, that once the concept of 'person' was launched into the stream of human ideas and became a regular item in the furniture of our everyday thought it inevitably tended to have an independent

[69] Heb. 1.3.

[70] Ps. 36.9.

[71] Cf. Hilary, *De Trinitate*, 2.2, 5; 4.1; 7.47; 10.53; and Calvin, *Institutio*, 1.8.1–2; 1.13.15. See also 'Calvin's Doctrine of the Trinity', *Trinitarian Perspectives*, ch. 3, pp. 44ff.

[72] Karl Barth, *Church Dogmatics* I.1 (2nd edn, 1975), p. 433. See his discussion of this from p. 428.

history of its own and in spite of cultural variations to give rise in people's minds to a general conception of what person denotes. It would be a serious mistake, however, to interpret what is meant by 'Person' in the doctrine of the Holy Trinity by reference to any general, and subsequent, notion of person, and not by reference to its aboriginal theological sense. Applied to God 'Person' must be understood in an utterly unique way appropriate to his eternal uncreated and creative Nature, but it may also be applied to human 'persons' made in the image of God in a very different creaturely way. Just as we may not understand what the Fatherhood of God means by analogical projection even *via eminentiae* out of human fatherhood, for human fatherhood is to be understood properly by reference to the Fatherhood of God beyond itself altogether, so we may not understand what it means to speak of God as Person or as personal in terms of what human beings are in themselves and in their relations to one another, for human personhood is to be understood properly by relation to the creative Personhood of God. We must think of God, rather, as *personalising Person*, and of ourselves as *personalised persons*, people who are personal primarily through onto-relations to him as the creative Source of our personal being, and secondarily through onto-relations to one another within the subject-subject structures of our creaturely being as they have come from him.

It is of course in and through Jesus Christ in particular that God's interrelations with us and our interrelations with God are acutely personalised, for Jesus is the personalising activity of God incarnated in the midst of our human existence and our subject-subject relations. He the incarnate 'I am' of God is the personalising Person in relation to whom in the Spirit we are personalised through the reconciling and re-creating activity of the Holy Trinity. In the Lord Jesus Christ himself the one Mediator between God and man, divine and human nature are united in one Person, as the Council of Chalcedon formulated it, without confusion, without change, without division and without separation. Classical Christology, under the illuminating guidance of Cyril of Alexandria,[73] explained this in relation to the twin concepts of *anhypostatos* (ἀνυπόστατος) and *enhypostatos* (ἐνυπόστατος). This was further developed by Severus of Antioch[74] and John of Damascus.[75] By 'anhypostatic' it was asserted that in the assumption of the flesh the human nature of Christ had no independent hypostasis or subsistence apart from the event of the incarnation, apart from hypostatic union, which ruled out any adoptionist error. By 'enhypostatic', however, it was asserted that in the assumption of the flesh the human nature of Christ was given a *real concrete hypostasis* or subsistence within the hypostatic union – it was enhypostatic in the incarnate Son or Word of God – which ruled out any Apollinarian or monophysite error. The concepts of *anhypostasis* and *enhypostasis* are complementary and inseparable.[76]

---

[73] Especially in Cyril's *Apologia contra Theodoretum*, *Patrologia Graeca*, 76, 397C, and *Thesaurus de Trinitate*, PG 75. 8, 101D–104B.

[74] Severus of Antioch, *Collected Letters*, tr. E. W. Brooks, *Patrologia Orientalis*, 1,14 (Paris, 1919–20), pp. 186–194. See Iain R. Torrance, *Christology After Chalcedon* (Norwich, 1988), pp. 114–116 & 125 f.

[75] John of Damascus, *De fide orthodoxa*, 3.3–9.

[76] Refer to Karl Barth, *Christliche Dogmatik* (Munich, 1927), p. 284; *The Göttingen Dogmatics*, I, tr. by G. W. Bromiley, (Edinburgh, 1991), p. 157f; and *Church Dogmatics* I.2 (Edinburgh, 1956), p. 163f; and Heinrich Heppe, *Reformed Dogmatics* (Eng. tr. Edinburgh, 1950), pp. 427ff.

In the incarnation the eternal Son assumed human nature into oneness with himself but in that assumption Jesus Christ is not only real man but *a* man. He is at once the *One* and the *Many*, for in Jesus the Creator become man, all human nature has been assumed. The point for our consideration here is the fact that it is in this union of the human hypostasis or person and the divine *Hypostasis* or Person that Jesus Christ is the personalising Person whose saving power is brought to bear directly upon us. In him the incarnate Son and Word of God, Creator and creature, divine and human nature, are united in one Person, so that in Jesus our human being is radically personalised and indeed humanised, and as such is brought into intimate union with God and into the Communion of the Holy Trinity. Since, as St Paul tells us, the very fullness of God or the entire Godhead dwells bodily in Jesus Christ (κατοικεῖ πᾶν τὸ πλήρωμα τῆς Θεότητος σωματικῶς), we must think of him as embodying within our human life the onto-interrelations which obtain not only between him and the Father but between the three divine Persons in their undivided Communion with One Another. It is as such that the Lord Jesus is the personalising Person with whom we have directly to do in the *parousia* of the Holy Spirit whom he breathes upon us and imparts to us on the ground of his reconciling and healing activity in life, death and resurrection.[77]

This personalising activity of God toward us in Christ and the Spirit, and the onto-relational way in which the three divine Persons are who they are in their Communion with One Another, revealed to us through God's trinitarian self-revelation in the Gospel, throw not a little light on the Nature of the one Being of God as Being in his internal relations, and on the nature of the homoousial Communion which the Father, the Son and the Holy Spirit constitute in their objective or hypostatic relations with one another. If the one Being of God is identical with the Communion of the three Divine Persons and the Communion of the three divine Persons is identical with the one Being of God, then we must think of the one God as a fullness of personal Being in himself.[78] He is not less personal in his one indivisible Being as whole God (ὅλος Θεός) than he is in each Person who is true God of true God and is in himself as the Son or the Spirit whole God (ὅλος Θεός) as well as the Father. However, to say that God is intrinsically personal does not mean that we must think of the one God as *a* Person in the relational sense of the three divine Persons in their objective relations to one another, in the same way that the Father, the Son and the Holy Spirit are each *a* Person in relation to the other two Persons, but rather that God is completely personal in himself. As the one God he is a Communion of personal Being in himself, a Trinity in Unity and a Unity in Trinity. God is perfectly Three in One and One in Three. In this case, the three Persons of the Holy Trinity in their difference from One Another and in their oneness with One Another, are to be heard, and known and worshipped and glorified by us 'as one Person (ἐν πρόσωπον)'.[79]

[77] See further *The Mediation of Christ* (Edinburgh, 1992), pp. 67ff.
[78] Cf. Augustine, *De Trinitate*, 7.6.11: 'For God it is not one thing to be, another to be a person, but it is absolutely the same thing.'
[79] Thus Didymus the Blind, *De Trinitate*, 2.36, and Cyril of Alexandria, *In Joannis Evangelium*, 15.1, without any trace of Sabellian unipersonalism. But cf. the warning of John of Damascus, *De fide orthodoxa* 3.5, against understanding this in terms of 'one hypostasis'.

2) THE MUTUAL INDWELLING AND LOVING OF THE FATHER, THE SON AND THE HOLY SPIRIT

In the outgoing movement of his eternal Love God himself has come among us and become one of us and one with us in the Person of his beloved Son in order to reconcile us to himself and to share with us the Fellowship of Love which he has within his own Triune Life. Since in the Lord Jesus Christ the fullness of God dwells bodily we must think of the entire Godhead as condescending in him to be 'God with us' in our human life and existence in the world. This does not mean of course that the Father and the Spirit became incarnate with the Son, but that with and in the incarnate Son the whole undivided Trinity was present and active in fulfilling the eternal purpose of God's Love for mankind, for all three divine Persons have their Being in homoousial and hypostatic interrelations with one another, and they are all inseparably united in God's activity in creation and redemption, not least as those activities are consummated in the incarnate economy of the Son. In refusing to spare his dear Son but in delivering him up in atoning sacrifice for us all, God the Father reveals that he loves us with the very Love which he bears to himself, and that with Jesus Christ he freely gives us all things. If God is for us in this way what can come between us? And in giving us his one Spirit who proceeds from the Father through the Son and sheds abroad in our hearts the very Love which God himself is, God reveals that there is nothing that can ever separate us from him in his Love. Through the Son and in the Spirit, we are taken into the triune Fellowship of God the Father, God the Son and God the Holy Spirit. Thus in an utterly astonishing way the Holy Trinity has committed himself to be with us and among us within the conditions of our human and earthly life in space and time, but, it need hardly be said, without being subjected to the processes and necessities of created space and time, and without in the slightest compromising the mystery of his divine transcendence.

The Love that God the Father, God the Son and God the Holy Spirit eternally are, has taken incarnate form in the Lord Jesus Christ for us and our salvation. The self-giving and self-sacrificial Love manifested in him flows from the self-giving and self-sacrificial Love of God and are that self-giving and sacrificial Love in redemptive action on our behalf in the world. To the fellowship of love which God establishes with us through the incarnation of his beloved Son in space and time there corresponds an eternal Fellowship of Love within God himself. The Freedom in which God enters into communion with us is grounded in and flows from the Freedom of the Father, the Son and the Holy Spirit in their love for one another. The Communion which God eternally is in the mutual indwelling of the three Divine Persons within the relations of his one Being, he is toward us and with us and for us in his saving presence and loving activity in history. This is what the doctrine of the Holy Trinity supremely means, that God himself is Love.[80] This is

[80] See F. W. Camfield, *Revelation and the Holy Spirit, An Essay in Barthian Theology* (London, 1933), p. 250f.

not a static unmoved and unmoving Love, for God's Being is an eternal movement in Love, and consists in the Love with which the Father, the Son and the Holy Spirit ceaselessly love one another. It is in the free gratuitous overflowing of this Love of God to what is other than God in creation and redemption that our salvation through Christ and sanctification in the Holy Spirit are grounded, and through its outward movement in the fulfilment of God's economic purpose in reconciling and unifying all things in heaven and earth that they are actualised in our existence in Christ, and therefore in the Church which as the Body of Christ is 'the earthly-historical form of his own existence'.[81]

In our discussion of the import of God's self-revelation to the people of Israel as 'I am who I am / I will be who I will be' we were concerned with the truth that God does not wish to live for himself alone, but has created mankind for fellowship with himself. We found that 'I am who I am / I will be who I will be' is not to be understood simply in terms of God's self-grounded Being, but as the Being of God *for others* with whom he seeks and creates fellowship, although this *for others* is to be regarded as flowing freely from the ground and will of his own transcendent Self-Being. While the Being of God is not to be thought of as constituted by his relations with others beyond himself, the free flowing of his Being outward in sheer love toward and for others reveals something of the inmost Nature of God's Being as *Being for* within himself. That is to say, the real meaning of the Being of God as he has revealed himself to his people has to do with the saving *self-determination* of God in his love and grace to be with them and for them as their God, as well as with his determination of them to be with him as his redeemed children.

It was this concept of *being for* (πρός τι) that Gregory Nazianzen found to characterise the profound hypostatic relation between the Father and the Son in terms of which what is meant by divine Fatherhood and Sonship may be understood at least in some measure. For God the Father to be Father is to be Father of the Son, and for God the Son to be Son is to be Son of the Father – they are who and what they are in their otherness as Father and Son in their hypostatic belonging to and being for one another. This *being for* one another naturally applies also to the interrelation between all three divine Persons in the Holy Trinity, which we spoke of as 'onto-relations' – the kind of relations between persons which belong to what they intrinsically are as persons. As we saw, it was in the course of the formulation of the doctrine of the Holy Trinity that this theological concept of person and of the personal first actually arose, but it took its beginning from the intimately personal self-revelation of God in Jesus Christ, the incarnate 'I am' of God. Our immediate concern at the moment is with the onto-relations of the three divine Persons as their *being for one another*, in which they dwell in one another, love one another, give themselves to one another and receive from one another in the Communion of the Holy Trinity.[82]

[81] Karl Barth, *Church Dogmatics* IV.2 (Edinburgh, 1958), pp. 614ff.
[82] I have in mind here an address given to the 1974 meeting of Society for the Study of Theology in Cambridge, entitled 'The Trinity in Prayer and Worship', by the late Dom Paul Ziegler, OSB, of Quarr Abbey, in which he discussed the concept of 'subsisting relations' between the divine Persons as 'their being for each other in the Trinity'.

It is particularly to the teaching of Jesus himself as given to us in the Gospel according to St John, followed up by St John in his first Epistle, that we must turn for the biblical account of the mutual movement of love immanent in the Holy Trinity, or the indwelling of the Father, the Son and the Holy Spirit in one another. It is to the connection between the Communion within the mystery of the Holy Trinity and the great mystery of godliness manifest in the flesh, in the hypostatic union in Christ, that our thought turns here, for it is in the incarnation of the Son of the Father in the Lord Jesus Christ that the inner trinitarian Life of the Love which God is has been thrust revealingly into our human existence and life, and it is through our union with Christ in the Spirit that we participate by grace in the eternal Life and Love of the Holy Trinity. It is, then, the indivisible relation in Being and Act between the Persons of Son and the Father actualised and manifested in the saving economy of Jesus' life and work in history that constitutes, so to speak, the axis on which there revolves our understanding of the Love that eternally flows between the Father, the Son and the Holy Spirit, that is, the axis of the oneness between the 'I am' of Christ and the 'I am' of God, or the dwelling of the Son and the Father in one another. It is in and through that indwelling that the ultimate mystery of the mutual indwelling of the three divine Persons in one God becomes disclosed to us, for it is through the Communion of the Holy Spirit sent to us by the Father that we may participate by grace in the Communion of the Father and the Son with one another, and thus in the Communion of the Holy Trinity.

In the Synoptic Gospels Jesus spoke to his disciples of 'the mystery of the Kingdom' which clearly referred to himself in their midst, in the light of which his teaching was to be understood.[83] In Johannine language the mystery is the *I Am* (Ἐγώ εἰμι) of him who is one with the Father: 'I am the way, the truth and the life; no one comes to the Father but by me.'[84] In the Synoptic language Jesus is *'Emmanuel, God with us'*,[85] but that Jesus is the Son of the living God is not revealed by flesh and blood, but only by the Father.[86] In the Fourth Gospel the teaching of Jesus centres throughout on his intimate relation as the incarnate Son to the Father which he described in terms of their existing and dwelling in one another and of their seeing, knowing and loving of one another. 'As the Father knows me, so I know the Father ... I and my Father are one ... the Father is in me and I am in him.'[87] 'He who has seen me has seen the Father ... Believe me that I am in the Father and the Father is in me.'[88]

It is on that ground of the unbroken relation in Being and Act between Jesus Christ and the Father, of their knowing and loving of one another, and through the mission of the Spirit of the Father and of the Son to be with us and dwell

---

[83] Mark 4.11; Luke 8.10; Matt. 13.11. For my discussion of this μυστήριον, see *Conflict and Agreement in the Church*, vol. 2 (London, 1960), pp. 82–92.

[84] John 14.6: Ἐγώ εἰμι ὁ ὁδὸς καὶ ἡ ἀλήθεια καὶ ἡ ζωή, οὐδεὶς ἔρχεται πρὸς τὸν Πατέρα εἰ μὴ δι᾽ ἐμοῦ. Cf. John 6.37, 44, 65.

[85] Matt. 1.23.

[86] Matt. 16.17; cf. 11.25; & Luke 10.22.

[87] John 10.15, 30, 38.

[88] John 14.9, 11.

within us, that the movement of Love eternally hidden in God has been revealed to us, and a corresponding movement of love has been generated in us toward the Father through the Son and in the Holy Spirit. The incarnation and the ascension are two complementary moments in the one saving movement of the Love of God the Father. Through the *coming* of Jesus Christ into the world as the only begotten Son loved by the Father, the Love which flows eternally between the Father and the Son in the Holy Trinity has moved outward to bear upon us in history and is made known to us above all in the sacrificial love of Jesus in laying down his life for us. And in the *ascending* of Jesus Christ to the Father the Love of God embodied among us in him and exhibited to us in his incarnate life and sacrifice, is shown to be grounded in the eternal Love of God the Father, the Son, and the Holy Spirit in their mutual indwelling in the Holy Trinity. The Love of God revealed to us in the economic Trinity is identical with the Love of God in the ontological Trinity; but the Love of God revealed to us in the economic manifestation of the Father, the Son and the Holy Spirit in the history of our salvation, tells us that God loves us with the very same love with which he loves himself, in the reciprocal love of the three divine Persons for Each Other in the eternal Communion of the Holy Trinity.

When we turn to the First Epistle of St John we learn that 'God is Love', and that this Love is defined by the Love that God bears to us in sending his Son to be the propitiation for our sins, and indeed for the sins of the world.[89] That is to say, the very Being of God as Love is identical with his loving, for he is himself the Love with which he loves: his Being and his Act are one and the same. This very Love that God is, therefore, is identical with Jesus Christ who laid down his life for us, and who in his own Being and Act as the Son of the Father embodies the Love of God. The self-giving of the Son in sacrificial love and the self-giving of the Father in sacrificial love are not separable from one another, for the Father and the Son dwell in one another, together with the Spirit of God, whom we know through his witness to the Son, and through whose dwelling in us God dwells in us. This means that we are to understand the Love that God is in his being-in-act and his act-in-being in a trinitarian way. The Father, the Son and the Holy Spirit who indwell One Another in the Love that God is constitute the Communion of Love or the movement of reciprocal Loving which is identical with the One Being of God. It is as God the Father, God the Son, and God the Holy Spirit that God is God and God is Love. As one Being, three Persons, the Being of God is to be understood as an eternal movement of Love, both in himself as the Love of the Father, the Son and the Holy Spirit for one Another, and in his loving Self-giving to others beyond himself.[90]

When we bring this together with the foregoing account of the onto-relations between the Father, the Son and the Holy Spirit in terms of their inter-personal relations for one another, we may speak of them as relations of the Love which the

---

[89] 1 John 4.7–16.

[90] See Karl Barth, *Church Dogmatics* II.1 'The Being of God as the One who Loves', pp. 272ff, and 4.2, 'The Basis of Love', pp. 751ff, helpful discussions to which I am indebted. Cf. also E. Jüngel, *God as the Mystery of the World* (Edinburgh, 1983), pp. 362ff; and Wolfhardt Pannenberg, *Systematic Theology* (Edinburgh, 1991), vol. 1, 'Love and Trinity', pp. 422ff.

three Divine Persons have in their bearing upon One Another as intrinsically ontic as well as dynamic. That is to say, expressed the other way round, the relations in reciprocal loving between the three divine Persons are onto-relations, for they are relations which belong to what they each are hypostatically in themselves as divine Persons and to what they are homoousially together in their love for one another, in their self-giving to one another and their receiving from one another. Thus in their Communion in Love with one another they are three Persons, one Being. Their differences from each other as Father, Son and Holy Spirit, instead of separating them from one another involve a 'sort of ontological communication' between them,[91] and as such are constitutive of their Unity in Trinity and their Trinity in Unity.

At the same time, the perfect oneness of the Being of God with his Loving, and the fact that the reciprocal relations between the Father, the Son and the Holy Spirit are the onto-relations in virtue of which they are who they are, mean that loving activity and personal being must be understood to qualify and define one another. This has the effect of deepening and reinforcing the theological concept of 'person', and 'personal', not only in respect of our understanding of the Father, the Son and the Holy Spirit as Persons in relation to one another, but in respect of our understanding of the Triune God as a fullness of personal and loving Being in himself. In the Communion of the Holy Trinity the Father is Father in his loving of the Son and the Spirit, and the Son is Son in his loving of the Father and the Spirit, and the Spirit is the Spirit in his loving of the Father and the Son. It is as such that the Love that flows between the Father, the Son and the Spirit, freely flows in an outward movement of loving activity toward us with whom God creates a communion of love corresponding to the Communion of Love which he ever is in himself.

While God loves us with the Love with which he loves himself that is not in any sense a selfish Love, but the mutual movement of love within the Holy Trinity in which the Father, the Son and the Holy Spirit dwell in one another and exist for one another in such a way that each is who he is only in his relations with the others. It is out of that selfless self-giving Love which God is eternally in himself that he gave himself freely in surrendering his dear Son in atoning sacrifice for our sins. Thereby God has revealed that he does not keep himself to himself but loves us without any reserve, more, astonishingly, than he loves himself. It is as this infinite, unlimited, transcendent self-giving Love that God is, that God the Father, the Son and the Holy Spirit, three Persons, one Being, seeks and creates fellowship with us in order to reconcile us with himself and to share with us his own eternal Life and Love.

In view of the teaching of the New Testament about the Communion (κοινωνία) of the Spirit, we can understand why the Church Fathers quickly thought of the Holy Spirit both in terms of the Communion of the Father, the Son and the Holy Spirit in God and in terms of the communion which he creates between us in the

---

[91] I have taken the expression 'ontological communication' from the essay of Nikos A. Nissiotis, in *The Orthodox Ethos*, edited by A. Philippou (Oxford, 1964), p. 43.

Church and the Holy Trinity. Thus early in the last quarter of the second century Athenagoras of Athens offered an account of the mutual relations between the Father, the Son and the Holy Spirit who are united with one another in their very differences and of the Spirit as constituting the union (ἕνωσις) between them.[92] This was developed in the teaching of Athanasius especially in his *Epistles on the Spirit to Serapion*,[93] which Basil followed up in his work *On the Holy Spirit* in which he spoke of the Holy Spirit as the Communion (κοινωνία) of the Father and the Son in the Godhead or as the Bond of Nature (κοινὸν τῆς φύσεως) in the Holy Trinity.[94] Likewise Gregory Nazianzen spoke of the Holy Spirit as intermediate (μέσον) between the Father and the Son,[95] while Epiphanius referred to the Holy Spirit as in the midst (ἐν μέσῳ) of the Father and the Son and as the Bond of the Trinity (σύνδεσμος τῆς Τριάδος).[96] This is the pneumatological teaching that Augustine took over and developed for Western theology in his influential account of the Holy Spirit as 'a kind of consubstantial Communion (*communio quaedam consubstantialis*)' between the Father and the Son.[97]

---

[92] Athenagoras, *Legatio pro Christianis*, 12.3.
[93] Athanasius, see especially *Ad Serapionem*, 1.16f, 20f; 2.5; 3.1-7; 4.3-7.
[94] Basil, *De Spiritu Sancto*, 45f; and *Epistulae*, 111: 'The Son includes the Spirit in his and the Father's Communion.' Basil is here indebted to Athanasius, *Ad Serapionem*, especially 1.20.
[95] Gregory Nazianzen, *Orationes*, 31.8.
[96] Epiphanius, *Anchoratus*, 4.7f; *Haereses*, 62.4; 74.11.
[97] Augustine, *De Trinitate*, 15.27.50.

7

Trinity in Unity and Unity in Trinity

I N our discussion of the formulation of the doctrine of the Holy Trinity in the third chapter we followed a movement of thought from the ground level of the incarnate self-revelation of God in a pattern of implicit trinitarian relations in the economic Trinity through two conceptual levels to a fully explicit pattern in the ontological Trinity. In the course of this movement there took place a refinement in our understanding of the basic concepts and relations of God's revealing and saving activity toward us and for us of which we learn in the Scriptures of the New Testament. This involved two stages: the interpretation of the soteriological content of God's three-fold self-revelation mediated to us in the biblical statements about the life, death, and resurrection of Jesus Christ in the light of their ontological sub-structure expressed in the Nicene *homoousion;* and the unfolding of the profound implications of the *homoousion* applied to the Spirit as well as to the Son for an understanding of the eternal relations of the Father, the Son and the Holy Spirit. At this third level use was made of the patristic concept of *perichoresis* to express something of the mystery of the Holy Trinity in respect of the coinherent way in which the Father, the Son and the Holy Spirit exist in one another and dwell in one another as one God, three Persons. We must now give further consideration to the notion of *perichoresis* and the help it gives us in deepening and clarifying understanding of the onto-relations of the three divine Persons to one another in respect of the coordination that obtains between them and their unity in the divine *Monarchia.*

It was undoubtedly Athanasius who in his elucidation of the dwelling of the Father and the Son in one another provided the theological basis for the doctrine of coinherence.[1] He did this by way of elucidating statements of Jesus to the disciples recorded by St John, particularly, 'I am in the Father and the Father in me'.[2] He deepened and refined the concept of the *homoousion* which gave expression to the underlying oneness in being and activity between the incarnate Son and God the

---

[1] For adumbrations of his thought here see Athenagoras, *Legatio pro Christianis*, 10, and Irenaeus, *Adversus haereses,* 3.6.2.
[2] John 14.11. Cf. also John 10.30, and 14.10.

Father upon which everything in the Gospel depended. As he understood it the *homoousion* pointed both to real distinctions between the three divine Persons and to their coinhering with one another in the one Being of God. For Athanasius this had to do not merely with a linking or intercommunication of the distinctive properties of the three divine Persons, which became known as *communicatio idiomatum* (κοινωνία ἰδιωμάτων), but with a completely mutual indwelling in which each Person, while remaining what he is by himself as Father, Son or Holy Spirit, is wholly in the others as the others are wholly in him. Although Athanasius did not give us a specific term for coinherence, mutual containing, or *perichoresis* (περιχώρησις) – that came later – its basic idea was already conceived in his refutation of the Arian disparagement of the Lord's Words, 'I in the Father and the Father in me', through their question, 'How can the one be contained (χωρεῖν) in the other and the other in the one?'[3] Athanasius pointed out that this would be to think of the relation between the Father and the Son quite inappropriately in accordance with the way material things can empty into and contain one another. He went on to explain that when it is said 'I am in the Father and the Father is in me' we are to understand this reciprocal relation as one in which the whole Being of the Father and the whole Being of the Son mutually indwell, inexist or coexist in one another, which is thinkable only in relation to God himself and of which we learn only in God's revelation of himself.[4]

In his *Letters on the Holy Spirit* written to his friend Serapion, Athanasius showed that we must think of this coinherence as applying equally to the homoousial interrelations between the Spirit and the Son, and the Spirit and the Father, and thus to the whole Trinity, for unless the Being and Activity of the Spirit are identical with the Being and Activity of the Father and the Son, we are not saved.[5] For the great Patriarch of Alexandria the Gospel of salvation as handed down from the apostles and expressed in the Nicene Confession depended entirely on the ontological connection between the saving life and activity of the incarnate Son of God and God the Father, which in turn revealed and imported the no less crucial ontological connection between the Holy Spirit and both the Son and the Father. Thus his stress upon the inner coinherent relations of the Holy Trinity was particularly significant in upholding the bond between the soteriological and ontological understanding of the Faith inherent in the *homoousion* that had been central to the Nicene appropriation and interpretation of the Gospel.

With reference to the Johannine verse, John 14.10, Hilary put forward much the same teaching in the West but with explicit account of the coinherence between the divine Persons in terms of their wholly *containing* one another as whole Persons without any diminishment to the honour and glory of one another. 'Although

---

[3] Athanasius, *Contra Arianos*, 3.1 – the Arian question ran: Πῶς δύναται οὗτος ἐν ἐκείνῳ, κάκεῖνος ἐν τούτῳ χωρεῖν; ἢ πῶς ὅλως δύναται ὁ Πατήρ, μείζων ὤν, ἐν τῷ Υἱῷ ἐλάττονι ὄντι χωρεῖν; See also *Contra Arianos*, 2.33.

[4] Athanasius, *Contra Arianos*, 3.1–6. See also 4.1–5; and *De synodis*, 26.

[5] Athanasius, *Ad Serapionem*, 1.19, 31; 2.2, 9; 4.4. See G. D. Dragas, 'St Athanasius on the Holy Spirit and the Trinity', in *Theological Dialogue between Orthodox and Reformed Churches*, vol. 2 (Edinburgh, 1993), Chapter 2, pp. 40ff.

these Beings do not dwell apart, they retain their separate existence and condition and can reciprocally contain one another, so that one permanently envelops and is also permanently enveloped by the other whom he yet envelops.' He argued that while this idea of mutual containing is unintelligible in respect of natural objects, it is not impossible with God who is both within and without all things, and contains all things although he himself is not contained by anything.[6] Hilary was very familiar with Athanasian and Cappadocian theology which he learned during his exile in the East, and although he wrote in Latin he clearly had in mind the Greek terms and χωρεῖν and χωρητικός in this account of the way in which the Persons of the Holy Trinity reciprocally contain one another while remaining what they are in their otherness from one another.[7] Here we evidently have developed the full concept that was to be given technical expression in the term *perichoresis* (περιχώρησις), which like the verb περιχωρεῖν derives from χωρεῖν meaning both 'to go' and 'to make room for' or 'to contain'.[8] The noun *perichoresis* may actually have been current in the East at that time, although there is no written evidence for it extant.

Gregory Nazianzen had used the verb περιχωρεῖν to help him express the way in which he thought the divine and human natures of Christ interacted or intermingled with one another in virtue of their union, but without any suggestion of the human nature interpenetrating the divine Nature, or any attempt to extend this to the inner relations of the divine Persons in the Holy Trinity.[9] The first actual use of the noun *perichoresis* in extant literature is found in the work of an unknown theologian on the Holy Trinity attributed to Cyril of Alexandria.[10] This is found in connection with the key text John 14.11, in a passage lifted without acknowledgement by John of Damascus but which had the effect of giving it currency as a technical theological term.[11] By *perichoresis* Pseudo-Cyril (and John Damascene) gave expression to the dynamic Union and Communion of the Father, the Son and the Holy Spirit with one another in one Being in such a way that they have their Being in each other and reciprocally contain one another, without any coalescing or commingling with one another and yet without any separation from one another, for they are completely equal and identical in Deity and Power. Each Person contains the one God in virtue of his relation to the others as well as his

---

[6] Hilary, *De Trinitate*, 3.1f; cf. also 2.6; 3.4; 4.10.

[7] Cf. Hilary's contemporary, Gregory Nyssen, *Contra Arianos et Sabellianos*, 12.

[8] Χωρέω is not to be confused with χορεύω which means to dance as in a Greek χορός or chorus. For the use of χωρεῖν in relation to the Greek Patristic notion of space, χώρα (which was carried over into the concept of the mutual containing of the three divine Persons) see my discussion in *Space, Time and Incarnation* (London, 1969), pp. 15f.

[9] Gregory Nazianzen, *Epistulae*, 101.6; cf. *Orationes*, 18.42; 22.4; and see *The Trinitarian Faith*, p. 234. But cf. John of Damascus, *De fide orthodoxa*, 3.3, who evidently following Maximus (*Disputatio cum Pyrro, Patrologia Graeca*, 91. 344–5) tried to apply the notion of mutual interpenetration to the divine and human natures of Christ, which easily slips into a Eutychian conception of Christ's humanity.

[10] Pseudo-Cyril, *De Sacrosancta Trinitate*, 10 and 23 (*PG*, 77, 1144D & 1164B). See the chapter on 'Co-inherence' by G. L. Prestige, *God in Patristic Thought* (London, 1952), pp. 282–301.

[11] John of Damascus, *De fide orthodoxa*, 1.8; see also 1.11.

relation to himself for they wholly coexist and inexist in one another. Human beings do not exist within one another, but this is precisely what the divine Persons of the Holy Trinity do. Explanatory reference is made to the statement of Gregory Nazianzen to the effect that the Godhead is undivided in divided Persons due to their identity of Being, rather like three suns cleaving to one another without any separation and giving out their light combined and conjoined into one.[12]

It is important to note that *perichoresis* has essentially a *dynamic* and not a static sense, with the meaning of mutual indwelling and inter-penetrating one another in the onto-relational, spiritual and intensely personal way discussed above.

It imports a mutual movement as well as a mutual indwelling, which gives expression to the dynamic nature of the homoousial Communion between the three divine Persons, in which, as we shall note, their differentiating qualities instead of separating them actually serve their oneness with each other. It was thus that Basil linked both the coactivity of the divine Persons in the Trinity and the oneness (ἕνωσις) of God's Nature to the Communion (κοινωνία) of the Spirit with the Father and the Son.[13] Since God is Spirit and God is Love, we must understand the *perichoresis* in a wholly spiritual and intensely personal way as the eternal movement of Love or the Communion of Love which the Holy Trinity ever is within himself, and in his active relations toward us through the Holy Spirit from within his homoousial relations with the Father and the Son. In this homoousial way the Holy Spirit is in himself the *enhypostatic* Love and the Communion of Love in the perichoretic relations between the Father and the Son, and as such is in himself the ground of our communion with God in the Love of the Father and Son. This was precisely the theme developed by the Apostle John in his Epistles, which had such a far-reaching impact on St Augustine.[14]

This teaching corresponds to the way in which theologians like Epiphanius of Salamis with considerable stress on the *homoousion* as applying to the inner relations of the Trinity as a whole, spoke of the Father, the Son and the Holy Spirit as three *enhypostatic* Persons eternally grounded and wholly coinhering in one another while remaining other than one another, without there being any deviation in the Trinity from complete oneness and identity. In the one Being of God the three Persons are always what they are, the Father always the Father, the Son always the Son and the Holy Spirit always the Holy Spirit, each being true and perfect God.[15] And it corresponds also to the thought of Cyril of Alexandria in his view of the living and dynamic coinherence or mutual containing of the Father, the Son and the Holy Spirit essentially and enhypostatically within the Holy Trinity. He brought together the emphasis of Athanasius upon the one Being of the homoousial Trinity with

---

[12] Gregory Nazianzen, *Orationes*, 31.14 – for the full citation see above at the beginning of chapter 4. See also 39.11, where Gregory speaks of the Godhead as 'divided indivisibly… and conjoined dividedly'.

[13] Basil, *De Spiritu Sancto*, 37, 45f.

[14] Augustine, *De Trinitate*, 5.11.12; 6.5.7; 15.27.50.

[15] Epiphanius, *Ancoratus*, 2, 5–10, 64, 67, 77, 81; *Haereses*, 36.6; 57.4f; 62.1ff, 6; 65.8; 69.67; 72.1, 11; 73.34; 74.1ff, 9; 76.16, 30; 77.22; *Expositio fidei*, 21.

Gregory Nazianzen's conception of an indivisible but internally differentiated Trinity of real hypostatic relations continuously and actively subsisting in the Godhead.[16]

We have spent some time in our consideration of 'the mystery of the *perichoresis*',[17] for its articulation in Nicene and post-Nicene theology of the immanent in-each-otherness of God the Father, God the Son and God the Holy Spirit in their homoousial Communion with one another, brought the Church's interpretation of God's revealing and saving acts in Jesus Christ and the Holy Spirit to its supreme point, in acknowledgement of the Triunity of the living God.[18] It expressed the truth that the Father, the Son and the Holy Spirit are distinctive Persons each with his own incommunicable properties, but that they dwell *in* one another, not only *with* one another, in such an intimate way, let it be repeated, that their individual characteristics instead of dividing them from one another unite them indivisibly together, the Father in the Son and the Spirit, the Son in the Father and the Spirit, and the Spirit in the Father and the Son. The Father is not Father apart from the Son and the Spirit, the Son is not the Son apart from the Father and the Spirit, and the Spirit is not the Spirit apart from the Father and the Son, for each is who he is in his wholeness as true God of true God in the wholeness of the other two who are each true God of true God, and yet in the mystery of their perichoretic inter-relations they are not three Gods but one only God, the Blessed and Holy Trinity.

We noted above that *perichoresis* is not a static but a dynamic concept, for it refers to an eternal movement in the Love of the Father, the Son and the Holy Spirit for one another, which flows outward unceasingly toward us. But it is important to note as well that *perichoresis* is not a speculative concept. It expresses the soteriological truth of the identity between God himself and the content of his saving revelation in Jesus Christ and in the Holy Spirit, and thereby assures us that what God is toward us in Jesus Christ and in his Spirit he is inherently and eternally in himself. Together with the conception of the *homoousion* the conception of the coinherent or perichoretic relations of the divine Persons enables us to read back the interrelations between the Father, the Son and the Holy Spirit in the economy of salvation into the eternal relations immanent in the one Being of God. It must be said, therefore, that the basic conception of *perichoresis* arises out of joyful belief in Jesus Christ as Lord and Saviour, and out of worship and thanksgiving for the saving Love of God as Father, Son and Holy Spirit who reconciles us to himself and takes us up into Communion with himself.

On the other hand, *perichoresis* is a truth about the intimate relations in the divine Life which we cannot but formulate in fear and trembling, with adoration and awe, and in recognition of the poverty and inadequacy of the language we use in trying to put into words understanding of the mystery of the oneness and three-foldness of God's self-revelation to us. We could not do this were it not for the incarnation of God's Word in Jesus Christ and his gracious condescension to address

---

[16] Cyril of Alexandria, see especially his comments on John 1.1, 3 & 18; 10.30 & 38; and 14.10. Refer to *The Trinitarian Faith*, pp. 338f.

[17] Thus Heinrich Vogel, *Gott in Christo* (Berlin, 1951), p. 278f.

[18] The term 'Triunity' is not found in Greek patristic literature, but is found in Latin. The first use of *Triunitas* appears to be that of Isidore of Seville in the 7th century, *Etymologia*, 7.4.

us in human forms of thought and speech. In speaking of the Holy Trinity especially we are aware not only of having to use human modes of expression provided for us in the biblical revelation which signify realities beyond themselves, but of having to employ non-biblical terms in venturing to make pronouncements beyond the actual statements of the Scriptures in order to clarify interpretation and refute error, yet we cannot disguise the fact that this is to tread upon holy ground where we may speak and think only with prayer for divine forgiveness.[19] As Karl Barth once wrote: 'In our hands even terms suggested to us by Holy Scripture will prove to be incapable of grasping what they are supposed to grasp.'[20] However, as Cyril of Alexandria once said, 'when things concerning God are expressed in language used of men, we ought not to think of anything base, but to remember that the wealth of divine Glory is being mirrored in the poverty of human expression.'[21] This is surely how we must think of *perichoresis* in our attempt to speak as carefully and faithfully as we can, within the limited range of our creaturely capacities, about the ineffable Trinity in Unity and Unity in Trinity of the inter-hypostatic onto-relations in the transcendent Life of God.

We must now go on to draw out several of the important implications of *perichoresis* for a doctrine of the Triunity of God in which we shall take up again and develop further some of the theological conceptions that have already come before us.

1) PERICHORESIS AND THE WHOLENESS OF THE HOLY TRINITY

Perichoresis reinforces the fact that the Holy Trinity may be known only as a *whole* for it is as a whole that God makes himself known to us through himself and in himself as Father, Son and Holy Spirit.[22] It enables us to appreciate more fully the truth that the Holy Trinity is completely self-grounded in his own ultimate Reality, and that God's self-revelation is a self-enclosed *novum* which may be known and interpreted only on its own ground and out of itself. This means that our knowing of God engages in a deep circular movement from Unity to Trinity and from Trinity to Unity, since we are unable to speak of the whole Trinity without already speaking of the three particular Persons of the Trinity or to speak of any of the three Persons

---

[19] Read the moving prayer of Hilary in his wrestling with the difficulties and problems of human thought and speech about God, *De Trinitate*, 1.37–38.
[20] Karl Barth, *Church Dogmatics*, I.1, p. 476 ; cf. p. 433.
[21] Cyril of Alexandria, *In Joannis Evangelium*, 10.33. The same point was made by Hilary, *De Trinitate*, 2.2; Augustine, *De Trinitate*, 5.10.9; 7.4.7; and Calvin, *Institutio*, 1.13.3, 5 – see 'Calvin's Doctrine of the Trinity', *Trinitarian Perspectives*, ch. 3, pp. 41ff.
[22] Cf. H. B. Swete with reference to Athanasius: 'He placed the whole subject of the interior relations in the life of the Holy Trinity on a scientific basis, so that the doctrine of the Father, the Son, and the Holy Spirit can be seen to form a coherent whole, no part of which can be abandoned without a general collapse of faith.' *The Holy Spirit in the Ancient Church* (London, 1912), p. 220.

without presuming knowledge of the whole Triunity, for God is God only as he is Father, Son and Holy Spirit, and cannot be conceived by us truly otherwise. Certainly, as we noted in the first chapter, in our apprehension of God's trinitarian self-revelation in its intrinsic wholeness we rely on a subsidiary awareness of the particular Persons of the Trinity and in our explicit apprehension of each particular Person we rely on an implicit awareness of the whole Trinity. This is precisely what *peri-choresis* tells us, that God is known only in a *circle of reciprocal relations*. In Karl Barth's words, 'Just as in revelation, according to the biblical witness, the one God may be known only in the Three and the Three only as the one God, so none of the Three may be known without the other Two but each of the Three only with the other Two.'[23]

The inner reason for this circular and holistic apprehension of God in his Triunity is already evident in the completely homoousial interrelations of the Father, the Son and the Holy Spirit in which as distinct Hypostases they share equally, individually and together, and are the one identical Being of the Lord God Almighty. But it is in the refining and developing of the *homoousion* in its application to the Trinity as a whole through the concept of *perichoresis* that this became fully confirmed, in realisation of the truth that no divine Person is he who he really and truly is, even in his distinctive otherness, apart from relation to the other two in their mutual containing or interpenetrating of one another in such a way that each Person is in himself whole God of whole God. Since each divine Person considered in himself is true God of true God (Θεὸς ἀληθινὸς ἐκ Θεοῦ ἀληθινοῦ) without any qualification, the whole God dwells in each Person and each Person is whole God. Since the fullness of the Godhead is complete in each of them as well as in all of them, it is as the one indivisible Holy Trinity that God is God and that God is one God, and therefore may be known and is actually and truly known only as a Triune Whole. No one Person is knowable or known apart from the others. Due to their perichoretic onto-relations with one another in which they have their Being in one another, the Father is not truly known apart from the Son and the Holy Spirit; the Son is not truly known apart from the Father and the Holy Spirit; and the Holy Spirit is not truly known apart from the Father and the Son. The Holy Trinity is revealed and is known only as an indivisible Whole, in Trinity and Unity, Unity and Trinity. This indivisible wholeness, as we shall see, must be allowed to govern our understanding of the divine processions or missions of the Son and the Spirit from the Monarchy which, without a lapse into a remnant of Origenist subordinationism, cannot be limited to the Father. The Father is not properly (κυρίως) Father apart from the Son, the Son is not properly Son apart from the Father, and the Holy Spirit is not properly the Holy Spirit apart from the Father and the Son.

[23] Karl Barth, *Church Dogmatics* I.1, p. 370.

2) PERICHORESIS AND DISTINCTIONS WITHIN THE TRINITY

The concept of *perichoresis* deepens and strengthens our understanding of the hypostatic distinctions within the Trinity. While it helps to clarify the circularity of our belief in the Trinity through belief in his Unity, and our belief in his Unity through belief in his Trinity, it does not dissolve the distinctions between the three divine Persons unipersonally into the one Being of God. On the contrary, it establishes those distinctions by showing that it is precisely through their reciprocal relations with one another, and in virtue of their incommunicable characteristics as Father, Son and Holy Spirit, that the three divine Persons constitute the very Communion which the one God eternally is, or which they eternally are. In so doing, however, *perichoresis* has much to say about the *order* or τάξις that obtains between the Father, the Son, and the Holy Spirit in their relations with one another, the relation of the Son to the Father as his Father, and the relation of the Holy Spirit to both as the Spirit of the Father and the Spirit of the Son. They all coexist enhypostatically in the Communion of the Holy Trinity without being confused with one another, and without differing from one another in respect of their homoousial Being and homogeneous Nature.

On the one hand, *perichoresis* asserts the full *equality* of the three divine Persons. Gregory Nazianzen and Didymus the Blind drew the attention of the Early Church to the fact that in the triadic formulations in the Scriptures of the New Testament a variation in the order in which the divine Persons are mentioned is found, which points to their indivisible nature and essential equality in Being.[24] Moreover, the New Testament refers to each Person, the Son and the Spirit no less than the Father, as 'Lord' or *Yahweh*, each, therefore, as true God or αὐτοθεός , as 'whole God' (ὅλος θεός), 'whole from whole' (ὅλος ὅλου), as Athanasius expressed it,[25] or 'God considered in himself', as Gregory Nazianzen expressed it.[26] This represented a rejection of any Arian or partitive conceptions of Deity, and was considerably strengthened by the concept of *perichoresis* without any detraction from the distinctive properties and interrelations of the three divine Persons, through the emphatic assertion, not only of their oneness in Being, but of their identity in will, authority, judgment, energy, power or any other divine attribute. In all but the incommunicable properties which differentiate them from one another as Father, Son and Holy Spirit, they share completely and equally – each of the divine Persons is entirely united to those with whom he is enjoined as he is with himself because of the identity of Being and Power that is between them.[27] This was clearly affirmed at the Council of Constantinople before the adoption of *perichoresis* as a technical term, when it promulgated and enlarged the Nicene Confession of Faith, later ratified at the Council of Chalcedon. Thus in taking their cue from the faith of

[24] Gregory Nazianzen, *Orationes*, 36.15; Didymus, *De Trinitate*, 1.18.
[25] Athanasius, *Ad Serapionem*, 1.16.
[26] Gregory Nazianzen, *Orationes*, 40.41.
[27] Gregory Nazianzen, *Orationes*, 11.14, 16; Pseudo-Cyril, op. cit., 10 – John of Damascus, op. cit., 8.

Baptism in the Name of the Father and the Son and the Holy Spirit, the Fathers of Constantinople wrote in their Encyclical or Synodical Epistle: 'According to the Faith there is one Godhead, Power and Being of the Father and of the Son and of the Holy Spirit, equal in Honour and Majesty and coeternal Sovereignty in three most perfect Hypostases, that is, in three perfect Persons.'[28] That was designed to set completely aside the twin heresies of Arianism and Sabellianism, or partitive and unipersonal conceptions of God, the very point which was taken up and made more precise by the perichoretic teaching of Pseudo-Cyril and John Damascene.

On the other hand, *perichoresis* affirms the real *distinctions* between the divine Persons in their hypostatic relations with one another, as well as their real oneness, and does so by providing the frame within which we may think and speak of the three divine Persons in their proper differences without detracting from their complete equality, in line with the order given in Baptism into the Name of the Father, the Son, and the Spirit – the Father first, the Son second, the Spirit third.[29] This priority in order or Monarchy of the Father within the trinitarian relations is consonant with the Father's relation to the Son and the Spirit within the indivisibility of the Triune Being of God. Hence the priority or Monarchy of the Father within the Holy Trinity must not be taken to imply a priority or superiority in Deity. It refers to the fact that 'the Son is begotten of the Father, not the Father of the Son',[30] which is the *order* manifested in the incarnation between the Father and his only begotten Son, and is reflected in the sending of the Holy Spirit by the Father in the name of the Son. This has to do in part, then, with the history of God's revealing and saving acts, but it is governed by the irreversible relation between the Father and the Son intrinsic to them in which, while the Father 'naturally' comes first, the Son is nevertheless everything the Father is except being Father.

While in the Father/Son relation the Father is the Father of the Son, he is in no sense the deifier of the Son, for he himself in his eternal Being as God is not Father without the Son, as the Son in his eternal Being as God is not the Son without the Father. As the Son of the Father he is not less than the Father but is himself true God of true God, for as St Paul tells us 'it pleased the Father that all the fullness of God should dwell in him' – 'the entire Godhead dwells in him.'[31] That is to say, the inner trinitarian order is not to be understood in an ontologically differential way, for it does not apply to the Being or the Deity of the divine Persons which each individually and all together have absolutely in common, but only to the mysterious 'disposition or economy' which they have among themselves within the unity of the Godhead, distinguished by position and not status, by form and not being, by sequence and not power, for they are fully and perfectly equal.[32]

A problem arose here in the Cappadocian theology of the post-Nicene era, due largely to their defence of Nicene Orthodoxy against the Aristotelianising

---

[28] Theodoret, *Historia ecclesiae*, 5.9.

[29] See 'Agreed Statement on the Holy Trinity', *Theological Dialogue between Orthodox and Reformed Theologians* (Edinburgh, 1993), vol. 2, Ch. 10; and *Trinitarian Perspectives*, ch. 7.

[30] Thus John of Damascus (and Pseudo-Cyril), *De fide orthodoxa*, 1.8.

[31] Col., 1.19; 2.9.

[32] Thus Tertullian, *Adversus Praxean*, 2.9; and Calvin, *Institutio*, 1.13.6. The term 'economy' is used here in Tertullian's sense as *dispositio*. Refer to *Trinitarian Perspectives*, pp. 65–69.

argumentation of Eunomius the Arian Bishop of Cyzicus.[33] The Cappadocian theologians helped the Church to have a richer and fuller understanding of the three Persons of the Holy Trinity in their distinctive 'modes of existence' or ways of origination (τρόποι ὑπάρξεως), as Basil and his brother, but not Gregory Nazianzen, spoke of them. They contributed considerably to the richly personal understanding of the Holy Trinity through their emphasis on the distinctive and objective existence, the peculiar nature and characteristics (ἰδιότητα, ἰδιώματα, χαρακτηριστικά) of the Father, the Son and the Holy Spirit as they are made known to us in the Gospel, and as they belong to one another in the Communion which they constitute together as μία οὐσία τρεῖς ὑποστάσεις, one Being three Persons. This was a significant move for faith and worship, for it meant that they completely set aside any anxiety about the Nature of God, or any temptation to think of God behind the back of his three-fold self-revelation – there is no such God. Apart from God as he is revealed to us in his three-fold economic or evangelical manifestation as Father, Son and Holy Spirit, there is no divine Being undefined by Jesus Christ which we need fear – as St John remarked, there is no room in the love of God for fear, for perfect love casts out fear.[34]

On the other hand, the rather dualist distinction drawn by Basil and his brother Gregory between the transcendent Being of God which is quite unknowable and the uncreated energies of his self-revelation,[35] had the effect of shifting the weight of emphasis from the Nicene doctrine of the identity of being to one of equality between the divine Persons, and of transferring the element of concreteness in the doctrine of God entirely on to the differentiating particularities of the three divine Persons in accordance with their modes of existence. Proper and salutary as this stress was upon the economic self-revelation of God as Father, Son and Holy Spirit mediated in the apostolic tradition of the Gospel and the liturgy, the way Basil and his friends sought to defend this had the effect of playing down the truth embedded in the Nicene *homoousion* of the oneness between the economic and the ontological Trinity, e.g. in respect of the fact that what God *now is* toward us as Father, Son and Holy Spirit in the economy of redemption, he *ever was* antecedently in his intra-divine Life. In the words of Athanasius: 'As it always was, so it is even now; and as it now is, so it ever was and is the Trinity, and in him the Father, Son and Holy Spirit.'[36] Consonant with his reservation about the identity of the economic Trinity and ontological Trinity is the rather strange fact that Basil never referred to the Holy Spirit as God or of one Being with him (Θεός or as ὁμοούσιος) in contrast to Gregory Nazianzen.[37]

However, Basil and his friends considered that the defence of Nicene theology required a clear distinction to be made between οὐσία and ὑπόστασις, for their

---

[33] For the following consult *The Trinitarian Faith*, pp. 211–221, 236ff, 313–326; and also J. N. D. Kelly, *Early Christian Doctrines* (London, 1958), pp. 258–269.

[34] 1 John 4.16–18.

[35] Basil, *Contra Eunomium*, 1.12ff; 2.32; *Epistulae*, 234.1, 235.2f.

[36] Athanasius, *Ad Serapionem*, 3.7. Cf. here also Karl Barth, *Church Dogmatics* I.2 (Edinburgh, 1956), p. 479f.

[37] Gregory Nazianzen, *Orationes*, 31.10.

identity could be used, and was used, though diversely, by Sabellians and Eunomians in support of their heretical unipersonal and subordinationist ideas. When the Cappadocian theologians argued for the doctrine of one Being, three Persons (μία οὐσία τρεῖς ὑποστάσεις) they did so on the ground that the *ousia* has the same relation to the *hypostasis* as the general or common to the particular. They pointed, for instance, to the way three different people have a common nature or φύσις.[38] They absorbed the Nicene *ousia* of the Father (οὐσία τοῦ Πατρός) into the *hypostasis* of the Father (ὑπόστασις τοῦ Πατρός), and then when they spoke of the three divine Persons as having the same being or nature, they were apt to identify *ousia* with *physis* or nature.[39] Thereby they tended to give *ousia* an abstract generic sense which had the effect of making them treat *ousia* or *physis* as impersonal.[40] Then when in addition they concentrated Christian faith directly upon the three distinct hypostases of the Father, the Son, and the Holy Spirit as they are united through their common action, they were charged with thinking of God in a partitive or tritheistic way, three Gods with a common nature, which of course they rejected.[41] They sought to meet this charge by establishing their belief in the oneness of God through anchoring it in the Father as the one Origin or Principle or Cause, 'Αρχή or Αἰτία, of divine Unity, and they spoke of the Son and of the Holy Spirit as deriving their distinctive modes of subsistence or coming into existence (τρόποι ὑπάρξεως) from the Father as the Fount of Deity (πηγὴ θεότητος). But they went further and argued that the Son and the Spirit derive their being (εἶναι) and indeed their Deity (θεότης) from the Father by way of a unique causation (αἰτία) which comprises and is continuous with its effects, and by that they meant the Father considered as *Person*, i.e. as ὑπόστασις, not οὐσία, which represented a divergence from the teaching of the Nicene Council. Thus Basil or his brother Gregory Nyssen thought of the relations between the Father and the Son and the Spirit as constituting a structure of a causal series or, as it were, 'a chain of dependence'.[42] And Gregory could speak of 'one and the same *Person* (πρόσωπον), out of whom the Son is begotten and the Spirit proceeds.'[43] The implication was that it is the *Person* of the Father who causes, deifies and personalises the Being of the Son and of the Spirit and even the existence of the Godhead![44] As Didymus pointed out, however, if one is to speak of the generation of the Son and the

---

[38] E.g. Basil/Gregory, *Epistulae*, 38.5; Basil, *De Spiritu Sancto*, 41.

[39] Cf. Basil/Gregory, *Epistulae*, 38.1ff; Basil, *Epistulae*, 52.2ff; 125.3; 189.2ff; 210.3–5; 214.3f; 236.6f; 265.2; *Homilia*, 111, etc.

[40] But cf. Basil, *Contra Eunomium*, 1.23 where he seems to modify the notion of a generic unity toward a notion of identity or ταυτότης.

[41] See especially Gregory Nyssen, *That there are not three Gods*; but also Basil, *Homilia contra sycophantes*; and Evagrius, *Epistulae*, 8.

[42] Basil or Gregory, *Epistulae*, 38.4; Gregory Nyssen, *De Spiritu Sancto*, 3; Basil, *De Spiritu Sancto*, 13, 45f; cf. *Contra Eunomium*, 3.1; *Contra Sabellianos*, 4.

[43] Gregory Nyssen, *Ex communibus notionibus* (Jaeger edn. Leiden, 1958), III.1, p. 25. See also *The Trinitarian Faith*, p. 318, and J. N. D. Kelly, *Early Christian Doctrines* (London, 1958), p. 265.

[44] The strange idea that God owes his existence to the *Person* or *Hypostasis* of the Father is compounded in error when a modern existentialising concept of 'personhood' is intruded into the doctrine of the Holy Trinity on the ground that existence precedes essence!

procession of the Spirit from the *Person* of the Father this is not to be equated with the *causation of their being*, but only with the *mode* of their enhypostatic differentiation within the one intrinsically personal Being of the Godhead.[45]

This centering of divine unity upon the *Person* of the Father rather than upon the *Being* of the Father, with its implication that the Person of the Father is the Fount of Deity, was to introduce the ambiguity into the doctrine of the Trinity that gave rise to difficulties regarding the procession of the Spirit as well as of the Son which we shall consider later. At the moment, however, it is the problem of a distinction drawn by the Cappadocians between the wholly uncaused or *underived* Deity of the Father and the caused or *derived* Deity of the Son and of the Spirit, that we must consider. As Gregory Nazianzen, himself one of the Cappadocian theologians, pointed out, this implied a relation of superiority and inferiority or 'degrees of Deity' in the Trinity, which is quite unacceptable, for 'to subordinate any of the three Divine Persons is to overthrow the Trinity'.[46] He was followed in this judgment by Cyril of Alexandria who, like Athanasius his theological guide, would have nothing to do with a generic concept of the divine οὐσία, or with causal and/or subordinationist relations within the Holy Trinity.[47]

It is at this very point that the introduction of the concept of *perichoresis* proved of decisive importance. It ruled out any notion of a 'before' and an 'after' or of degrees of Deity and set the doctrine of the Trinity back again on the basis laid for it by Athanasius in terms of the coinherent relations and undivided wholeness in which each Person is a 'whole of a whole', while nevertheless gathering up and reinforcing the strong hypostatic and intensely personal distinctions within the Trinity which the Cappadocian theologians had developed so fruitfully especially for spiritual life and worship. This perichoretic understanding of the Trinity had the effect of restoring the full doctrine of the Fatherhood of God without importing any element of subordinationism into the hypostatic interrelations between the Father, the Son and the Holy Spirit, and at the same time of restoring the biblical, Nicene and Athanasian conception of the one Being or Οὐσία of God as intrinsically and completely personal. Moreover, it ruled out of consideration any conception of the trinitarian relations arising out of a prior unity, and any conception of a unity deriving from the underived Person of the Father. In the perichoretic Communion of the Father, Son and Holy Spirit who are the one Being of God, Unity and Trinity, Trinity and Unity mutually permeate and actively pass into one another.

When we consider the order of the three divine Persons in this perichoretic way we do indeed think of the Father as first precisely as Father, but not as the Deifier

---

[45] Didymus the Blind, *De Trinitate*, 2.1; 2.2, 5; 2.26f; *De Spiritu Sancto*, 26. See *The Trinitarian Faith*, pp. 323ff.

[46] Gregory Nazianzen, *Orationes*, 43.30, 43. And refer to *The Trinitarian Faith*, pp. 239ff and 319ff. There lurked in the Cappadocian stress upon the Father as the Principle or Arche of Godhead (Πατήρ = Ἀρχή), to borrow an expression from Karl Barth (used in a different but similar context), 'an unsubdued remnant of Origenist subordinationism', *Church Dogmatics*, 1.1, p. 482.

[47] Cyril of Alexandria, *Thesaurus de Trinitate*, *Patrologia Graeca*, 75. 128; *De Trinitate dialogus*, II, *Patrologia Graeca* 75. 721, 733, 744, 769, etc.

of the Son and the Spirit.[48] Thus while we think of the Father within the Trinity as the Principle or Ἀρχή of Deity (in the sense of *Monarchia* not restricted to one Person, which we shall consider shortly), that is not to be taken to mean that he is the Source (Ἀρχή) or Cause (Αἰτία) of the divine Being (τὸ εἶναι) of the Son and the Spirit, but in respect simply of his being Unoriginate or Father, or expressed negatively, in respect of his not being a Son, although all that the Son has the Father has except Sonship. This does not derogate from the Deity of the Son or of the Spirit, any more than it violates the real distinctions within the Triune Being of God, so that no room is left for either a Sabellian modalism or an Arian subordinationism in the doctrine of the Holy Trinity. The statement of Jesus, 'My Father is greater than I',[49] is to be interpreted not ontologically but soteriologically, or 'economically (οἰκονομικῶς)', as Gregory Nazianzen, Cyril of Alexandria and Augustine all understood it.[50] In other words, the subjection of Christ to the Father in his incarnate economy as the suffering and obedient Servant cannot be read back into the eternal hypostatic relations and distinctions subsisting in the Holy Trinity.[51] The mediatorial office of Christ, as Calvin once expressed it, does not detract from his divine Majesty.[52] Since no distinction between underived Deity and derived Deity is tenable, there can be no thought of one Person being ontologically or divinely prior to another or subsequent to another. Hence while the Father in virtue of his Fatherhood is first in order, the Father, the Son, and the Spirit eternally coexist as three fully co-equal Persons in a perichoretic togetherness and in-each-otherness in such a way that, in accordance with the particular aspect of divine revelation and salvation immediately in view, as in the New Testament Scriptures, there may be an appropriate variation in the trinitarian order from that given in Baptism, as we find in the benediction, 'The grace of the Lord Jesus Christ, and the love of God and the communion of the Holy Spirit be with you all.'[53] Nevertheless both Athanasius and Basil counselled the Church to keep to the order of the divine Persons given in Holy Baptism, if only to counter the damaging heresy of Sabellianism.[54]

3) PERICHORESIS AND THE DIVINE MONARCHY

Perichoresis has far-reaching implications, as became apparent above, for our understanding of the divine *Monarchia*. We saw earlier that *perichoresis* reinforces

[48] Cf. John Calvin's comment: 'The name of God is restricted to the Father only in respect of his being the Principle of Godhead (*Deitatis Principium*), not because he is the source of divine Being (*non essentiando*), as the fanatics babble, but by reason of order (*ratione ordinis*).' *Institutio*, 1.13.26.
[49] John 14.28.
[50] Gregory Nazianzen, *Orationes*, 40.31, 43; 43.30; Cyril of Alexandria, *Thesaurus de Trinitate*, *Patrologia Graeca* 75.144–45, 177–78, 380–81; *In Joannis Evangelium*, 10.29ff; 14.28; cf. 6.38f; Augustine, *De fide et symbolo*, 18; *In Joannis Evangelium*, 14.27–28.
[51] This is surely part of the significance of 1 Cor. 15.24ff.; cf. Phil. 2.7–10.
[52] John Calvin, *Institutio*, 1.13.24, 26.
[53] 2 Cor. 13.14.
[54] Athanasius, *Ad Serapionem*, 4.5; Basil, *Epistulae*, 125.3.

the fact that the Holy Trinity may be known only as a whole, for it is as a whole that God makes himself known to us through himself and in himself as Father, Son and Holy Spirit. The self-revelation of God as triune is a self-enclosed *novum* which may be known and interpreted only on its own ground and out of itself. Hence our knowing of God engages in a perichoretic circular movement from Unity to Trinity and from Trinity to Unity, for God is God only as he is Father, Son and Holy Spirit, and cannot be conceived by us truly otherwise. This means that we understand the Monarchy of God not in a partitive way moving linearly, as it were, from one divine Person to Another, but in the same holistic way as we know the Trinity, although, as we have been trying to do, we may develop modes of thought and speech with which to bring out the distinctive individualities and objectivities of the three divine Persons, as the Cappadocian theologians sought to do while seeking to steer a way between the extremes of unipersonalism and tritheism.

It has been remarked at several points hitherto that 'Father' was constantly used in the New Testament Scriptures and in the Early Church in two cognate ways with reference to the Godhead and to the Person of the Father.[55] They were never separated from one another, but with the Cappadocian theologians these two senses of paternity were elided with one another. At the same time, as we have just pointed out, their way of distinguishing between *ousia* as a general concept and *hypostasis* as a particular concept, imported a shift in their approach (for two of them at least) away from the central significance of *homoousios* as the theological key to understanding the identity, intrinsic oneness, and internal relations of the Holy Trinity. In the course of this development they threw the emphasis upon the three *Hypostaseis* as individual modes of existence united through the *Monarchia* of the Father and as thereby having their Being in common, three *Hypostaseis*, one *Ousia*. Thus the main thrust of the Cappadocian teaching, even with reservations and qualifications, was to make the uncaused Person of the Father the Cause or Source of the Deity and of the personal Nature of the Son and the Spirit. Although they claimed that everything of the Father belongs to the Son, and everything of the Son belongs to the Father, the general trend was to weaken the Athanasian axiom that whatever we say of the Father we say of the Son and the Spirit except 'Father'.

For Athanasius as for Alexander, his predecessor as Archbishop of Alexandria, the idea that the Father alone is *Arche* ('Ἀρχή), Principle, Origin or Source, in this sense was an Origenist concept that had become a main plank in Arian deviation from the Apostolic and Catholic Faith.[56] Athanasius, on his part, held that since the whole Godhead is in the Son and in the Spirit, they must be included with the Father in the one originless Source or 'Ἀρχή of the Holy Trinity.[57] Admittedly, the Cappadocian way of expounding the doctrine of the One Being, Three Persons or

[55] Cf. Augustine, *De Trinitate*, 5.11.12ff.
[56] See the letter of Arius to Eusebius, *apud* Theodoret, *Historia ecclesiae*, 1.4; Athanasius, *De synodis*, 16. Thus also Hilary, *De Trinitate*, 4.13, and Epiphanius, *Haereses*, 69.8,78 ; cf. also 73.16, 21.
[57] Athanasius, *Ad Antiochenos*, 5; *Contra Arianos*, 4.1–4. Thus also Epiphanius, *Haereses*, 69.29; 73.16; *Expositio fidei*, 14.

Hypostases, helped the Church, as we have said, to have a richer and fuller understanding of the Three Persons of the Holy Trinity in their distinctive modes of existence. However, this was done at the expense of cutting out the real meaning of *ousia* as *being in its internal relations*, and of robbing *ousia* of its profound *personal* sense that was so prominent at Nicaea, and had been reinforced by Athanasius and Epiphanius.[58] It also had the support of Hilary in the West.[59] Moreover, the Cappadocian interpretation, under a lingering Origenist influence, concealed a serious ambiguity. From one point of view the so-called 'Cappadocian settlement' meant the rejection of subordinationism, but from another it implied a hierarchical structure within the Godhead.[60] This carried with it an ambiguous element of subordinationism that kept disconcerting thought within the Church and opening the way for division, yet it was the Latins who stressed even more strongly the role of the Father as *principium et fons totius Deitatis.*[61]

The formulation of the doctrine of the Trinity at the Council of Constantinople was certainly indebted to the Cappadocian theologians, especially to Gregory Nazianzen who presided over its opening session, and as with them care was taken to steer between unipersonalism and tritheism. However, the main development did not follow the line advocated by the Cappadocians in grounding the unity of the Godhead in the Person of the Father as the unique and exclusive Principle of the Godhead, but reverted to the doctrine of the Son as begotten *of the Being* of the Father and made a similar affirmation of the Holy Spirit.[62] In deliberate reaffirmation of Nicene theology it operated on the basis laid down by Athanasius, particularly as filled out and strengthened by the doctrine of the Holy Spirit. This had seen further clarification through Epiphanius regarding the interrelation between the Unity and the Trinity of God, and was to see full-orbed development through Cyril of Alexandria. For Athanasius the concept of Triunity was already embedded in his understanding of the *homoousion* which, with its rejection of any notion either of undifferentiated oneness or of partitive relations between the three divine Persons, carried with it the conception of eternal distinctions and internal relations in the Godhead as wholly and mutually indwelling one another in the one identical perfect Being of the Father, the Son and the Holy Spirit. It was through the Trinity, Athanasius held, that we believe in the Unity of God, and yet it is only in recognition of the indivisible oneness and identity of Being in the Son and the Spirit with the Father that we rightly apprehend the Holy Trinity.[63]

It is in this very light that we are to understand how Athanasius regarded the divine *Monarchia*. He certainly thought of the Father as the *Arche* ('Αρχή – and Αἴτιος, but not Αἰτία or Cause) of the Son in that he has eternally begotten the

---

[58] Refer to *The Trinitarian Faith*, p. 310f.

[59] Hilary, *De Trinitate*, 1.5f.

[60] Thus Gregory Nyssen taught that the being of the Spirit was caused by and grounded in the existence of the Son whose being was in turn caused by and grounded in the Father, e.g. *Contra Eunomium*, 1.36, 42; see also *De Spiritu Sancto*, 3.

[61] For the bearing of this upon the hierarchical structure of the Roman Church, see *Theological Dialogue between Orthodox and Reformed Churches*, vol.1 (Edinburgh, 1985), pp.108–120.

[62] Theodoret, *Ecclesiae historia*, 5.11.

[63] Athanasius, *Contra Arianos*, 3.1ff; 4.1ff; *Ad Serapionem*, 1.16, 20, 28; 3.1,6, etc.

Son. He thus declared 'We know only one *Arche*', but he immediately associated the Son with that *Arche*, for, he added, 'we profess to have no other Form of Godhead (τρόπον Θεότητος) than that of the only God.'[64] While the Son is associated with the *Arche* of the Father in this way, he cannot be thought of as an *Arche* subsisting in himself, for by his very Nature he is inseparable from the Father of whom he is the Son. By the same token, however, the Father cannot be thought of as an *Arche* apart from the Son, for it is precisely as Father that he is Father of the Son. 'The Father and the Son are two, but the Unity (Μονάς) of Godhead is one and indivisible. And thus we preserve the one Ἀρχή of the Godhead, not two Ἀρχαί, so that there is strictly a Monarchy (Μοναρχία).'[65] It is in this light also that we must understand the Synodal Letter of Athanasius to the people of Antioch in which he joined with others in acknowledging 'a Holy Trinity, but one Godhead, and one *Arche*, and that the Son is of one Being with the Father, while the Holy Spirit is proper to and inseparable from the Being of the Father and the Son.'[66]

Thus while accepting along with the Cappadocians the formulation of *One Being, Three Persons*, Athanasius had such a strong view of the complete identity, equality and unity of the three divine Persons within the Godhead, that he declined to advance a view of the Monarchy in which the oneness of God was defined by reference to the Father alone or to the Person of the Father. The *Mone Arche* (μονὴ Ἀρχή or Μοναρχία) is identical with the Trinity, the *Monas* with the *Trias* (the Μονάς with the Τριάς), and it is precisely in the *Trias* that we know God to be *Monas*. Athanasius actually preferred to speak of God as *Monas* rather than as *Arche*, since his understanding of the *Monas* was essentially as the *Trias*: God is eternally and unchangeably Father, Son and Holy Spirit, three Persons who, while always Father, Son and Holy Spirit, in their coindwelling relations *are* the Triune God. The *Monarchia* or the *Monas* is essentially and intrinsically trinitarian in the inner relations of God's eternal *Ousia*.[67] An early statement attributed to Athanasius appears to represent his concept of the Triunity of God rather faithfully:

The Trinity praised and worshipped and adored, is one and indivisible, and without degrees (ἀσχημάτιστος). He is united without confusion, just as the *Monas* is distinguished in thought without division. For the threefold doxology, 'Holy, Holy, Holy is the Lord' offered by those venerable living beings, denotes the three perfect Persons (τρεῖς ὑποστάσεις τελείας), just as in the word 'Lord' they indicate his one Being (μίαν οὐσίαν).[68]

When we turn to Epiphanius we find him taking essentially the same line, for he presented his doctrine of the Son and the Spirit within an understanding of the whole undivided Trinity, not just the Father, as the *Monarchia*.[69] He did not speak

[64] Athanasius, *Contra Arianos*, 1.14; 3.15.
[65] Athanasius, *Contra Arianos*, 4.1; cf. 2–3.
[66] Athanasius, *Ad Antiochenos*, 5.
[67] Athanasius, *Contra Arianos*, 4.1, 3; *De decretis*, 26; *De sententia Dionysii*, 17, etc.
[68] Athanasius, *In illud, omnia*, 6.
[69] Epiphanius, *Ancoratus*, 7f, 67f, 70f, 119f; *Haereses*, 69.17, 52; 70.5; 72.4f; 73.16, 18; 74.5, 7, 11f; *Expositio fidei*, 14.

of the three divine Persons as 'modes of existence', like Basil, Gregory Nyssen and Amphilochius, but as 'enhypostatic' in God, that is, having real, objective personal subsistence in God and as coinhering homoousially and hypostatically in him. His conception of the *homoousion* as applying to the Trinity as a whole deepened the notion of the coinherence of the Father, the Son and the Holy Spirit in their subsistent enhypostatic relations. Moreover, he did not share the Cappadocian way of trying to ensure the unity of God by tracing it back to the one uncaused or underived Person of the Father. He held the whole Trinity, and not just the Father, to be the Principle or Ἀρχή of the oneness of the Godhead. Hence he laid immense emphasis upon the full equality, perfection, eternity, power and glory of the Father, the Son and the Holy Spirit alike, and thus upon the perfection of God's Triunity. Each of the divine Persons is fully, equally and perfectly Lord and God, while all three have and are one and the same Godhead. As Augustine wrote: 'There is so great an equality in the Trinity, that not only the Father is not greater than the Son, as regards divinity, but neither are the Father and the Son together greater than the Holy Spirit; nor is each individual Person, which ever it be of the three, less than the Trinity itself.'[70] No one of the divine Persons is prior to or greater than another.[71] 'In proclaiming the divine *Monarchia* we do not err, but confess the Trinity, and Trinity in Unity, one Godhead of the Father, Son and Holy Spirit (τὴν Τριάδα, Μονάδα ἐν Τριάδι, καὶ Τριάδα ἐν Μονάδι, μίαν Θεότητα Πατρός, καὶ Ὑοῦ, καὶ Ἁγίου Πνεύματος).'[72] 'There are not three Gods, but there is only one true God, and since the Begotten is One from One, and One also is the Holy Spirit who is One from One, a Trinity in Unity, and one God, Father, Son and Holy Spirit.'[73] 'There is one Trinity in Unity, and one Godhead in Trinity.'[74] For Epiphanius, God *is* the Trinity, and the Trinity *is* God. The Father, the Son and the Holy Spirit are essentially and intrinsically and coinherently One.[75] While each one of the three divine Persons ever remains enhypostatically and perfectly what he is in himself (καθ' ἑαυτό), they all bear upon one another mutually and coinherently in the one identical Being of the Godhead, and are the Godhead.[76] 'The relation of the Father is with the Son and the relation of the Son is with the Father, and both proceed in the Holy Spirit, for the Trinity ever consists in one Unity of Godhead: three Perfections, one Godhead.'[77]

It has been important to say something in detail of the teaching of Athanasius and Epiphanius, for in pressing further the biblical stress of Athanasius on the 'I am' of the one ever-living ever-acting Being of God understood in his internal relations, Epiphanius did more than any other to clear away problems that had arisen in the doctrine of the Holy Trinity and to prepare the ground for the

[70] Augustine, *De Trinitate*, 8. Preface.
[71] Epiphanius, *Ancoratus*, 6–8; 22. 81; *Haereses*, 66.69; 69.33, 37, 43; 72.1; 73.3; 74.8,12; 76. *Refutatio Aetii*, 4.20f, 32f, 35; *Expositio fidei*, 14.
[72] Epiphanius, *Haereses*, 62.3; see also 4–7.
[73] Epiphanius, *Ancoratus*, 2.
[74] Epiphanius, *Haereses*, 76. *Refutatio Aetii*, 33 & 35.
[75] Epiphanius, *Ancoratus*, 10.
[76] Epiphanius, *Haereses*, 63.6; 65.1f; 72.1f, 10; 73.16ff; 74.11f; 76.2, 12, 20, 15; *Ancoratus*, 6ff, 10.
[77] Epiphanius, *Haereses*, 69.54.

ecumenical consensus that was registered in the Nicene-Constantinopolitan Creed. It is important to throw the spotlight on this development today for it is actually somewhat different from what is found in the usual text-book tradition: it was upon the Athanasian-Epiphanian basis that classical Christian theology developed into its flowering in the great work of Cyril of Alexandria. In our day it has been upon the Athanasian-Epiphanian-Cyriline basis, together with the trinitarian teaching of Gregory Nazianzen who insisted that the *Monarchia* may not be limited to one Person,[78] that doctrinal agreement on the doctrine of the Holy Trinity has been reached between Orthodox and Reformed Churches.[79] It is of particular significance for our discussion here that the conception of *perichoresis* played a crucial role in clarifying and deepening the conception of the *Monarchia* for the understanding of the interlocking of Unity and Trinity, Trinity and Unity, in the doctrine of God. It may be helpful to cite here a paragraph from a document of the Orthodox/Reformed Commission commenting on the *Monarchia* in this connection.

> Of far-reaching importance is the stress laid upon the Monarchy of the Godhead in which all three divine Persons share, for the whole indivisible Being of God belongs to each of them as it belongs to all of them together. This is reinforced by the unique conception of coinherent or perichoretic relations between the different Persons in which they completely contain and interpenetrate one another while remaining what they distinctively are in their otherness as Father, Son and Holy Spirit. God is intrinsically Triune, Trinity in Unity and Unity in Trinity. There are no degrees of Deity in the Holy Trinity, as is implied in a distinction between the underived Deity of the Father and the derived Deity of the Son and the Spirit. Any notion of subordination is completely ruled out. The perfect simplicity and indivisibility of God in his Triune Being mean that the *Arche* (ἀρχή) or *Monarchia* (μοναρχία) cannot be limited to one Person, as Gregory the Theologian pointed out. While there are inviolable distinctions within the Holy Trinity, this does not detract from the truth that the whole Being of God belongs to all of them as it belongs to each of them, and thus does not detract from the truth that the Monarchy is One and indivisible, the Trinity in Unity and the Unity in Trinity.[80]

4) PERICHORESIS AND THE PROCESSION OF THE HOLY SPIRIT

The doctrine of the one Monarchy together with the doctrine of the perichoretic

---

[78] Gregory Nazianzen, *Orationes*, 29.2; 31.14; 40.41; 42.15, 16. See *The Trinitarian Faith*, p. 321f.

[79] See the two memoranda for the proposed dialogue in volume one of *Theological Dialogue between Orthodox and Reformed Churches*, ed. T. F. Torrance (Edinburgh, 1985), pp. 3–18; and the text of 'Agreed Statement on the Holy Trinity', in vol. 2. 1993, ch. 7, pp. 219–226.

[80] *Theological Dialogue between Orthodox and Reformed Churches*, vol. 2, 'Significant Features, a Common Reflection on the Agreed Statement', ch. 7, p. 231. See also my 'Commentary on the Agreed Statement on the Holy Trinity', the section 'Trinity in Unity and Unity in Trinity, the one Monarchia', *Trinitarian Perspectives*, ch. 9, pp. 137–139.

interpenetration of the three divine Persons in one another within the one indivisible Being or Communion of the Holy Trinity, puts our understanding of the procession of the Holy Spirit from the Father on a deeper and proper basis, as procession from the one Being of God the Father which is common to the Son and the Spirit. Moreover, it is to be borne in mind that 'the Father', when considered absolutely or simply, refers to the Godhead, that is to the one Being (οὐσία) of God, but when considered relatively refers to the Father of the Son, i.e. to the Person (ὑπόστασις) of the Father. We recall that the conflation of these two senses by the Cappadocians gave rise to serious difficulties, not least in connection with their conception of the Unity of God as deriving 'from the Person of the Father (ἐκ τῆς ὑποστάσεως τοῦ Πατρός)', thereby replacing the Nicene formula 'from the Being of the Father (ἐκ τῆς οὐσίας τοῦ Πατρός).' In the Cappadocian framework this meant that procession is regarded as taking place between different modes of existence or relations of origin, which is hardly satisfactory for it falls short of affirming the *homoousion* of the Spirit.[81] However, in holding that the Spirit proceeds from the Person of the Father, thus understood, rather than from the Being of the Father, the Cappadocians were nevertheless intent on rejecting any suggestion that the Spirit, who is not begotten of the Father like the Son, is to be regarded as created by God as he was held to be by Arian and Macedonian heretics. While their intention was certainly right in rejecting Arian error, the problematic role they gave to the Person of the Father *vis-à-vis* the Son and the Spirit provoked the reaction associated with the *ex Patre filioque* clause which the Western Church inserted unecumenically into the Creed, thereby creating a serious impasse in the relations between the East and the West.[82]

In view of the idea that the Spirit proceeds from the Father, although he is sent by the Son, Western churchmen felt obliged to hold that the Spirit proceeds from the Son as well as the Father, otherwise, they held, the Son would be regarded as subordinate to the Father, as an adopted creature of God, and not really as God of God – thus they too were rejecting Arianism. Following St Augustine, however, they held this in a modified form according to which the Spirit is understood to proceed from the Father principally (*principaliter*).[83] Eastern churchmen, on the other hand, felt that any idea of a procession of the Spirit from the Son as well as the Father, appeared to posit two ultimate Principles or 'Αρχαί in the Godhead – hence they opted for a formula expressing the procession of the Spirit *from the Father only* (ἐκ μονοῦ τοῦ Πατρός). They defended this with reference to the teaching of Jesus in the Fourth Gospel,[84] which implies a distinction between *procession* and *mission*, that is, as they interpreted it, between the *eternal* procession of the Spirit from the Father, and the *historical* mission of the Spirit from the Son. The pattern exhibited in the latter reflects the former in virtue of the fact that what

---

[81] But contrast Gregory Nazianzen, *Orationes*, 31.8,10f.

[82] For a fine succinct account of this question see Walter Kasper, *The God of Jesus Christ* (London, 1984), pp. 214ff.

[83] Augustine, *De Trinitate*, 15.26.47. For the teaching of St Thomas, see *Scriptum super sententiis*, I, d. 28, q. 1, a. 1; and III, d. 25, q. 1, a. 2.

[84] John 15.26 & 16.7.

the Father does he does *through* the Son, as Basil pointed out.[85] Does this mean that the sending of the Spirit by the Son has to do only with revelation and faith, and is not grounded immanently in the eternal Being of God? If so, would that not call in question the full homoousial relation of the Holy Spirit to God the Father?

Frequently associated with the defence of this distinction between the eternal procession and the historical sending of the Spirit is the Basilian and Palamite distinction between the divine Being and the divine energies. This tends to have the effect of restricting knowledge and speech of God apophatically (ἀποφατικῶς) to his divine energies or operations (ἐνεργείαι, or δυνάμεις) and ruling out any real access to knowing God in himself or in the intrinsic relations of his eternal Being.[86] But it also implies that to know God in the Spirit (ἐν Πνεύματι) is not to know God in his divine Being – to know God is only to know the things that relate to his Nature (τὰ περὶ τὴν φύσιν) as manifested through a penumbra of his uncreated energies or rays.[87] When applied to the procession and mission of the Spirit this appears to be influenced by a dualism inherited from Origenistic tradition,[88] which is made to operate in such a way as to drive a wedge between the inner Life of God and his saving activity in history or between the ontological Trinity and the economic Trinity.[89] This would not be to take the key Nicene concept of identity of being or *homoousion* seriously but to operate instead with some notion of likeness in being or *homoiousion*, which is precisely the sort of subtle error that Athanasius attacked in his *Letters to Serapion on the Holy Spirit*. Quite clearly a dualistic approach of this kind detracts from a realist doctrine of the Holy Spirit and from a realist conception of the homoousial and perichoretic interpenetration of the three divine Persons in one another in accordance with which each Person is whole God and all three are together the one Triune God.[90]

---

[85] Basil, *De Spiritu Sancto*, 19f. Cf. also Cyril of Alexandria, *In Joannis Evangelium*, 7.16; 13.3; 16.27f.

[86] Cf. Basil, *Epistulae*, 234.1f; *Contra Eunomium*, 1.6; 2.4, 33. Palamas even speaks of the divine energies as 'inferior Deity' in contrast to the divine Being as 'superior Deity', in a passage cited by V. Lossky, *In the Image and Likeness of God* (New York, 1974), p. 55; but Lossky himself denies that this distinction between essence and energies introduces any sort of division within the divine Being. *The Vision of God* (Clayton, Wisconsin, 1963), p. 127.

[87] Thus John of Damascus, *De fide orthodoxa*, 1.4, where he misuses a passage from Gregory Nazianzen, *Orationes*, 38.7 and 45.3. See 'The Doctrine of the Holy Trinity in Gregory Nazianzen and John Calvin', in *Trinitarian Perspectives*, ch. 2, pp. 21–40. Athanasius had explicitly rejected the restriction of thought and speech of God to 'the things which are round about him (περὶ αὐτόν)' – *De decretis*, 22.

[88] Cf. Origen's distinction between 'the eternal Gospel' and 'the temporal Gospel', *In Joannis Evangelium*, 1.8–10; 2.6; *De principiis*, 3.6.8; 4.2.6; 4.3.13.

[89] Cf. V. Lossky, op. cit., p. 34f and 53, who speaks of the line of demarcation that passes 'between the abyss of the Father and the Son who reveals him', and of 'a mysterious distinction in God's very Being'!

[90] Cf. Gregory Nazianzen who spoke of 'the One Godhead and Power, found in the Three in Unity, and comprising the Three separately, not unequal in beings or in natures, neither increased nor diminished by superiorities or inferiorities, in every respect equal, in every respect the same – just as the beauty and the greatness of the heavens is one – the infinite conjunction of three Infinite Ones, each God when considered in himself, as the Father so the Son, as the Son so the Holy Spirit, each preserving his own properties, the Three One God when contemplated together, each God because homoousial, one God because of the Monarchy.' *Orationes*, 40.41.

Any kind of disparity or disjunction between the Holy Spirit and God the Father was definitely ruled out by the Constantinopolitan form of the Creed in its stating that the Spirit is the Lord and the Giver of Life, and is to be worshipped and glorified together with the Father and the Son, for in the Holy Spirit God communicates *himself* to us, not just something of himself in his uncreated energies – the divine Giver and the divine Gift are one and the same. And of course the Council of Constantinople affirmed, as we have had occasion to mention, the truth that the Spirit is of one and the same being as the Father and proceeds from the Being of the Father.

If we probe behind this state of affairs to the implications of the Nicene *homoousion* and of the Athanasian doctrine of coinherence, we find a rather different situation governed by the conception of the *Monarchia* consisting of three perfectly coequal and coeternal enhypostatic Persons in indivisible Communion with one another in the Holy Trinity. What is crucial here, as Athanasius taught, is that the Spirit and the Son coinhere in one another, and that the Spirit is ever in the hands of the Father who sends and the Son who gives him as his very own, and from whom the Spirit on his part receives. The Spirit is from the Father but from the Father in the Son. Since the Holy Spirit like the Son is of the Being of God, and belongs to the Son, since he is in the Being of the Father and in the Being of the Son, he could not but proceed from or out of the Being of God inseparably from and through the Son. Moreover, for Athanasius the proceeding of the Spirit from the Father is inextricably bound up with the generation of the Son from the Father which exceeds and transcends the thoughts of men.[91] Since it would not be reverent to ask *how* the Spirit proceeds from God, Athanasius did not and would not entertain the question, for that would have implied an ungodly attempt to intrude into the holy mystery of God's Being. Thus the problem of the so-called 'double procession' of the Spirit did not come into the picture. However, he was bound to understand the Spirit's being 'of God' and 'from God', and even 'from and through' the Son, in the light of the Nicene *homoousion* and the explanation given at the Council that 'from the Father' meant 'from the *Being* of the Father'. Hence Athanasius' application of the *homoousion* to the Holy Spirit had the effect, not only of asserting that the Spirit is also of one Being with the Father, but of implying that the procession of the Spirit is from the *Being* of the Father, and not from the *Person* (ὑπόστασις) of the Father, in distinction from his *Being*. For Athanasius the Son and the Spirit are both *of the Being* of the Father so that the idea that the Spirit derives from the *Being* of the Son just did not arise and could not have arisen for Athanasius.[92]

In line with this teaching Epiphanius thought of the Holy Spirit as having personal subsistence, not only 'out of the Father through the Son', but 'out of the same Being', 'out of the same Godhead' as the Father and the Son, for the Holy Spirit is ontologically (οὐσιωδῶς) inseparable from the Father and the Son. As the Spirit of the Father and the Spirit of the Son he is 'in the midst of the Father and the Son' and is 'the bond of the Trinity', but he is that Bond as he who is fully

[91] Athanasius, *De decretis*, 12.
[92] See Athanasius, *Ad Serapionem*, especially 1.20f. Consult *The Trinitarian Faith*, pp. 231ff & 331 ff.

homoousial and perfectly coequal with the Father and the Son. The Holy Spirit is ever with the Father and the Son, coinhering with them in the one eternal Being of God, but coinhering enhypostatically (ἐνυποστατικῶς) with them in such a way that in the one Being of God the Holy Spirit is always Holy Spirit, as the Father is always Father and the Son is always Son, each being 'true and perfect God', as Epiphanius loved to express it.[93] That is to say, the Holy Spirit belongs to the inner Being of the one God, and to the constitutive internal relations of the Godhead as Father, Son and Holy Spirit. He is central to the Triunity of God, for God the Father is not the Father nor God the Son the Son, without God the Holy Spirit. Thus understood in this way it may be said that the Holy Spirit proceeds, in Nicene language, as Light from Light from both the Father and the Son.[94] It is in virtue of this developed doctrine of the Triunity of God, which holds together the conceptions of the identity of the divine Being and the intrinsic Unity of the three divine Persons, that the procession of the Holy Spirit is surely to be to be considered.

It was then in this direction that Epiphanius interpreted and filled out the succinct Athanasian statement that 'the Holy Spirit proceeds from the Father and receives from the Son', yet in such a way that the enhypostatic realities and distinct properties of the Father, the Son and the Holy Spirit always remain the same in the perfect equality and homoousiality of the Holy Trinity.[95] The Holy Spirit is 'of one and the same being as the Father and the Son'.[96] And it was in these terms that he put forward the credal statement, including the crucial clauses about the Holy Spirit, which was taken up by the Council of Constantinople in 381. 'We believe in one Holy Spirit, the Lord and Giver of Life, who proceeds from the Father, who with the Father and the Son is worshipped and glorified, who spoke through the prophets.'[97]

Unfortunately the original Tome promulgating the Creed was lost, but we do know from Theodoret that the Council spoke of the Holy Spirit as 'of one and the same being (μιᾶς καὶ τῆς αὐτῆς οὐσίας) as the Father and the Son.'[98] While the original Creed of Nicaea spoke of the incarnate Son as of one and the same being with the Father, the clause 'God from God' applied to him was sometimes held to imply a difference between the underived Deity of the Father and the derived Deity of the Son, as in the thought of two of the Cappadocians, but any implication of subordination (ὑποταγή) in the Trinity was completely ruled out by the Fathers of the Constantinopolitan Council. In dropping the words 'God from God' (which might be taken to suggest a difference between underived and derived Deity), the Council laid all the emphasis upon 'true God from true God', thereby rejecting any difference in Deity, Glory, Power and Being between the Father and the Son. The Deity of the Son is as true and unqualified as the Deity of the Father. While the Son is

[93] Epiphanius, Ancoratus, 10, 81; Haereses, 69.44, 56; 72.1; 76.21; Expositio fidei, 18.
[94] Epiphanius, Haereses, 62.4; 69.54; 73.12, 16; 74.7f, 10ff; 76.11; Ancoratus, 7f, 67, 71f.
[95] Epiphanius, Ancoratus,. 72ff; Haereses, 74.9ff, 12.
[96] Epiphanius, Haereses, 74.11–12.
[97] Epiphanius, Ancoratus, 119.
[98] Theodoret, Historia ecclesiae, 5.11.

begotten of the Father, he is, with the Spirit, equal in every respect to the Father, apart from his being Father. The same completely mutual relation obtains between the Holy Spirit and the Father, and between the Holy Spirit and the Son. As there is only one Being of the Father, the Son and the Spirit, so the hypostatic Reality of each of them is as eternal and perfect as that of the others. The three divine Persons of course do not share with one another their distinguishing properties as Father, Son and Holy Spirit, but they do share completely and equally in the one homogeneous (ὁμογενής / ὁμοφυής) Nature and Being of God. The whole Godhead (ὁλόκληρος Θεότης) belongs to each divine Person as it belongs to all of them, and it belongs to all of them as it belongs to each of them.

It is when we apply the concept of *perichoresis* rigorously to this doctrine of the Holy Trinity together with the concept of the triune *Monarchia* that it becomes possible for us to think through and restate the doctrine of the procession of the Holy Spirit from the Father in a way that cuts behind and sets aside the problems that divided the Church over the *filioque*. If we take seriously the understanding of the Trinity in Unity and the Unity in Trinity in which each Person is perfectly and wholly God, and in which all three Persons perichoretically penetrate and contain one another, then we cannot but think of the procession of Holy Spirit from the Father through the Son, for the Son belongs to the Being of the Father, and the Spirit belongs to and is inseparable from the Being of the Father and of the Son. In proceeding from the Being of the Father, however, the Holy Spirit proceeds from the One Being which belongs to the Son and to the Spirit as well as to the Father, and which belongs to all of them together as well as to each one of them, for each one considered in himself is true God without any qualification. The Spirit proceeds perichoretically from the Father, that is, from out of the mutual relations within the one Being of the Holy Trinity in which the Father contains the Son and is himself contained by the Spirit. Thus the procession of the Spirit cannot be thought of in any partitive way, but only in a holistic way as 'whole from whole' (ὅλος ὅλου), that is, as proceeding from the wholly coinherent relations of the three divine Persons within the indivisible Being of the one God who is Trinity in Unity and Unity in Trinity. Strictly speaking, then, it must be said that the Holy Spirit proceeds from the one Monarchy of the Triune God. Interpreted in that sense it would appear that both the expressions 'from the Father and the Son', and 'from the Father through the Son', are in order – *but not* if they are understood in accordance with the view that the Monarchy is limited to the Father which both the Western and the Eastern Church have held in their different ways; *not* if they are understood in accordance with the view that there is a distinction between the underived Deity of the Father and the derived Deity of the Son and the Spirit; *and not* if they are understood in accordance with the view that the Holy Spirit does not belong equally and completely homoousially with the Father and the Son in their two-way relation with one another in the divine Triunity.

It should now be evident that the effect of this understanding of the Holy Spirit, who is of one and the same being as the Father and who proceeds homoousially or consubstantially from the one indivisible Being of God, is to cut behind the division between the East and the West over the *filioque*.[99] It does not allow of any procession of the Spirit from the Father and the Son alone, as if the Spirit himself did not belong to the Father-Son relation in the Holy Trinity equally with the Father and the Son. Nor does it allow of any procession of the Spirit from two ultimate Principles or Origins, or Άρχαί,[100] although it does allow for a procession of the Spirit from the Father *through* the Son. But 'through the Son', perichoretically understood, cannot but mean through the Son who has one Being with the Father, and so from out of the Communion of the Son with the Father and the Communion of the Father with the Son, which the Holy Spirit himself *is* in his coequal and homoousial relation with the Father and the Son as himself God of God, God the Holy Spirit. In other words, here we have to do not just with a two-way relationship between the Father and the Son in which the Spirit is some kind of connecting link, but with an active three-way or perichoretic relationship between the Father, the Son and the Holy Spirit.[101]

This approach is reinforced by consideration of the truth that since *God is Spirit*, 'Spirit' cannot be restricted to the Person of the Holy Spirit, but must apply to the whole Being of God to whom the Father and the Son with the Spirit belong. This implies that any proper understanding of the procession of the Spirit must be of procession from the whole spiritual Being of God the Father which the Holy Spirit has entirely in common with the Father and the Son. Thus in a real sense, the Spirit is to be thought of as proceeding from the Being of God the Father which as Spirit he himself is. As Epiphanius expressed it: 'The Holy Spirit ever is from the same Being of the Father and the Son, for God is Spirit.' 'He is the Spirit of the Son, but in the midst of the Father and the Son, from (ἐκ) the Father and the Son, the third in Name.' 'The Holy Spirit is from both (παρ' ἀμφοτέρων), Spirit from Spirit, for God is Spirit.'[102] The Holy Spirit is the Spirit of the Son by Nature as well as the Spirit of the Father by Nature, and it is as such that the Spirit proceeds from the Father and is given by the Son, as from the one Being which they both equally share, but share also with the Holy Spirit himself, for the Father is not Father and the Son is not Son apart from the Holy Spirit.

Here we may recall again the remarkable passage from Athanasius in which he puts into the mouth of Christ words interpreting the relation of the Spirit to the

---

[99] Consult 'Spiritus Creator: A Consideration of the teaching of St Athanasius and St Basil', in *Theology in Reconstruction* (London, 1965), pp. 217ff.

[100] It should be pointed out that Latin theology in the West insisted that the procession of the Spirit from the Father and the Son is 'not from two Principles but from one Principle (*non tanquam ex duabus principiis, set tanquam ex uno principio*)' – Council of Lyons, 1274, Denzinger-Schönmetzer, *Enchiridion Symbolorum* (Freiburg, 1965), 850. This was confirmed at the Council of Florence in 1445, ibid. 1300.

[101] Cf. Karl Barth, *Church Dogmatics* I.1 (Edinburgh, 2nd edn, 1975), p. 487: 'What is between them [the Father and the Son], what unites them, is no mere relation. It is not exhausted in the truth of their being alongside and with one another. As an independent mode of being over against them, it is the active mutual orientation and interpenetration of love, because these two, the Father and the Son, are of one essence, and indeed of one divine essence, because God's Fatherhood and Sonship as such must be related to one another in this active mutual orientation and penetration. That the Father and the Son are one God is the reason why they are not just united but are united in the Spirit in love; it is the reason, then, why God is love and love is God.'

[102] Epiphanius, *Ancoratus*, 7, 8; *Haereses*, 74.8.

Son. 'I, being the Father's Word, I give to myself become man, the Spirit, and in him I sanctify myself become man, so that henceforth in me who am the Truth ('For Your Word is Truth') all may be sanctified.'[103] The point for us to note here is that while the Holy Spirit is given to us through the incarnate Son, he gives it to us from out of himself as eternally his own, that is, out of the fullness of his divine Being.[104] Thus Epiphanius could say of the Holy Spirit that though he is not begotten he is 'out of the same Being as the Father and the Son.'[105] As Cyril of Alexandria expressed it: 'The Holy Spirit proceeds from the Father and the Son (ἐκ Πατρὸς καὶ Ὑοῦ), for he belongs to the divine Being and inheres in it and issues from it substantially (οὐσιωδῶς).'[106] Properly understood, then, when it is said that the Spirit proceeds from the Father and the Son, or from the Father through the Son, what is meant is that the Spirit proceeds from the Community of Being of the Father and the Son, or from the Communion (Κοινωνία) between the Father and the Son which the Holy Spirit himself is, and the three Divine Persons are in their eternal perichoretic relations with one another. It is, then, the conception of *perichoresis*, the doctrine of coinherence in the one identical Being of God, according to which the Father, the Son, and the Holy Spirit mutually indwell one another and contain one another, while remaining what they are in their otherness from one another, that must be allowed to govern our understanding of the procession of the Spirit from the Father through the Son. But if we think in this way of the Spirit as proceeding from the Father and the Son we must do so in the conviction that the Father and the Son are *with the Spirit* the one identical Being of the Godhead, the Triune Monarchy.

The question must now be asked whether the difficulties that have arisen over the procession of the Holy Spirit do not have to do, in part at least, with the fact that we do not know at all what 'proceeding (ἐκπόρευσις) from the Father' really means, any more than we know what 'begotten of the Father' really means. As we noted in an earlier chapter we do not really know what 'father' and 'son' mean even when they are applied to God by divine revelation. As Gregory Nazianzen said, they stand for relations, real or substantive relations, in God which transcend our finite comprehension. What we are concerned with is the substantive and personal relation between the Father and the Son, the Son and the Father, to which the human words 'father' and 'son' are used by divine revelation in such a way as to point beyond themselves. Problems arise immediately we try to understand divine Fatherhood and Sonship, and not least the concept of 'the begotten Son', in terms of what human fatherhood, sonship, and begetting mean. This problem is particularly acute when we think of the Spirit as going forth (ἐκπορευόμενον) from the Father in a way that is different from the begetting of the Son by the

---

[103] Athanasius, *Contra Arianos*, 1.46. Cf. the comments of George D. Dragas on this passage, *Athanasiana*, I (London, 1980), p. 62f.
[104] The same point is made by Cyril of Alexandria, *Adversus Nestorium*, 4.
[105] Epiphanius, *Ancoratus*, 7.7f, 70.
[106] Cyril of Alexandria, *Thesaurus de Trinitate*, *PG*, 75, 577, 580f, 585, and the whole section 575–617.

Father, and have to find a way of expressing that difference.[107] What does *procession*, or its equivalent *spiration* mean?

The three basic relations with which we have to do in the doctrine of the Trinity were variously referred to by the Church Fathers as 'fatherhood' or 'unbegottenness', 'sonship' or 'begottenness', and 'procession' or 'spiration' – the principle they followed is that each of these relations must be understood in accordance with the revealed nature and the hypostatic properties or particular characteristics of the Person or Persons concerned, thus υἱικῶς in respect of the Son, and πνευματικῶς in respect of the Spirit. What is theologically significant about the expressions 'procession' or 'spiration', is that they speak of a distinctive relation of the Holy Spirit, in accordance with the nature of his particular Person, to the Father in comparison with and in difference from the distinctive relation of the Son to the Father. But these expressions, Fatherhood, Sonship and Procession, are used not because they have been applied by us to the Godhead but because, as Pseudo-Cyril pointed out, 'they are communicated to us by the Godhead'.[108] That is to say, as divinely given they are irreplaceable ultimate terms which we cannot but use and which are always to be used only with godliness, reverence, and fidelity. They denote ineffable relations and refer to ineffable realities, of which we know only in part through the incarnation of the Father's only begotten Son in Jesus, through the teaching of Jesus about his Father and the gift of the Holy Spirit, through his breathing the Spirit upon the disciples after his resurrection and his pouring out of the Spirit upon the Church after his ascension. But what do 'breathing' and 'pouring' or 'proceeding' mean beyond indicating divine actions which in their nature are quite incomprehensible to us? As Karl Barth pointed out, we can no more offer an account of the 'how' of these divine relations and actions that we can we define the Father, the Son and the Holy Spirit and delimit them from one another.[109]

It is instructive to note the adverbial qualifications of these relations that were used, e.g. by Gregory Nazianzen and Epiphanius: without beginning (ἀνάρχως), without time (ἀχρόνως), without cause (ἀναιτίως), without explanation (ἀνεκδιηγήτως), etc. They signify to us that when we speak of the begetting of the Son or the proceeding of the Spirit we have to suspend our thought before the altogether inexpressible, incomprehensible Nature of God and the onto-relations of the Communion of the Father, the Son, and the Holy Spirit, which the Holy Spirit eternally is. To cite Athanasius once again, 'Thus far human knowledge goes. Here the cherubim spread the covering of their wings.'[110] If 'Father', 'Son' and 'Holy Spirit' stand for inexpressible although real relations, 'begetting' and 'proceeding' which are relations between relations are no less ineffable, and should surely be left undefined – we cannot but use them if we are not to be altogether

---

[107] See Augustine, *De Trinitate*, 5.14.15, where he deals with the question; 'why the Holy Spirit is not also a Son, since he too comes forth from the Father, as we read in the Gospel (John 15.26).' He answers 'Because the Spirit came forth, not as born, but as given.' Cf. also *In Joannis Evangelium*, 16.15, 99.4–9.

[108] Pseudo-Cyril, *De Sacrosancta Trinitate*, 8 – John of Damascus, *De fide orthodoxa*, 8.

[109] Karl Barth, *Church Dogmatics* I.1, p. 475f.

[110] Athanasius, *Ad Serapionem*, 1.7; cf. *In illud, omnia*, 6.

silent, but let us use them only with apophatic reserve and reverence. With Basil again, 'We confess to knowing what is knowable of God, and yet what we know reaches beyond our apprehension.'[111]

5) PERICHORESIS AND THE COACTIVITY OF THE HOLY TRINITY

It is very easy when using technical terms of thought and speech like *'homoousion'*, 'hypostatic union', *'perichoresis'*, and even 'Unity' and 'Trinity', to think concepts rather than the realities denoted by them, and to lapse into some static mode of thought. This applies to all our theological terms which through their use may acquire an independent authority in themselves in virtue of which they tend to exercise a determinative and formative function over the truth, as if that only is true which can be reduced to conceptual expression. Rather do we have to use these technical theological terms as under the formative impact of divine revelation they take shape as aids to our weakness in saying something about realities which cannot be mastered in human forms of thought and speech, and as a means of pointing to those realities which may shine through them but which are to be known apart from them and independent of them, and by which the forms of thought and speech we use are themselves relativised. Theological concepts are used aright when we do not think the concepts themselves, thereby identifying them with the truth, but think through them of the realities or truths which they are meant to intend beyond themselves.[112] This applies not least to the concept of *perichoresis* in which we are concerned with real objective onto-relations in the eternal movement of Love in the Communion of the Holy Trinity as they have been disclosed to us in the incarnate economy of God's revealing and saving acts in Jesus Christ and the Holy Spirit.

We recall that the biblical and patristic concept of the Being or οὐσία of God, governed by the self-revelation of God as *I am* in his incarnate Son, is concretely personal and dynamic in its significance. Likewise the compound concept of the *homoousion*, was used in Nicene theology to signify the oneness in Being and Act between the incarnate Son and the Father, and later also the oneness in Being and Act between the Holy Spirit and the Father. God's triune Being is to be understood as his Being-in-Act, and his Act as his Act-in-Being (to borrow Karl Barth's expressions), which was recognised and expressed by Athanasius in his concept of God's activity as inherent in his Being, ἐνούσιος ἐνέργεια.[113] He had already discerned that the *homoousion* implies a mutual indwelling or a mutual coinherence of the three divine Persons not only in their Being but in their Activity. It is that triune *coactivity* of the Father, the Son and the Holy Spirit that we are now to consider with the help of the concept of *perichoresis* which, as we have seen, is to be

---

[111] Basil, *Epistulae*, 235.2.

[112] Refer to Torrance, *Theology in Reconstruction*, pp. 30ff & 46ff; *Divine Meaning. Studies in Greek Patristics* (T&T Clark, Edinburgh, 1995), ch. 1: 'The Complex Background of Biblical Interpretation'; and ch.11: 'The Logic and Analogic of Biblical and Theological Statements in the Greek Fathers'.

[113] Athanasius, *Contra Arianos*, 2.2; cf. 2.28; 3.65; 4.1f.

understood as essentially active in its basic significance without any split in its wholeness between ontological and dynamic aspects.

The original understanding of coinherence which was developed and refined through the concept of *perichoresis* arose as an interpretation of the mutual indwelling of the Son and the Father of which we learn in the discourses of Jesus relayed to us in the Fourth Gospel, especially in its reports of his 'I am' sayings and of his teaching about his relations with the Father, and about the Holy Spirit who proceeds from the Father in the Name of the Son and acts in his place as 'another Paraclete'. This account of the reciprocal indwelling or inexisting between the Father, the Son, and the Spirit, however, is presented to us in evangelical contexts which have to do with the interrelation between the miraculous *works* of Jesus and the *works* of God the Father. Thus when Jesus was challenged by the Jewish authorities about his act in healing on the Sabbath day a man who had been lying helpless at the Pool of Bethesda for thirty-eight years, which they deemed had broken the Sabbath, Jesus replied with the terse sentence: 'My Father works up to now, and I am at work.' He was thereby claiming that in his miracle of healing he was in fact continuing the creative activity of God,[114] by implication, beyond the sixth day when the original creation ended,[115] and was engaged in bringing it to its completion.[116]

Throughout this fifth Chapter of St John's Gospel we have recorded words of Jesus concerning a oneness in act as well as in being between himself and the Father, even in respect of the ultimate acts of God in resurrection and judgment, for the Father has given the Son both to have life in himself and to do all that he the Father does. That is to say, here we are told that the message of the Gospel, the truth of Jesus, is grounded in and arises out of complete coinherence *in being and act* between the Father and the Son. This is followed, of course, in the Fourth Gospel by the statements we have already discussed in which Jesus claims that he and the Father are one, for the Father is in him and he is in the Father, and that it is in virtue of this living relation of being, doing and loving between the Father and himself that he undertakes his work of redemption in laying down his life for us and taking it up again, and in sending the Holy Spirit to act in his place in the actualising of his saving presence and power in the life and faith of his followers. Throughout the Gospel we learn that the self-revelation of God as Father, Son and Holy Spirit takes place through the Word and Work of Christ as they are integrated in his Life and Being, who as the incarnate *I am* of the Lord constitutes the one exclusive Way to the Father, for he who sees Jesus sees the Father. 'Do you not believe', Jesus asked Philip, 'that I am in the Father and the Father is in me? The words that I say to you, I do not speak on my own authority, but the Father who dwells in me does the works. Believe me that I am in the Father and the Father in me or else believe me for the sake of the works themselves.'[117]

The threefold coactivity of God manifested in the missions of the Son and the Spirit from the Father was given summary expression in the words of St Paul: 'For

114 John 5.17.
115 Gen. 2.1–3.
116 John 5.36.
117 John 14.10f.

of him, and through him, and to him are all things (ἐξ αὐτοῦ καὶ δι᾽ αὐτοῦ καὶ εἰς αὐτὸν τὰ πάντα)'.[118] And again: 'There is one God and Father of all who is above all, and through all, and in all.'[119] This was paraphrased in the Council of Constantinople, 'For one is the God and Father, from whom are all things, and one Lord Jesus Christ, through who are all things, and one Holy Spirit in whom are all things.'[120] There is a significant coordination and unity of Being (οὐσία) and Activity (ἐνέργεια) in the Holy Trinity, *from* the Father, *through* the Son and *in* the Holy Spirit, although the distinctive mode of operation by each of the three divine Persons is maintained, indicated by the prepositions 'from (ἐκ)', 'through (διά)', and 'in (ἐν)'.[121] All three divine Persons have one Activity which is ever the same for 'the Father does all things through the Word and in the Spirit'.[122]

Particular attention must be given to the middle term in the one coordinate activity of God, 'through', for it is through the *incarnate* Son of God, the one Mediator between God and Man, that the activity of God as Father, Son and Holy Spirit is disclosed to us in the life and works of Jesus as objective events and truths of God's saving activity in history.[123] There is no separate activity of the Holy Spirit in revelation or salvation in addition to or independent of the activity of Christ, for what he does is to empower and actualise the words and works of Christ in our midst as the words and works of the Father. Everything in the message of the Gospel, and everything in the doctrine of the Holy Trinity, hinges upon the concrete mediatorial activity of Christ in space and time, for it is through the incarnate *parousia* of the Son of God in Jesus that the activity of God in its nature and reality is revealed to us and its saving power is actualised among us in the Spirit whose coming to us is made possible on the ground of Christ's atoning and reconciling work. Calvary and Pentecost, the blood of Christ and the Spirit of Christ, may not be separated from one another.[124]

The proper evangelical understanding of the procession of the Holy Spirit from the Father in the Name of the Son and his sending by the Son in union with the Father is very important (apart from the problem which we have discussed above), for two reasons. On the one hand, it is on the inseparable relation of the Spirit in his Being and Activity to the incarnate Being and Activity of Jesus Christ that our participation in the economic Activity of God depends; but on the other hand, it is on the oneness of the historical mission of the Spirit from the incarnate Son with the eternal outgoing of the Spirit from the Father that the truth of the Gospel is

---

[118] Rom. 11.36.

[119] Eph. 4.6.

[120] *Enchiridion Symbolorum Definitionum et Declarationum de rebus fidei et morum*, H. Denzinger & A. Schönmetzer, 33rd edn (Freiburg, 1965), 421 / p. 144.

[121] Athanasius, *Ad Serapionem*, 1.20 – see also 1.14 & 3.5; and Basil, *De Spiritu Sancto*, 5.7ff.

[122] Athanasius, *Ad Serapionem*, 1.28, & 30–31.

[123] Karl Barth objected to the expression 'through the Son' for he held that, unlike the *filioque*, it 'does not lead…to the thought of the full consubstantial communion between the Father and the Son', *Church Dogmatics* I.1, p. 481f. That would be unfortunate, but actually it is the διὰ τοῦ υἱοῦ which preserves the incarnational or economic factor in the doctrine of the procession of the Spirit, which, to say the least, is not prominent in the Western *filioque*. After all, the Nicene *homoousion* was asserted of Jesus Christ the *incarnate* Son and Saviour.

[124] Cf. Leo the Great, *Sermones*, 87.1–4.

ultimately grounded. If the ontological bond between the historical Jesus Christ and God the Father is cut then the substance falls out of the Gospel, but if the ontological bond between the Holy Spirit and the incarnate Son of the Father is cut, so that there is a discrepancy between the economic Trinity and the ontological Trinity, or between the saving activity of the love of God in history and the transcendent activity of God in eternity, then we human beings are left without hope and can have no part or lot in *God's* saving activity in Jesus Christ. This is why the Church found it of the utmost importance and necessity in the proclamation of the Gospel under constraint of its divine truth to assert the *homoousion* both of Christ and of the Spirit, for, as Athanasius argued so powerfully, the *homoousion* of the Son and the *homoousion* of the Spirit belong inseparably together – neither can be maintained apart from the other. It is in this all-important homoousial bond between them that the procession of the Spirit *through* the Son is to be appreciated, for it is a procession through him in God and from the Father in the Son – the Spirit is sent by the Son in the Father. It is worth noting in this connection Athanasius' comment on the trinitarian benediction: 'The Grace of the Lord Jesus Christ and the love of God and the communion of the Holy Spirit be with you all.'[125]

> For the grace and gift that is given is given in the Trinity, from the Father, through the Son, in the Holy Spirit. As the grace given is from the Father through the Son, so we can have no communion in the gift except in the Holy Spirit. For it is when we partake of him that we have the love of the Father and the grace of the Son and the communion of the Spirit himself.[126]

The truth of this trinitarian understanding of the Father, the Son and the Holy Spirit in their personal onto-relations with one another and in the unity of their Being and Activity is considerably deepened and reinforced with the help of the concept of *perichoresis* in which we are not concerned simply with a one-way set of relations but with a dynamic three-way reciprocity. This enables us to think of the Triunity of God both in terms of the mutual containing of the particular divine Persons in one another, and in terms of the reciprocal interpenetration of their distinctive activities, and think of them at one and the same time, or in perichoretic circularity and wholeness. Just as we think of the particular properties of the three divine Persons not as holding them apart from one another but rather as contributing to their inseparable Communion with one another, without in any way diminishing their respective characteristics; so we think of the different activities of the Father, the Son and the Holy Spirit, not as dividing them from one another but as constituting their dynamic oneness with one another, without in any way diminishing their differences. Perichoretic relations characterise both the hypostatic subsistences and the hypostatic activities of the three divine Persons, so that they are not only Triune in Being but are Triune in Activity. Since God's Being and Activity completely interpenetrate each other, we must think of his Being and his

---

[125] 2 Cor. 13.14.
[126] Athanasius, *Ad Serapionem*, 1.30.

197

Activity not separately but as one Being-in-Activity and one Activity-in-Being. In other words, the Father, the Son and the Holy Spirit always act together in every divine operation whether in creation or redemption, yet in such a way that the distinctive activities of the Father, the Son and the Holy Spirit, are always maintained, in accordance with the propriety and otherness of their Persons as the Father, the Son and the Holy Spirit. This may be called the 'perichoretic coactivity of the Holy Trinity'.

In every creative and redemptive act the Father, the Son and the Holy Spirit operate together in fellowship with one another but nevertheless in ways peculiar to each of them. It is not possible for us to spell that out in terms of any demarcations between their distinctive operations, if only because within the coactivity of the three divine Persons those operations perichoretically contain one another and pass over into one another while remaining what they distinctively are in themselves.[127] It is only from within the incarnate economy of God's saving self-communication to us as Father, Son and Holy Spirit that we can say anything at all about this. The primary distinction was made there, of course, for it was the Son or Word of God who became incarnate, was born of the Virgin Mary, was crucified under Pontius Pilate, and rose again from the grave, and *not* the Father or the Holy Spirit, although the whole life and activity of Jesus from his birth to his death and resurrection did not take place apart from the presence and coactivity of the Father and the Spirit. And it is in the light of what the Lord Jesus himself revealed about his relation to the Father and the Spirit, and what he did for us in his miraculous works and saving acts, thereby manifesting on earth the works of the Father, that we are able to discern something of the way in which the Father and the Spirit participated in the economy of redemption. This enables us to believe that what God is toward us in Jesus Christ and in his manifestation in the history of salvation as Father, Son and Holy Spirit, he really is antecedently and eternally in his triune Self.

It is, then, in the activity of the economic Trinity alone that we may learn something of the activity of the ontological Trinity, for we believe that the pattern of coactivity between the Father, the Son and the Holy Spirit in the economic Trinity is through the Communion of the Spirit a real reflection of the pattern of the coactivity of the Father, the Son and the Holy Spirit in the ontological Trinity. It is indeed more than a reflection of it, for it is grounded in it, is altogether inseparable from it, and actually flows from it. While not everything that took place in the historical economy can be read back into eternity, the intrinsic oneness between the coactivity of the Father, Son and Holy Spirit in the economic Trinity

---

[127] Cf. the interesting way in which Basil distinguished in his account of creation between the work of the Father as 'the original cause of all things that are made', and the work of the Son as 'the operative cause', and the work of the Spirit as 'the perfecting cause' – his account of the 'royal freedom' of the Spirit is particularly helpful. While he held that the three divine Persons are inseparable from one another, he nevertheless distributed their distinctive activities in accordance with his conception of the Unity of the Trinity as deriving from and governed by the Ἀρχή of the Father and the distinctions between the Son and the Spirit in respect of the origins of their subsistence, the τρόποι ὑπάρξεως . *De Spiritu Sancto*, 16.37. See my discussion of this in *Theology in Reconstruction* (London, 1965), pp. 220ff.

and their coactivity in the ontological Trinity are soteriologically and epistemologically absolutely essential.

We cannot say precisely what the Father does and what the Spirit does in distinction from what Christ has done and continues to do for us. Nevertheless we cannot but say that both the Father and the Spirit participated in ways appropriate to their distinctive natures and properties in the birth of Jesus, in his servant ministry as Son of Man, in his atoning sacrifice on the Cross for sin, in his triumphant resurrection, in his ascension to the Father, in his heavenly intercession for us, and his rule over all things at God's right hand. And so we cannot but hold that the Father and the Spirit continue to participate in the saving work of God's Love, and will participate with Christ in the consummation of all things at the final judgment and resurrection. We can also say in the light of the incarnation that as the Word made flesh, the Word by whom all things that are made were made, Jesus Christ is the fulfilment of God's eternal purpose for his creation, that it is in Jesus Christ himself that all things in heaven and earth are reconciled, and that the whole created universe consists in him as its Head. Thus in virtue of the incarnation and the renewing and redeeming activity of Christ we can say something of his participation as the Word and Wisdom of God in the creation of all things, and in the covenant of grace established by God as the inner basis and framework of the created order which we read back from its fulfilment in Christ into the very beginning. As the First and the Last, the Alpha and Omega, the Lord Jesus Christ gathers up all things from the beginning in himself as the Head of the created universe in the consummation of God's eternal purpose of Love – all this also belongs to our understanding of the oneness of the economic Trinity with the ontological Trinity.

There are two further considerations that need to be taken into account.

First, the fact that in God's eternal purpose it was God the Son, *not* God the Father and *not* God the Holy Spirit, who became incarnate for us and our salvation once for all, sets aside as evangelically and theologically unentertainable any other alternative such as the possibility that the Father or the Holy Spirit could have or might have become incarnate. Certainly the incarnation and the atoning death of Christ are inconceivable apart from the Trinity for it was precisely in his differentiation as Son from the Father and from the Holy Spirit that Christ was born of the Virgin Mary and died on the Cross as the Saviour of the world. However, it was and is the *actuality* of God's exclusive revelation and communication of himself once for all in the incarnation of his only begotten Son that decides the hypothetical question whether the incarnation of another divine Person was a possibility. That also definitely rules out any suggestion that there may still be a *Deus absconditus* behind the back of Jesus Christ or some hidden God for which Jesus Christ does not stand surety. We cannot argue hypothetically (let alone reverently) from what God *has done* to what we think he might otherwise have done, for that would assume that the absolute singularity of Christ and his mission of love from the Father to be the Saviour of the world has no real or revelatory bearing upon the inner Life and Nature of God, so that in fact God remains ultimately unknown to us. It would deny the supreme truth that God himself is the content of God's self-revelation in Jesus Christ, for it would assume that divine Nature and human natures are not inseparably united in the one Person of Christ.

It would presuppose that there is only a transient functional and not an ontological relation between the economic self-revelation of God consummated in him and what God is antecedently and eternally in himself. To say the least, that would disregard the uniqueness of the one Word of God, and the comprehensiveness and absolute finality of God's economic self-revelation in the incarnation of his only begotten Son! And that, as Karl Rahner pointed out, would create havoc with theology, for in that case there would no longer be any connection between 'mission' and the intra-divine Life.[128] That is why he insisted so strongly that the economic Trinity *is* the immanent Trinity, although as we have noted that 'is' may not be construed in a logically necessary or reversible way.

Second, in view of the complete perichoretic interpenetration of the three divine Persons and their distinctive activities in one another, the so-called 'law of appropriations' brought in by Latin theology to redress an unbalanced essentialist approach to the doctrine of the Trinity from the One Being of God,[129] which obscured the evangelical approach from the economic Trinity,[130] falls completely away as an idea that is both otiose and damaging to the intrinsic truth of Christ who, as the Word and only begotten Son of God, constitutes the *one* revelation of the Father and the *one* way by which we can go to the Father.[131] This principle of appropriation carried the idea that some attributes and activities common to the whole Trinity may be specially assigned or 'appropriated' to one Person rather than another in order to reveal his distinctive hypostatic character.[132] However, since God is Triune, all his acts toward us cannot but be acts of the Trinity in Unity and of the Unity in Trinity, while in all these acts each Person who is himself whole God acts without any surrender of his distinctive hypostatic properties as Father, Son or Holy Spirit, so that the problem addressed by the principle of appropriations need not have arisen in the first place. This would seem to be the way in which Karl Barth restated the doctrine of appropriation, in his radically economic and trinitarian way of appropriating 'creation', 'reconciliation' and 'redemption' to the hypostatic distinctions between Father, Son and Holy Spirit, in which the order of God's economic self-revelation is grounded in the order of the ontological Trinity.[133]

[128] Karl Rahner, *The Trinity* (Eng. tr. London), 1970, p. 39.

[129] Thus Karl Rahner said of 'The Augustinian-Western conception of the Trinity, as contrasted with the Greek conception', 'It begins with the one God, the one divine essence as a whole, and only *afterwards* does it see God as three in persons', ibid., p. 17.

[130] See Hugo of St Victor, *De sacramentis*, 1.2, 8; and Thomas Aquinas, *Summa Theologiae*, 1.39.7; *De Veritate*, 7.3. Following St Augustine, St Thomas regarded 'power' as appropriated to the Father, 'wisdom' to the Son, and 'goodness' and 'love' to the Spirit, *Scriptum super Sententiis*, 1, d. 31, q. 1 & 2. This law of appropriations depends on the concept of the Father as the *principium deitatis* which is similar to the Basilian understanding of the role of Ἀρχή in the unity of God and his threefold activities.

[131] Cf. Karl Rahner, *The Trinity*, pp. 24–30; and Catherine M. LaCugna, *God for us. The Trinity and Christian Life* (San Francisco, 1993), pp. 99f & 211f.

[132] There is another way in which appropriation might be considered to apply, in attributing to one divine Person what is strictly proper to another, as when St Paul spoke of God as having gained the Church his own 'through his own blood'. Acts 20.28.

[133] Karl Barth, *Church Dogmatics* I.1, section 9.2, 'Trinity in Unity', pp. 353ff; cf. 579ff.

The perichoretic coordination and unity of God's saving purposes and their once for all fulfilment in Christ Jesus, and the perichoretic understanding of the one Triune Monarchy, have the effect of setting trinitarian theology upon a sure basis in the homoousial and inter-hypostatic relations between the Father, the Son and the Holy Spirit as they are revealed in the irreversible events of the incarnate economy of redemption, the mighty deeds of the Lamb of God slain before the foundation of the world. Any idea which would make the incarnation an adventitious or arbitrary event as one among other possibilities would undermine the ground of soteriological reality in the essential relation between the incarnate self-revelation of God and the Truth of God as he ever is in his Triune Being.

By way of bringing this chapter to a close it may be helpful to recall a significant contribution made by John Calvin to the doctrine of the Holy Trinity.[134] Of particular importance for him was the expression the Triunity of God given by Gregory Nazianzen.

> I cannot think of the One without immediately being surrounded by the radiance of the Three; nor can I discern the Three without at once being carried back to the One. When I think of the Three I think of him as a Whole... I cannot grasp the greatness of the One so as to attribute a greater greatness to the rest. When I contemplate the Three together, I see but one Luminary, and cannot divide or measure out the undivided Light.[135]

In Gregory's 'Oration on the Holy Spirit' there is a similar passage in which he declares:

> To us there is one God, and one Godhead, and all that issues from him is referred back to him as to be one with him, although we believe that there are Three. And One is not more and another less God, nor is One before and another after... But differentiated as the Persons are, the entire and undivided Godhead is One in each Person, and there is one mingling of light, as it were three suns joined to each other.[136]

Calvin had another way of expressing the nature of this Unity of the One Godhead in whom a Trinity of Persons coexist in Communion with One Another, when he borrowed the unusual expression *in solidum* from Cyprian.[137] This was originally intended to speak of the episcopate as essentially corporate which is held in *solidum* by one and all alike. The one episcopate belongs to each bishop only as it belongs to all. Calvin adopted this to present his own doctrine of the ministry as a corporate episcopate or presbyterate held by all pastors alike in such a way that, while it involves a parity of ministers before God, it also allows for administrative

---

[134] For the following see 'Calvin's Doctrine of the Trinity' in *Trinitarian Perspectives. Toward Doctrinal Agreement*, ch. 3, pp. 54ff.

[135] Gregory Nazianzen, *Orationes*, 40.31 – Calvin, *Institutio*, 1.13.6..

[136] Gregory Nazianzen, *Orationes*, 31.14; see 31.3.

[137] Cyprian, *De Unitate Ecclesiae*, 3.5, 6. See Calvin, *Institutio*, 4.2.6, 6.17, etc.

distinctions within the ministry. Here, however, he adapts and transfers 'in solidum' to help him express the mysterious Unity in Trinity and Trinity in Unity of God, that is, to say something of how the three Persons relate to one God without losing their distinctiveness and interrelations as three. Each of the divine Persons, Calvin declares, *in solidum* is God (*quorum quisque in solidum sit Deus*),[138] and the Being of God is totally and *in solidum* common to the divine Persons, such that with respect to their Being there is no difference between the one and the other (*restat ut tota et in solidum Patris et Filii sit communis*).[139] In other words, all three divine Persons, who do not share with one another their distinguishing properties, nevertheless share together completely and equally, not partially, in the one indivisible Being of God: the whole Being of God belongs to each of them as it belongs to all of them, and belongs to all of them as it belongs to each of them.

The language that Calvin used about what the Father shares with the Son and what they both hold in common,[140] points to the Athanasian statement that the Deity (Θεότης) flows unbrokenly and ineffably between the Father and the Son and the Holy Spirit.[141] In this way Calvin used the concept of *in solidum* to fill out the Nicene and Athanasian conceptions of *ousia* as self-existent being considered in its internal relations (*in se*) and of *hypostasis* as subsistent being considered in its objective otherness (*ad alios*). Thus while he thought of the whole Being of God as dwelling in each Person, he thought of each Person and of all three Persons, with their differentiating properties and in their mutual interrelations, as dwelling hypostatically and consubstantially in the one indivisible Being of God. The *in solidum* concept enabled Calvin to give firm expression to the intrinsically interpersonal cohesion of the Three in One and One in Three, in which there is no confusion or separation between the Persons. The incommunicable properties distinguishing them do not divide them from one another but on the contrary integrate them in their subsistent reciprocal relations. The whole Being of God belongs to each Person as it belongs to all three Persons, and belongs to all three Persons as it belongs to each Person, and so the Unity of God, utterly simple though it is, is to be understood not in an abstract generic way, nor as an undifferentiated oneness, but as the indivisible consubstantial Communion of the Father, the Son and the Holy Spirit. Moreover, the fullness of God dwells in each Person, and the fullness of each Person dwells in God, such that the one God is intrinsically hypostatic and completely *personal*, the eternal *I am who I am*, the Father, the Son and the Holy Spirit. To say that God is personal is not to say that he is *a* Person (i.e. *una persona*) in the relational sense of the three divine Persons, who are Persons *ad alios*, but that, far from being impersonal, he is a Communion of personal Being within himself, for the whole God dwells in each Person, and each Person is the whole God. Thus we may rightly think *in solidum* of the Triune God as intrinsically, perfectly and sublimely Personal.

[138] Calvin, *Institutio*, 1.13.2.
[139] Calvin, *Institutio*, 1.13.23.
[140] Calvin, *Institutio*, 1.13.23.
[141] Athanasius, *Expositio fidei*, 1–4.

8

The Sovereign Creator

THROUGHOUT the last two chapters our thought has centred on the Triunity of God as three Persons, one Being, and towards the end of the last chapter attention was directed particularly to the concept of *perichoresis* for our understanding of the coactivity of the Holy Trinity. It was pointed out that it is very easy when using technical terms to think concepts rather than the realities denoted by them. Technical terms are a kind of theological shorthand which helps us to give careful expression to basic truths and their conceptual interconnections, as we noted earlier, in the passage of theological clarification from one level of understanding to another and back again. However, in the last resort they are no more than empty abstract propositions apart from their real content in the specific self-communication of God to us in his revealing and saving acts in history in which he has made himself known to us as Father, Son and Holy Spirit. It was such an essentially dynamic approach to the coactivity of the three divine Persons that we found to be entailed in the theological shorthand of *perichoresis*. In this chapter we will be concerned to pursue that further in regard to the doctrine of God as the Sovereign Creator.

In the Nicene-Constantinopolitan Creed which gives expression to the basic doctrinal content of divine revelation, belief in God as the Sovereign Creator is presented within a trinitarian structure: one God the Father Almighty, Maker of heaven and earth and of all things visible and invisible, one Lord Jesus Christ through whom all things were made, and the Holy Spirit the Lord and Giver of life. Integrated with these three statements there are clauses about the saving incarnation of the Son of God, his crucifixion, resurrection, and final advent, while clauses on the forgiveness of sins, the resurrection of the dead and the life of the world to come are included in the third article on the Holy Spirit. This signifies to us that the doctrine of the Creator belongs to the heart and substance of the Gospel, so that belief in him is appropriately formulated within the evangelical interrelations of the economic Trinity. While the concept of God as the Creator of the universe derived originally from the Old Testament revelation and had been developed by Judaism, it was radicalised through the New Testament teaching about the Lord Jesus Christ as the Word of God by whom all things that came into being have been created, from whom they derive their intelligible and lawful order, and through whom and in whom the whole universe of visible and invisible realities consists or is held together. In Jesus Christ the Lord God has himself become man, and the Creator of all things has himself become a creature, without of course ceasing to be God the Creator, and therefore interacts creatively with the world not just from without but from within. And so it is in Christ that we creatures may meet with the Creator face to face, and it is in and through his life and work within the creation, not least through his redemptive triumph over all evil and darkness in his resurrection from the grave, that we may really understand something of the wonderful nature and work of the Creator himself, as it would be quite impossible otherwise. Moreover, since it is in the life and work of Jesus Christ that God has been manifested to us in his reality as Father, Son and Holy Spirit, our knowledge of the Sovereign Creator may not be abstracted from the incarnate power of the saving love of the triune God mediated to us and activated among us in salvation history or from the creative power of the Holy Spirit poured out upon all flesh who sheds abroad that love of God in our hearts.

It is, then, within the economy of redemption, and in the two-fold mission of the Son and the Spirit from the Father, that the distinctive nature of the sovereign power of God is made known. It is, perhaps above all, the first Chapter of St Paul's Epistle to the Colossians to which we must return here, for there we learn that in God's eternal economic purpose for the creation brought to its redemptive fulfilment in the incarnation, Jesus Christ is the central and pivotal reality of the universe, for all things were created through him and for him. In him the fullness of God was pleased to dwell, and in him as the Head of creation all things hold together while through his Cross all things, visible and invisible, are reconciled to God. With the incarnation, the death and resurrection of Christ in space and time a portentous change has taken place in the universe affecting the way in which we are to understand divine creation as proleptically conditioned by redemption.[1]

THE ALMIGHTY FATHER

In the Nicene Creed we begin with confessing belief in one God the Father Almighty, Maker of heaven and earth. He is Almighty and Father, Father and Almighty, at one and the same time, for he *is* Father, and *is* Almighty. Let us note in passing that this means that we must reject all abstract notions of divine omnipotence, for omnipotence is not to be understood in terms of what we think God can do, defining it as potence raised to the nth power, i.e. as omni-potence, but in terms of what God actually *is* and actually *has done*. Thus we do not define God by omnipotence but define omnipotence by the Nature and Being of God as he has revealed himself to us in his creative and redemptive activity. His power is not

---

[1] See H. R. Mackintosh, *Doctrine of the Person* (Edinburgh, 2nd edn, 1913): 'Christ is conceived as Creator of the world *qua* the Person in whom the universe was in due time to find its organic centre in virtue of his work of reconciliation; he was the initial cause of all things, as being destined to be their final end. His function as Creator is proleptically conditioned by his achievement as Saviour', p. 70.

different from his Nature, for it is the power of his Nature, the power of his Being in action, the power of what he is in his Being and ever will be. He *is* God the Father Almighty. Since his almightiness is to be understood strictly in accordance with his divine Being, we may say that he does not do, and cannot do, what is other than what he actually and eternally is as the Lord God, or what is other than the nature of his Being as God the Father. There is and can be no valid or meaningful discussion of God's sovereignty or power in detachment of his sovereignty from his Being or in abstraction of his power from his being God the Father. We cannot even think of God's power from any point above him or apart from what he actually is and has been revealed to be, for, to say the least, that would be an empty movement of thought. Hence abstract questions postulated about what God can do and can not do are empty of meaning and give rise to nonsensical answers, for they are false questions posed apart from the reality and nature of God's being. A proper and realistic understanding of the almightiness of God must be formed on the basis of the identity between God's transcendent reality and his power – they are one and the same. God's power is as unlimited as God himself is, and is limited only by what God himself is. God and God alone has real power for his power is the power of his transcendent reality as the one and only God.

In the Nicene Creed we confess belief 'in one God, the Father Almighty, Maker of heaven and earth and of all things visible and invisible', but we also confess belief 'in one Lord Jesus Christ, the only-begotten Son of the Father. ...homoousial with the Father, through whom all things were made.' These clauses have to be taken together, for any Christian and rigorously theological doctrine of the Sovereign Creator must be true and faithful to his personal Nature as God revealed in Jesus Christ his Son who is of one and the same being as God the Father. It is as Father Almighty that God *is* Creator, and it is through the Son who is in act as well as being one with the Father that all things are made. The *homoousion* tells us that the sovereignty of the Father is identical with the sovereignty of the incarnate Son, and the sovereignty of the incarnate Son is identical with the sovereignty of God the Father. We may not forget, however, the distinctive characteristics of the Persons of the Father and the Son for they also obtain in creation, but there as elsewhere they serve not to divide but to unite the Father and the Son.

When we speak of God the *Father*, then, in relation to creation as well as redemption, we mean the God and Father of our Lord Jesus Christ. Certainly, as we have reminded ourselves more than once, in the New Testament and the Early Church the term 'Father' is understood in a twofold but indivisible way, as referring both to the Godhead, and to the Father of the Son. While 'Father' in the sense of the ultimate Godhead is the one almighty Source of all other being, he is so only as he is eternally Father of the eternal Son. That is to say, the one and only God is God precisely in that he is the Father of his Son, and it is as such that he is the Source of all being, not through any intermediary but directly in virtue of his very nature as God. The Fatherhood and the Sonship of God are as ultimate and eternal as one another, for the Father and the Son are who they are in their mutual inter-personal relations with one another. Therefore we do not and cannot know God as Father either in himself or as our Father, apart from the Person of his only begotten Son incarnate in Jesus Christ, through whom alone in one Spirit God gives us access to

THE CHRISTIAN DOCTRINE OF GOD

knowledge of himself in accordance with what he is in his transcendent Nature. We know God strictly in accordance with his Nature, then, when our knowledge of him is governed by the Nature of Jesus Christ as he is made known to us in the Gospel. There is no way of knowing the sovereignty or almightiness of God by going behind the back of Jesus Christ, for there is no God but he who is immutably this God and Father whom we know in the face of the Lord Jesus Christ, for it is through him the one and only Son of the Father that we know the Father. God's sovereign Power is, therefore, not other than the power manifest in the incarnation, for God does not act otherwise than he has acted and does act in the Lord Jesus Christ who is the Word and Will and Power and Love of God incarnate among us. Since what Jesus Christ is and does is what God is and does, God cannot be thought of as being other than what Jesus Christ is, the same yesterday, today and for ever. God does not and cannot go back on the incarnation or become different from what he ever was, has become and for ever will be in Jesus Christ. Because Jesus Christ is the only-begotten Son of the Father, he is the one way whereby God makes himself known as Father, and is in fact the exclusive revelation of the Fatherhood of God and of the almighty Power of God the Father. As there is no other God than this God, there is no other almighty Power than the almighty Power of God revealed in Jesus Christ. God's almighty Power, omnipotence or sovereignty is therefore to be understood in terms of what he unalterably and immutably is in Jesus Christ, for he remains in all his acts eternally true to and consistent with his eternal nature as revealed in the incarnation.

It must be added, however, that this intrinsic relation between the Father and the Son is not rightly and properly known except within the oneness and wholeness of the triadic relations of the Godhead, and therefore not apart from the Holy Spirit, for in the Holy Trinity the Father is not properly Father apart from the Son and the Spirit, and the Son is not properly Son apart from the Father and the Spirit, and the Spirit is not properly Spirit apart from the Father and the Son. Owing to this oneness of nature between the Father, the Son and the Spirit, there is also a oneness of activity between them. Since the Father is never without the Son and the Spirit, all that the Father does is done in, through and with the Son and the Spirit, and all that the Son and the Spirit do is coincident with what the Father does. It is, then, of God the Father in this full sense, in his mutually homoousial and completely perichoretic relations with the Son and the Spirit, that we are to think of him as the Sovereign Creator, or in credal language as 'God the Father Almighty, Maker of heaven and earth and of all things visible and invisible'.

Within this trinitarian perspective, the power or almightiness of God is revealed to be essentially *personal*, defined by God's triune Nature and Being as Father, Son and Holy Spirit. This personal power of God is not power that overrules the creature but sustains the creature, not power that negates the freedom of the creature, but the power of the Love that God is, power therefore that sustains the relation and freedom of the creature before God, for it is always creative, and in relation to his human creatures always personalising and humanising power. It is essentially being-constituting, creature-constituting power. Hence when we confess in the Creed belief in God the Father Almighty we believe that the almightiness of God is the almightiness of God the Father – God's almightiness and God's Fatherhood inhere in one another, and are as such intrinsically and undeviatingly personal within the fullness of personal Being in the Holy Trinity.

Two cognate points call for our consideration right away: that while God is always Father he is not always Creator; and that it is as Father that God is Creator, not vice versa.[2]

(a) God is always Father, not always Creator

It was Athanasius who first put forward this statement in showing that the kind of relation between God and what he has created is altogether different from the kind of relation between the Father and the Son within his eternal Being.[3] He distinguished sharply between the eternal generation of the Son from the *nature* of God, with whom he ever lives without any beginning, and the creation of the world by the *will* of God who in accordance with his good pleasure has freely brought it into existence out of nothing and given it a finite beginning.[4] As the Nicene Creed tersely expressed it, the incarnate Son 'was begotten, not made'. There is thus a oneness in being and an identity in nature between the Father and the Son, but a total otherness in being and a complete disparity in nature between the Creator and the creature. An entirely different kind of relation obtains in each case, for one is ontological and belongs to the intrinsic life and eternal Being of God, and the other is contingent and relates to the temporal existence of the creature. Just as there is no necessary relation between God and the world which he has freely created, for God does not need the world to be God, so the Fatherhood of God is in no way dependent on or constituted by relation to what he has created outwith himself. Of course we do not know any God who is completely locked up in himself but only the God who interacts with us. We learn from his incarnate self-revelation that God does not will to exist for himself alone and does not wish to be without us, but has in his eternal purpose of love freely created a universe, within which he has placed human beings made after his own image and likeness in order that he may share his love with them and enable them to enjoy his divine fellowship.

---

[2] See *The Trinitarian Faith*, ch. 3, 'The Almighty Creator', pp. 76ff.

[3] See Georges Florovsky's illuminating discussion, 'The Concept of Creation in Saint Athanasius', *Studia Patristica*, vol. IV (1962), p. 45f.

[4] The creation of the universe out of nothing does not mean the creation of the universe out of something that is nothing, but out of nothing at all. It is not created out of anything – it came into being through the absolute fiat of God's Word in such a way that whereas previously there was nothing, the whole universe came into being. Nor of course is the creation to be regarded an emanation of God, something which is in God or part of God, or created out of God. The creation of the universe is the unique positive act in which God freely brings into being another reality utterly different from his own transcendent reality, yet contingent on it and existing and continuously existing under the affirming and sustaining power of his sovereign will as the Lord God Almighty. For a scientific account of creation *ex nihilo* see Wm. Lane Craig, 'The Caused Beginning of the Universe: a Response to Quentin Smith', *The British Journal for the Philosophy of Science*, vol. 44, No. 4 (Dec. 1993), pp. 623–639.

What Athanasius encountered in the teaching of Origen, in his failure to distinguish between the eternal generation of the Son and the creation of the world, between ontological and cosmological dimensions, is not unlike, it may be said, what is found today in process theology according to which the external relations of God are held in some measure to be constitutive of what he is as God. God is always Father, but he is not always Creator, for in his creative activity God has to do with what is 'external' to his Being, freely giving existence to what did not exist before, and sustaining it by his will and grace in a creaturely coexistence with himself. Origen's rather hellenistic failure to distinguish between the ontological and cosmological dimensions in his understanding of God as Father and as Creator had the effect of ultimately resolving 'the temporal Gospel' into 'the everlasting Gospel', thus undermining the particularity and concrete reality of God's revealing and saving acts in history.[5] It is the same danger that frequently crops up today in a failure to take seriously the temporal relevance and concrete reality of the incarnation and the resurrection.[6]

While God was always Father and was Father independently of what he has created, as Creator he acted in a way that he had not done before, in bringing about absolutely new events – this means that the creation of the world out of nothing is something *new even for God.* God was always Father, but he *became* Creator. This is not to say, of course, that God did not always have the power to create, nor is it to say that creation was not in the Mind of God before he actually brought it into being, but that he brought it into being by a definite act of his gracious will. It is in a similar way that we must think of the incarnation, for although God was always able to become incarnate, he chose to become incarnate in what the Bible calls 'the fullness of time'; and must likewise also think of Pentecost and the radical change in the nature and mode of his presence in the world which it initiated. Taken together these new decisive acts of God in creation, incarnation, and the coming of the Spirit, have breath-taking implications for our understanding of the unlimited *freedom* of God. They tell us that far from being a static or inertial Deity like some 'unmoved mover', the mighty living God who reveals himself to us through his Son and in his Spirit is absolutely free to do what he had never done before, and free to be other than he was eternally: to be Almighty Creator, and even to become incarnate as a creature within his creation, while nevertheless remaining eternally the God that he always was.

The fact that while God was always Father he freely chose to become Creator, and what is more, the fact that he freely and astonishingly chose to become a creature within his creation, reveals something about the astonishing nature and freedom of God's dynamic Being, and the inconceivable way in which his ever-living acting Being is always *new* while always remaining what it ever was and is and ever will be. By his very nature, in the unlimited, uninhibited overflow of his love and grace, God always takes us by surprise, the ever-living, ever-moving, eternally new

---

[5] Origen, *De Principiis*, 4.3.13; cf. 3.6.8; *In Joannis Evangelium*, 1.8–9.

[6] This is what Karl Barth called a 'horror of physis, of externality, of corporeality', *Church Dogmatics* I.2, p. 130. He had the idealist and Hegelian theologians particularly in mind, but also Paul Tillich.

Lord God Almighty, the one Source and Lord of all being whatsoever. His almighty power and freedom are not exhausted in what he has done, does do, and will do. The fact that in his unlimited freedom God has brought and does bring things to pass that have never taken place before and are new for God means that there is, if we may express it thus, a 'before' and 'after' in God's activity, which calls for a consideration of the unique nature of 'time' in the eternal Life of God. But that must wait till later on in our discussion.

(b) It is as Father that God is Creator, not vice versa

The fact that God is always Father, not always Creator, but *became* Creator, means that it is precisely *as Father* that he is Creator, and not that he became Father because he was Creator. It is God in the power of his eternal Fatherhood who is the sovereign Creator. And so we confess in the Creed, 'We believe in *God the Father* Almighty, Maker of heaven and earth, and of all things visible and invisible.' We do not confess that God is Father *and* Almighty, for God's almightiness is the almightiness of his Fatherhood from everlasting to everlasting; his being Father does not result from his being Almighty, although he was eternally Almighty. While creation of the universe, in form and matter out of nothing, certainly involved omnipotent power, we must think of that power not in an abstract way as bare unlimited power in itself,[7] not as the power of some 'God' complete and enclosed and inactive in his loneliness, but as the living power of the eternal Father flowing from his intrinsic nature as Love, as the movement of the Love that God is ever in himself as Father, Son and Holy Spirit. It is out of that movement of sublime Love within himself, and its free movement outward from himself toward us in his will not to exist for himself or in himself alone but to share the fullness of his Love in fellowship with others, that God the Father became Creator and continues unceasingly to sustain his creation in relation to himself.

In virtue of his intrinsic and eternal Fatherhood God always had the power to create, and did actually create because he was and is the Father of the Son. Expressed otherwise, since God is Father in himself, as Father of the Son, he is essentially generative or fruitful in his own Being, and it is because he is inherently productive as *Father* that God could and did freely become Creator or Source of all being beyond himself. Creation arises, then, out of the Father's eternal love of the Son, and is activated through the free ungrudging movement of that Fatherly love in sheer grace which continues to flow freely and unceasingly toward what God has brought into being in complete differentiation from himself. This is a truth which we have come to grasp only through the incarnation of his Love in Jesus Christ, God's beloved Son whom he did not spare but delivered him up for us all. The utterly astonishing truth revealed in the fact that God did not spare his beloved Son but freely gave him up for us on the Cross is that 'God loves us better than he

---

[7] Cf. Karl Barth, *Dogmatics in Outline*, pp. 46ff.

209

loves himself',[8] and that, with the gift of his dear Son in atoning sacrifice for our sin, God the Father will continue freely to give us all things. This is why it may be said, not only that our understanding of creation is proleptically conditioned by redemption, but that the actual creation of the universe in the outward movement of the Father's love was proleptically conditioned by the incarnation of that love within it in order to redeem the creation and to reconcile all things, things visible and invisible alike, to himself. This is another way of expressing what the New Testament Scriptures refer to as the divine act of 'predestination' before the foundation of the world, but of course an act of *pre*destination in which we may not and cannot rightly interpret that 'pre' in terms of the kind of temporal priority, or indeed causal and logical priority, with which we have to do in the universe of created space and time.

Because God *is* Love, we cannot and may not try to press our thought speculatively behind that Love to what might have happened, had not the fall taken place, had not the world become disordered through evil. We can no more do that than we can think beyond the ultimate Being of God in his inner divine Life. On the other hand, because the Love of God did not have a temporal beginning but is as eternal as his very Being, because the Father *first* loved the world that he gave his only-begotten Son for our salvation, and because he *first* loved us that he has reconciled us to himself, our understanding of the movement of his redeeming love, precisely under the thrust of that free spontaneous movement, cannot but reach back beyond time, through what he has done for us in history, to the eternal Fountain of divine Love out of which it flowed.[9] Hence when by the redeeming love of Christ we are brought to love God in time, we love him with the very love with which he *first* loved us, and adore his love in and for itself. In the love of God incarnate in Jesus Christ and shed abroad in our hearts by the Holy Spirit we learn to love the Love of the Father ultimately for himself alone and not for any gain to ourselves. In trinitarian terms this means that the Love of God the Father historically manifest in the economic Trinity directs us back to the Love that God eternally is in himself in the ontological Trinity apart from his relation to the world. Hence, while clapping our hands upon our mouth, without knowing what we say, we may nevertheless feel urged to say that in his eternal purpose the immeasurable Love of God overflowing freely beyond himself which brought the creation into existence would have become incarnate within the creation even if we and our world were not in need of his redeeming grace.[10] Certainly we cannot and may not think of God's eternal purpose apart from the way that his Love has actually taken among us in incarnation and redemption; nevertheless, in being loved with that Love, we know it to be both unbeginning and unending Love that transcends all space and time and all human thought processes in the infinite dimensions of its divine fullness.

[8] H. R. Mackintosh, *The Person of Jesus Christ* (London, 1912), p. 91. See also his contribution to *Monthly Visitor*, Edinburgh, June 1932, on 'The Sacrifice of the Father'; and my essay, 'Hugh Ross Mackintosh, Theologian of the Cross', *The Scottish Bulletin of Evangelical Theology* (Edinburgh, 1987), vol. 5, no. 2, p. 165.

[9] Cf. John Calvin, *Institutio*, 2.16.1–4.

[10] Cf. James B. Torrance and Roland C. Walls, *John Duns Scotus Doctor of the Church* (Edinburgh, 1992), p. 9. Cf. also Iain Mackenzie, *The Anachronism of Time* (Norwich, 1994).

Let me repeat the point that we cannot think truly of God the Father Almighty, Maker of heaven and earth and of all things visible and invisible, and of the essential nature of his omnipotent power, except on Christian ground, for we have no other source of knowledge than that given us in Christ. It is in him that the ultimate power of God who is Love became incarnate. 'My Father is working still, and I am working.'[11] The Kingdom of God has merged with his Person,[12] in whom all the fullness of God dwells bodily. In him the Kingdom of God is embodied and becomes visible and active in the world in the power and freedom of his redeeming and transforming Love. It is thus that we are to understand the words of the Lord Jesus spoken in his great commission to the disciples after his resurrection, 'All power is given unto *me* in heaven and on earth ... And, lo, *I* am with you always, even to the end of the world.'[13] In thinking of God the Father as Almighty Creator, therefore, we cannot but think of him in terms of the unbroken and perfect oneness between his Beloved Son and himself. This knowledge of the Sovereign Creator arises within the economic manifestation of God's saving acts made known to us in the Gospel of the life, death and resurrection of Jesus Christ and in the Holy Spirit he sends to us. It is knowledge controlled both by what Jesus affirmed of the unqualified omnipotence of God the Father,[14] and by his own passion on the Cross and his triumphant resurrection over death and darkness.[15]

Far from being some irrational arbitrary power in itself, the sovereign power of the Creator is not empty of his Holy Reality as God, so that it is to be understood strictly in accordance with the Nature of his divine Being who is not and cannot be, and who does not do and cannot do, what is other than what he actually and eternally is and does do as Father, Son and Holy Spirit. The power of his Triune Being is not different from the personal power of his revealed Nature and the power of his Will is not different from what he is in himself and ever will be. His omnipotent power is in absolute accord with the infinite perfections of his Being, for it is the omnipotent power of his wisdom, love and grace as God the Father. His unbounded almightiness is the sovereignty of his Holy Love revealed to us in the Gospel, the power of the Triune God who is a transcendent Communion of Love in himself and who in the ungrudging and unrestrained overflow of his Love delights to give being and freedom to his creatures. He respects their integrity and nature as his creatures,[16] and redeems them from all that conflicts with their being and freedom or corrupts their integrity and creaturely nature. The relation of God to the world is completely positive for it is never anything else than creative; he loves it, upholds it and blesses it and coordinates its continuing creaturely existence

---

[11] John 5.17.
[12] Cf. H. R. Mackintosh, *Doctrine of the Person* (Edinburgh, 1913), p. 54; and E. Jüngel, *God as the Mystery of the World* (Grand Rapids, 1983), p. 353.
[13] Matt. 28. 18 & 20.
[14] Matt. 19.26: 'With God all things are possible'.
[15] John 16.33, 'Be of good cheer, I have overcome the world'.
[16] Cf. Jesus' rebuke to the disciples who wanted to call down divine fire upon the Samaritan villagers who would not receive him: 'You do not know what manner of spirit you are of, for the Son of Man came not to destroy men's lives but to save them' (Luke 9.54).

with his own ever-living uncreated existence, as the one Source of all being and order, all existence and rationality.

God's Holy Love is defined for us above all by what took place in the birth, life, death and resurrection of Jesus Christ, and in his pouring out of the Holy Spirit upon the Church at Pentecost. It is defined therefore in its triune reality as *the Grace of the Lord Jesus Christ, the Love of God and the Communion of the Holy Spirit.* It is ultimately in that *triune* way that we must think of the intrinsic Nature and Power of God the Father Almighty, Maker of heaven and earth, and of all things visible and invisible. Colin Gunton has very rightly said that 'the only satisfactory account of the relation between the creator and the creation is a trinitarian one', but he also points out that 'giving of priority to the Father is not to take away from the distinctive modes of action of the Son and the Spirit, but on the contrary, to guarantee that full weight is given to them.'[17]

We recall that in the Holy Trinity the Father is not properly Father apart from the Son and the Spirit, the Son is not properly Son apart from the Father and the Spirit, and the Spirit is not properly Spirit apart from the Father and the Son. Owing to this oneness of Nature between the Father, the Son and the Holy Spirit there is a oneness of Activity between them, although each in accordance with his own hypostatic reality engages in the creative work of God in his own distinctive way. Since the Father is never without the Son and the Spirit, all that the Father does is done in and through and with the Son and the Spirit, and all that the Son and the Spirit do is continuous with what the Father does. It is then of this one God in his intrinsically homoousial and perichoretic relations as Father, Son and Holy Spirit, that we are to think of him as Sovereign Creator.

1) The Activity of God the Father

Creation is the work of the Triune God, but there are relative distinctions in his three-fold activity appropriate to the Persons of the Father, the Son, and the Spirit, which bear upon the creation, although they overlap with one another and penetrate one another. This is very evident in the activity of divine Love which is peculiarly appropriate to the Father, for it is from him that the Son and the Spirit eternally proceed, each in his own way. It is to the ultimate Love of God the Father that the 'reason' for the creation is to be traced, why it exists at all, but also why it is what it is and not something else. Expressed the other way round, there is no reason why the creation came to be, why there is something and not nothing, apart from the eternal movement of Love in the inner Life of God, which in love freely overflows from God who does not will to exist for himself alone but for others also. It is then, as grounded in that ultimate Love which God the Father is, that the rational order of the creation is to be understood, for that Love precisely as Love is inflexibly opposed to all that is not love or that resists the fulfilment of God's love for his creation and his affirmation and justification of it as his good creation. It is intrinsically Holy Love which is not and cannot be anything other than itself, and

---

[17] Colin E. Gunton, *Christ and Creation* (Carlisle, 1992), pp. 75 and 80.

cannot, therefore, condone anything that conflicts with it. The Holy Love of God is thus the Law of his own divine Being and Activity which withstands and negates all that is contrary to God's Love, judges all that resists it, and inexorably condemns it. It is this Holy Lawful Divine Love that constitutes the ultimate invariant ground of all rational and moral order in the created universe, and it is under its constraint that all physical and moral laws functioning within the universe operate and are in the last resort to be recognised and formulated.

As such the whole realm of heaven and earth is to be understood as framed and designed by God to bear witness to himself and reflect the glory of his Love and Holiness. It constitutes the *theatrum gloriae Dei*, as John Calvin fittingly expressed it,[18] wherein all things invisible and visible bear witness to God and praise his transcendent Glory, Goodness and Beauty. It belongs in particular to the role of man and woman whom God has created after his own image, and made the crown of his creation, to bear witness to that Glory and serve the purpose of God's wonderful Love. Nature itself is mute, but human being is the one constituent of the created universe through whom its rational structure and astonishing beauty may be brought to word in praise of the Creator.

2) The Activity of God the Son

Since God the Father is not Father apart from the Son, while the Son is not Son apart from the Father, the incarnation of the Holy Love of the Father in Jesus Christ tells us that he works along with the Father in the creating and ordering of the universe. In Jesus Christ none other than the Creator, the ultimate Ground and Source of all being, order and rationality, the Creator Word of God who is God, has himself become man within our creaturely existence and operates creatively within it imparting to all things their form and order. St John tells us that all things were made by him, and without him there was not anything made that was made, and that he was the Light shining in the darkness of the world whose Life was the light and life of mankind.[19] And St Paul tells us not only that all things were created, earthly and heavenly, visible and invisible, realities alike, through Christ and for him, but that they all consist or are held together in him, for he is before all things and the Head of all things, and in him all things in heaven and earth, invisible and visible are reconciled.[20] As the Word and the Wisdom of God who was in the beginning with God and was God, he it is who has imparted to the universe its rational order, but who as the Word and Light of God incarnate has come into the midst of our dark, sinful and alienated world in order to redeem and reconcile it to the Father and thereby to overcome its strangely lawless state and restore it to the law of his divine Love.

Here in Jesus Christ made known to us in the Gospel as Lord and Saviour we are given a revelation of God who does not hold himself aloof from the world of

---

[18] John Calvin, *Institutio*, 1.6.2; 1.14.20; 2.6.1; 3.9.2, etc.
[19] John 1.1f.
[20] Col. 1.16f; cf. Heb. 1.1ff.

space and time which he has brought into orderly existence out of nothing, but is continuously active in creative preservation and redemptive intervention in the affairs of mankind and the world. Thus the biblical revelation of God as the ever-living and ever-acting Lord is finally established for us by the incarnation of the Word by whom all things are made, by the personal Presence of God himself in space and time, and his redemptive and providential interaction with the world. This interaction is not to be thought of as involving a suspension or interference in the natural order of things, for the natural order came from the Word of God in the first place, and is now to be regarded as brought under the reordering activity of God through the redemptive intervention of the Creator Word and given a deeper dimension in which it reaches its fulfilment in God's eternal purpose of Love. In the incarnation the order of redemption has been made to intersect with and overlap the order of creation in such a way that the whole history of mankind and the universe comes under the Kingdom of Christ as the First and the Last, the *Protos* and the *Eschatos*, the origin and the goal of creation – and so we have the Christological and soteriological interrelation between eschatology and cosmology that is apocalyptically indicated for us in The Revelation of St John the Divine.

Through his incarnation God the Son made himself one of his own creatures and one with them, penetrating through time to the very beginning of the creation and gathering it all up in himself as its Head. He made its alienation and lost condition his own and through his reconciling life and atoning passion he brought the love and power of God to bear upon its deep-seated disorder so as to make an end of it for ever. Through his cross and resurrection the incarnate Saviour penetrated into the ontological depths of creation where in death created being borders upon non-being, and set it upon an altogether new basis, that of Grace in the triumph of God's Holy Love in what the Bible speaks of as a new heaven and a new earth. It is, then, *in Jesus* in whom the Creator himself became a creature, God became man, that the mystery of his creative activity really becomes disclosed to us. It is the *new creation* effected in the midst of the old, inaugurated in Jesus' birth of the Virgin Mary and consummated in his resurrection from the dead, that opens our understanding to the unique nature of God's creation and the distinctive activity of his Holy Love within it. It is in Jesus the Saviour and Redeemer of the world that we learn how the Sovereign Creator operates, for in him the almighty power of God's Holy Love is revealed as *omnipotent Grace*.

It will be helpful to consider this omnipotent Grace more pointedly in respect of the incarnation, the death of Christ and the resurrection of Christ, and the renewal of Creation in him.

The incarnation. This is the new act of the eternal God whereby God himself becomes man without ceasing to be God, the Creator becomes creature without ceasing to be Creator, the transcendent becomes contingent without ceasing to be transcendent, the eternal becomes time without ceasing to be eternal. This is an even more astounding act than that of the creation of the universe out of nothing, for in the incarnation the almighty living God becomes little without ceasing to be the mighty omnipotent eternal God. The self-humiliation of God in Jesus Christ, his *kenosis* or *tapeinosis*, does not mean the self-limitation of God or the curtailment of his power, but the staggering exercise of his power within the limitations of our contingent existence in space and time. Thus in it the omnipotent sovereign Lord God is revealed to have the inconceivable power of becoming little and contingent, while remaining what he eternally and almightily is. The sovereignty of God is here revealed to be omnipotence clothed in littleness, and it is as such that God exerts and exhibits his indescribable, inconceivable power in his revealing and saving acts for us in space and time.

The death of Christ. This is the act in which God himself enters into our death and reduction to immobility and nothingness, in order to take it all upon himself, and redeem us from it, the expiatory act whereby he penetrates back through the guilt-laden irreversibility of time into the very beginning in such a way as to undo the past and undo our sin and guilt. This is the manifestation of divine sovereign power or omnipotence in which God crucified dies our death, descends into the chasm or abyss of our alienation from him in order to effect atonement and propitiation. This is the act whereby God gives *himself,* his all in the sacrifice of Christ on the Cross, for our redemption. This is an act of astonishing divine omnipotence in which God reveals that he loves us more than he loves himself – the transcendent sovereignty of the eternal love of God. What God's omnipotence really is we learn from the identity between the almightiness of God and the weakness of the Man on the Cross – that is a revelation of the distinctive kind of power that God is, which is the very opposite of what we would think or could ever imagine. As H. R. Mackintosh once wrote,

> the supreme example of divine almightiness at work is supplied by the New Testament picture of the world's salvation through the Cross. God will not prevent the crucifixion, but what he does is greater, namely, use the human crime as the unintended means whereby to accomplish his loving plan to reach and win the sinful.[21]

The resurrection of Christ. This is the act whereby God incarnate penetrates into death, annulling its power, manifesting his lordship over life and death, and thereby demonstrates his omnipotent power over all being and non-being. But at the same time God has demonstrated for us in the death and resurrection of Christ the altogether distinctive kind of power his omnipotence is, which is so unique that we cannot describe it by analogical reference to any other kind of power. The omnipotence of God is to be understood, as far as it may be by us, only out of its own uniqueness, and the incredible acts of God Almighty in incarnation, atonement and resurrection – the omnipotence of God in the highest acting from the lowest, becoming what we are in our lost and damned condition in order to save us and reconcile us to himself in the undoing of all disorder and in the triumph of divine Love and Light over all darkness and evil. In the resurrection of Jesus God has manifested the measureless extent of his power to share with us to the uttermost

---

[21] H. R. Mackintosh, *The Originality of the Christian Message* (London, 1920), p. 44f.

our perdition and condemnation in order to lift us up to share with him his divine Life and Light, delivering us from the power of darkness and translating us into his Kingdom. In other words, the sovereignty of God is the grace of the Lord Jesus Christ, who, though he was rich, for our sakes became poor that we through his poverty might become rich. If that is the way in which God's almighty sovereignty has operated in Jesus Christ from his birth to his resurrection, then that is the way in which it operates now and will always operate. God manifests his infinite power in his ability to condescend to the level of his creatures and to lower himself to be one of them in their littleness. God is not limited by the incapacity or limited ability of his creatures, and reveals his unlimited measureless power in meeting his creatures within the narrow limits and measures of their finite and spatio-temporal existence, without ceasing to be what he is in his own transcendent Being and Reality.

The incarnation was not just a transient episode in the interaction of God with the world, but has taken place once-and-for-all in a way that reaches backward through time and forward through time, from the end to the beginning and from the beginning to the end. Jesus Christ is not just an instrument in the hands of God arbitrarily to be taken up, used, and laid aside at will; he *is* God become man, and remains God even though he has come among us as man. It is in the indivisible oneness of God and man in the one Person of Jesus Christ that God Almighty has for ever chosen to work and exercise his almighty power and sovereignty for us and our salvation. If, then, Jesus Christ in his own incarnate Person is the Kingdom of God in action, if the way Jesus Christ acted in the Gospel is the way the Father Almighty acts, then that is how God will always act throughout all space and time into the consummation of his purpose of love.

3) The Activity of God the Holy Spirit

The Holy Spirit is also Creator in union with the Father and the Son, no less than they, and in perfect communion and conjunction with them, but Creator in his distinctive nature and activity as *Spirit*. In this respect the sovereign power of God is to be understood particularly as his transcendent and unlimited *freedom*. We have already had to touch upon this in regard to the fact that there was and is no necessary relation between God and the world he has created, for he had no need of the creation to be who he is, while the world he creatively brought into existence out of nothing contains no reason in itself why it should be what it is and should continue to exist as it does. It exists and continues to exist in complete dependence upon the free Grace of the Creator, and in unqualified differentiation from his transcendent Being and Reality. While in that differentiation the universe is given a reality of its own and a relative independence, that reality and independence are themselves dependent upon God and his unceasing continuous creative presence.[22]

---

[22] Cf. John Duns Scotus: 'The creation of things proceeds from God not out of any necessity whether of being or of knowledge or of will but out of pure freedom which is not moved, much less necessitated, by anything outside of itself so as to be brought into operation.' *Quaestiones disputatae de rerum principio*, q. 4, a. 1, n. 3.

This is what is meant by speaking of the created universe as *contingent* not only in its absolute origin through *creatio ex nihilo* but in its continuing spatio-temporal existence and its rational order. As I have written elsewhere,

> By contingence is meant that as created out of nothing the universe has no self-subsistence and no ultimate stability of its own, but that it is nevertheless endowed with an authentic reality and integrity of its own which must be respected. By contingent order is meant that the orderly universe is not self-sufficient or ultimately self-explaining but is given a rationality and reliability in its orderliness which depend on and reflect God's own eternal rationality and reliability.[23]

Regarded in itself this orderly universe is not a closed but an open system, not a complete but an incomplete system, whose physical and moral laws depend for their validity and ultimate explanation on a transcendent ground of rationality in God the Creator as their sufficient and ultimate reason. We have already considered the astonishing nature of the sovereign power of God in regard to the fact that both in his creation of the world and in his incarnation God has done what he had never done before, and thus acted in ways that were quite new even for himself. God is so free that he is able, without ceasing to be what he eternally is, to be other than himself, and to bring into being what is entirely different from what he has done before. In them the transcendent Power of God is revealed in terms of his *unlimited and unrestricted freedom*.

The fact that he who freely created the universe has once and for all become incarnate within it, means that as the Creator God wills freely to coexist with his creaturely children, and therefore that the continuing existence of the universe is ontologically bound to the crucified and risen Jesus and destined to partake in the consummation of God's eternal purpose in him. It also means that the whole universe is brought to share in the unlimited freedom of the Creator, although always in a differentiated way appropriate to its creaturely reality and contingent nature. It is given an authentic freedom of its own, one which is certainly limited, but limited only by the unlimited inexhaustible freedom of the Creator upon which it is contingent and with which it is indissolubly interlocked, for in his outgoing Love and ungrudging Grace God irreversibly binds the created universe to his own Existence and his own Existence to the universe. That is the aspect of God's triune Sovereign Power which has to do particularly with the liberating and quickening activity of the *Spiritus Creator* whereby the creature is creatively upheld and sustained in its existence beyond its own power in an *open-ended relation* toward God in whom its true end and purpose as creature are lodged.

In the Nicene Creed the Holy Spirit is spoken of as 'the Lord and Giver of Life' which is linked in triadic formulation of the Faith to statements about the creative work of the Father and of the Son. The Holy Spirit shares in the *Sovereign Power* (βασιλεία) of the Father and the Son, but his distinctive sovereign activity is that

---

[23] *Divine and Contingent Order* (Oxford, 1981), p. viif.

of quickening or giving life to the creature.[24] That is to say, while there is only one creative activity of God, from the Father, through the Son and in the Spirit, the special work of the Holy Spirit is to be discerned in that he brings the life-giving power of God to bear upon the creature in such a way that through his immediate presence to the creature and in spite of its creaturely difference from God he sustains it in its being and brings its relation to the Creator to its true end in him. This is what St Basil called 'the perfecting cause' of the Spirit, or the *sovereign freedom of the Spirit.*[25] We may recall here the way in which Karl Barth wrote of the distinctive activity of the Spirit. Coming from the inner Life and Communion of the Trinity, the Holy Spirit is the Creator God who in virtue of his presence to the creature, not just externally nor just from above, but from within and from below, effectuates the relation of the creature to himself by way of a relation of himself to himself.

> The Spirit of God is God in his freedom to be present to the creature, and therefore to be the life of the creature. And God's Spirit, the Holy Spirit, especially in revelation, is God himself in that he can not only come to man, but also to be in man, open up man and make him capable and ready for himself, and thus achieve his revelation in him.[26]

This means that God does not 'deistically abandon' (Barth's expression) what he has brought into existence but in his Love justifies and affirms its creaturely reality in its utter differentiation from his own Reality. He continuously holds it in being over the chasm of nothingness out of which it was created and through the freedom and presence of his Spirit embraces its frail contingent reality within the everlasting power of his divine presence, thereby affirming its 'goodness' as well as its reality. As 'the Lord the Giver of Life' the Holy Spirit is none other than the transcendent Lord of all being from whom we derive our own being, by whom we are upheld and undergirded in our creaturely existence day by day, and through whose presence to us and in us we are immediately in touch with the living dynamic Reality of God Almighty, Creator of heaven and earth, and of all things visible and invisible. It is through the presence of his Spirit that we live and move and have our being in God.

The supreme end for which God has designed his creation and which he activates and rules throughout all his relations with it is the purpose of his Holy Love not to live for himself alone but to bring into being a creaturely realm of heaven and earth which will reflect his glory and within which he may share with others the Communion of Love which constitutes his inner Life as Father, Son and Holy Spirit. It is in the incarnation of God's beloved Son in Jesus Christ, and in our sharing in that relation of the Son to the Father through the Holy Spirit, that the secret of the creation, hidden from the ages, has become disclosed to us. It was of this that St Paul wrote in the Epistle to the Ephesians:

---

[24] See John 5.21; 6.63; and 1 Tim. 6.13.
[25] Basil, especially *De Spiritu St.*, 16.38, and *Contra Macedonios*, Athens edn. vol. 68, pp. 194–199. See my account of this in *Theology in Reconstruction* (London, 1965), pp. 220f.
[26] Karl Barth, *Church Dogmatics* I.1, p. 450 – cf. also p. 472.

Blessed be the God and Father of our Lord Jesus Christ, who has blessed us in Christ with every spiritual blessing in heavenly places, even as he chose us in him before the foundation of the world, that we should be holy and blameless before him. He destined us in love to be his sons through Jesus Christ, according to the purpose of his will, to the praise of his glorious grace which he freely bestowed on us in the Beloved. In him we have redemption through his blood, the forgiveness of our trespasses, according to the riches of his grace which he has lavished upon us. For he has made known to us in all wisdom and insight the mystery of his will, according to his purpose which he set forth in Christ, as a plan for the fullness of time, to unite all things in him, things in heaven and things on earth.

In him, according to the purpose of him who accomplishes all things according to the counsel of his will, we who first hoped in Christ have been destined and appointed to live for the praise of his glory. In him you also, who have heard the word of truth, the Gospel of your salvation, and have believed in him, were sealed with the promised Holy Spirit, which is the guarantee of our inheritance until we acquire possession of it, to the praise of his glory.[27]

Our immediate concern in this passage is not with the redeemed life of the people of God in the history of salvation, but with the truth that in his eternal purpose God established between himself and the creation an *all-embracing framework of grace* within which and through which to share with us the fellowship of his Love. We have to fill out our understanding of this with what we learn elsewhere in the Holy Scriptures. Regarded in one way this framework has to do with the Father/Son, Son/Father relation which through the incarnate Son constitutes the central axis round which the whole universe is made to revolve. Regarded in another way the framework may be described as having to do with a relation between the faithfulness of God and the created order, or the relation between *covenant* and *creation*. As Karl Barth has expounded it, the covenant may be regarded as 'the internal basis of the creation' and the creation may be regarded as 'the external basis of the covenant'.[28] Since the creation is the unique work of the Father, the Son and the Holy Spirit it would not be surprising if, in view of that correlation between the covenant and the creation fulfilled in the incarnation of God's Love in Jesus Christ and the pouring out of the Holy Spirit upon humanity, the creation and its history should bear the imprint of the Trinity upon it. This is indeed what Barth affirmed when he spoke of the creation as a 'temporal analogue', taking place outside of God, of that event in himself by which God is Father of the Son.[29] This is not to be thought of in terms of an analogy of being (*analogia entis*), for the Creator and the creation are ontologically utterly disparate, but it does mean that in the wonder of his free out-going love and grace the universe took form as a created counterpart to the uncreated movement of Love within the Holy

[27] Eph. 1.3–14.
[28] Karl Barth, *Church Dogmatics* III.1, pp. 42ff, and 228ff.
[29] Karl Barth, *Dogmatics in Outline*, p. 52.

219

Trinity. What may be envisaged is an 'analogy of relation (*analogia relationis*)', that is a created correspondence in the relationship between the eternal generation of the Son within the life of the Holy Trinity (begotten, not made), on the one hand, and the relationship between the creation of the universe (made not begotten) outwith the life of the Holy Trinity, on the other hand. It is not to be understood, therefore, in terms of analogical relations on one and the same logical or ontological level, but rather in terms of meta-relations or cross-level relations. What is involved here, then, is an *ana*-logy with an utter difference between the creature and the Creator, but one freely posited by the Creator in the omnipotence of his Grace.[30]

Through the freedom of his Spirit the Triune Creator relates us to himself as the Father who is the one and only Father Almighty, who mysteriously exists and moves eternally in himself alone, but who also is the one Source of all other beings whom he does not beget out of himself but wonderfully brings into being out of nothing. Thus corresponding to the mystery of God's uncreated Being there is the wonder of our created being which while freely given a reality and a freedom of its own, is yet wholly contingent upon God's transcendent reality and Freedom to be what it is in its ontological difference and created likeness to him. It is an analogical correspondence of opposites into which we are brought by the power of the Creator Spirit, but it is one posited by his Grace that does not disintegrate into nothingness for in his outgoing Love God the Father wills us to coexist appropriately with him as his dear children, and through the presence of his Spirit to share in the Communion of his own eternal Life and Love. Moreover, through the Freedom of his Spirit the Triune Creator is present to us in such an immanent way as to realise in our human existence the creative, reconciling and personalising power of the Word and Son of God incarnate in Christ Jesus the Light of the world, so that in our creaturely rationality enlightened by him we may *reflect by grace*[31] but in an appropriately differentiated way, something of the uncreated Rationality of God. Far from suppressing, crushing or extinguishing the frail forms of contingent rationality with which we are endowed as human beings created after the image of God, the presence of the Holy Spirit empowers, integrates and establishes them while overcoming the alienating deficiencies and contradictions which we have introduced into them, so that they may be made to realise their true end in the Love and Wisdom of God the Father, the Maker of heaven and earth and of all things invisible and visible.

A differentiated analogical correspondence between the Creator and the creation may be traced between the heavenly Life of God and the earthly life of creaturely beings, between the uncreated Time of God and the created time of our world, between uncreated Light and created light, and not least between the transcendent Communion of the three divine Persons in God and the communion of persons in the Church. Various aspects of this correspondence come before us when we spell out the interrelations involved within the all-embracing framework of Grace as it

---

[30] Cf. Karl Barth, *Church Dogmatics* III.1, pp. 11ff & 49; and H. Hartwell, *The Theology of Karl Barth: An Introduction* (London, 1964), p. 114.

[31] This is the Athanasian concept of 'the grace of the image', ἡ κατ' εἰκόνα χάρις, e.g. *De Incarnatione*, 11.

has been consummated in the Lord Jesus Christ, the one Mediator between God and man. But at this juncture it may be helpful to think specifically of the bearing of the Trinitarian Order immanent in God upon the contingent order immanent in our world, and take our cue from the way in which divine and human natures have been united in the one incarnate Person of Jesus Christ, 'without confusion, without change, without division, without separation', as the Council of Chalcedon formulated it. It is, I believe, in the overlapping of the Trinitarian Order and the contingent order in and through the incarnation of God the Son in space and time, that we may gain a deeper understanding of the Sovereign Power of the Triune God in the fulfilment of his redemptive and providential purpose for his creation. At the same time this will help us to grasp something of the truth of what is traditionally called the 'immutability' and the 'impassibility' of God.

DIVINE PROVIDENCE

In turning to the doctrine of divine providence we must bear particularly in mind two truths that have come before us in our account of the Sovereign Power of the Creator. First, the Triune Being of God is a Communion of Love, whose activity revealed to us through Christ and in his Spirit is perfectly and completely personal. This is activity that always affirms the integrity and sustains the freedom of the creature with the power of the Love that God is. Like his creative activity God's providential activity has positive Trinitarian content, for through their perichoretic interrelations the Father, the Son and the Holy Spirit are creatively and redemptively at work in fulfilling God's eternal purpose of love for his creation and for men, women and children within it. Second, in his overflowing love God freely created the universe of space and time, doing something utterly new which he had never done before and bringing into existence what did not exist before. Moreover, in the incarnation of his beloved Son in Jesus Christ, and in delivering him up on the Cross in atoning sacrifice for the sin and guilt of his human creatures, and then in pouring out his Spirit upon all flesh, God has again done quite new things that he had never done before. God is so wonderfully and omnipotently free that he is able do things and bring about events that are new even for himself, all in fulfilment of the purpose of his measureless Love not to exist for himself alone but to bring other beings into coexistence with himself that he may share with them his triune fellowship of Love.

Quite clearly the doctrine of divine providence must be one that is governed by the incarnation of the eternal Son of God as the new act of Almighty God whereby he became man without ceasing to be God, became creature without ceasing to be Creator, allied himself with us in space and time, without ceasing to be transcendent over all space and time. This is an event more astounding than that of the creation of the universe out of nothing. In Jesus the Lord God Almighty has come among us to exercise his sovereign power within the frail conditions of our mortal life. This is for us an altogether incomprehensible, inexpressible act of God's power within the parameters of our little and contingent existence in space and time.

Here there is revealed the nature of the sovereignty of God incarnate in Jesus Christ – unbounded omnipotence clothed in creaturely littleness and human weakness. Hence if we want to know *how* God exercises his sovereignty we must turn to the evangelical presentation of it in the conception, birth, life, death and resurrection of Jesus. In him we find that God does not exercise his sovereign Power upon us from above and beyond us like some impersonal *force majeure*, but in an intensely personal patient way from below, by penetrating into the dark disordered depths of our alienated creaturely existence in order to work savingly, healingly and preservingly within it.

It is supremely in the sacrificial death of Christ on the Cross that the power of God is manifest, for there God crucified enters our death, unites himself to us in the abysmal chasm of our alienation from him in order to effect atonement, propitiation and reconciliation. It is a kind of power entirely different from any power which we human beings can ever conceive. It is the aweful and awesome act of the total self-giving of God the Father in the sacrifice of his Beloved Son in which God revealed that he loves us unreservedly and unstintingly. It is power which is absolutely supreme over all being and non-being, over all life and death, over anything in heaven and earth or under the earth, over all that can separate us from God – the transcendent almightiness of God's redeeming Love. As H. R. Mackintosh has finely written

> Its [Christianity's] faith in divine providence is simply the converse of faith in redemption; the two are so indissolubly and organically one, that if either be amputated the other slowly bleeds to death. The same Father who saves the world at the cost of Jesus is he who omnipotently guides the world, and the single lives within the world, to a blessed end. Providence is correlative to the Cross.[32]

The birth, life, death and resurrection of God incarnate, together with the fact that God is able to do things and bring about events that are new even for himself, and even to lay hold of all that is contrary to his will and make it serve the purpose of his love, tell us that we must think of him as completely free to relate himself to the world in innumerable multivariable ways while being consistently true to his own nature as Holy Love and consistently true to his creation of the world with a contingent rational order of its own. In his relations with the world the unlimited freedom of God in his transcendent rationality and the limited freedom of the world in its contingent rationality overlap and intersect in such a way as to give rise to refined and subtle patterns of order in the on-going spatio-temporal universe which we cannot anticipate but which constantly take us by surprise. That is why nature is so elusive and unpredictable at its deepest levels – it is marvellously coordinated with the transcendent rationality and infinite freedom of its Triune Creator.

Divine providence is to be understood not as continuing or perpetuating the original act of creation as if the act of creation were still incomplete, but as the continuation of God's creation through his disposing and ordering presence within

---

[32] H. R. Mackintosh, *The Originality of the Christian Message* (London, 1920), p. 70.

it through the incarnate Word. We must think of this, however, as conditioned by his redemptive activity. There is, and cannot but be, an inseparable relation between divine creation and divine providence, for God does not withdraw his activity from the world which he has once for all brought into being, but correlates the creation with himself in a new way by embodying his creative Word and redemptive activity within the created order. He thereby continues to conserve the creation in a covenanted coexistence with himself. He interacts positively and constructively toward it and within it, in a life-giving and preserving activity in which he cares for it and supplies all its needs out of his limitless grace, constantly upholding all things by the Word of his power and through the presence of his Spirit. Thus it may be said that providence has to do with God's creative and redemptive relation with the creation in which all that happens within it comes under the Fatherly rule and provision of God the Creator and Redeemer, whose covenant purpose for the whole history of the creation is disclosed in the birth, life, death and resurrection of Jesus Christ. Providence has to do with the execution and fulfilment of God's eternal purpose of love and grace which is revealed and incarnated in Jesus Christ. It is thus by reference to the Father's Will embodied in Jesus Christ that we are to understand the purpose, nature and scope of divine providence in its inseparable relation with the creation while nevertheless distinct from it.

If the covenant of grace is held to be the internal basis of the creation, and the creation to be the external basis of the covenant, then providence may be regarded as having to do with the history of the creation as the external basis of the covenant of grace, and therefore with the redemptive overruling of history in the service of God's purpose of love not through absolute fiat but through incarnate grace. Providence is concerned, then, with the continuation and preservation of the creation grounded in the covenant of God's grace and directed by the fulfilment of that covenant in the order of redemption. In creation God brought into existence a world other than himself but with which he has entered into a covenanted relation such that he will not hold himself apart from it or be known except in relation to the world he has made. This relationship implies a purposed coexistence between God and the world, a totally unequal coexistence of God with the world and an utterly contingent coexistence of the world with God. The doctrine of providence is the doctrine of the interaction between God's transcendent coexistence with the creation and the contingent coexistence of the creation with God, in which he exercises not just oversight and disposal over all created existence, but is personally and actively present to it all, redemptively effecting its preservation under his unceasing cooperation and under his immediate direction. God does not exercise his providence over the creation, therefore, from afar, deistically detached from it as a sort of absentee God, but is personally near to it as one who has graciously bound himself to the creation even in its fallen condition, and has assumed the fearful cost of its redemption, reparation and preservation upon himself. From beginning to end God is directly and immanently present to it in the midst of all its vicissitudes, without of course cancelling his complete difference from the creation or surrendering his transcendence over it.

It is in accordance with God's mighty acts of creation, incarnation and redemption, and in the light of what God has revealed of his unlimited freedom and infinite flexibility in those acts, that we may understand something of the wonderful operation of his gracious providence within the history, structures and laws and the on-going processes of our space-time existence in the created universe. As God created all things through his Word and Wisdom, and impressed upon them their rational form and order, so he maintains and rules over all things by the ordering activity of his Word and Wisdom. He does not abandon the world to blind chance or impersonal necessity, or determinist law, far less to irrational and malign forces. On the contrary, as we have seen, God endows it with a creaturely rationality and a contingent freedom of its own which he undergirds and affirms through the freedom of his Spirit to be present within it and realise its relation to himself. Thereby he correlates its creaturely rationality with his own transcendent Rationality, and its limited creaturely freedom with his own unlimited freedom. This is why God's providential sovereignty over all things is to be understood in terms of the utterly free personal operations of the Creator and Redeemer, and thus correspondingly only through our personal relations with the Creator and Redeemer, and his mighty personal deeds in space and time.

It is only through God's personal self-revelation of himself as the eternally self-living God, the Creator and Redeemer, that we may know something of the origin of all things and the purpose of their creation. Thus in Jesus Christ we learn that all things are in the hands of the merciful and loving Father, who having given his only Son for our salvation will with him also freely give us all things. He can no more abandon his creation that he can abandon his beloved Son. As the Creator and Redeemer, God personally and wisely upholds the world in coexistence, an asymmetrical coexistence to be sure, but in genuine coexistence with himself in such a way that while he is supremely transcendent over it, he is also immanently present within it, affirming its relative independence and freedom and its distinctive contingent nature and order. As both transcendent and immanent he rules over the universe and all that goes on within it, and does not abandon it to the rule of chance or fate or any necessitarian system at variance with his creative purpose of love. He rules over all things in the world without detracting from their reality or impairing their contingent nature, freedom or order, yet in such a way that in his absolute freedom he makes everything to serve his ultimate purpose of love and of fellowship with himself. In his transcendent freedom God exercises his providence over all that inexplicably defies his ways or seeks to make itself independent of him – that is, he exercises his lordship over all evil and death, but it is a lordship not of naked power but of his love and grace and in patient and wise fulfilment of his purpose of redemption and renewal.

Before we go further we must consider the baffling problem of evil or 'the mystery of iniquity', as the New Testament calls it, for with the emergence of evil, a malign power has lodged itself in the midst of God's good creation, which is not just privative but directly negative in its character. It involves what the New Testament calls a bottomless chasm in the relation between man and God which cannot be bridged from the side of creation. The fearful depth of evil has been exposed by the fact that in the incarnate life and death of his beloved Son *God himself* had to descend into the very heart of the world's evil and into its terrible darkness and enmity, even into the depths of its ultimate domain in death itself and its fearful finality. Thereby he brought the power of his divine love to bear upon it, and penetrated it, at the point of its supreme thrust against him in the crucifixion of Christ in order to judge and reject it, and at the same time to save the world from its doom and reconcile all things visible and invisible to himself. That astonishing paradoxical activity of God sharply exhibited in the *Eli, Eli, Lama sabachthani* of Jesus on the Cross,[33] is the very same activity in which the Triune God ceaselessly engages in the Persons of his incarnate Son and of the Holy Spirit throughout his providential overruling and ordering of all things in the spatio-temporal existence and continuity of the universe. This is not to be understood in any way as an extending of the incarnation or a prolonging of the atonement into history for they have taken place once for all and cannot be repeated. On the contrary, it is the triumphant extending of the effect of that finished work into the history of the world through the reconciling and renewing power of the crucified and risen Christ as the Lamb of God enthroned at the right hand of God the Father Almighty, Creator of heaven and earth, and of all things invisible and visible. The crucified and risen Jesus is now exalted to be the organic centre of all things in heaven and earth from where he extends his sovereign rule over the whole history of material and spiritual reality. He reigns from there, however, as one in whom God has aligned himself with his creatures and is unceasingly present with them in all their distress and desperate need under the menace of the powers of evil. He remains the Lord who will not allow them to be overwhelmed by the powers of darkness, but is working out the perfect fulfilment of his will for the whole of his creation.

We have to think of this triumph of the Kingdom of God merged with the Person of the crucified and risen Lord Jesus as a triumph not just over a difference, vast as it is, between the created realm, to which we belong, and God, but a triumph over a fallen, twisted and alienated world which exists in direct *opposition* to God, while nevertheless being continuously sustained by his omnipotent grace. At the same time God does not condone evil in any way or permit evil in any form finally to triumph, but judges, contains and circumscribes it, and makes it through the atoning death and resurrection of Christ to serve his eternal purpose of love and redemption.[34] It is important to note that God does not deal with evil impersonally by bringing the almighty force of his divine Majesty to bear directly and coercively upon it in order to reduce it to nothing. Rather does he penetrate with his holy will and living power personally into its ultimate stronghold in evil, sin and death, and absorbs its attack upon himself in order to vanquish it from within through his own holy love. That is what he does in Jesus Christ in identifying himself with his human creatures, without ceasing to be who he eternally is in his holiness and love, making himself one with them in their desperate godlessness and inextricable misery, even in their lostness and damnation, and takes it all upon himself in order to overcome evil and destroy it from within its own malign force and twisted movement. The astonishing nature and extent of that self-identifying of God with

---

[33] Cf. my account of the *Eli, Eli, lama sabachthani* in ch. 7, 'Questioning in Christ', in *Theology in Reconstruction*, pp. 117–127.

[34] See here especially F. W. Camfield, *The Collapse of Doubt* (London, 1945), ch. 5, on 'The Mystery of Evil', pp. 61ff.

us in Christ is such that St Paul could even say of Christ, that God made him who knew no sin to be sin for us, that we might be made the righteousness of God in him.[35] We cannot grasp what this really involves, but whatever else it means it does mean that God in Christ does not just obliterate our sin by absolute fiat or naked divine power, but actually substitutes himself the Holy One in our place and takes our sin and judgment upon his own heart, and our death into his own divine life, exchanging the poverty of our existence for the riches of his grace, in order to undo evil completely through his atoning love and grace, and replace our life with another upon an altogether different basis of unbroken communion with himself.

Several significant points must be borne in mind here which in their interconnection have a bearing upon how we are to think of the ongoing activity of divine providence.

First, human existence and history are not separable from the material universe, for man precisely as man is body of his soul as well as soul of his body and it is in the wholeness of that soul-body, body-soul relation that he has been created for fellowship with God. This means that the human being is not exempt from the material forces immanent in the spatio-temporal universe, or therefore exempt from the control of its physical laws impressed upon it by the Creator. Somehow it is not just man who has fallen but the whole created order along with him, so that we may not isolate our understanding of human evil from natural evil, or moral evil from material evil, the pain and suffering of human being from the suffering and misery, the pain and travail of the whole creation. There is what may be called a principle of evil in nature, but of course a perverted principle.[36] It is not surprising, therefore, as the Holy Scriptures tell us, that real redemption from the power of human sin and guilt involves a radical change in the material world and calls for the complete redemption of the created order. That is why both the Old and the New Testaments speak prophetically of a new heaven and a new earth. Our understanding of what this means is governed by the physical or bodily nature of the death and resurrection of Christ, an event with space-time coordinates. Redemption is somatic as well as spiritual, for moral and physical evil infecting the creation may not finally be separated from one another. This cannot but apply to the providential activity of God which involves material as well as spiritual power, and therefore an on-going interaction of God as Creator and Redeemer with the physical universe. The power by which he redeems the world and exercises his providential care over its history is the very same power as that by which he created the world in matter and form out of nothing. Just as his creative power brought the world into physical existence and endowed it with a rational order, so it is in virtue of the same creative power that his redemptive and providential activity operate within the space-time structures of the ongoing world. But just as we cannot comprehend *how* God created the world out of nothing, or *how* he brought Jesus Christ forth from the grave, so we are unable to grasp *how* his redemptive and providential activity makes all things, material as well as spiritual, to serve his eternal purpose of love.

---

[35] 2 Cor. 5.6; cf. Rom. 8.3.
[36] Cf. F. W. Camfield, op. cit., p. 68.

Second, by its very nature, moral or natural evil is essentially anarchic. It is an utterly irrational factor that has inexplicably entered into the created order. Whatever else evil is it involves the introduction of a radical discontinuity into the world that affects the relation of mankind to God, of man to himself, and of man to woman and woman to man, and of course of men and women to nature. It affects the entire relation of the universe to God, infecting its contingent nature or the relative independence given by God to the created order. As such evil defies human comprehension and any rational explanation. It is a virulent, demonic force radically antagonistic to all that is holy and orderly, right and good. St Paul spoke of it as the mystery of lawlessness (ἀνομία)[37] of a strangely personal kind, in fact a malevolent will. It was in similar terms that Jesus referred to the Devil as the father of lies, the Satan with whom Jesus himself struggled in his temptation. And it is in similar terms that the Gospels tell us of the conflict of Jesus with the demonic powers of darkness that infested people's lives in mind and body, but which he denounced as the enemy, rebuked and cast out of people's lives, thereby showing that with his presence the Kingdom of God had been ushered in and deliverance from the power of darkness had been brought about. The sharp personal conflict of Jesus with evil reveals it to be more than the hypostatisation of a principle of contradiction between God and the world, and to be in fact an organised kingdom of evil and darkness with a kind of headquarters of its own, the power house of an utterly rebellious evil will or spirit which the Holy Scriptures call Satan.[38] We are unable to understand how God continues to deal with the forces of darkness, but we believe that as he dealt miraculously with sickness and death, miraculously fed the hungry thousands on the hills of Galilee with food, and miraculously brought the turbulent winds and waves under his command, 'Peace, be still;'[39] so we believe that he will bring his divine peace and power to bear marvellously and triumphantly upon the physical conditions of human existence in history, not to be sure in accordance with our conceptions, but in accordance with his transcendent wisdom.

Third, by its very nature evil has a kind of impossible, although a deadly real, existence. It is impossible because it is utterly alien to the will of God, and yet has a strange contradictory form of existence under the divine rejection of it. This is 'the impossible possibility' of evil with which Karl Barth valiantly grappled in his difficult concept of 'nothingness' (*Das Nichtige*), and in connection with which he raises some intriguing questions to which there are no answers.[40] In no sense does God will evil or even permit it, but somehow in ways that we cannot understand, the very *No* of God to evil in which he delimits and marks it off from what is good and right thereby 'hardens' it as the evil that it is in the very act of forbidding it. This has the effect of lending evil a mode of reality which it does not have and cannot have of itself. It is a similar point that St Paul made when he spoke of 'the

---

[37] Thus St Paul, 2 Thess. 2.3, 7.
[38] Refer to William Manson, *Jesus and the Christian* (London, 1967), 'Principalities and Powers: The Spiritual Background of the Work of Jesus in the Synoptic Gospels', pp. 77ff; and 'Early Christian Eschatology,' pp. 163ff.
[39] Mark 4.34, where the Greek Σιώπα, πεφίμωσο literally means 'Be quiet, be muzzled'.
[40] Karl Barth, *Church Dogmatics* III.2, pp. 289–378.

law as the strength of sin'.[41] In some sense, then, the very possibility of evil and its power are, so to speak, indirectly and strangely related to the will of God who nevertheless remains Lord over it and wholly rejects its usurpation of his will. Expressed the other way round, in its cunning duplicity evil takes cover under the good and the right and uses them to exert its malevolent force against God and his good creation. As such evil has infected and is somehow present throughout the whole realm of material and spiritual reality. We who are evil and partake of its deception and duplicity cannot know this of ourselves, but evil and its deceptive ways are exposed precisely through God's total rejection of it and triumph over it in the Cross, for it is there that the appalling abysmal depth of evil is exposed. It is only as we cross over that abyss through the atoning sacrifice of Christ that we are able to look down into its terrifying abysmal depth and discern evil for what it actually is, as attack upon God. But it is through the power of the Cross, the power of salvation, that God the Creator and Redeemer exercises his overruling sovereignty and providential care for the creation in such a way as to make all things work together for good. How God does this is again something that we are unable to grasp, but we believe that just as he made the crucifixion of Jesus, the wickedest act of evil ever perpetrated, to serve his supreme purpose of love and redemption, so by the same Cross he will make the very worst things that can happen to us in the history of the world actually serve the design of his wisdom and the purpose of his grace. Divine providence is correlative to the Cross, and the obverse of divine redemption.

If the providential activity of God is as sovereign as his creation, and as sovereign as the incarnation of the Son of God within the frail contingent structures of creaturely existence, then it involves a quite unique kind of power which by its very nature cannot be demonstrated. As the Lord Jesus told his disciples when there arose demands for visible and tangible signs of the Kingdom, 'the Kingdom of God does not come with observation'. Let it be repeated that the unique kind of power of God which broke into the world of space and time in Jesus is *grace*, which is material as well as spiritual power, but it is not to be observed or demonstrated in the way that we observe or demonstrate matters in our sciences. God's ways are unsearchable and past finding out. Objectively, and supremely real though God's activity is, it may only be acknowledged by faith, be believed and trusted, in precisely the same way in which we believe in and rely on Jesus Christ as our Lord and Saviour. The kind of demonstration that is appropriate here is what St Paul called 'demonstration of the Spirit and of power' (ἀπόδειξις τοῦ πνεύματος καὶ δυνάμεως).[42] This reminds us of the words of Jesus, 'If I by the *finger* of God cast out devils, then the kingdom of God has come upon you',[43] which in the Synoptic parallel reads 'If I cast out devils by the *Spirit* of God, then the kingdom of God is come upon you.'[44] That is to say, Jesus identifies the mighty power of God over evil with the power of the Holy Spirit, which may not be coordinated on the same level

[41] 1 Cor. 15.56.
[42] 1 Cor. 2.4.
[43] Luke 11.20.
[44] Matt. 12.28.

with the kind of power with which we have to do in physico-causal relations. But this is not to say that the spiritual power operating in miraculous events may not have space-time coordinates on a different level of reality. Our best cue for understanding the power of the Spirit must surely be taken from the bodily resurrection of Jesus Christ from the grave, which was at once a pure act of the Spirit and an event that took place in space and time. How those two levels are coordinated we are unable to understand, any more than we can understand, for example, the Virgin Birth of Jesus which altogether transcends our grasp and cannot be explained in biological terms.

We must also take into account the fact of the Church of Christ which he has united to himself through the Holy Spirit as his Body and sent out into history as 'the earthly-historical form of his own existence' in the world.[45] The Church stands for the establishing of the mighty acts of redeeming grace in the midst of our human life and history, and thus for the earthly correlate of the Kingdom of God which in Christ had broken redemptively and creatively into the midst of our alienated and violent existence in order to deliver it from the forces of darkness and evil, to reclaim it for the heavenly Father and to restore it to its true end in the creative love of the Holy Trinity. Hence to the eye of faith the life and mission of the Church as the Body of Christ – the Christ who died and rose again and constitutes the organic centre of all things in heaven and earth – carry into the ongoing history of the world the sovereign Word of God's saving grace. Through the proclamation of the Gospel this saving grace is critically and creatively at work in the midst of all the recalcitrant forces of evil, spiritual and material, which threaten the fulfilment of God's will to reconcile all things in heaven and earth and create fellowship with himself throughout the whole of his creation. As St Paul tells us, the whole creation groans and is in travail waiting for the triumph of that divine purpose over all the forces of the cosmos – that is the way in which faith discerns the triumph of God's redemptive overruling not just over tribulation, distress, persecution or famine or nakedness or peril or sword, but over the whole realm of 'angels, principalities and powers', as St Paul calls them, or spirits and superhuman powers.[46] There is a much deeper dimension to God's sovereign activity in redemption and providence than is often realised.

It may help us at this point to pause and reflect on the distinctive role of *angels* in biblical accounts of God's redemptive and providential activity.[47]

In the Holy Scriptures angels are uniquely related to the direct action of God, not as personified concepts, symbolical agencies or etherial figures that merely appear in dreams and visions, but as real beings of an incomprehensible nature which eludes us. They appear from time to time fleetingly on the edge of our earthly existence, and are, as it were, both tangential to the Being of God and tangential to human being. They have their existence in standing before the throne

[45] See Karl Barth, *Church Dogmatics* IV.2, pp. 614ff.
[46] Rom. 8.19–39.
[47] For the following see my essay 'The Spiritual Relevance of Angels', in *Alive to God. Studies in Spirituality, presented to James Houston*, ed. J. I. Packer & L. Wilkinson (Downers Grove, 1993), pp. 122–139.

of God and functioning in the relation between God and humanity as God's commissioned witnesses and representatives in the history of salvation. They tell us that something being done on earth is the counterpart of what is being done in heaven, but are not themselves the operative nexus between the two things. They are a sort of window opening into the invisible heavenly establishment of God's covenant of grace with the people of Israel, to its messianic fulfilment in the incarnation of his beloved Son in Jesus Christ, but also in the fulfilment of the Kingdom of God inaugurated in history with the birth, death, and resurrection of Christ. Angels are not sent to indwell us, like the Holy Spirit, and we are not united to them as we are united to Christ through his Spirit, but they are present and active in our midst as God's agents fulfilling his behests. That is surely how we are to assess the marginal presence of angels at decisive points in the Gospel story, but also at crucial points in the history of the Church through which the message of redemption is carried into all the world. Throughout the whole history of salvation they serve the covenant community at the boundaries, so to speak, of its pilgrim existence, witnessing to the mystery of divine revelation and signalling the advent of salvation promised by God, when he would deliver his people from the harsh restriction of oppression and captivity and bring them into a 'large place', thereby making space in their life for communion with himself. Angels themselves are not restricted or hemmed in by space and time as we are,[48] but they direct us at the boundary of our earthly existence within space and time and at the frontiers of human knowledge to listen to the voice of God from beyond and to distinguish it from all earthly voices.

It is within this perspective that we may think of the role of angels in the providential and eschatological activity of God in the history of his human children, and indeed of the creation as a whole. As the Apocalypse tells us, the Lamb of God is in the midst of the throne, from first to last triumphant over the forces of darkness.[49] It is the ascended Lord Jesus Christ himself who rules over all things through the power of his Cross and resurrection, but angels are given a subordinate function to fulfil in the great apocalyptic strife between the Lamb of God and Satan, between the Kingdom of God and the bestial powers of darkness. Angels are found at the very heart of redemptive history as it presses victoriously forward to its final consummation when the Saviour will come again in radiant glory to judge both the quick and the dead and to make all things new.

Angels have to do only with a subsidiary service which they are sent to exercise where heaven touches earth and earth is open to the touch of heaven, in the saving economy of God's creative and critical interrelations with mankind. As heavenly messengers they cannot be conceived in terms of human or earthly corporeality, or as subject to the limits and laws of space and time in our world. Unlike God they have no creative or redemptive power, but by their concomitant presence and operation they are meant to indicate to us that salvation events are due entirely to God's gracious intervention on our behalf, and are not to be put down to chance or

---

[48] This is the significance of the medieval discussion about how many angels can dance on the point of a pin! In their tangential relation to our world they are like spaceless mathematical points.
[49] Rev. 5–6.

necessity, nor to be explained in terms of physical laws, even if those laws are open-structured as indeed relativity and quantum theory now regard them. Thus, for example, the all-important relation between the forgiveness of our sins and the atoning death of Christ on the Cross, or between our new birth and the resurrection of Jesus from the dead, may not be accounted for by the kind of logico-causal nexus that obtains between intra-mundane events in our finite and fallen world, but only by the inexplicable power of the immediate presence and operation of God himself.

It was by the Holy Spirit that Jesus was conceived by the Virgin Mary;[50] by the Spirit or Finger of God that he cast out demons, thereby showing that the kingdom of God had come;[51] through the eternal Spirit that he offered himself up in atoning sacrifice for our sins;[52] and through the Holy Spirit that he was raised from the dead.[53] It is precisely in virtue of this same power of the Spirit that we are purged from our sins by the blood of Christ: Calvary and Pentecost belong inseparably together. It is an essentially divine and spiritual nexus that operates in all God's mighty acts of creation and redemption, and in judgment too. All the works of God are characterised by an infinite flexibility and differentiality which cannot be caught in the mesh of our conceptual connections and constructs, for, as we have already noted, they manifest an entirely different kind of force from anything we know or can imagine in this world: it is none other than the inherent transcendent power of God's own eternal being, the power of the Spirit.

It is the part of angels, in their divine mission, to bear witness to the distinctive nature of God's power and to the unfettered freedom of God in all his interactions with us in space and time. This is the same freedom with which he brought the vast universe into being out of nothing, and with which he became man in Jesus Christ in space and time without ceasing to be the God he eternally is. It is in fact the unlimited freedom of the love of God which God himself is; it is the ultimate power of all order, and the final judgment of all disorder. The baffling and incomprehensible nexus of divine events is so utterly inexpressible in the mundane grammar of our human thought and speech that the Holy Scriptures in the Old and New Testaments alike resort to the strange broken forms of what is called *apocalyptic* to indicate it. The visionary sections of Daniel and Revelation are the classic examples. The mode of divine disclosure does not take place, however, without the witness of angels which forbids us to interpret those apocalyptic visions in any literal or linear way, while nevertheless bidding us to take them seriously as pointing to what really happens when God himself penetrates into the chaotic violence of our alienated and guilt-laden existence in order to judge and redeem humankind by the power of the Lamb and his atoning sacrifice on the Cross.

The witness of angels to this humanly unaccountable character of divine activity is relevant to our understanding of both salvation and judgment, and of the

---

[50] Matt. 1.20; Luke 1.35.
[51] Matt. 12.28; Luke 11.20.
[52] Heb. 9.34.
[53] Rom. 1.4.

interaction of God with the world not only in the past or present but also in the future. Our clues to the unfolding pattern of God's providential activity must certainly be taken from the whole history of salvation, but above all from the incarnate form which that activity has taken once for all in the birth, life, death and resurrection of Jesus Christ, whereby in our stead and for our sake, God has penetrated the strongholds of guilt and death and hell, and vanquished the power of the devil and all his demonic minions. This is just what we find in the book of Revelation, in the eschatological account it presents of what takes place behind the scenes in the interaction of the Kingdom of God with the cosmic powers and forces that seek to dominate the history of humanity and the course of the created order. At its heart the spotlight of revelation is focused on the life and mission of the Church in history, interpreted after the pattern of the incarnate life and ministry of Jesus, and the proleptic unfolding of its cosmic impact in the final events of judgment, resurrection and renewing of heaven and earth. Here the eschatological thrust of the Gospel of the incarnation, as it penetrates into the very centre of world history and presses toward the final day of reckoning, is presented in terms of the evangelical humiliation and exaltation, the veiling and unveiling, of the Lamb of God in the heart of human affairs, as a sort of extended Christology or soteriology projected into the historical process. But all through that account the witness of angels enables us to discern the redemptive purpose and pattern of the mystery of God.

By virtue of the angels' presence the eyes and ears of faith penetrate the apocalyptic imagery to discern something of the invisible and inaudible heavenly background to all that happens on earth. As angelic heralds they testify to the triumph of the Kingdom of Christ over all forces of evil and darkness and enable us here and now to glimpse the silver lining behind the fearful wrath of history. Angels in different forms participate at every stage in the unfolding of the apocalyptic drama, bearing witness to the fact that God himself is at work judging evil and making all things to serve his creative and redemptive purpose. At the same time they link earth to heaven in such a way that they both present the prayers of the martyrs and saints like incense before the throne of God and make the triumphant songs of the heavenly host of the redeemed to resonate in the worship of the Church on earth.

The intermingling of divine Providence and mission in which the angels are charged with their spiritual ministry operates not only on the vast scale of the cosmic panorama, but in relation to the lives of individuals as well. Their providential service was clearly indicated in the Old Testament account of the angel of the Lord who was sent on special errands to particular people like Gideon or Manoah or Daniel. This was usually in connection with the deliverance of the people of God from alien oppression, for as the Psalmist expressed it 'the angel of the Lord encamps round those who fear him, and delivers them.'[54] The bearing of that service on mission was strikingly indicated by the call of Isaiah of Jerusalem as one of the seraphim touched his lips with a burning coal taken from the altar: 'Then I heard the voice of the Lord saying, "whom shall I send? And Who will go for us?" And I said, "Here am I. Send me.'"[55] In the New Testament the presence of angels is recorded at crucial points in the Gospel story and in the Acts of the Apostles where it is made clear that God's providential overruling of the course of events serves the supreme purpose of the salvation of mankind entrusted to the mission of the Church sent out into the world as the Body of Christ himself, or as Karl Barth has spoken of it, as 'the earthly-historical form of Christ's existence'.[56]

While creation, redemption and providence are inseparable, the operation of divine providence within the ongoing space and time of the created cosmos does not happen simply through divine fiat, but through the self-abnegating movement of God who in the incarnation has entered into our creaturely existence and in the sacrificial death of his dear Son has taken the enmity and antagonism of our sinful world upon himself and subdued it in such a way as to let the power and grace of his divine Life flow into in the life of his creatures and thereby to open to them the healing power of his eternal Being and Love. Here there can be no deterministic notion of providence whereby all things are ruled in accordance with rigidly imposed laws, but one through which God reaffirms the contingent nature of his creation with a relative independence and freedom and order of its own, while re-establishing its coexistence with himself. This means also that we may not think of the ongoing universe as somehow at the mercy of blind chance and irrational process, which would be merely the obverse of a thoroughly fatalistic and determinist conception of the world. Nor may we think of it as furnished by God with such an independent order and self-consistent set of rational laws that it is entirely self-governing in all its immanent processes and changes. Rather must we think of the created universe in its covenanted relation to God as in itself incomplete and open-structured, with built-in freedom and unpredictability characterising its essentially contingent nature which cannot be understood consistently through necessary modes of reasoning. As Creator and Redeemer, God alone holds the key to the mystery of the ongoing created order. We must think of its history as one in which God's unlimited freedom intersects with and overlaps with the relative independent reality and contingent and limited freedom of the world, in such a way as to make all that happens serve the purpose of his love and reflect his divine glory.

Let it be repeated, however, that just as we cannot understand the 'how' or nature of God's original creative act in bringing the universe into existence out of nothing, so we cannot understand the 'how' or nature of his transcendent operation and of his unlimited freedom in interacting with the contingent order and disorder of our world and its history. This takes place in such a way as to give it meaning through completion beyond itself, and in such way as to make all that is random and chaotic or disorderly in it to cooperate and converge in serving and fulfilling the supreme end of God's wisdom and love. The 'how' of providence like the 'how' of creation remains ultimately an incomprehensible mystery – we may understand it only in so far as it is revealed as the activity of the Father through the Son and in

[55] Isa. 6.8.
[56] Karl Barth, *Church Dogmatics* IV.2 (Edinburgh, 1958), pp. 614 ff.

the Holy Spirit. It is the unique kind of activity by the Word and Spirit of God, of which the paradigm acts of God are provided in the virgin birth and in the resurrection of Jesus. It is in the same way that we must think of the renewal of the creation when Christ comes again.

9

The Unchangeableness of God

THE unchangeableness of God is one of the major themes of the Old Testament
Scriptures. In them we hear from God that he has revealed himself to mankind
as *Yahweh*: 'I am who I am – I shall be who I shall be,'[1] the self-existing, self-living,
self-affirming God whose being is his ever-continuing life and whose life is his
ever-continuing being. God does not speak of himself simply as the One who is,
but introduces himself as *Yahweh* in the first person as 'I am – I shall be', and even
then not in a static but in a dynamic mode, as 'I am who I am – I shall be who I
shall be'. And he goes on to characterise himself as he who is the God of Abraham,
Isaac and Jacob, he who will deliver his people from bondage, who will always be
their God and claim them as his own people. 'This is my name for ever, my memorial
unto all generations.'[2] And so through the prophets sent to Israel, God kept
proclaiming himself to Israel throughout their history: 'I am *Yahweh* your God
from the land of Egypt.'[3] 'I am *Yahweh*, the first and the last, I am he.'[4] It is as such
that God reveals and names himself as the living, speaking and acting God who
is who he is in the undeviating self-determination of his own Life and Activity,
and is who he is in covenanted relation with his people and who ever will be their
Lord and Saviour. *Yahweh* is he who is and invariably will be in the living reality
and self-consistency of his own eternal being. He is Lord God who made heaven
and earth and all that is, and makes himself known to mankind in and through his
Word and Act as he who never will be other than he is in his Word and Act. There
is no other God than this God who makes himself known to mankind and who
reveals himself to them in this way, and who thereby denies reality to any other god
and discounts any other possible way for human beings to know him. As we have
already noted, that is the import of the those Old Testament passages which speak
of God as 'the jealous God',[5] which is not what it appears in English to be, for it
means that the very nature of the Lord God excludes the possibility of there being

---

[1] Exod. 3.13, 14.
[2] Exod. 3.15.
[3] Hos. 12.9; 13.4.
[4] Isa. 41.4; 43.10, 13, 25; 44.6; 48.12.
[5] Exod. 20.5, 34.14; Deut. 4.24, 5.9, 6.15, 29.20, 32.16, etc.

other gods. 'I am God, there is none else.'[6] 'Hear Oh Israel, the Lord your God is one God.'[7]

This incomparable God is not to be understood on the analogy of our finite creaturely human being with whom word, act and person are different from one another. With us word is different from act. We speak but exert additional power in order to carry out what we say. We finite beings act but our acts are not personal in themselves. Our word and act do not coincide in the unity and power of our personal being – act and person, word and person, word and act are all separate in finite beings. With God it is not so, for his eternal uncreated Being is not characterised by the kind of distinctions found in finite creaturely beings. He meets us, speaks to us, acts toward us as One whose Word and Act and Person are inseparable from one another in the intrinsic simplicity and homogeneity of his divine Being. The Word that he speaks takes place of itself, for it is filled with the power of his Person, the power by which he is who he is and by which he lives his own personal life in absolute self-sufficiency and freedom. His power to act is not other than the power of his Person or the power of his Word. He is in Person identical with his Word, and his Word is itself his Act. Nor are the Word and Act of God separated from his Being, for they inhere in his Being, and indeed are his Being speaking and acting. God speaks to us and acts toward us personally in such a way that his Being is wholly present in his Word and Act. Hence God's Being is neither mute nor inactive, but is inherently eloquent and active. His Being is his Being in his Act and his Act is his Act in his Being; his Word is his Word in his Being and his Being is his Being in his Word. Such is the dynamic eternal reality of the mighty living God who names himself 'I am who I am – I will be who I will be.' God is no other than he who he is and always will be in the Word and Work which are integral to his ever-living unchangeable personal Being. He is the one self-revealing, self-naming God who is and always will be one and the same in his eternal faithfulness.[8] Hence we must think of all the changes in God's mighty acts of creation and redemption which constantly surprise us as flowing from and reposing upon his eternally unchanging life.

In the New Testament Scriptures this same living God has revealed himself through the consummating of his creating and saving acts in Jesus Christ, the Word made flesh, God become man. He has given us access to himself through Christ and in one Spirit, naming himself as Father, Son and Holy Spirit in such a way that we know that there is no other God but he who is Father, Son and Holy Spirit. *Yahweh* was the ineffable Name of God in his self-revelation to Israel as the one Lord God, Creator of heaven and earth; but in his self-revelation in Jesus Christ, Father, Son and Holy Spirit is the triune Name whereby God makes himself personally and familiarly known to us as he is in his divine Nature. As we have already noted, the name *Yahweh*, translated *Kyrios*, is applied to the Lord Jesus

---

[6] Isa. 46.9; cf. 37.16, 44.5, 45.22.
[7] Deut. 6.4; Mark 12.29, 32.
[8] Exod. 15.3; Ps. 83.19; Hos. 12.6; Isa. 42.3.

Christ, who confronts us in the Gospel as *Ego Eimi*. He is 'the First and the Last', the 'Alpha and the Omega', 'He who is, who was and who is to come', 'the beginning and the End'.[9] 'Jesus Christ is the same yesterday, and today, and for ever',[10] the unchanging One. And it is in and through him that the dynamic constancy of the eternal self-living and self-moving God is fully made known.

This is properly to be understood in the light of God's trinitarian self-revelation as Father Son and Holy Spirit effected in the saving acts of incarnation and redemption. What God is toward us in the Gospel as Father, Son and Holy Spirit he is antecedently, inherently and eternally in himself. He did not become a Trinity in the incarnation but became toward us what he eternally is, and what he became toward us in his trinitarian self-revelation he eternally is in himself. The one being of God is thus revealed to be intrinsically and eternally dynamic being, not static being but unique divine becoming. It is as such that God is unchangeable, ever one and the same. How are we to understand this dynamic unchangeableness?

Let us think again of the creation as an utterly new event in which the world was brought into being by the sheer fiat of God's Word 'let there be'. God was always Father, but not always Creator. God did not have to create the world, for he was perfectly free to create or not to create. Nevertheless in the unlimited freedom of his love God created the world out of nothing, and did not grudge bringing into being an altogether new reality utterly different from his own. While this was something completely new, nevertheless even in that new event God did not change but remained and continues to remain ever one and the same, for in that astonishingly new act, as Duns Scotus used to point out, God revealed himself as completely free to bring new ideas and realities into existence without contradicting himself.[11]

Thus in fact God's creation of the universe is to be regarded as the demonstration of his inexhaustible freedom as the mighty living God who is eternally one and the same throughout all change. As the Psalmist said:

> Of old thou hast laid the foundations of the earth:
> and the heavens are the work of thy hands.
> They shall perish but thou shalt endure;
> yea all of them shall wax old as a garment;
> as a vesture shalt thou change them, and they shall be changed;
> but thou art the same, and thy years have no end.[12]

Yet 'new' as the act of creation was, it is not to be regarded just as an 'after-thought', for it flowed and continues to flow freely from what God eternally is in his divine life and love. All this is finally to be understood only in the light of the utterly astonishing supreme event of the incarnation when in Jesus Christ God himself became man, the Creator became a creature.[13]

---

[9] Rev. 1.4, 8, 17; 2.8; 21.6; 22.13.
[10] Heb. 13.8.
[11] For references consult my *Divine and Contingent Order*, p. 153.
[12] Ps. 102.25–27; Heb. 1.10–12.
[13] *Divine and Contingent Order*, p. 87f.

Consider again, then, the Incarnation, as an absolutely new event for God: 'the Word became flesh.'[14] God was not always incarnate. He was always God the Son as well as God the Father and God the Holy Spirit, but not always God become man in Jesus Christ in whom divine and human nature are for ever united in the one incarnate Person of God the Son. Yet in this utterly new event God does not change but remains ever one and the same – in his transcendent freedom he became man, one with us in our contingent mutable existence, without ceasing to be what he eternally was and is and ever will be in himself. Far from being a deviation in his constancy or a limitation of his essential being, or a compromising of his divine nature, the incarnation was the supreme manifestation, transcending that of the creation, of God's constancy in unbounded freedom and unlimited perfection. As such the incarnation cannot be regarded just as an 'after-thought' but as freely issuing from the overflowing life and love of the eternal God, Father, Son and Holy Spirit. It is above all through the incarnation, the Word of God become flesh, that God reveals to us something of his own nature as the mighty living God who is who he eternally is and yet who will not be without us whom he has created for fellowship with himself and with whom he freely shares his own divine Life and Light and Love. It is in Jesus Christ, therefore, that we really understand and think aright about God's unchanging constancy, for it is in him, the only-begotten Son of the Father, that we may really know God in accordance with the inmost nature of his eternal being.

Along with the incarnation, of course, we must take fully into consideration, the death and resurrection of Jesus, that is, the death and resurrection of God incarnate in space and time. What event could be more astonishing, and utterly new even for God, than *God crucified and risen again*? And what are we to think of the cognate event that followed fifty days after at Pentecost, when God poured out his Spirit upon human beings in a way that he had never done before? This self-giving of God to the apostles and disciples at Pentecost was not just a once for all event in space and time when the Church was launched into history as the Body of Christ, but a really new event in the relations between God and the human race. On the ground of the atoning death and resurrection of Christ, finished and perfected once and for all, God the Father sent his Spirit into the world to make himself present to his creatures in such a way as to open himself to direct personal access through the mediation of Christ. The transcendent Spirit of God had always been actively present in the world immanently sustaining its continuing relation to God the Creator, but what happened at Pentecost manifested a change not only in the form of his activity but in the mode of his immanence which it is difficult for us to conceive or express. It certainly illuminates for us the changed situation between God and man brought about by the incarnation, but at the same time it brings home to us the fact that what happened at Pentecost was not only quite new in the experience of mankind, but something incomprehensibly new in the life and activity of the eternal God and the mode of his presence to all flesh.[15]

---

[14] John 1.14: ὁ λόγος σάρξ ἐγένετο.
[15] Cf. H. J. Wotherspoon, *What Happened at Pentecost and Other Papers* (Edinburgh, 1937), pp. 4ff.

Quite clearly the mighty living God of the Old Testament revelation and the Triune God of the New Testament revelation is neither the 'Unmoved Mover' of Aristotelian scholastic theology nor the 'Moved Unmover' of Whiteheadean process theology.[16] The former represents an inertial Deity who does not personally intervene in our mutable world of space and time, and the latter represents a panentheistic Deity who is not detached from the ongoing process of this world and is not the transcendent Lord of space and time. Both these conceptions, the Unmoved Mover and the Moved Unmover, imply different forms of immobility or immutability, one of complete detachment from the world, and one of inextricable attachment to the world. Neither involves the biblical conception of the *freedom of God* who, while remaining constantly the one who he is, is also the one who is eternally new and constantly surpasses himself in all that he does. Unlike the fundamental constants of nature upon which the invariance and limits of all physical law depend, the constancy of God does not limit his freedom, for it is the constancy of his freedom as the ever self-living and ever self-moving Being. In fact it is the constancy of God which provides the very ground for the infinite mobility, newness and variability of his activity, and at the same time the very ground for his remaining always the same mighty living God in every change. It is the constancy of the self-existing, self-living and self-affirming, self-revealing God who is eternally new while always one and the same, who is never other than he who he is in the unlimited freedom and inexhaustible newness of his creative and saving acts, and whose unpredictable deeds unceasingly take us by surprise. This God is immutably free, for his freedom is the constancy of his self-living, self-affirming and self-moving personal being. That is why Karl Barth could write so movingly and powerfully about the constancy of God's personal being and life in all his activity as the perfection of his unbounded freedom in which he keeps on surpassing his own acts of love and grace.[17]

The contrast between the immutability of the Unmoved Mover or of the Moved Unmover and the immutability of the mighty living God of revelation could not be greater. As the one Lord God who is who he is in his acts of creation, revelation and redemption, the God and Father of our Lord and Saviour Jesus Christ, he surpasses those kinds of immutability altogether. He is the *Self-moved God* who is transcendently and majestically free to become one with us in our creaturely existence and even to enter into the depths of our misery and alienation, while remaining he who he always is as the mighty living God, and who is therefore perfectly free and able to redeem and save us from our bondage and degradation. As I have written elsewhere, 'If God is merely immutable (i.e. in the abstract sense) he has neither place nor time for frail evanescent creatures in his unchanging existence. But the God who has revealed himself in Jesus Christ as sharing our lot is the God who is really free to make himself poor that we through his poverty might be made rich, the God of invariant love but not impassible, constant in faithfulness but not immutable.'[18]

[16] The term 'Moved Unmover' is the expression used by Colin Gunton to describe the God of process theology – cf. my *Ground and Grammar of Theology* (Charlottesville, 1980), p. 247.

[17] Karl Barth, *Church Dogmatics* II.1, pp. 491–522.

[18] *Space, Time and Incarnation* (Oxford, 1969), p. 75.

It is in the incarnation above all that the constancy of the self-moving God is revealed, for although he did not have to do so, in Jesus Christ God freely became man without ceasing to be God, he freely became a creature without ceasing to be the Creator. Thus F. W. Camfield, expounding Barth's account of the constancy of God, has written:

> Paradoxically enough, to all appearance, the great affirmation of the permanence (or constancy) of God is made in the act in which in Jesus Christ he becomes one with the creature. That the creator should himself become creature would seem to involve a change so radical that the permanence of God could no longer be spoken of. The very opposite is however true. In himself becoming creature, God demonstrates in the most conclusive way that in setting up an existence other than his own, the existence of the creature, he is in no way ceasing to be what he was before or becoming something other than what he was before, but is living his own free life. The life of the creature belongs absolutely to him: he in his freedom is its absolute Lord. What then can hinder him from living that life? When once we have got rid of the abstract idea of unchangeableness as applied to God, an idea that can only serve to designate immobility and death, and put in its place the true idea of the one free living God who, in that he is such, has a history and indeed is a history, and who in that history remains the same one free living God whose being and nature is love, we perceive that there is no contradiction between the unchangeableness of God now rightly understood, and his moving and acting towards and within the created order.[19]

We may now turn to consider several aspects of God's unchangeableness or immutability, rightly understood as the constancy of his self-living, self-moving and self-affirming personal Being.

1) The Life of God

The self-revelation of God as 'I am who I am – I will be who I will be' together with his self-revelation in Jesus Christ as he who was, is and will be, tells us something about the inconceivable nature of God's eternal life, that it is not immobile but continually self-moving, that while it is from everlasting to everlasting without beginning and end, it is continually new and carries within it the eternal purpose of God's love, moving uninterruptedly toward its perfect fulfilment. The eternal life of God has *direction*. This is made clear to us by God's act of creation in which he revealed that he does not want to live alone and will not be without us, for he has made us for fellowship with himself in order to share with us his divine Life

---

[19] F. W. Camfield, *Reformation Old and New* (London, 1947), p. 62f. See Karl Barth, *Church Dogmatics* 2.1, pp. 499ff, 502f, 512ff.

and Light and Love. As we have seen, the creation of the world and of mankind was an utterly new event for God, for while he was always Father he was not always Creator, so that although God was not different after the creation from what he was before it, the creation registered a distinct 'moment' in the eternal life of God. We have also seen how it is in the light of the incarnation, an even more astonishing act of God than his original creation, that we may grasp something of the significance of his eternal purpose, its *direction* and its *fulfilment*, for in Jesus Christ God has become what he never was before, a human being, the Creator has become a creature, and the eternal has become time, all that he may share what we are and have become in order to share with us what he is in his eternal Life and Love and ever will be.

This means that we must think of the constancy of God which is his unchanging eternal Life as characterised by *time*, not of course our kind of time which is the time of finite created being with beginning and end, and past, present and future, but God's kind of time which is the time of his eternal Life without beginning and end. While he creates time along with all that is changeable, he does so without any temporal movement in himself.[20] The time of our life is defined by its fleeting creaturely nature, but the time of God's Life is defined by his everlasting uncreated Nature in which he transcends our temporality while nevertheless holding it within the embrace of his divine time. Just as we distinguish sharply between the uncreated reality of God and the created reality of the world, between the uncreated rationality of God and our created rationality, or between the uncreated Light of God and our created light, so we must distinguish between God's uncreated time and our created time. On the other hand, just as we think of our creaturely being as contingently grounded upon the eternal being of God, so we must think of our creaturely time as contingently grounded upon the eternal time of God. Thus we may think of the time of our world, which God has created out of nothing along with the world he has made, as unceasingly sustained by him in a created correspondence to the uncreated time of his own eternal Life. And so far from being some kind of timeless eternity or eternal now that devalues or negates time, the real time of God's eternal Life gives reality and value to the created time of our life through coordinating its contingent temporality with its own movement and constancy. What does this have to say to us about the unchangeableness or constancy of God which is identical with his self-moving eternal Life? The fact that God has time for us in the partnership he maintains with us in which our fleeting time for all its dissimilarity reflects his eternal time, reinforces the conviction that the nature of God's time is not static but essentially dynamic and as such is the constant power upon which our contingent temporality rests.

The time of our human life is characterised by finite distinctions and limits between past, present and future, which do not characterise the eternal Life of God. And yet, as we have seen, there is a purpose of love and so a definite direction in God's eternal Life, marked by distinct *moments* in it such as that before and after the creation or before and after the incarnation, in which it moves toward the

---

[20] Cf. Augustine, *De Trinitate*, 1.1.3.

divinely determined fulfilment revealed in Jesus Christ when God will be all in all.[21] There is thus direction and onward movement in the eternal Life and Activity of God. Hence we may well say, in Karl Barth's startling statement, that God has a 'history'[22] – but of course 'history' in a unique sense defined by God the unique subject of this history, the one ever-living God. Just as the finite distinctions between word, act, and person that characterise human beings may not be projected into our understanding of God, so our finite distinctions between past, present and future may not be projected into our thought of God's being and activity which transcend them altogether. There is and can be no conflict between the unchanging constancy of God's eternal time and the movement and activity of God toward the fulfilment of his eternal purpose of love.

This must be thought out in the light of the happening of the incarnation when the eternal Word of God *became* historical event, and the eternal *became* time. The fact that in the incarnation God became man without ceasing to be God, tells us that his nature is characterised by both repose and movement, and that his eternal Being is also a divine *Becoming*.[23] This does not mean that God ever becomes other than he eternally is or that he passes over from becoming into being something else, but rather that he continues unceasingly to be what he always is and ever will be in the living movement of his eternal Being. His Becoming is not a becoming on the way toward being or toward a fullness of being, but is the eternal fullness and the overflowing of his eternal unlimited Being. Becoming expresses the dynamic nature of his Being. His Becoming is, as it were, the other side of his Being, and his Being is the other side of his Becoming. His Becoming is his Being in movement and his Being in movement is his Becoming in a way which we cannot adequately grasp or express, but which we discern in the incarnate life and activity of God within the space and time of our creaturely existence which affirmed the reality of that space and time for ever in God's interrelations with us throughout all history. That is to say, we must think of the constancy of the mighty living God as essentially dynamic and never as static, for it is none other than the constancy of the self-living, self-moving God himself revealed in the Lord Jesus Christ, the same yesterday, today and for ever, the incarnate 'I am' of the eternal Lord God. As our Lord once said, 'Before Abraham was, I am.'[24]

2) The Faithfulness of God

The self-affirming and self-determining of God as 'I am who I am – I will be who I will be', together with the decisive once-for-all event of the incarnation, speak to us of the unswerving faithfulness of God in all his divine acts toward us and for us in time and eternity. Here we have to do with the irreversibility of God's eternal

[21] 1 Cor. 15.28.
[22] Karl Barth, *Church Dogmatics* II.1, p. 502f.
[23] Consult especially Eberhard Jüngel, *The Doctrine of the Trinity, God's Being is in Becoming*, Monograph Supplements to the *Scottish Journal of Theology*, vol.4, tr. Horton Harris (Edinburgh, 1976).
[24] John 8.58.

time in its forward movement toward the complete fulfilment of his eternal purpose of love in creation and redemption. In Jesus Christ God has revealed himself not only as he who he really is, but as he who he always will be, who does not go back upon what he has become and has undertaken for our sakes, and who does not retract his word or break his promises, sealed as they are with the blood of his dear Son. As such he is the God who keeps faith and truth with his creation and with the people he has created and continues unceasingly to sustain for fellowship with himself. The everlasting self-consistency, the unswerving constancy, the uninterruptible invariance of God's purpose of love, manifest in his covenant relation built into the very foundation of the creation, and renewed and sealed in the covenant of grace embodied in space and time in Jesus Christ, speak to us of the permanent faithfulness of God. His self-naming and self-affirming as *Yahweh*, and his absolute self-giving and self-commitment to us as the God and Father of our Lord Jesus Christ, assure us that God is absolutely reliable. God does not, cannot go back upon the sacrifice of his dear Son with whom he has freely given us all things. He does not, cannot deny himself or retract his promises to bring to complete fruition what he has already perfected in Jesus Christ.[25] He is both the Alpha and the Omega, the Beginning and the End, the First and the Last, he who is and was and ever will be, and he who will at the last make all things new.

Let us consider what this means to us personally and to the whole universe in which God has planted us.

On the one hand, it means that there is a relation of complete fidelity and reliability between what God is in Jesus Christ toward us and what he is eternally in his unchangeable being. 'God is faithful'; we may commit our souls to him as unto 'a faithful Creator'.[26] God is not one thing in himself and another thing in Jesus Christ – what God is toward us in Jesus he is inherently and eternally in himself. That is the fiducial significance of the central clause in the Nicene Creed, that there is a oneness in Being and agency between Jesus Christ the incarnate Son and God the Father. What God is in eternity, Jesus Christ is in space and time, and what Jesus Christ is in space and time, God is in his eternity. There is an unbroken relation of Being and Action between the Son and the Father, and in Jesus Christ that relation has been embodied in our human existence once for all. There is thus no God behind the back of Jesus Christ, but only this God whose face we see in the face of the Lord Jesus. There is no *deus absconditus*, no dark inscrutable God, no arbitrary Deity of whom we can know nothing but before whom we can only tremble as our guilty conscience paints harsh streaks upon his face. No, there are no dark spots in God of which we need to be afraid; there is nothing in God for which Jesus Christ does not go bail in virtue of the perfect oneness in being and nature between God and himself. There is only the one God who has revealed himself in Jesus Christ in such a way that there is perfect consistency and fidelity between what he reveals of the Father and what the Father is in his unchangeable reality. The constancy of God in time and eternity has to do with the fact that God

[25] Cf. Heb. 6.12ff.
[26] 1 Cor. 10.13; 1 Pet. 4.19.

243

really is like Jesus, for there is no other God than he who became man in Jesus and he whom God affirms himself to be and always will be in Jesus.

On the other hand, the irreversible event of the incarnation, in which the Word of God by whom all things are made became flesh, in which God the Creator became man and the eternal became time in Jesus Christ, all for us and our salvation, means that God has decisively bound himself to the created universe and the created universe to himself, with such a unbreakable bond that the Christian hope of redemption and recreation extends not just to us human beings but to the universe as a whole. All that God has done, is and will do, is bound up with Jesus Christ, the same yesterday, today and for ever, by whom all things visible and invisible were created and in whom they consist.[27] That this created universe in which God has set us will one day be utterly obliterated in some final catastrophe is as inconceivable for Christians as the obliteration of Jesus Christ, and with him the undoing of the eternal purpose of God's love embodied in him in space and time and fulfilled in his saving life, death and resurrection. Thus it is in the bodily resurrection of Jesus Christ from the dead, in which the final immobility of death, or the immobility which is death, was utterly vanquished, that we may clearly discern the essentially dynamic nature of God's unchangeableness or constancy. This is the living immutability of his eternal Being which is the very antithesis of all inertial immutability or immobility. This is the triumphant freedom of the divine constancy revealed and enacted in Jesus: 'I am the resurrection and the Life.'[28]

3) The Eternal Love of God

We return to the point that in his creative and redeeming acts God has revealed that he will not live alone without us and that his nature is such that he has created beings other than himself in order to establish fellowship between them and himself. God did not have to create the world. He had no need for others to be able to love, nor was there any reason outside of himself for what he has done. God's love knows no *why* beyond itself – there is no reason for God's love apart from his love. God loves us because he loves, because his loving is the primary act of his Being, because his loving is his very Being. What God did, therefore, in creating fellowship between himself and others, he did in the sheer freedom of his overflowing love. This is made clear to us above all in the incarnation when God became man and became one with us, thereby committing himself to us in his love in an absolutely irreversible way. 'God so loved the world that he gave his only begotten Son that whoever believes in him should not perish but have everlasting life.'[29] The infinite extent of God's self-commitment in that act of love was stressed by St Paul in words that suggest to us, as we have already noted more than once, that God loves us more than he loves himself. 'He who spared not his own Son but delivered him up for us all, how shall he not with him also freely give us all things?'[30] In giving to us his

[27] Col. 1.16f.
[28] John 11.25.
[29] John 3.16.
[30] Rom. 8.32.

beloved Son God gives us not something of his love but his very self and in giving himself he gives us everything – his love for us was such that he did not hold back anything from the supreme sacrifice.

This reveals that what God is in that movement of his love he is in the ultimate reality of his inmost Being, and so St John tells us that 'God *is* love'.[31] God does not merely love, for he is Love and apart from his Love God is not at all. That is, God's loving and living are one and the same, for he is not different in the eternal constancy of his divine living from what he is in the outreach of his loving. God is in himself in his own eternal Life he who he is in the activity of his love toward us; and that activity is defined specifically in terms of the sending of God's only Son into the world that we might live through him, and thus in terms of the concrete act of God's love in space and time in giving his Son to be the propitiation for our sins on the Cross.[32] God does not love us because of the atoning propitiation enacted in the sacrificial death of Christ. Rather does that propitiation flow freely from the consistent self-movement of the Love that God himself is. It is through the sheer overflow of his eternal love that God has provided for mankind atoning propitiation in the blood of Christ, in order thereby to draw near to us and to draw us near to himself in such a way as to do away with all barriers of sin, hostility and fear between us and himself.[33]

It is, then, in the incarnation and the atonement that the unchangeableness or constancy of the love of God is fully demonstrated as the essential movement of God's own eternal Life and Being. The constancy of God's love is the dynamic constancy of God himself who ever loves and is Love, not in such a way that the eternally living God also loves, but in such a way that God's loving is eternally his living and his living is eternally his loving. The unchangeableness of the love of God is the unchangeableness of his self-living and self-moving being. Hence all that is to be said about the constancy and freedom of God applies to the constancy and freedom of his love.

Since God is Love, his love can no more cease to be love than God can cease to be God. Like God himself his love is always consistently the same in every change, and yet always new in its free spontaneous outflow unconditioned by anything beyond itself. As such the love of God is characterised by a total freedom from rigid immutability or inflexibility and by an infinite range of variability and mobility in which its dynamic constancy as love is brought to bear consistently and yet differentially upon every and any state of affairs beyond itself, whether it is good or bad, orderly or disorderly, rational or irrational. This does not mean that the love of God is indifferent to states of affairs, for that would not be consistent with what it is as love. The love of God will never be other than it eternally is, so that it always acts faithfully and appropriately with the just and the unjust, the merciful and the froward alike.

This is what we find in the biblical revelation again and again when, although it may appear otherwise, the notion of repentance is anthropomorphically applied to

---

[31] 1 John 4.8, 16.
[32] 1 John 4.9f.
[33] Eph. 2.13ff.

God in statements about his repenting or not repenting of some word or act.[34] They are rather to be understood in terms of the intrinsic freedom and variability of divine love which precisely in its dynamic constancy and consistency as love bears upon people by way of forbearance or rebuke, election or rejection, redemption or judgment, unconstrained by any considerations beyond its own free movement as sheer grace.[35] It is precisely because the love of God never repents of being love that it acts differentially and appropriately with different people or in different events. Because the love of God is always and everywhere immutably the same, unconditioned in its nature as love by anything beyond itself, that it functions unreservedly and equally as love even in the judgment of the sinner. It is his loving of the sinner which resists his sin that is his judgment of the sinner.

The love of God revealed in Jesus Christ is his total unconditional self-giving to mankind, love in which he does not withhold himself from loving to the utmost or cut short its full movement, and it is upon that love that our hope of redemption and resurrection is grounded. It is the love of the eternally self-affirming and self-giving God, and so the love he pours out freely upon us through the Holy Spirit is love that affirms itself as love against all that is not love or resists his love. That is why the total self-giving of the self-affirming God in love is and cannot but be the judgment of his love upon the sinner. He does not hold back his love from the sinner, for he cannot cease to be the God who loves and loves unreservedly and unconditionally. Is that not why St John in the Apocalypse could speak of the wrath of God as 'the wrath of the Lamb',[36] for his wrath is the total unrestrained self-giving of God's love upon the Cross which he does not withhold even from those who reject it, and which is and cannot but be wholly opposed to evil and sin? And that is surely why St Paul could speak of his ministry of the Gospel as a savour to one of life unto life and to another of death unto death. In God there is no Yes and No, but only Yes.[37] It is upon the Yes of God's eternal love for us that our salvation rests, but that Yes is also the judgment of those who perish.[38] Why people may want to reject the love of God is quite inexplicable, but whether they believe in Jesus Christ as the incarnate love of God or refuse to believe in him, the love of God remains unchangeably what it was and is and ever will be, the love that is freely, unreservedly and unconditionally given to all mankind.

4) The Impassibility of God

The unqualified Deity of Christ means that his incarnate life as the one Mediator between God and man falls within the life of God, and that his passion belongs to the very Being of God, and thus of God the Father and God the Spirit as well as God the Son. Through his resurrection and ascension all that Christ Jesus has done

---

[34] Cf. the illuminating discussion of Karl Barth, *Church Dogmatics* II.1, pp. 495–499.
[35] Cf. St Paul's account of God's relations to Jacob and Esau, Rom. 9.13–23.
[36] Rev. 6.17; 11.18; 16.1; 19.15.
[37] 1 Cor. 1.19f, 2.15f.
[38] This is how John Calvin interpreted St Paul's teaching about election. See my *Kingdom and Church* (Edinburgh, 1956), pp. 104ff.

for us in his historical life and death in offering himself for the sins of mankind has not only been accepted by the Father but has been taken up into God and is anchored in his eternal unchangeable reality. Unless that is the case, unless the atoning exchange effected through the suffering and death of Christ was indeed the vicarious act of God himself in order to bring about our salvation, then what took place in his crucifixion would have been in vain. Only if the Lord God himself were directly and immediately engaged in the vicarious passion of his incarnate Son could it be the vicarious means of redeeming and liberating the creation.

'God crucified'! That is the startling truth of the Gospel. Of course only if God is a Trinity, does this make sense, for it was not the Father or the Spirit who was crucified but the incarnate Son of God, crucified certainly in his differentiation from the Father and the Spirit, but nevertheless crucified in his unbroken oneness with the Father and the Spirit in being and activity. The whole Trinity is involved in the sacrifice of Christ on the Cross.[39] In an Easter Oration Gregory Nazianzen once spoke of this awesome fact, 'God crucified', as a downright 'miracle'. 'We needed an incarnate God, a God put to death, that we might live. We were put to death with him, that we might be cleansed; we rose again with him, because we were put to death with him; we were glorified with him, because we rose again with him.'[40] In a letter to Epictetus about the suffering and crucifixion of Christ written in rebuttal of Arian error Athanasius wrote:

> Let them confess that the crucified was God, for the Scriptures bid them, and especially Thomas, who, after seeing upon him the print of the nails, cried out, 'My Lord and my God'. For the Son, being God, and Lord of Glory, was in the Body which was ingloriously nailed and dishonoured; but the Body while it suffered, being pierced on the tree, and water and blood flowed from its side, yet because it was a temple of the Word, was filled full of the Godhead.[41]

In the Nestorian controversy it became quite clear to Cyril of Alexandria that because of the hypostatic union of divine Nature and human nature in the one incarnate Nature or Reality (μία φύσις σεσαρκωμένη) of the Son of God we cannot but think of the passion of Christ as taking place in his indivisible divine-human Person. 'If the Word did not suffer for us humanly, he did not accomplish our redemption divinely; if he who suffered for us was mere man and but the organ of Deity, we are not in fact redeemed.'[42] It was God who suffered in Christ, for no mere man can be

[39] His insistence upon this is one of the merits of Jürgen Moltmann's book *The Crucified God* (London, 1974), but his somewhat tritheistic understanding of the unity, rather than the oneness, of the Father, the Son and the Holy Spirit, in spite of what he intends, damages this insight.

[40] Gregory Nazianzen, *Orationes*, 45.28f.

[41] Athanasius, *Ad Epictetum*, 10. But cf. *Contra Arianos* 3.34, where Athanasius remarks that while in his own nature the Word is impassible, he suffered in the flesh and the body for they were proper to him as the Saviour. His nature, however, was such that instead of being harmed by those passions he obliterated and destroyed them. In this sense we ourselves also become impassible in him. Athanasius operated with a bi-polar conception of divine suffering, for God suffers in the suffering of his Son not in the way creatures do.

[42] Cyril of Alexandria, *Epistula ad monachos Aegypti*, 25–26. Elsewhere Cyril says 'he suffered impassibly – ἔπαθεν ἀπαθῶς' *Scholia de incarnatione unigeniti*, 35 and 37, and *Dialogus contra Theodoretum*, 3. See R. V. Sellers, *Two Ancient Christologies* (London, 1940), p. 88f.

our Saviour. It was Christ *as God* and God *as Christ* who suffered for us and our salvation, but in such a way as to redeem mankind from suffering and redeem suffering in mankind.

It is surely within this perspective, that of the incarnate and crucified Saviour and the revelation mediated to us through his life and passion of the nature of God, that we must consider the question of divine *passibility* and *impassibility*. God is certainly impassible in the sense that he is not subject to the passions that characterise our human and creaturely existence, and it is certainly true that God is opposed to all suffering and pain. He is, moreover, intrinsically impassible for in its own divine Nature he is not moved or swayed by anything other than himself or outside of himself.[43] That is the sense of divine impassibility on which ancient and medieval theology often laid such stress, although it tended to fall under the influence of a metaphysical conception of the inertial Nature or Being of God. But it was rather otherwise whenever a powerful soteriological approach to the doctrine of God was dominant, governed by the self-revelation of God as Father, Son and Holy Spirit in the history of salvation. That had the effect of setting aside static notions of God's being and activity in favour of one in which God is in himself as a trinitarian Communion a movement of love, and on the ground of which he freely and actively enters into relations of love with others thereby opening himself to them and establishing reciprocal relations with them.

In this approach God is not thought of as characterised by apathy (ἀπαθεία) in holding himself aloof from the pain and suffering of his human creatures, for his heart goes out to them in redemptive sympathy in what Moltmann has called his 'active suffering'.[44] In his overflowing love he allies himself with his people in their afflictions and takes them upon himself in order to reverse their suffering and redeem them from it.[45] This is the point made by Athanasius when, with reference to Jesus' pain, agitation and distress in soul, he said 'one cannot say that these things are natural to Godhead, but *they came to belong to God by nature*, when it pleased the Word to undergo human birth and to reconstitute in himself, as in a new image, that what he himself had made but which had been disorganised by sin, corruption and death.'[46] What pains God above all is the sin and wickedness of his human creatures, their rebellion against his holy will and their persistent rejection of his grace. His opposition to evil and his wrath with evildoers, however, are not just negative, for they arise positively out of the steadfastness and immutability of his holy love which by its very nature is completely opposed to evil and rejects it in every form as sin against the very love that God himself is. The conflict between God and evil is the obverse of his love for the world, but it is in that love that God provides a way for the saving and healing of the world, and the vanquishing of all its evil, and he does so by paying for it at infinite cost to himself in the sacrifice of Christ as the Lamb of God sent by him to bear and bear away the sins of the world.

---

[43] Cf. G. L. Prestige, *God in Patristic Thought* (London, 1952), pp. 6ff, 11; and O. C. Quick, *Doctrines of the Creed* (London, reprint 1947), pp. 122f and 184ff.

[44] Jürgen Moltmann, *The Crucified God* (New York, 1974), p. 230.

[45] Cf. Isa. 63.9f where this is spoken of in relation to the Spirit of God.

[46] Athanasius, *Contra Apollinarem*, 1.5.

That is the significance and message of the Cross. God does not obliterate evil by absolute irresistible power, but in his boundless mercy lays hold of it in the incarnate birth, life and death of his beloved Son and makes it serve the supreme purpose of his love for the world. It is in that self-abnegating compassionate act of God's transcendent love in delivering up his beloved Son for us all, and in suffering his death, that his fathomless passion is revealed, the pain of which is as infinite as his love.

It is, then, the mediatorial passion of Christ in life and death in bearing the wrath of God upon the sin of the whole human race, the fearful anguish of his soul in making that sin his own and bearing the infliction of divine judgment upon it, the indescribable agony and sorrow that overwhelmed him in the Garden of Gethsemane and in the darkness of dereliction which he endured on the Cross, in which spiritual and physical pain interpenetrated each other, all that unveils for us something of the infinite depth of the active suffering of God.[47] That was the inexpressible agony of the Saviour as true God and true man in the depth of his incarnate being as one indivisible Person. What Christ felt, did and suffered in himself in his body and soul for our forgiveness was felt, done, and suffered by God in his innermost Being for our sake. The suffering of Christ is the incarnate manifestation and expression of the vicarious suffering of God, the self-sacrifice of the Son is the correlate of the self-sacrifice of the Father. 'At bottom the atonement is something provided, something done by God; it is an expression of his nature, for the atonement really is the cost to God of forgiveness.'[48] That was not a cost which God the Father counted too high. Hence, as Karl Barth wrote:

It is not at all the case that God has no part in the suffering of Jesus Christ even in his mode of being as the Father. No, there is a *particula veri* in the teaching of the early Patripassians. This is that primarily it is God the Father who suffers in the offering and sending of his Son in his abasement. The suffering is not his own, but the alien suffering of the creature, of man, which he takes to himself in the Son. But he does suffer it in the humiliation of his Son with a depth with which it never was or will be suffered by any man – apart from the One who is his Son. And he does so in order that, having been borne by him in the offering and sending of his Son, it should not have to be suffered in this way by man. This fatherly fellow-suffering of God is the mystery, the basis, of the humiliation of his Son; the truth of that which takes place historically in his crucifixion.[49]

We have to do with a paradoxical relation between passibility and impassibility in our understanding of God in the light of the incarnate Mediator of God to which theologians as different as Cyril of Alexandria and Theodoret of Antioch

---

[47] How appropriate it is in Handel's *Messiah* to be directed to the words from the prophet in Lamentations 1.12: 'Is it nothing to you, all you that pass by? Behold, and see if there is any sorrow like unto my sorrow, which is done unto me, wherewith the Lord has afflicted me in the day of his fierce wrath.'

[48] H. R. Mackintosh, *Some Aspects of Christian Belief* (London, 1924), p. 93.

[49] Karl Barth, *Church Dogmatics* IV.2, p. 357.

gave expression in the statement '*he suffered impassibly*.'[50] The emphasis tended to be laid sometimes on one side of the paradox, and sometimes on the other, but Cyril was always concerned not to detract either from the integrity of human nature or from the integrity of divine nature.[51] On the one hand the notion of divine passibility would appear to call in question the steadfastness or immutability of God in face of the pressure of outside forces upon him as if he could be moved by what is other than God. On the other hand the notion of divine impassibility would evidently exclude the possibility of any real movement of God in a loving and vicarious self-identification with us in incarnation and redemption which would posit a deep gulf between God as he is in himself and God as he is toward us. On the one hand, therefore, we cannot but hold that God is impassible in the sense that he remains eternally and changelessly the same, but on the other hand, we cannot but hold that God is passible in that what he is not by nature he in fact became in taking upon himself 'the form of a servant'.[52] He became one of us and one with us in Jesus Christ within the conditions and limits of our creaturely human existence and experience in space and time, although without in any way ceasing to be God who is transcendent over all space and time. That is surely how we must think of the passibility and impassibility of God: their conjunction is as incomprehensible as the mode of the union of God and man in Christ. Just as in creation and incarnation God acted in entirely new ways while remaining unchanged in his divine nature, just as he became man without ceasing to be God and became a creature without ceasing to be the Creator, so he became passible (παθητός) in one sense without ceasing to be impassible (ἀπαθής) in another sense.[53] This means that we cannot approach the apparent contradiction or paradoxical relation between the passible and impassible in any logical way, but only in a dynamic way in terms of God's active self-humiliation in the compassionate assumption of passible human nature in order to redeem it.

The guiding thought here must be that of the *reconciling exchange* expressed by St Paul in his Epistle to the Corinthians, 'You know the grace of our Lord Jesus Christ, that, though he was rich, yet for your sakes became poor, that you through his poverty might be rich.'[54] This was the great soteriological principle of sacrificial atoning exchange (ἀντάλλαγμα), *the unassumed is the unredeemed*, expounded by the Greek fathers, and sharpened particularly in the face of Apollinarian heresy by Athanasius, Gregory Nazianzen and Cyril of Alexandria.[55] Since this soteriological

[50] Cyril of Alexandria, *Scholia de incarnatione unigeniti*, 35 & 37, ἔπαθεν ἀπαθῶς; and Theodoret of Antioch, *Eranistes seu polymorphus*, 3. Refer to Athanasius, *Contra Apollinarem*, 1.10–11; 2.2; *Ad Epictetum*, 6. The paradoxicality of the passible/impassible conjunction is evident in various statements of Cyril, e.g. *Scholia de incarnatione unigeniti*, 34: 'He suffers and does not suffer, after one manner and another (πάσχει, καὶ οὐ πάσχει, κατ' ἄλλο καὶ ἄλλο); for he suffers humanly in the flesh as man; he is impassible divinely as God (πάσχει μὲν γὰρ ἀνθρωπίνως· ἀπαθὴς δέ ἐστι θεϊκῶς, ὡς θεός).'
[51] Cf. Cyril of Alexandria, *Adversus Nestorium*, PG 76, 17B, 72C, 132D, 232D–233A; *Scholia de incarnatione geneti*, PG 75, 1407B, 1409D; *Quod unus sit Christus*, PG 75, 1341A–D.
[52] Refer again to Athanasius, *Contra Apollinarem*, 1.12.
[53] See the discussion of Cyril, *Quod unus sit Christus*, PG 75, 1341–1362.
[54] 2 Cor. 8.9; cf. 5.21.
[55] See *The Trinitarian Faith*, pp. 179–184. Cf. also John of Damascus, *De fide orthodoxa*, 3.6: 'For what has not been taken cannot be healed.'

exchange takes place within the incarnate constitution of the Mediator who is both God and man in his one Person, it takes place not without but within the very Life of God himself. That is to say, we cannot but think of the saving passion of Christ as internal to the Person of God the Son become man. In this connection David Brown has shrewdly written: 'To say that the divine nature remains entirely impassible in the union would, I think, undermine any claim to there being a single person present since there is no way of distinguishing between God the Son's relationship to that particular human nature and any other human nature.'[56] He goes on to add, however, that 'this shows that "impassible" cannot be used in exactly the same sense when applied to the divine nature in the Incarnation, as when applied to the Godhead at other times.'

We must be quite definite about the fact that in the Lord Jesus Christ *God himself* has penetrated into our suffering, our hurt, our violence, our sinful alienated humanity, our guilty condition under divine judgment, and even into our dereliction. 'My God, my God, why hast thou forsaken me?' Behind that cry of Jesus on the Cross there is a mysterious movement in the divine Triunity, a counterpoint between the *pathos* in the crucified Jesus and the *pathos* in God.[57] The cry of Jesus in dereliction was followed by another cry, 'Father into thy hands I commend my spirit.' There on the Cross at the deepest point of our relations with God in judgment and suffering the incarnate Son of God penetrated into our *pathos* in such a profoundly redemptive way that in the very heart of it all, he brought his eternal serenity or ἀπάθεια to bear transformingly upon our passion. Thus we cannot but say that in Christ God both suffered and did not suffer: through the eternal tranquillity of his divine impassibility he took upon himself our passibility and redeemed it. As indicated above, this is not to be understood logically but economically, that is dynamically and soteriologically, on the ground of what actually took place in the vicarious life and passion of God's incarnate Son. This excludes altogether any thought of God as impassible in the Greek or Stoic sense, and any thought of God as passible in the way human beings are, or even as Jesus was in the flesh when, for example, he was subjected to temptation, and was crucified under Pontius Pilate. Rather is the suffering of God to be understood in terms of his boundless love and compassion when in oneness with Christ he took upon himself our passion, our hurt and suffering and indeed our judgment, in order to exhaust it all in his divine impassibility (τὸ παθητόν ἐν ἀπαθείᾳ)[58] in such a way that he masters and transmutes it within the embrace of his own immutable peace and serenity. It is an essential aspect of the atoning exchange in Jesus Christ that through his sharing in our passion (πάθος) he makes us share in his own peace and imperturbability (ἀπάθεια).[59] Through his atoning exchange in

[56] David Brown, *The Divine Trinity* (London, 1985), p. 264.
[57] I have in mind here again Bruno Brinkman's sensitive discussion, *To the Lengths of God. Truth and the Ecumenical Age* (London, 1988), pp. 45–86. Cf. also my essay on the *Eli, Eli, lama sabachthani* of Mark 15.34, 'Questioning in Christ', *Theology in Reconstruction* (London, 1965), pp. 117–127.
[58] Athanasius, *Contra Apollinarem*, 2.11.
[59] Cf. Didymus, *De Trinitate*, 3.12; cf. 1.26 & *De Spiritu Sancto*, 1.11.

taking our place we are given his place, through his profound sympathy with our weaknesses in his priestly self-abasement and compassionate oneness with us, the Lord has given us peace through his wounds, rest through his sorrow, and life through his death.

In the perfect oneness of his human and divine nature it cannot be said that Christ suffered only in his humanity and not in his divinity. How are we to understand that? As the incarnate Saviour, Jesus did not fulfil this priestly and mediatorial activity on his own, but only in an unbroken oneness in being and activity with God, and thus only in an unbroken oneness in being and activity of God with him. But how far and in what way may we read his suffering back into the ultimate Being of God which he the Son of God fully shared? How far and in what way is the very Godhead involved in the struggle of Christ against the forces of darkness and in his self-sacrifice in the expiation of our guilt? Certainly the kind of physical and emotional suffering Christ endured in his incarnate historical existence in body and spirit is not the kind of suffering that we may attribute to God,[60] but in him there is, if it may be said reverently, a suffering of a deeper and more terrible kind behind the suffering of the incarnate Son, the pain of God the Father in giving up his beloved Son, his only begotten Son, in atoning sacrifice for the sin of the world and its redemption of mankind from the antagonistic powers of darkness.[61] The passion of Christ considered apart altogether from the passion of the Father would be no more than the noblest martyrdom for it would be empty of ultimate divine validity. It is in his perfect oneness in being with God that the passion of Christ is saving. If our bond with the Creator is most acute in our suffering, as Bruno Brinkman has argued, then a God totally untouched by suffering would not be 'the God-for-man'.[62]

Of absolutely fundamental importance to our thinking here is the truth of the coinherent relations of the Father, the Son and the Holy Spirit, and of their perichoretic coactivity in all that they do in which their distinctive characteristics and hypostatic properties far from dividing them in their activities serve their perfect oneness in an eternal movement of love. The whole undivided Trinity is involved in our salvation, and thus in the central atoning passion of Christ, God the Father and God the Spirit, as well as God the Son, in their different but coordinated ways.[63] The passion of the Lord Jesus Christ who offered himself on the Cross in atoning propitiation for our sin and guilt flows from the passion of the Father who at infinite cost and out of his measureless love did not spare his own Son but gave him up for us all – the fearful pain of the Cross and self-sacrifice of the Son goes back to the pain in the heart of the Father that infinitely exceeds all that we could ever conceive. This is a passion in which the Holy Spirit shares equally with the

[60] Cf. Jürgen Moltmann, *The Crucified God* (New York, 1974): 'The Son suffers and dies on the Cross. The Father suffers with him, but not in the same way.'

[61] Cf. Origen, *Homilia in Ezekielem*, 6.6: *Ipse Deus non est impassibilis. Die Griechen Christlichen Schrifteller der ersten drei Jahrhunderte* (Berlin), vol. 8, p. 384.

[62] Bruno R. Brinkman, op. cit., p. 54.

[63] Cf. Augustine, *De Trinitate*, 13.11.15: 'Together both the Father and the Son, and the Spirit of both, work all things equally and harmoniously; yet we are justified in the blood of Christ, and we are reconciled to God by the death of his dear Son.'

Father not only because the nature of the Father is Spirit but because the Person of the Holy Spirit is in himself the consubstantial Communion of the Father and the Son, and as such participates in the intercessory passion of the Son and resonates unutterably in our prayers the saving intercession of the Son, thereby coming to aid us in our weakness when we do not even know how to pray.[64] The Father and the Spirit suffer with the Son and no less than the Son but in their own distinctive hypostatic realities and different ways. Just as the whole undivided Trinity is active in our redemption, so the whole undivided Trinity shares in the saving passion of the incarnate Son. As such the Holy Trinity constitutes the ontological and dynamic frame for the saving economy, and provides the Gospel and the Christian Faith with the ultimate unchangeable ground on which they rest.

That ultimate ground is the eternal Love that God is. The Gospel does not rest simply on the fact that God loves us, but on the fact that he loves us with the very same Love which he is in the eternal Communion of Love which God is in his Triune Being. F. W. Camfield has written very finely about this.

> The doctrine of the Trinity alone ultimately safeguards the truth that God's nature is love. It is not merely that subject and object of God's love are within his own being, thus making his love an eternal thing, something that belongs to his nature as such, and not merely an attitude and disposition which he takes up. The mere relation of Father and Son would mean simply that God loves himself. But God does not simply love himself, he loves *in* himself. That is to say, beside the subject-object relation, the relation of the Father and the Son, there is yet another which involves that God can love that which is not himself with the same love wherewith he loves himself. There is the Holy Spirit. Through the Holy Spirit the love of God can enfold us and our world with no other than, but with the same love as God bears to himself. Our lives can be rooted in no mere external relation to God, but in those internal relations in which his being consists. The love which binds man to God in the Holy Spirit is none other than the love which binds the Son to the Father in God's eternal being. This is the mystery of the love of God, the height and depth and length and breadth of it. This is man being 'filled with the fullness of God'.[65]

Moreover since the whole Trinity is involved in our redemption the saving passion of Christ cannot be regarded as merely a passing event in history, or something that is completely bound up with the temporal processes and causal connections of a fallen world. It derives from and is grounded in the eternal Communion of Love which God is in his one indivisible Being as Father, Son and Holy Spirit. The crucial point for us to note is the oneness (incomprehensible though it is) between the passion of God the incarnate Son in his union with us in history and the transcendent passion of God the Father. What is at issue here is the supreme truth of the Deity of Christ and the Holy Spirit, and thus the homoousial relation of

---

[64] Rom. 8.26.
[65] F. W. Camfield, *Revelation and the Holy Spirit* (London, 1933), p. 251.

both the incarnate Son and the Holy Spirit with God the Father. Everything stands or falls, then, with the profound oneness between the evangelical or economic Trinity and the ontological or immanent Trinity. If there is no such oneness the saving passion of Christ in history is ultimately superficial and finally evanescent, for it would not be grounded in the transcendent passion of the eternal Being of the Father, and our hearts would not then be filled with the love of God poured into them by the Holy Spirit. However the *homoousion* applies to the incarnate Saviour and his saving passion, and to the Holy Spirit who himself shares in the intercession of Christ and whose dwelling in us makes us participate in the saving benefits of what Christ has done for us. In that event our salvation is grounded immutably in the self-abnegating Love of God which flows freely to us from the eternal Communion of Love in his Triune Being.

The fact that God the Father and God the Holy Spirit are fully involved with God the Son in our redemption, means that the doctrine of the economic and ontological Holy Trinity is of the greatest evangelical relevance to us in our daily life of faith. Expressed the other way round, the saving import of the Gospel reaches its climax in the Triune God. Its importance to us in our daily life becomes particularly clear in prayer. If God is utterly unchangeable and impassible, and is not touched like Christ Jesus with the feeling of our infirmities but is immutably aloof from our creaturely cries and conditions, if there is no ontological bond between what he is in his transcendent Reality and the Lord Jesus Christ who loved us and gave himself for us, died and rose again for our salvation, then there can be no place for human prayer or any expectation that it will be answered. Human faith and hope can only shrivel up and wither away in the face of such a cold, remote, and impassible Deity. But if God himself has condescended out of sheer love at infinite cost to himself to come among us in our weakness and misery in order to make our cause his very own, and bring his divine serenity to bear upon our suffering, then the situation is very different. Prayer is then something very real, for it is directed in the name of his beloved Son to the Father in the light of his immense compassion, his unlimited freedom, the infinite outreach of his grace, and his boundless capacity for care in healing and redemptive provision for us in life and death. Far from being some cold metaphysical deduction, or second-order construction the doctrine of the Holy Trinity gives supreme theological expression to the evangelical truth that through Christ Jesus and his Cross we have access by one Spirit to the Father. It affirms in no uncertain terms that the God and Father of our Lord Jesus Christ has given himself to us as our Father, so that through the Holy Spirit whom he pours into our hearts, we may indeed know him and love him as our God and Father.

The Resurrection of the Crucified Christ

From very early times Christians looked upon the suffering of Christ the crucified Son of God through the triumphant event of his resurrection in which pain had been transmuted into joy, passion into glorification. This is reflected in the Homilies entitled *Peri Pascha* (Περὶ Πάσχα) frequently delivered at the celebration of the

Eucharist, which took their cue from St Paul's statement that 'Christ our passover (πάσχα) is sacrificed for us'.[66] The Greek word *pascha* was used to refer in the first instance to the celebration of the Jewish passover, but in view of Jesus' celebration of the Passover with his disciples on the night he was betrayed which transformed it into a memorial (*anamnesis*) of his sacrifice, *pascha* soon came to be used of the Christian Passover or the Lord's Supper, which in turn was further transformed by the presence among his disciples of the risen Lord into the Eucharist. This was a celebration of the real presence or *parousia* of the risen Saviour, which enshrined both a present and a future reference. As the Eucharist, the Lord's Supper was regularly and significantly celebrated on the Lord's Day or the day of his resurrection. Hence influenced by the fact that the Greek word *pascha* was derived from πάσχειν, to suffer, it soon came in common use to refer to the *passion* of Christ, but significantly, as understood from the perspective of the resurrection.[67] It was a celebration both of the sacrificial death of Christ as the Lamb of God and of his triumphant resurrection from the grave. That is to say, *pascha* referred at once to passion and the resurrection of the Lord, and later indeed simply to Easter, as today in the French *Pâque*. The effect of this in the mind of the early Church was to bring inseparably together understanding of the passion and the resurrection of Christ as one great redeeming event upon which the faith of Christian people rested. The fact that in raising the crucified Jesus Christ from the dead, God the Father acknowledged him as his own beloved Son, means that it was his own self-sacrifice that lay behind and empowered the atoning passion and resurrection of Christ. Moreover, the fact that in his ascension Christ offered himself through the eternal Spirit to the Father, means that the whole undivided Trinity was involved in the atoning passion of Christ. The risen and ascended Lord Jesus bears for ever the imprint of the Cross in his hands, feet and side – it is as such that he is enthroned as the Lamb of God.

In the fifth chapter of Revelation the apostle tells us that as he looked through a door in heaven he glimpsed something of the triumphant outcome of God's overruling of the fearful events of world history. Two things riveted his attention: a scroll and a lamb. The scroll was the book of human destiny sealed and firmly held in the hand of God. When no one in heaven or earth was able to open the scroll and look inside, John wept bitterly. Then he was told that the Lion of the tribe of Judah, the Root of David, had gained the power to break the seals and open the scroll. John turned to see the *Lion*, the mighty power of God, but what he saw standing in the midst of the throne of God was a *Lamb* with the marks of sacrifice upon him who took the scroll from the right hand of God, and when he did so a new song was heard to break out in heaven:

> You are worthy to receive the scroll and break its seals, for you were slain and by your blood you have redeemed for God people of every tribe and

---

[66] 1 Cor. 5.7.
[67] Cf. Irenaeus, *Adversus haereses*, 2.21.2 & 4; and Melito of Sardis, *Peri Pascha*, and my exposition of it in *Divine Meaning. Studies in Patristic Hermeneutics* (Edinburgh, 1995), ch. 4.

language and nation and race. You have made them a royal house of priests for our God, and they shall reign on earth. This was echoed by countless angels, singing 'Worthy is the Lamb who was slain, to receive power and riches, wisdom and glory and praise.'

This surely means that the atoning passion of Christ must for ever be allowed to govern our understanding of God in all his creative, providential, and redemptive relations with us. Is that not why we cannot but think of passion and serenity, passibility and impassibility as interpenetrating one another in the ultimate nature of God? And is that not how we continue to worship him?

Just as the whole undivided Trinity was involved in redemption so the whole undivided Trinity is worshipped in our celebration of the Eucharist. The liturgy of the Church was aboriginally and intrinsically trinitarian, so that it is not surprising that it was out of the sacramental worship of the Church in Baptism and Eucharist shaped through the inspired witness of the apostles handed down to us in the Scriptures of the New Testament, that the doctrine of the Holy Trinity, One God Three Persons, came into explicit formulation.

Praise and thanksgiving be unto you, O God, who brought again from the dead our Lord Jesus Christ and set him at your right hand in the kingdom of glory.

Praise and thanksgiving be unto you, O Lord Jesus Christ, you Lamb of God who has redeemed us by your blood, you heavenly Priest who ever lives to make intercession for us, you eternal King who comes again to make all things new.

Praise and thanksgiving be unto you, O Holy Spirit, who has shed abroad the love of God, who quickens us together with Christ, and makes us to sit with him in heavenly places, and to taste the good Word of God and the powers of the age to come.

Amen. Blessing, and glory, and wisdom, and thanksgiving, and honour, and power, and might, be unto you our God for ever and ever. Amen.

Index

Breinigsville, PA USA
14 August 2010
243532BV00004B/1/A